ECONOMICS *and* EMPIRE
in the ANCIENT NEAR EAST

CENTER AND LIBRARY FOR THE BIBLE AND SOCIAL JUSTICE SERIES

Matthew J. M. Coomber, series editor

The Center and Library for the Bible and Social Justice Series produces scholarship for the academy, churches and seminaries, and activist communities so as to fulfill The Center's mission to connect biblically informed activists and justice-oriented scholars.

Laurel Dykstra and Ched Myers, editors
Liberating Biblical Study
Scholarship, Art, and Action in Honor of
the Center and Library for the Bible and Social Justice

Norman K. Gottwald
Social Justice and the Hebrew Bible
3 volumes

Elaine Enns and Ched Myers
Healing Haunted Histories
A Settler Discipleship of Decolonization

Richard A. Horsley
Jesus and the Politics of Roman Palestine

Matthew J. M. Coomber
Re-Reading the Prophets through Corporate Globalization
A Cultural Evolutionary Approach to Economic Injustice
in the Hebrew Bible

ECONOMICS
and EMPIRE
in the ANCIENT
NEAR EAST

Guide to the Bible and Economics, Volume 1

Edited by
Matthew J. M. Coomber

CASCADE *Books* • Eugene, Oregon

ECONOMICS AND EMPIRE IN THE ANCIENT NEAR EAST
Guide to the Bible and Economics, Volume 1

Center and Library for the Bible and Social Justice Series

Cascade Books
An Imprint of Wipf and Stock Publishers
199 W. 8th Ave., Suite 3
Eugene, OR 97401

www.wipfandstock.com

PAPERBACK ISBN: 978-1-5326-5798-6
HARDCOVER ISBN: 978-1-5326-5799-3
EBOOK ISBN: 978-1-5326-5800-6

Cataloguing-in-Publication data:

Names: Coomber, Matthew J. M., editor.

Title: Economics and empire in the ancient Near East : guide to the Bible and economics, volume 1 / edited by Matthew J. M. Coomber.

Description: Eugene, OR: Cascade Books, 2023. | Center and Library for the Bible and Social Justice Series. | Includes bibliographical references and indexes.

Identifiers: ISBN 978-1-5326-5798-6 (paperback). | ISBN 978-1-5326-5799-3 (hardcover). | ISBN 978-1-5326-5800-6 (ebook).

Subjects: Bible. Old Testament—Criticism, interpretation, etc. | Economics in the Bible. | Economics—Religious aspects. | Religion—Economic aspects. | Jews—History—To 70 A.D.

Classification: BS1199.E35 E20 2023 (print). | BS1199 (ebook).

VERSION NUMBER 02/22/23

In memory of Norman K. Gottwald (1926–2022)

Scholar, mentor, friend, and cofounder of the Center
and Library for the Bible and Social Justice

Contents

Acknowledgments

In a project of this breadth it is difficult to know how to begin thanking all of those who made it possible, so I will start at the beginning. The series to which this volume is connected was born out of an idea that Neil Elliott had during his years at Fortress Press: to create a repository of what is known about biblical economics and how this subfield of biblical studies is relevant to both the academy and also to the nonacademic world. Elliott had been in close communication with the newly created "Economics in the Biblical World" section of the Society of Biblical Literature (founded by Richard A. Horsley and Samuel L. Adams), which seeks to foster more comprehensive and critical investigation into economic aspects of biblical texts in their historical contexts. The original plan was to create a single volume that brought together substantial articles from scholars who are knowledgeable in key areas so as to create a repository in which further investigation of biblical economics might be more appropriately grounded. Elliott then expanded the project into a multivolume series that included both exegetical essays focused on the economic dimension and also essays exploring implications for economic justice today. Elliott invited me to edit the series, and we brought together a fantastic group of scholars, as is evident in the tables of contents.

Due to a change in company structure at Fortress Press, however, the project was let go. Elliott assisted me in finding a new home for the series and its contributors' works, which were already under way. I cannot thank him enough for his dedication to this series and assistance in finding it safe harbor. K. C. Hanson and Cascade Books was that safe harbor, and I am immensely grateful to him for his assistance in helping me to shape this series into what it has become. Hanson's years of experience in the publishing world, alongside his academic expertise in the field of biblical studies, were invaluable in helping to move the project forward.

Next, I wish to thank the late Norman Gottwald. Shortly after completing my doctoral studies, Gottwald read my book, *Re-Reading the Prophets through Corporate Globalization*, and invited me to join the board of directors for the Center and Library for the Bible and Social Justice (CLBSJ). I jumped at the chance to be involved with an organization that connects sound biblical scholarship with activist communities that endeavor to create a just world. Gottwald's guidance and encouragement were highly formative in both my development as a scholar and also in how I approached my editorial work in this volume. My colleagues at the Center and Library for the Bible and Social Justice have been incredibly supportive in the development of this series, for which I am very thankful.

Lastly, I would like to express my gratitude and respect to those who continue to shape my scholarship and lead me in new directions of study. Their influences have played no small part in the creation of this series. I do not believe I would have been approached to edit the CLBSJ Series Guide to the Bible and Economics had it not been for the experience and guidance that I gained through editing *The Old Testament and Apocrypha: The Fortress Commentary on the Bible* with Gale Yee and Hugh Page Jr. Yee and Page were outstanding colleagues with whom to work and gracious mentors. I am also profoundly thankful to the contributors to the CLBSJ Series Guide to the Bible and Economics. Their contributions, both in these volumes and also in their other work, have helped to shape my scholarship, priestly vocation, and advocacy work for a more just world. I am honored to have had this chance to collaborate with them.

My understandings of ancient Near Eastern micro- and macroeconomics and the Bible's relationships with economics today have been greatly impacted by the research of Roland Boer, Christina Petterson Roger Nam, Samuel Adams, Kelly Murphy, Ronald A. Simkins, M. Daniel Carroll R., Davis Hankins, Brendan Breed, and Kenneth Hirth. The postcolonial scholarship of Jione Havea, Monica Melanchthon, Steed Davidson, Margaret Aymer, and Raj Nadella have shaped my understandings of biblical interpretation and how imperialism has shaped its trajectories. Their work has not only given me insight into modern receptions of the Bible, but has helped me to explore new questions pertaining to the experiences of colonized peoples in the ancient world. Examining biblical realities through the gender-focused works of Elisabeth Schüssler Fiorenza, Gale Yee, Davina Lopez, Mitzi Smith, Jessica Keady, Cynthia Shafer-Elliot, Katie Edwards, Carolyn Osiek, Lynn Huber, and Christy Cobb has filled a hole in my scholarship. Their work will continue to impact mine. And the activist-centered scholarship of Gerald West, Diana

Swanncutt, Crystal Hall, Noelle Damico, Ched Myers, Amy Dalton, and so many others have helped to open my eyes to the possibilities that exist for both asking new questions of the Bible's ancient contexts and also seeing various points of relevance that biblical texts hold for today. I am grateful for my supportive colleagues at St. Ambrose University, with whom I exchange research ideas, including Micah Kiel, Lisa Powell, Ella Johnson, Mara Adams, Fr. Bud Grant, Keith Soko, Neil Aschliman, Dennis Tarasi, and Grant Tietjen. I would also like to extend my gratitude to Richard Horsley, a mentor and friend who has been an invaluable consultant in the development of this series.

In a project such as this, there are so many folks to thank that I fear it is inevitable there will be key individuals and groups whom I have missed. I offer them my sincere apologies and extend my gratitude.

Abbreviations

ABD	*Anchor Bible Dictionary.* Edited by David Noel Freedman. 6 vols. New York: Doubleday, 1992
ABS	Archaeology and Biblical Studies
AfO	*Archiv für Orientforschung*
AJA	*American Journal of Archaeology*
ANEM	Ancient Near East Monographs
ANESSup	Ancient Near Eastern Studies Supplement Series
ANET	*Ancient Near Eastern Texts Relating to the Old Testament.* Edited by James B. Pritchard. 2nd ed., corr. and enlarged. Princeton: Princeton University Press, 1956
AOAT	Alter Orient und Altes Testament
AT	author translation
BA	*Biblical Archaeologist*
BASOR	*Bulletin of the American Schools of Oriental Research*
BETL	Bibliotheca Ephemeridum Theologicarum Lovaniensium
Bib	*Biblica*
BibInt	*Biblical Interpretation*
BibInt	Biblical Interpretation Series
BibSem	The Biblical Seminar
BM	British Museum
BMA	Babylonian Marriage Agreement
BTB	*Biblical Theology Bulletin*
BthSt	Biblisch-theologische Studien
BZABR	Beihefte zur Zeitschrift für Altorientalische und Biblische Rechtsgeschichte

BZAW	Beihefte zur Zeitschrift für die alttestamentliche Wissenschaft
CA	*Current Anthropology*
CBOTS	Coniectanea Biblica Old Testament
CBQ	*Catholic Biblical Quarterly*
CahRB	Cahiers de la Revue biblique
CG	Clermont-Ganneau Ostraca as in A. Dupont-Sommer, "Un ostracon inedit d'Elephantine (Collection Clermont Ganneau)," in *Hebrew and Semitic Studies Presented to G. R. Driver*, edited by D. W. Harris and W. D. McHardy, 53–58. Oxford Oxford University Press, 1963
CTH	*Catalogue des textes hittites.* Emmanuel Laroche. Paris: Klincksieck, 1971
CHANE	Culture and History of the Ancient Near East
COS	*The Context of Scripture.* Edited by William W. Hallo. 3 vols. Leiden: Brill, 1997–2002
CurBR	*Currents in Biblical Research*
DJD	Discoveries in the Judean Desert
DMOA	Documenta et Monumenta Orientis Antiqui
EA	Tell el-Amarna. *The Amarna Letters.* William L. Moran. Baltimore: Johns Hopkins University Press, 1992
EJL	Early Judaism and Its Literature
FAT	Forschungen zum Alten Testament
FOTL	wForms of the Old Testament Literature
FRLANT	Forschungen zur Religion und Literatur des Alten und Neuen Testaments
GAT	Grundrisse zum Alten Testament
HBT	*Horizons in Biblical Theology*
HCOT	Historical Commentary on the Old Testament
HdO	Handbuch der Orientalistik
HeyJ	*Heythrop Journal*
HThKAT	Herders Theologischer Kommentar zum Alten Testament
HUCA	*Hebrew Union College Annual*
HUT	Hermeneutische Untersuchengen zur Theologie

IBC	Interpretation: A Bible Commentary for Teaching and Preaching
ICC	International Critical Commentary
IEJ	*Israel Exploration Journal*
JAAR	*Journal of the American Academy of Religion*
JBL	*Journal of Biblical Literature*
JCS	*Journal of Cuneiform Studies*
JESHO	*Journal of the Economic and Social History of the Orient*
JNES	*Journal of Near Eastern Studies*
JSJ	*Journal for the Study of Judaism*
JRS	*Journal of Roman Studies*
JSJSup	Journal for the Study of Judaism Supplements
JSOT	*Journal for the Study of the Old Testament*
JSOTSup	Journal for the Study of the Old Testament Supplement Series
JRS	*Journal of Roman Studies*
JJS	*Journal of Jewish Studies*
LAI	Library of Ancient Israel
LEC	Library of Early Christianity
LHBOTS	Library of Hebrew Bible / Old Testament Studies
LSTS	Library of Second Temple Studies
NEA	*Near Eastern Archaeology*
NICOT	New International Commentary on the Old Testament
NovTSup	Novum Testamentum Supplements
NTS	*New Testament Studies*
NTT	*Norsk Teologisk Tidsskrift*
OBT	Overtures to Biblical Theology
OTL	Old Testament Library
OTR	Old Testament Readings
PEQ	*Palestine Exploration Quarterly*
PRU I	*Le Palais royal d'Ugarit, IV, Textes accadiens des archives sud.* Edited by J. Nougayrol. 2 vols. Paris: Imprimerie nationale, 1956
SAA	State Archives of Assyria

SBAB   Stuttgarter biblische Aufsatzbände

SBL   Society of Biblical Literature

SBLDS   Society of Biblical Literature Dissertation Series

SemeiaSt   Semeia Studies

STDJ   Studies on the Texts of the Desert of Judah

StudBib   Studia Biblica

SNTW   Studies of the New Testament and Its World

SWBA   Social World of Biblical Antiquity

SymS   Society of Biblical Literature Symposium Series

TAD   Porten, Bezalel, and Ada Yardini, eds. *Textbook of Aramaic Documents from Ancient Egypt*. Vol. 3, *Literature, Accounts, Lists*. 4 vols. Jerusalem: Winona Lake, IN: Eisenbrauns, 1993

TNTC   Tyndale New Testament Commentaries

URJ   Union for Reformed Judaism

VT   *Vetus Testamentum*

VTSup   Vetus Testamentum Supplements

WAW   Writings from the Ancient World

WBC   Word Biblical Commentary

WGRW   Writings from the Greco-Roman World

WMANT   Wissenschaftliche Monographien zum Alten und Neuen Testament

ZA   *Zeitschrift für Assyiologie*

ZNW   *Zeitschrift für die neutestamentliche Wissenschaft und die Kunde der älteren Kirche*

Contributors

Samuel L. Adams is the Mary Jane and John F. McNair Chair of Biblical Studies and Professor of Old Testament at Union Presbyterian Seminary in Richmond, Virginia, and a Presbyterian minister. Adams' interests include wisdom literature, wealth and poverty in the biblical world, apocalypticism, the Dead Sea Scrolls, Egyptology, and the Bible and American politics. His publications include *Wisdom in Transition* (2008), *Social and Economic Life in Second Temple Judea* (2014), *The Blackwell Companion to Wisdom Literature* (2020), *Sirach and Its Contexts* (2021), and *Ben Sira: A New Translation with Introduction and Commentary* (forthcoming). He is the editor of the journal *Interpretation*.

Roland Boer is a professor in the School of Philosophy at Renmin University of China, Beijing. While his earlier work concerned Marxist approaches to the Bible, his more recent work has been devoted to Marxist philosophy. Among his publications are *Marxist Criticism of the Bible* (2003), *Idols of Nations: Biblical Myth at the Origins of Capitalism* (2014), *Postcolonialism and the Hebrew Bible* (2013), *The Sacred Economy of Ancient Israel* (2015), and *Socialism in Power: On the History and Theory of Socialist Governance* (Springer 2022).

Matthew J. M. Coomber is professor of biblical studies and theology at St. Ambrose University in Davenport, Iowa, and an Episcopal priest. Coomber's research focuses on how biblical texts that challenge systemic poverty might provide tools for confronting modern injustice. His publications include *Re-Reading the Prophets through Corporate Globalization* (2010; paperback ed., Cascade Books, 2022), *Bible and Justice* (2011), and *The Common Good: A Biblical Ethos against Poverty* (forthcoming). He is also coeditor of *The Fortress Commentary on the Bible: The Old Testament and Apocrypha* (2014) and editor of the six-volume Guide to the Bible and Economics (Cascade Books).

Anne Fitzpatrick-McKinley is associate professor of Second Temple Judaism at Trinity College Dublin. Fitzpatrick's current research focuses on the period of restoration within the context of imperial rule in the ancient Near East. Her publications include *Transformation of Torah from Scribal Advice to Law* (1999), *Religion in the Achaemenid Persian Empire* (2015), *Assessing Biblical and Classical Sources for the Persian Period* (2015), and *Empire, Power and Indigenous Elites* (2015).

Davis Hankins is associate professor of religious studies at Appalachian State University in Boone, North Carolina. Hankins' research focuses on biblical literature, religion, and society in light of modern literary theory and philosophy. He has published a number of articles and edited volumes, as well as the monograph *The Book of Job and the Immanent Genesis of Transcendence* (2015).

Kenneth Hirth is professor of archaeology at Pennsylvania State University. Hirth researches the origin and development of ranked and state-level societies in the New World. His publications include *Household, Compound, and Residence* (1993), *Ancient Urbanism at Xochicalco* (2000), *Mesoamerican Lithic Technology* (2003), *The Aztec Economic World* (2016), *The Organization of Ancient Economies: A Global Perspective* (2020), and *Economy and Ritual in a Central Honduran Chiefdom* (forthcoming).

Douglas A. Knight is the Drucilla Moore Buffington Professor of Hebrew Bible Emeritus at Vanderbilt University. Knight's research in the Hebrew Bible engages sociohistorical approaches, ideological criticism, ethics, history of interpretation, and the social and political world of the first millennium BCE. His publications include *Rediscovering the Traditions of Israel* (1975), *The Hebrew Bible and Its Modern Interpreters* (1998), *Ethics and Politics in the Hebrew Bible* (1995), and *Law, Power, and Justice in Ancient Israel* (2011).

Rainer Kessler is emeritus professor of Protestant theology within the field of Old Testament at the University of Marburg, Germany, and is an ordained minister. Kessler's areas of specialization include the social history of the Hebrew Bible, prophetic literature, and ethics. His publications include *State and Society in Pre-Exilic Judah* (1992), *Social History of Ancient Israel* (2006), *The Way to Life: Old Testament Ethics* (2017), and *Leben und Handeln in der Gesellschaft* (2021).

Christina Petterson is an honorary lecturer at Australian National University in Canberra, Australia. Petterson's primary research considers Christianity through the lenses of theology, history, and cultural theory. Her publications include *From Tomb to Text: The Body of Jesus in the Book of John* (2018), *Apostles of Revolution? Marxism and Biblical Studies* (2020), *Acts of Empire: The Acts of the Apostles and Imperial Ideology* (2020), and *The Moravian Brethren in a Time of Transition* (2021).

Cynthia Shafer-Elliott is associate professor of Hebrew Bible/Old Testament at Baylor University in Waco, Texas. Shafer-Elliott specializes in the historical, cultural, and social contexts of ancient Israel and Judah, with a focus on daily life of the average Israelite and Judahite household. She is an experienced field archaeologist and is part of the archaeological excavations at Tell Halif and Tell Abel Beth Maacah in Israel. Her publications include *Food in Ancient Judah* (2013), *The Five-Minute Archaeologist in the Southern Levant* (2016), and the *T. & T. Clark Handbook of Food in Ancient Israel and the Hebrew Bible* (2021).

1. The Importance of Biblical Economics to the Field of Biblical Studies

Matthew J. M. Coomber

Biblical economics is a quickly developing subfield within the discipline of biblical studies, and for good reason. Neither the Bible as a whole nor its individual books can be fully understood without an awareness of their economic underpinnings. As is the case with any religious culture, either ancient or modern, Hebrew religious beliefs and practices cannot be divorced from the economic environments in which they were developed and formalized. It is for this reason that the first volume of the Center and Library for the Bible and Social Justice Series Guide to the Bible and Economics was created: to offer what is currently understood about the economic contexts of the ancient Near East, so as to facilitate further research on the economic environments that both shaped and were also challenged by Hebrew communities.

The chapters within this book illuminate the economic realities that underpin Hebrew legal texts, prophetic oracles, narrative stories, and wisdom and apocalyptic writings that were composed in the late second and first millennia BCE. Before delving into the volume's main body of work, this introduction explains the importance of the field of biblical economics and addresses some of the challenges faced by those who pursue its study.

Importance of the Study of Biblical Economics to Biblical Studies—and Beyond

It is understandable that the Bible is most often read without consideration for either its economic underpinnings or their implications. More often than not, the Bible is thought of in regard to its devotional value, with readers' first encounters often taking place in devotional settings like houses of worship or religious education programs. Others gain their first exposure to the Bible through the evangelism of its devotees, through such organizations as Gideons International, which offers free Bibles on the street and in hotel rooms. At other times, the Bible may be introduced through the promotion of a specific verse. During televised sporting events in the United States, for example, it is not uncommon to see "John 3:16" held aloft on poster board or written under an athlete's eyes. But while the Bible is unquestionably religious, it is also undeniably economic. That economic nature of the Bible is a very important factor for both academics who study biblical literature and also for scholars of other disciplines that consider the cultures and geographic settings that surrounded the Bible's development.

Economics and economic concerns do not run parallel to the field of biblical studies: they run straight through it. Recognizing and understanding the influence of the Bible's economic underpinnings affords two primary benefits. First, a recognition of the Bible's economic backdrop reveals previously unnoticed levels of meaning in even the most familiar of texts. For scholars, a recognition of these underpinnings cultivates a greater awareness of the recurring economic themes and values—adopted from yet earlier West Asian societies—that recur in various parts of the Hebrew Bible. Such awareness can also facilitate a recognition of previously unseen connections between texts as disparate as the legal texts of the Holiness Code, apocalyptic visions, prophetic oracles, and narrative texts. Conversely, cultivating this knowledge can also help us to better recognize and dispel eisegetical interpretations. Understanding the economic systems of the ancient world, which functioned differently than our own, better equips readers to recognize when modern paradigms—such as free-market or socialist ideologies—are imposed on biblical texts. Additionally, for scholars and nonscholars alike, paying attention to the Bible's recurring economic themes can help bring into view those texts that confronted ancient forms of exploitation that are also present today, such as political corruption, predatory resource extraction, and other financial abuses.

A second benefit to be gained from recognizing the Bible's economic underpinnings is the potential to discover clues pertaining to the economic realities that colonized peoples were made to face in the ancient Near East. Beyond value to the field of biblical studies, insights that can be gleaned from the Bible are of great importance to scholars who study economic anthropology, ancient history, or other humanities and social-scientific disciplines that have an interest in the lives of West Asia's inhabitants during the first and second millennia BCE. Extracting such insights from Hebrew texts, however, is complicated and fraught with potential for missteps—these complications are addressed in the section "Challenges to Creating an Overview of Hebrew Economics," below. Before outlining these challenges, the intertwining nature of economic development and religious formation should be addressed.

Centrality of Economics in Religious Activity

Concerns over the allocation and distribution of resources have propelled almost every aspect of human life since kinship groups started banding together into larger communities. From the development of the earliest hunting and foraging societies to the modern ambitions of billionaires who wish to colonize Mars, communities have developed and augmented strategies to procure, secure, and distribute goods. In addition to motivating humans to form societies for cultivating and storing food, broadening genetic diversity, and securing alliances, economic activity has also shaped the creation, development, and evolution of religious beliefs, ethics, and practices.

In the ancient world, little divided environmental phenomena from the spiritual realm. Rates of rainfall and the flow of rivers, the spread of crop-killing diseases and pests, and other natural events were often connected to either the will or the neglect of divine actors. It was for this reason that communities believed the pursuit of divine favor to be essential. Ensuring fruitful harvests and avoiding the catastrophic consequences of successive crop failures were believed to depend upon the successful navigation of religious rituals and observances. Thus, these religious practices were designed to guide planting and harvest seasons, to regulate relationships between neighbors, and to determine the management of arable lands.[1] Numerous texts within the Hebrew Bible represent these same concerns.

Hebrew communities depended upon deities like YHWH and Ba'al to send rains to water their fields and replenish their aquifers. They turned to the divine to navigate planting seasons and the successful growth of crops. Hebrew communities developed holidays such as the festivals of Weeks (Exod 23:16, 34:22) and of Booths (Lev 23:34 and Deut 16:13–17) to either secure or give thanks for successful harvests. The authors of the Hebrew Bible also believed that the divine realm could protect the fruits of their labor, shielding them from extraction by regional administrators, imperial forces, or their combined efforts: evidence of this is found among texts within the Covenant, Holiness,

1. Hirth, *Organization*, 117–23; Rappaport, "Sacred," 37–39.

and Deuteronomic legal codes. Additionally, some Hebrew people sought the assistance of goddesses, like Asherah, to bless them with viable offspring to work and inherent their fields, as well as to protect them from their enemies (Jer 44:16–19). In addition to such divine favors, administrators relied upon the celestial realm to legitimize their rule.[2]

Connections between economics and engagement with the divine realm, however, went beyond simply seeking deities' favor and avoiding their rage; religious rituals and beliefs were used to facilitate economic administrators' ambitions. As economic systems gained complexity and evolved, religious beliefs shifted to meet and support the resulting new societal goals. Bernard Knapp notes that as a result of the strong connections that develop between agrarian strategy and divine engagement, "ritual activities serve as the interface between religion and techno-economic or socio-political activities."[3] Such connections between farming and religious practices in the ancient Near East are found in communities ranging from small, autonomous collectives to the large temple complexes that served as centers of land management, resource extraction, and allocation of goods.[4] The intertwining nature of religion and economics in ancient agrarian societies blurs any lines between resource management and religious belief.

As spiritual-economic traditions solidify over time, the ritualization of producing, storing, and allocating goods erodes any divisions that may have once existed between religious ethics and economic activity; the economic system becomes imprinted onto the deity or deities to which the rituals are connected.[5] Consequently, the characteristics of divine actors become indistinguishable from the community or society's economic systems and goals. This process happens so completely that shifts in economic goals are rarely mitigated by religious doctrine or tradition. The reverse, rather, is more often the case. Doctrine and tradition—as well as the deities to which they are connected—undergo a transformation that facilitates the desired economic changes of local and regional administrators, and/or their imperial overlords. This appears to have been the case in the late eighth century BCE, when the Kingdom of Judah was absorbed into an expanding Assyrian Empire and the

---

2. For more on this aspect of divine reliance, see Ekholm-Friedman, "On the Evolution," 161.

3. Knapp, "Copper Production," 157.

4. Boer, *Sacred Economy of Ancient Israel*, 113–14.

5. Coomber, "Caught in the Crossfire?," 419–21.

region experienced numerous religious reforms, particularly in relation to the temple cult in Jerusalem.[6]

Marriages between economics and religion, and the pull that economic forces exert on religious belief and practice, are not limited to the ancient world. An increase in trade between Europe and Asia during the fifteenth century CE overturned numerous long-held religious taboos, such as making various Chinese spices—which had once been strictly reserved for ceremonial use— available for general consumption on European tables.[7] So too in the twentieth century CE, Libyan dictator Mu'ammar Qadhdafi reinterpreted Muslim doctrine and altered the Islamic calendar in his country in an effort to reshape his nation's economic strategy. For example, in order to liberalize Libya's economy to more effectively engage with international capitalism, Qadhdafi privatized the nation's sacred lands, known as the *waqif*, which had been religiously managed for centuries in order to offer subsistence farming for impoverished agrarian workers.[8] Such examples of economics influencing religious practice and their connected belief systems and institutions go on into the present day, including the rise and spread of prosperity theology in the United States.

Considering the links that bind religious development and economic practice, it is no surprise that economic desires and shifts underpin the laws, oracles, stories, and other writings of the Hebrew Bible. Recognizing biblical authors' reactions to economic change—whether in support of those changes or as forms of resistance to them—can offer insights into the effects of the continual economic developments that took place in the first millennium BCE. These include advancements in the processing and manipulation of iron, the introduction of monetary economics, a centralization of oil and wine production, the advent of speculative taxation, and the introduction of sustained imperial control over a region that had previously enjoyed cyclical autonomy.[9] While an awareness of how such societal changes affect religious systems can highlight those economic realities that are imprinted onto the texts of the Hebrew Bible, such an awareness can also shed light on biblical interpretations that are born out of economic shifts in those societies that would later adopt the Hebrew Bible's writings as sacred.

---

6. Coomber, *Re-Reading the Prophets*, 97–134. For example, King Hezekiah's decision to remove worship sites from Judah's countryside and centralize worship, and its flow of temple revenue, in the capital city of Jerusalem (2 Kgs 18:22; 2 Chr 32:12).

7. Bayly, "'Archaic,'" 52–53.

8. Anderson, *State and Social Transformation*, 266.

9. Coote and Whitelam, *Emergence of Early Israel*, 72–80.

Much is to be gained by studying the economic environments out of which the Hebrew Bible developed, but the region's economic systems can be exceedingly difficult to decipher. The following section addresses some of the challenges that scholars of biblical economics face, and which have been met by the contributors of this volume.

Challenges to Creating an Overview of Hebrew Economics

The economic information provided by the Hebrew Bible is far from clear. Hebrew religious texts represent perspectives that are largely, if not entirely, limited to those of male, urban elites. They are driven by religious and other cultural biases, and only present their audiences with what the authors wanted to reveal. Furthermore, the books of the Hebrew Bible underwent several levels of revision before being set in those forms from which our modern translations are derived—some quite clumsily and haphazardly, as can be found in the book of Micah. In short, there is no *original text* with which to work.[10] To simply receive the Hebrew Bible's accounts of its economic environments would result in images that are either incomplete or wholly inaccurate: take, for example, the false claims of King Solomon's unmatched wealth (2 Chr 9:13–29), for which there is evidence to the contrary. But when read in concert with contemporaneous literature, histories, and archaeological evidence, and the heuristic aid of social-scientific theories, the Hebrew Bible can serve as an indispensable partner in uncovering those economic realities and challenges that shaped Hebrew communities. While our understandings of Hebrew economics are incomplete, clues within the Hebrew Bible—whether presented overtly or hidden within context—can serve as useful tools for developing a clearer picture. The contributors to *Economics and Empire in the Ancient Near East* have incorporated such tools in order to offer the clearest picture that we currently have of those economic environments, goals, and challenges that shaped the composition of the texts that would eventually become a part of the Hebrew Bible. Outlined here are a few of the more overt challenges to engaging this process.

Scarcity and Nature of the Literary Evidence

A common challenge faced by those who study the economic practices surrounding the Hebrew Bible is a lack of literary evidence, much of which—including all original texts—has been lost to time. Whereas the Assyrians and

---

10. A helpful treatment of the urban-dominant perspectives of the Hebrew Bible is found in Davies, "Urban Religion and Rural Religion."

Babylonians left legal texts and accounting records preserved in baked clay—some dating as far back as the third millennium BCE[11]—such was not the case among the biblical authors' communities. Scholars of biblical economics must conduct their research without original texts: there are no original texts. Aside from the fact that much of the Hebrew legal corpus appears to have originated and continued as oral tradition, those law codes, contracts, and supply lists that were committed to writing were recorded on animal skins, which decayed; devoting the time, energy, and resources necessary to create copies was essential to their literary survival. The oldest examples of Hebrew texts are but fragments, centuries younger than their originals, reflecting generations worth of redactions that augmented previous copies to fit the evolving circumstances and ideologies of the redactors and their audiences.

In addition to the literary limitations addressed above, certain kinds of documents that would help researchers to better understand rural economic practices of ancient Hebrew communities are entirely absent. For example, we scholars are missing key documents pertaining to how land tenure was managed (usufruct is the legal right of an individual or kin-group to the productive capabilities of farmable land). While some Hebrew legal, prophetic, wisdom, and narrative texts address usufruct (e.g., Lev 25; 1 Kgs 18; Prov 22:28; Isa 6:8), legal documents pertaining to land conveyance and deeds of land ownership are entirely absent from the biblical record. Not only do scholars work without either land-conveyance documents or landholding deeds, but Baruch Levine notes that there are no official correspondence or royal edicts from either the Kingdom of Israel or the lack of literary evidence, scholars of biblical economics have found various means through which to glean information, including comparative studies with neighboring cultures and various social-scientific methods.

Contextual, Cultural, and Paradigmatic Differences in the Authors' Times

Another set of challenges faced by those who research the economic realities of the Hebrew Bible are the sociocultural gulfs that exist between biblical texts and their modern audiences. While this is challenging enough in itself—considering differences in economic goals, strategies, and religious norms between ancient and modern cultures—scholars of biblical economics must also

11 The Code of Ur-Nammu dates to between 2100 and 2050 BCE.

consider the disparities that existed between the different ancient communities that gave rise to the texts of the Hebrew Bible.

Many ancient authors of the Bible were separated from each other by culture, time, geography, and theology, and their works represent and reflect theological assertions, questions, and assumptions of communities that had worked apart and, therefore, came to differing conclusions. These divergent societal and religious contexts led to (what would later become) intrabiblical conflicts pertaining to economic rules and ethical outlooks. For example, in the Covenant Code it is commanded that a male slave should be freed without debt in the seventh year of bondage (Exod 21:2), but no command for manumission is afforded to female slaves (Exod 21:7). In the Deuteronomic Code, however, both men and women are to be freed in the seventh year (Deut 15:12; see also Jer 34:9). Gleaning economic information from the Hebrew Bible is further complicated by the fact that its writings emerged and were copied before notions of intellectual property had developed. Thus, biblical texts were frequently subject to additions and revisions so that they came to represent later writers' theological and ethical viewpoints. While theological differences existed between various biblical authors, far greater are the socioreligious and paradigmatic dissimilarities between the ancient authors and their modern audiences. For many who have learned to view the Bible as a unified whole, such differences are difficult to either see or accept and therefore are frequently ignored.

Projecting Modern Economic Paradigms onto the Ancient Past

A key impediment to understanding the economic landscapes of the ancient Near East, as addressed by both Hirth and also by Boer in this volume, is the temptation to impose modern paradigms onto the ancient past, whether consciously or involuntarily.

When a person is presented with a situation or object that they do not understand, the mind looks for potential connections to what *is* understood in order to make sense of it. It has been explained that this may be why so many foods with nondescript flavors appear to taste like chicken when tried for the first time. While the primary hopes and anxieties of ancient and modern humans are quite similar, their paradigmatic worlds—their separate cultural, religious, scientific, and economic environments—are foreign to each other. It is only natural, therefore, for modern readers of the Bible to approach those texts with what tools they have at hand: for example, labeling a particular economic strategy as *protocapitalist* or *protosocialist*. While this process may be natural, forcing modern systems and ideas onto the ancient past can impede our attempts to develop clearer understandings of ancient economic contexts as they were.

In the context of the field of medieval studies, Norman Cantor addressed the issue of imposing modern realities onto earlier cultures. He found that people had a high propensity to project their worldviews onto the medieval world, which led them to reinvent the past in their own image: an issue addressed by current medievalist Courtney Luckhardt in relation to White supremacist impositions of modern biases onto medieval Europe.[12] Just as modern people project contemporary biases into the study of medieval Europe, students of the biblical world sometimes do the same. Examples of this are frequently found in artworks that portray biblical characters, such as Gerard van Honthorst's seventeenth-century painting *King David Playing the Harp*. In this painting, van Honthorst presents David as primarily a European-style king, save a few orientalist adornments. In much the same way, biblical scholars are prone to think of and express biblical-economic concepts and goals in terms of the capitalist, socialist, or other economic systems to which they are accustomed. Such anachronisms—like Juan Alfaro's interpretation of the land-seizing antagonists in Micah 2 as mafiosos[13]—might readily make sense to author and audience alike, but do not represent their ancient contexts. While it is difficult to avoid the projection of modern paradigms onto earlier contexts—to escape doing so entirely is scarcely possible—attentiveness to this hazard can help scholars to avoid its worst effects as they work to understand realties outside their own worldview.

While the challenges outlined above may impede our understandings of the economic realities that surrounded the Hebrew Bible's authors and their communities, hope is not lost. As readers will find in the following chapters, scholars of ancient Near Eastern history, culture, and religion are able to employ numerous models, tools, and strategies to help decipher the macro and microeconomic realities of the Southern Levant. Based on clues derived from the Hebrew Bible, archaeological evidence, literary resources from neighboring civilizations, and social-scientific models that can be tested against the evidence we have, the field of biblical economics is offering new insights into the economic realities in and around ancient Palestine. Additionally, studies in biblical

---

12. Cantor, *Inventing the Middle Ages*, 156–58; Luckhardt, "Confronting Race and Medieval Fantasies."

13. Alfaro, *Justice and Loyalty*, 22.

economics are shedding light on long-hidden meanings behind numerous biblical texts.

Lack of Consensus within the Field of Biblical Economics

As in any academic area of study, scholars will interpret data in different ways, which leads to divergent conclusions. Such disagreements are not unwelcome, as the differing viewpoints that emerge from such disputes can be incredibly fruitful to both sharpening and also furthering discussion and discovery. Debate is the whetstone of the mind, and when collegially and successfully engaged, its friction grinds the false away so as to lead us closer to truth. Within this volume, readers will occasionally find differing viewpoints in areas where our contributors' research overlaps. This was to be expected and it is welcomed by the editor. *Economics and Empire in the Ancient Near East* was by no means intended to be the last word on biblical economics. The goal is to present what is currently known about the economic landscapes out of which the Hebrew Bible developed and to facilitate further exploration into their study. To present a univocal collection of essays would be a great disservice to that end. Readers can be assured, however, that any discrepancies between our contributors' interpretations of evidence do not stem from a lack of academic rigor from one author or the other. Rather, areas of difference should be recognized as guideposts for the sort of reflection and exploration that this volume intends to promote, highlighting areas for further investigation.

On behalf of the contributors, the editor wishes to express our hope that *Economics and Empire in the Ancient Near East* will offer valuable insights into how the Hebrew Bible's economic environments—both real and imagined—shaped the communities and individual lives of those living in ancient Israel/Palestine, while also highlighting what the area of biblical economics has to contribute to the field of biblical studies, and beyond.

Bibliography

Alfaro, Juan. *Justice and Loyalty: A Commentary on the Book of Micah.* International Theological Commentary. Grand Rapids: Eerdmans, 1989.

Anderson, Lisa. *The State and Social Transformation in Tunisia and Libya: 1830–1980.* Princeton Studies in the Near East. Princeton: Princeton University Press, 1986.

Bayly, C. A. "'Archaic' and 'Modern' Globalization in the Eurasian and African Arena: c. 1750–1850." In *Globalization in World History,* edited by A. G. Hopkins, 47–73. London: Pimlico, 2002.

Boer, Roland. *The Sacred Economy of Ancient Israel.* LAI. Louisville: Westminster John Knox, 2015.

Cantor, Norman F. *Inventing the Middle Ages: The Lives, Works, and Ideas of the Great Medievalists of the Twentieth Century*. Cambridge: Lutterworth, 1992.

Coomber, Matthew J. M. "Caught in the Crossfire? Economic Injustice and Prophetic Motivation in Eighth-Century Judah." *BibInt* 19 (2011) 396–432.

————. *Re-Reading the Prophets through Corporate Globalization: A Cultural-Evolutionary Approach to Understanding Economic Injustice in the Hebrew Bible*. Biblical Intersections 4. Piscataway, NJ: Gorgias, 2010. Paperback ed., Center and Library for the Bible and Social Justice Series. Eugene, OR: Cascade Books, 2022.

Coote, Robert B., and Keith W. Whitelam. *The Emergence of Early Israel: In Historical Perspective*. Social World of Biblical Antiquity Series 5. Sheffield: Almond, 1987.

Davies, Philip. "Urban Religion and Rural Religion." In *Religious Diversity in Ancient Israel and Judah*, edited by Francesca Stravrakopoulou and John Barton, 104–17. London: T. & T. Clark, 2010.

Ekholm-Friedman, Kajsa. "On the Evolution of Global Systems, Part I: The Mesopotamian Heartland." In *World System History: The Social Science of Long-Term Change*, edited by Robert A. Denemark et al., 152–84. London: Routledge, 2000.

Hirth, Kenn. *The Organization of Ancient Economies: A Global Perspective*. Cambridge: Cambridge University Press, 2020.

Knapp, Bernard A. "Copper Production and Eastern Mediterranean Trade: The Rise of Complex Society in Cyprus." In *State and Society: The Emergence and Development of Social Hierarchy and Political Centralization*, edited by John Gledhill et al., 149–72. One World Archaeology. London: Unwin Hyman, 1988.

Levine, Baruch A. "Farewell to the Ancient Near East: Evaluating Biblical References of Ownership of Land in Comparative Perspective." In *Privatization in the Ancient Near East and Classical World*, edited by Michael Hudson and Baruch A. Levine, 223–52. Peabody Museum Bulletin 5. Cambridge: Peabody Museum of Archaeology and Ethnology, 1996.

Luckhardt, Courtney. "Confronting Race and Medieval Fantasies: Teaching the Middle Ages in the Modern South" (September 2021). https://www.historians.org/publications-and-directories/perspectives-on-history/october-2021/confronting-race-and-medieval-fantasies-teaching-the-middle-ages-in-the-modern-south?fbclid=IwAR2N1N33gi2LTolZoyyrCH2cuQ87ZrkuXTkumRNtbvKdZ2bWmozuEOsLTdY.

Rappaport, Roy A. "The Sacred in Human Evolution." *Annual Review of Ecology and Systematics* 2 (1971) 23–44.

Stravrakopoulou, Francesca, and John Barton, eds. *Religious Diversity in Ancient Israel and Judah*. London: T. & T. Clark, 2010.

2. Introducing Economy in the Ancient World

KENNETH HIRTH

Introduction

Ancient economies were different from our modern twenty-first-century economic systems. Modern economies employ different production and communication technologies that have fostered an increase in depersonalized buying and selling options both through the internet and via large commercial shopping malls.[1] Modern economies are much more complex, interdependent, and interconnected at the global level than were ancient economies. Nevertheless, there are still a number of similarities between ancient and modern economic systems that carry over between them. Goods are produced and change hands in a variety of ways to reach the individual and institutional consumers that want or need them. While material goods are the focus of the economy, many of the supply, production, finance, and distribution networks of small business

1. The pattern of depersonalized economic interactions as the dominant way of establishing economic interaction does not have a deep history. While the development of marketplaces enabled individuals to interact on a level economic playing field without regard for social differences, ethnographic research has established that many supply and buyer-seller relationships within traditional marketplaces often developed social relationships as a precondition of their operation (Khuri, "Etiquette of Bargaining"; Mintz, "Employment of Capital"). Similarly, the operation of retail-shop economies has always depended on developing strong social relationships between buyers and sellers (Braudel, *Wheels of Commerce*, 73; Cox, *Complete Tradesman*, 146; Dyer, *Country Merchant*; Holleran, *Shopping in Ancient Rome*). The depersonalization of economic transactions in historical terms is a relatively recent development that occurred in the wake of the industrial revolution.

start-ups in the modern world have continued to rely on informal and inter-personal networks to grow and operate just as they did in the ancient past.[2] While ancient economies operated at smaller scales and under the constraints of less developed transportation and communication networks, premodern forms of organization can still be found in world today. The challenge for investigators interested in studying premodern economies is to exercise care not to overlay their experiences and modern views of the economy onto the ancient past.

This chapter provides a basic analytical framework for understanding how ancient and premodern economies were organized and operated. It presents a model of economy relevant for discussing the economic behavior in both large and small-scale societies in the ancient and premodern past.[3] The model was constructed for purposes of the cross-cultural comparison of ancient economies. It is intrinsically an anthropological approach that draws upon a broad range of historical, archaeological, and ethnographic information from many societies around the world. Despite this perspective it does not promote a single theoretical orientation to explain the development of ancient economy. Instead its foundation rests on the broad patterns of economic interaction documented in both ancient and premodern societies, which provide a useful framework for examining how past economic systems operated across ancient Palestine.

This chapter is organized in three sections. It begins with a general discussion of the ancient economy and some of the modern assumptions that are commonly and unknowingly transposed onto past societies we hope to understand. This is followed by a presentation of a model for studying economic organization that divides economic activities into three broad behavioral and organizational sectors. These are (1) the domestic economy of individual families and households, (2) the informal institutions found within communities by means of which households supported themselves and their neighbors, and (3) the formal institutions that embraced society as a whole. Because each of these behavioral sectors consumed resources, it is possible to examine them as spheres of intersecting economic behavior involved in the production and

2. As an example, we need to only point to ongoing recent business revolutions in both China and India that have occurred largely through informal lending relationships and mobilizing capital along kinship lines, which have dominated ancient and premodern societies for thousands of years. While formal banks and banking institutions exist in both China and India, they did not provide the capital to fund the majority of recent small business ventures in these two large countries (Ayyagaria et al., "Formal versus Informal Finance"; Dong et al., "Effects of Credit Constraints"; Kumar, "Credit Rationing"; Turvey and Kong, "Informal Lending").

3. Hirth, *Organization*.

mobilization of the resources they consumed. The chapter concludes by evaluating how the specific and unique circumstances of ancient Palestine fit within this general framework.

The Nature of Ancient and Premodern Economies

The economy has been defined in different ways with no end of debate over what the economy is, and whether it actually can be studied as a separate field apart from the broader society in which it operates. Scholars following a neoclassical tradition have defined the economy as "the science which studies human behavior as a relationship between ends and scarce means which have alternative uses."[4] This approach views the economy through the lens of individual choice and is based on Adam Smith's contention that all individuals have the natural propensity to truck and barter.[5] Karl Polanyi, on the other hand, saw barter and other forms of commercial negotiation as disruptive forces that could lead to conflict within society if they were left unchecked by social controls. For Polanyi the economy did not grow organically through individual decision making but was created and operated through society's social, political, and religious institutions.[6] These two approaches have created what has been called the Formalist–Substantive debate, depending on whether scholars view the economy from a Modernist perspective based on principles of maximization, or a Primitivist perspective that sees the economy as an instituted entity shaped by the social institutions that created it. To this must be added the Marxist theorists who study the development and evolution of economic systems through a series of modes of organization (see Chapters 3 and 4 in this volume). While Marxists bring a worthwhile diachronic perspective to the study of past economic systems, they are prone to overestimating the role of class conflict in economic development or to characterizing multifaceted economic systems by a single dominant form of organization.

While each of these theoretical orientations has their strengths, the important question is, What perspective is the most useful for studying and understanding the ancient economy? I believe the economy is best viewed as a *socially mediated form of material provisioning and interaction involving the production and allocation of resources between alternative ends.* This perspective combines the strengths of both Formalist and Substantive views and provides the basis for examining diachronic changes in modes of organization in the

4. Robbins, *Essay*, 16.
5. Smith, *Inquiry*.
6. Polanyi, *Great Transformation*; Polanyi, "Economy."

Marxist tradition. Defining the economy in this way recognizes three important features of how ancient economies operated.

First, it focuses on *material provisioning of everyday life* and the behaviors and interactions associated with it. People always were responsible for their own subsistence livelihoods, and they did what they had to do to ensure that their families had enough to eat. The main adaptive unit to meet subsistence needs was the household, which had to balance the demands of producing resources for its own internal consumption with the demands of others outside the household. Material provisioning involved the interplay of individuals with the resources distributed across the natural environment and the groups who used or controlled them. The effort invested in subsistence activities together with their ultimate productivity defined the ability of households and other economic units in society to grow and survive in an unstable and fluctuating social landscape. If history and ethnographic research has taught us anything, it is that work effort varied from production unit to production unit and that free riders existed in every society.

Second, the economy was, and still is, a *socially mediated* realm of human behavior. This perspective recognizes that societies define the values and behaviors that shape their provisioning decisions. This substantive view of the economy believes that processes of material provisioning cannot be understood apart from the broader social structures that shaped and created them.[7] Where people put their effort and what they valued were learned and acquired in the course of growing up in the societies where they lived. Because work and economic goals are learned behaviors, they can vary greatly from society to society. For this reason Polanyi and other substantivists have argued that the economy is shaped and *embedded* in the social systems where provisioning takes place, and that behaviors like maximization, utility, and rational choice can only be understood in terms of the specific culture in which they occur. In this sense a good deal of material provisioning at both the household and institutional levels was influenced by, or embedded in, other social, religious, and political activities.

Third, the production and allocation of resources refers to the *decision-making processes* that individuals and groups establish in order to produce, distribute, and consume the resources that they require or want. Here self-motivated or altruistic choices meet the cultural norms that shape them. It is an empirical fact that humans are problem solvers and make decisions that affect the physical and social well-being of the groups to which they belong.

7. See Polanyi, *Great Transformation*; and Dalton, "Economic Theory."

People must eat to survive, obtain mates to reproduce, and raise children that represent the next generation of society. To do this people have to be decision-makers and mediate these issues through their own calculations and by using the advice and guidance of others. People are both rational and pragmatic in making these choices, but they are far from the emotionless and fully informed *homo economicus* of neoclassical economics. Individuals are bounded by their beliefs, emotions, and cultural experiences,[8] and judging the rationality or irrationality of their choices depends on understanding the cultural vantage point from which they are made.

What are some of the modern assumptions and beliefs that commonly are transposed onto ancient economies? There are a number. The first is the myth of self-sufficiency. The idea of self-sufficiency at the household or community level was a product of early ethnographic studies where researchers observed that households in both tribal and peasant societies produced large quantities of food and fiber resources for their own internal consumption. Self-sufficiency was the goal of all ancient households just as it is today; modern households like ancient ones support themselves by the fruits of their labor. But complete self-sufficiency was not an attainable or sustainable economic strategy in the ancient past. It was not attainable because few households had enough labor and access to all the resources that they needed for their livelihood. It was not sustainable because complete self-sufficiency in an environment with fluctuating resource levels like those found in ancient Palestine (see Chapter 3 in this volume) was a very high-risk strategy. Unanticipated resource shortfalls were a constant threat in even some of the most productive environments, and societies developed a range of strategies to offset the subsistence risk that they presented.[9]

One long-standing way to mediate the problem of unanticipated resource shortfalls was to develop interhousehold exchange networks through which resources could move as both gifts and balanced reciprocal exchanges. Evidence for exchange can be found in the archaeological record extending back more than forty thousand years into the Upper Paleolithic.[10] Exchange has been documented ethnographically and historically as a means of obtaining access to resources in societies at all scales of complexity from small forager and

8. Sandstrom, "Ritual Economy"; Thaler, *Misbehaving*.

9. Halstead and O'Shea, eds., *Bad Year Economics*; O'Shea, "Role of Wild Resources."

10. Hagstrum, "Goals of Domestic Autonomy"; Izuho and Hirose, "Review"; White, "Systems."

horticultural groups to large-scale state societies.[11] Establishing exchange relationships with other households in the same or different communities or with groups exploiting different ecological zones helped to minimize risk and provide access to resources when localized or regional shortfalls occurred.

The evidence for exchange early in human history and its positive adaptive value for the households and societies that engaged in it contradicts the modern opinion held by some scholars that interactions involving barter and market exchange did not occur because they were disruptive to social cohesion. Nothing could be further from the truth. Negotiated and reciprocal exchange transactions *always* occurred within socially defined and mediated contexts of interaction whether they were trading partnerships, social linkages, or fictive kinship relationships.[12] They were the linkages through which emergency support could be mobilized, credit could be extended, or regular provisioning could be counted on.[13]

Rather than threatening the cohesion of early human groups, the presence of negotiated, reciprocal exchange as a regular feature of ancient and premodern societies provided another mechanism to acquire necessary resources and guard against unanticipated shortfalls. Heated bargaining does not necessarily disrupt the social fabric of society. One only has to witness the heated negotiation of brideprice between two soon-to-be-linked households in the marriage of their children[14] to realize that this was a regular feature of many societies around the world including in the ancient Near East (see Chapter 7 in this volume). It is more often the case that social disruptions occur when resource flows are forced or unbalanced, and when negotiation does not take place, or when it is not reciprocal.[15]

Another misconception promulgated by scholars following substantive economics is that the economy is so deeply embedded in the social institutions of society that it cannot be examined as a separate field of study.[16] If that was true, this volume would not have been undertaken or produced meaningful results. Yes, the economy was deeply embedded within the social institutions

11. Harding, *Voyagers*; Harding, "Precolonial New Guinea." Malinowski, *Argonauts*. Renfrew et al., "Obsidian"; Silver, *Economic Structures*; Wiessner, "Hxaro."

12. Blakeslee, "Origin and Spread"; Heider, "Visiting"; Hirth, *Organization*; Khuri, "Etiquette of Bargaining"; Malinowski, "Kula"; Wiessner, "Hxaro"; Wood, "Plains Trade."

13. Firth, "Capital, Saving, and Credit"; Hodder, *Merchant Princes*, 226; Mintz, "Employment of Capital," 262.

14. Gray, "Sonjo Bride-Price."

15. Sahlins, *Stone Age Economics*.

16. Polanyi, *Great Transformation*; Polanyi, "Economy."

of society, but that does not make it subordinate to larger social and political processes. On the contrary, it has been strenuously argued and demonstrated that control of the economy and the resources flowing through it was the basis for the development of a good deal of wealth inequality, political complexity, and centralized leadership at both the local and regional levels.[17]

Ideology whether sacred, political, or economic in nature structures human interaction. The exchange of material goods has always accompanied social interactions and cemented alliance relationships between individuals and societies.[18] One view for why the economy was embedded within society is because it provided a more enduring mechanism for solving economic problems involving risk than individual decision-makers, who are notorious short-term problem solvers with imperfect knowledge about the long-term consequences of their economic decisions. After all, even Adam Smith recognized the advantage of embeddedness when he said, "Economic actors tend to make strenuous efforts to re-entangle economic relations in a nexus of social relations for the stability and predictability of the markets."[19].

What then are some features of the economy that ancient, premodern, and modern economies have in common? The first of these is that households, no matter how they were defined or composed, were in business for themselves. The domestic sector always was, and still is, the largest component of the economy. It also was where the majority of resources were produced and consumed to support the society's large commoner population. This point is emphasized by Roland Boer (see Chapter 3 in this volume), but it is often lost in discussions by scholars who focus on the political economy that supported the elite and their attendant institutions rather than the small-scale, quotidian activities of everyday households. The dynamic relationship that has intrigued scholars for the past hundred years is how elites accessed, expropriated, or utilized the labor and resources produced in non-elite households for their own and/or institutional purposes. The goal of households, on the other hand, was to use the resources they produced to support themselves. From the point of view of domestic households there was no "surplus" in society,[20] and understanding how resources were mobilized or produced for institutional use requires

17. Blanton et al., "Dual-Processual Theory"; Earle, *How Chiefs Come to Power*; Flannery and Marcus, *Creation*; Fried, *Evolution*; Friedman and Rowlands, *Evolution of Social Systems*; Johnson and Earle, *Evolution of Human Societies*; Stanish, *Ancient Andean Political Economy*; Trigger, *Understanding Early Civilizations*.

18. Dalton, "Economic Theory."

19. Oka and Kusimba, "Archaeology," 365.

20. Harris, "Economy Has No Surplus."

understanding the social and ideological obligations that linked elite and non-elite sectors of society.

A common feature of ancient and modern economies is that they grow and develop in similar ways. That is, they are economically plastic. *Economic plasticity* refers to the growth in the number, size, and complexity of economic activities in society without replacement.[21] New technologies, forms of organization, or types of activities often appeared as solutions to problems (e.g., famine, resource shortfalls) or new opportunities (e.g., trade, cartage). New economic activities usually were initiated as small undertakings by individuals or in sectors of the society with enough resources to attempt non-traditional endeavors. What is important is these new initiatives spread throughout society alongside established forms of work as they demonstrated their efficiency, their capacity to increase productivity, and their ability to reduce labor while still conforming to existing ideological norms. But this does not mean that traditional forms of work or less efficient technologies disappeared. They did not. Instead they coexisted alongside new economic solutions if they continued to fulfill the needs of the groups that used them.

All economic systems are by nature economically conservative. Traditional ways of doing things continue because they incur no new costs of investment, labor needs are known, and the outcomes of production are predictable given past experience. This leads to *economic heterogeneity* within societies as new forms of economic organization are added to economic systems without replacing traditional forms.[22] The result is that older and less efficient economic arrangements coexist alongside new, more efficient, and even industrial forms of work as long as they meet the needs of their users.[23] Older technologies and economic practices will continue if they get the job done and are often perpetuated in domestic sectors of the economy where they are suitable for small-scale or intermittent production and distribution activities. The conservative nature of traditional economies explains why farmers in Cyprus, Greece, and Turkey continued to thresh their grain throughout the twentieth century using threshing sledges (*dhoukani*) edged with sharp chert flakes and blades.[24]

Established forms of organization are also durable if they can be adapted to new conditions or opportunities. This is the case in many parts of the

21. Hirth, *Organization*; Hirth and Pillsbury, "Redistribution."

22. Hirth, *Organization*.

23. Langlands, *Craft*.

24. Anderson and van Gijn, "Functional Riddle," Figure 5. Kardulias and Yerkes, "Microwear"; Pearlman, "Threshing Sledges."

modern world where the putting-out system, a precursor to modern factory labor, continues to produce textiles, tourist items, and other goods for the global
economy.[25] Émile Durkheim described the heterogeneity of complex economic
systems in terms of their organic and mechanical solidarity and the interdepen-
dence they created between producers and consumers.[26] One contributing feature of this complexity was the way alternative forms of economic organization
coexisted alongside one another producing and distributing goods through a
range of different but complementary distribution networks.

The Organization of Ancient Economies

Ancient and premodern economies were diverse and multifaceted entities.
They differed from one another in terms of the resources available in the regions they occupied and whether they adapted to these regions using different
combinations of hunting, foraging, herding, fishing, and/or agricultural strategies. Whatever the mix of subsistence strategies, tremendous variation can be
found in how work groups were organized, how the means of production were
allocated, and what principles were used to assign ownership rights to resources within societies. Economic change most often occurred slowly and incre-
mentally as a series of small changes in different sectors of the economy rather
than as large-scale shifts across the society as a whole. The shift in agricultural
societies from general usufruct of land held at the community level to restricted
or assigned control and eventually to individual ownership is an example of this
type of complex change.

Despite the variation in economic arrangements found from society to
society, it is possible to classify forms of economic organization in ways that
permit comparisons across the ancient world. The three divisions used here for
examining ancient economic organization are the domestic economy and the
informal and formal sectors of the institutional economy.

Domestic Economy

The *domestic economy* was the foundation of all human societies. It was organized to support and provision individual families and households with the
food and fiber required for their successful biological and social reproduction.
One of the best ways to understand the domestic economy is to examine what

25. Geertz, *Peddlers and Princes*; Lazerson, "Factory or Putting-Out?"; Lazerson, "Putting-Out Production." Littlefield and Reynolds, "Putting-Out System."

26. Durkheim, *Division of Labor*.

households actually do in an effort to support themselves. First and foremost, survival and reproduction were the business of every household, and their productivity determined the success and well-being of their members.[27] Annual fluctuations in resource availability made it difficult for households to consistently predict the level of work required to avoid resource shortfalls. One solution was for households to set their production goals at levels to meet their needs during below-normal years.[28] The result in normal and good years was the production of a food surplus that could be used in community sharing and intergroup feasting of various kinds.[29] Unlike modern society, however, there were few formally financed safety nets in the ancient past to assist a failing household. Instead the mechanisms of assistance that existed tended to operate informally and inconsistently. Small household size was often viewed as a limitation or weakness of the domestic economy. In fact, small size allowed households to respond quickly to both problems and opportunities, making them highly adaptive and flexible economic entities. When small size was a problem for households, it could be solved by mobilizing labor through informal work parties or forms of collective labor at the community level (see below).

Second, households were not passive in their subsistence pursuits. Many households displayed a high level of initiative to support themselves. One way this was accomplished was by investing labor and intensifying production within the productive landscape, using terracing and irrigation. Alternatively, households could follow a diversification strategy where subsistence risk was minimized by investing in a range of different production activities that could offset seasonal resource shortfalls throughout the year.[30] Rural agricultural households in ancient Greece used a mixture of intercropping, crop diversification, and small field dispersal as ways to maximize agricultural yields while minimizing risk.[31] James Scott has argued that households consciously opt for a safety-first subsistence strategy,[32] although that does not mean that households don't take risks when their basic food needs are met, and when they know that an alternative activity might increase their overall economic well-being.[33]

27. Johnson and Earle, *Evolution of Human Societies*.

28. Halstead and O'Shea, eds., *Bad Year Economics*.

29. Allan, *African Husbandman*, 38; Halstead, "Economy Has No Surplus."

30. Arnold *Famine*; Davies, *Adaptable Livelihoods*; Halstead and O'Shea, eds., *Bad Year Economics*; Messer, "Seasonality."

31. Gallant, *Risk and Survival*, 38–42.

32. Scott, *Moral Economy*.

33. Popkin, *Rational Peasant*, 21.

But there is another common and overlooked strategy of household diversification that needs to be mentioned beyond food production. That was the practice of incorporating part-time or intermittent craft production into the normal work regime of both agricultural and nonagricultural households.[34] The strategy involved producing craft goods that could be exchanged for food and other durable goods that households needed. Crafting enabled households to utilize the labor available during slack periods of the annual work cycle, such as during the agricultural dry season, without disrupting other subsistence activities.[35] Furthermore, the presence of trained craftsmen in domestic settings was highly adaptive for the society as a whole because it made them available for institutional use on a periodic basis when needed.

Another source of household diversification was providing services within society. Ethnographic research has shown that households commonly diversified their economic activities by engaging in a mix of both subsistence and commercial activities.[36] Even participation in corvée work projects and labor drafts could have positive returns to households when the sponsoring person or institution provided the mobilized labor with a meal as compensation for the work supplied. In a very real sense agricultural households that also produced goods or services for sale did so with what can be considered an entrepreneurial orientation. These alternative activities were geared to improving the household's overall economic well-being and self-sufficiency even when they were conducted on a small scale.[37]

The Institutional Economy: Formal and Informal

The *institutional economy* consisted of the regularized and agreed-upon structures of socioeconomic interaction that operated within society above the level of individual households. Economic institutions carry with them the norms, values, and rules that govern socioeconomic interaction as well as the forms of organization created to carry them out.[38] While the nature of these institu-

34. Netting, *Balancing*; Rosen, "Early Multi-Resource Nomadism."
35. Hagstrum, "Household Production."
36. Netting, *Balancing*; Netting, *Smallholders*; Sundström, *Exchange Economy*.
37. See, for example, Tax, *Penny Capitalism*.
38. Defining institutions in this way differs from the way that the New Institutional Economics defines them as simply as the rules of the game, distinguishing and separating institutions from the groups of players (the organizations) that carry them out (North, "Institutions," 22). This distinction is useful for studying contemporary societies (North, *New Institutional Economics*), but it is difficult to apply to the ancient past when the physical

tions ranged along a continuum in terms of their formality and durability, two general categories have widespread cross-cultural relevance for all ancient and premodern economies. These are (1) informal institutions, which households established to support and assist themselves and their neighbors in pursuit of their common subsistence and social needs, and (2) formal institutions that were special-purpose organizational structures operating at the level of the whole society.

Informal Institutions

Informal economic institutions encompass the array of special practices and economic arrangements that households employed on a regular or ad hoc basis to access or produce resources, mobilize labor, and obtain other forms of interhousehold support required for their maintenance and social reproduction. They were structured through the social linkages and kinship relationships that households initiated and maintained with one another. They represent mutual assistance networks that operated on a voluntary or quasi-voluntary basis between households. The function of these networks and the level of support that they could provide varied with the specific risks that households faced in their respective environments. Some of the most common problems that households faced and that informal institutions attempted to address were mobilizing labor for work projects, establishing predictable and sustainable resource yields through production and exchange, and providing assistance when unanticipated events placed households in peril.[39] Because they structured interactions between households, they are often subsumed within discussions of community-level behavioral networks.

Informal institutions are difficult to identify in ancient societies because they leave few durable traces in the archaeological record and are only occasionally referred to in historical sources. Nevertheless, they have been repeatedly documented ethnographically in a wide array of large and small societies around that world. They occur in both state and prestate societies, and since they provided valuable support to the households that organized them, there is every reason to assume that they also were widespread throughout the ancient world. The trick is to look for evidence for their operation where that evidence exists. One common practice was the mobilization of labor through reciprocal

remains and organizational structures are easier to identify than the behavioral rules with which they operated.

39. Hirth, *Aztec Economic World*, 22.

labor exchanges and festive work parties.[40] Work parties of this sort could be organized at either the household or community level as a means of getting work done at key points in the agricultural or resource cycle,[41] or to intensify production, and/or to initiate large-scale work projects beyond the capacity of a few households.[42] Labor-exchange relationships between households could be spontaneous or regularized depending on the predictable need for labor and whether they were organized with or without formal leadership oversight.

Another very common function of informal institutions was the formation of social networks that provided a range of important functions for households. Interhousehold social networks were indispensable for accessing resources, providing protection, conducting exchange, moving to better economic opportunities, and fleeing famine, plague, or other disasters. As societies grew in size, some of these activities were formalized at the institutional level modeled after and supplementing the networks forged at the household level without replacing them. One of the most common ways of forming and maintaining social networks was through feasting, which occurred at all levels of society from individual households to whole communities. Everybody loves a party, and as a result food sharing and feasting were ways to build social capital and political relationships through communal celebrations.[43] Social and family networks were the linkages through which spouses were obtained and children were fostered when they were orphaned or moved between families for other reasons.[44] Finally, informal institutions provided the final safety net when natural disasters, war, or unanticipated deaths put households at risk.

Formal Institutions

Formal Institutions developed alongside informal institutions and created the social cohesion and organizational structures that integrated whole societies. Formal institutions were what held societies together as they grew in size and internal complexity. They represent the special arrangements, modes and rules of operation, and organizational structures created by groups and their leaders

40. Erasmus, "Culture Structure."

41. Conklin, Hanunóo Agriculture; Steward, Basin Plateau.

42. Håkansson and Widgren, "Labour and Landscapes"; Håkansson and Widgren, Håkansson and Widgren, eds., Landesque Capital.

43. Dietler and Hayden, Feasts; Hayden, Power of Feasts.

44. Goody and Tambiah, Bridewealth and Dowry; Scelza and Silk, "Fosterage."

to accomplish specific ends.[45] They constitute the many diversified social, political, and religious organizations found in early chiefdom and state-level societies. From an archaeological perspective, formal institutions represent many of the stand-alone "bricks-and-mortar" organizations identified as temples, shrines, marketplaces, and the variety of installations associated with political governance, including palaces, fortifications, courts, armories, and assembly halls. Four important evolutionary forces helped shape and provided the integration for these societywide institutions: the formation of landholding and resource pooling associations, the need for mutual protection, the intensification of agricultural production including the development of irrigation technology, and the need to mediate political relationships with neighboring groups.[46] It is within the development of formal community or societywide institutions that social and economic inequality appeared,[47] and leaders emerged who acquired special privileges under the guise of fulfilling community needs and producing or managing the resources necessary to meet them.[48]

A common feature of formal institutions is that they required resources to carry out their normal functions and activities. These activities included sponsoring celebrations, constructing special-purpose facilities, and supporting the administrative personnel involved in institutional activities. The quantity of resources or labor required depended on the type and scale of their operations. How labor and resources were obtained varied greatly from society to society given the opportunities and strategies they employed. Resources could be mobilized on a voluntary basis from the populations that the institutions served or coerced through a variety of means, including different forms of taxation. Alternatively, and very important for the development of systems of institutional resource control, resources could be produced by the institutions themselves with only minimal infringement on resources or labor of the commoner population. Institutional economies usually were a mix of direct production, taxation, voluntary contributions, institution-directed commerce, and charges rendered for services provided.[49] How the institutional economy developed in any specific society is a complicated task for historians and archaeologists to unravel.

45. Acheson, "Welcome to Nobel Country."
46. Hirth, *Organization*.
47. Flannery and Marcus, *Creation*.
48. Hirth, "Political Economy."
49. Hirth, "Political Economy"; Hirth, *Organization*.

Community contributions and leader (i.e., patron) sponsorship were common ways that community-based activities were sponsored in small-scale societies. As societies grew in size and complexity, more resources were required, and other forms of institutional support emerged. Foremost among these were systems of direct production where the institutions that needed resources undertook to produce them with minimal infringement on the domestic economy of the households that they served. In agricultural societies a common practice was to set aside agricultural land to support the operation of temples, the leader, the palace, or other specific activities deemed necessary in society. The labor needed to cultivate these lands was often mobilized through corvée work groups from the households that the institution purportedly served. The result was the emergence of temple and institutional estates like those found throughout Mesopotamia and early state societies in other areas including the New World. Whether estates were formed around the institutions that needed resources or around the leaders in charge of their operation varied from society to society. But the result was the same; the stage was set for the differential accumulation of wealth within institutional and leader households.

The important point about systems of set-aside and direct production within institutions is that the rationales and mechanisms for their creation were already embedded in and adopted from the domestic economy. Temples across the Near East were regularly conceptualized as the *house of god*. Since all households in agricultural communities normally had usufruct rights to communal land, it was relatively easy to set aside land for the support of the deity's household. Likewise, because all households had the ability to mobilize labor through informal institutions such as festive and reciprocal labor groups, it was within the domain of the deity's household to do the same, which provided a rationale for corvée labor drafts. Whether corvée was a large or small infringement on contributing households depended on many factors, including the number of households involved, the time the work draft was called, the amount of time required to complete the work, and whether the obligation was fixed or rotated between participating households. Direct production was the foundation of institutional economy for both the Inca and Aztec states. This form of organization allowed institutions to be supported without drawing food resources directly from the domestic economy. The resources produced on the lands allocated to commoner households for their support stayed in their households.

An alternative and more intrusive form of institutional support was that of direct taxation. In commenting on the uncertainties of the new American constitution, Benjamin Franklin wrote, "in this world, nothing can be said to be certain, except death and taxes." Without question taxation was a very important way to mobilize resources for institutional support in the ancient world. Its definitive feature was that it mobilized resources from the individuals and households that produced them. Rather than mobilizing labor, forms of taxation extracted finished goods from households after all inputs and risks of production were invested. In this sense it was a heavier burden on the contributing households regardless of whether taxes were calculated as tariffs, head taxes, luxury taxes, or special levies in times of war. But like direct production the rational for taxation already existed in prestate societies in the voluntary contributions that households made to institutional feasts and celebrations. In fact, if taxation is focused on as an isolated entity we miss the fact that taxes lay at one end of a spectrum of voluntary and involuntary contributions that households made for institutional support. Coercive taxation lay at one end of this spectrum and the voluntary support of state institutions by elite members of society lay at the other. Elite patronage and euergetism were an important foundation of institutional support across the Greco-Roman world.[50]

Systems of taxation were highly varied in the ancient world, and in many cases they are difficult to distinguish in historical documents from forms of institutional rent.[51] Perhaps the most important distinction to be made about taxation is whether the resources collected were from members of the society that the institution served or from a conquered population. The authors in this volume make that distinction by assigning the term *tax* to resources drawn from the insider population, and the term *tribute* to the resources extracted from conquered populations. That distinction is a good one because as a rule the taxes levied on members of society that institutions served were low in comparison to the levies on conquered groups, where there is less compunction at extracting resources that might threaten the livelihood of member households. In all cases, however, institutional economies were usually a mixture of different resource-mobilization strategies.

The Economy of Ancient Palestine

The question of course is how well the model presented above furthers our

50. Hands, *Charities*; Veyne, *Bread and Circuses*; Zuiderhoec, *Politics of Munificence*.

51. The difference between tax and rent as the terms are used here is whether something direct and tangible like access to agricultural land or a house is received for the payment made. For rent access to something physical is received while for a tax the return on the payment made is indirect and often quite nebulous.

understanding of the structure of the economy in ancient Palestine. It conforms to the model in several ways. The *domestic economy* was the foundation of society whether households operated as freeholders within the context of their rural villages or as debt laborers on village or estate properties. The work of Boer[52] emphasizes the importance of subsistence agriculture and its organization at the household and community levels. Households were concerned primarily with providing a livelihood for their families, and when that livelihood was threatened unrest or resistance could result.

A number of scholars have argued for the centrality of the patrimonial household as the foundation of subsistence production in ancient Palestine.[53] Not only was the household the foundation for domestic subsistence, but it also served as the conceptual model for organizing both temple (e.g., the house of God) and palace (e.g., the house of David) institutions. Kinship also was an important integrative mechanism, but households regularly incorporated nonkin into their social fabric, which made them a good model for larger institutional organizations. How households accessed the land they cultivated certainly changed over time as freeholders became debt laborers, and estates grew at the expense of village land holdings. Indirect evidence for this change is chronicled in the work of Samuel Adams[54] and Douglas Knight (see Chapters 7 and 10 in this volume) where they note a change from bridewealth to dowry in marriage practices during the Second Temple period, a pattern usually associated with land shortages and the high cost and risk of a raising a family under conditions of shrinking resource availability. Understanding how elite households emerged and controlled land at the village and regional levels is key for reconstructing the relationship between the domestic and institutional sectors of the economy.

Roland Boer believes that households did not have continual usufruct control over specific land within the traditional Jewish community, but that land parcels were regularly rotated and reallocated to farming households by village assemblies. The evidence to support this practice is unclear, and while it would have reinforced an egalitarian ethos within the community, it would have been detrimental to the long-term survivability of households in a region where rainfall was highly variable, and where landscape improvements that households could make, such as terracing, would have improved soil and moisture

---

52. Boer, *Sacred Economy*; and Chapter 3 in this volume.
53. Adams, *Social and Economic Life*; Schloen, *House of the Father*.
54. Adams, *Social and Economic Life*.

retention important for agricultural productivity.[55] More importantly, rotating land assignments would have discouraged the investment of labor in improvements such as vineyards and olive orchards that take years to develop before they bear fruit. Archaeological research indicates that orchard cultivation was established between the fourth and second millennium BCE, producing wine, olive oil, and dried fruit for consumption in towns and urban centers across the southern Levant.[56] Land improvement and the cultivation of multiyear fruit-bearing tree species are two well-documented practices of households in many societies to extend usufruct control over land in the commons.[57] I suspect the same rationale very likely operated across ancient Palestine.

All aspects of ancient society were permeated by religious beliefs that shaped the moral economy at the community level. While Fitzpatrick-McKinley (see Chapter 6 in this volume) argues that the Torah codes were not the basis for legal or economic decisions by judges, Horsley (in volume 2 of this six-volume set) finds that the moral economy of rural villages followed many of the general principles, commandments, and customs of Mosaic law. One of the most vibrant aspects of economic philosophy in ancient Palestine was a concern for the well-being of community members whether they were widows, orphans, or individuals who had fallen into debt. This comes out in the descriptions of a range of informal institutions recorded in the Hebrew Bible.

Informal institutions, as discussed above, are those mechanisms that operated on a voluntary or informal basis within society. One account that reveals several interconnected informal institutions designed to assist failing families is found in the book of Ruth. Here a Moabite women (Ruth) marries a Jewish man who died without having a brother to provide her with a spouse through the informal institution of the levirate. Rather than returning to her home village, Ruth accompanies her widowed mother-in-law (Naomi) back to her natal village of Bethlehem where they live together and eke out a living. Ruth goes out to glean the fields at harvest time and to search out the intentionally uncut corners of the fields (*pe'ah*), the uncollected stalks or grain (*leket*) that had fallen to the ground, and any broken sheaves of grain (*shikh ah*) that farmers left in their fields for the poor in their communities. Finally, a relative of Naomi named Boaz voluntarily steps in through the practice of the *go'el* as a substitute to fulfill the responsibilities of the levirate and marry Ruth. All of these

55. Donkin, *Agricultural Terracing.*
56. Fall et al., "Agricultural Intensification."
57. Conklin, *Hanunóo Agriculture*; Earle, "Archaeology"; Håkansson and Widgren, "Labour and Landscapes."

practices were voluntary, and while the moral economy emphasized the need to be concerned for the poor, the decision to leave a lot or very little of their grain uncut in the corners of agricultural fields rested entirely with individual households.

Other types of informal institutions are also reflected in the Hebrew Bible. The practice of brideservice is illustrated in the story of Jacob (Gen 28–29), who goes to live with his maternal uncle (Laban) where he works for a period of fourteen years to obtain two wives (Leah, Rachel). Brideservice is an alternative to brideprice, where instead of compensating the family of the bride-to-be with material goods, the groom donates his labor to his wife's household. After Jacob's period of brideservice is completed, this same account describes how a labor contract is arranged between Jacob and Laban, whereby Jacob agrees to tend Laban's flocks on a reproduction-shares basis. Similar labor contracts are known from Mesopotamia during the sixth and seventh centuries BCE where shepherds were subcontracted to tend temple flocks for a percentage increase of the herd.[58] It was a way that shepherd households through both skill and luck could support themselves and build their own herds.

One of the most pressing needs at both the household and community levels was mobilizing labor for specific types of work. As discussed above, one way this was done was through reciprocal labor arrangements and festive work parties. An example of a voluntary work party organized at the community level was the rebuilding of wall of Jerusalem in the mid-fifth century BCE (Neh 2–6). In this account Nehemiah organizes groups in the region surrounding Jerusalem to enclose the city and rebuild the lower courses of the wall in a period of only fifty-two days. How accurate this account is remains to be seen, but two things are clear. First, participation in the project was voluntary. Nehemiah did not have the participation of the whole province of Judah to rebuild the wall,[59] and there was considerable resistance to the project from local leaders. Second, the work was carried out as a form of unsupervised, segmental construction like that found in traditional villages of the Third World. The task was accomplished by Nehemiah dividing the construction project into forty-one unequal parts with one segment of the wall assigned to each participating group according to the labor and resources they could mobilize. In this case there was no need for direct supervision because groups followed the wall's preexisting foundation, utilized stone from the previous wall, and only had to connect their work to the segment of the wall located on either side.

58. Kozuh, *Sacrificial Economy*.
59. Blenkinsopp, *Ezra–Nehemiah*, 226.

Informal institutions were an important component of every society, and the three examples cited above illustrate how they are represented in the Hebrew Bible. They operated within the context of the moral economy of ancient Jewish society. The Sabbatical and Jubilee Years also were intended to help families in economic difficulty. These were the years of release, when debts were to be canceled, bond servants were to be freed, fields were to be left unplanted, and olive orchards and vineyards were to be left unpicked so that they could be harvested by the poor. Whether the laws governing these years were formally or informally practiced is unclear, and the observance probably varied from region to region over time. As Fitzpatrick-McKinley points out in her chapter (Chapter 6 in this volume), economic practices in Jewish communities in Egypt and Babylonia during the sixth to the fourth century BCE tended to follow local customs rather than a strict adherence to Levitical law.

Formal institutions were societywide organizations intended to provide services and integration for all members of the society whether they used them or not. The transition of Israel and Judah from independent kingdoms to tributary provinces of the Assyrians, Babylonians, Persians, and Romans transformed their autosufficient economies into surplus exporters that enriched their overlords while impoverishing residents. The two primary institutions in ancient Palestine were the temple and the palace. While both were connected under the umbrella of theology, the fact that each kept their own treasury (see Chapter 8 in this volume) allows us to examine them separately at least in conceptual terms. The degree that their resource streams were merged, reorganized, or eliminated under periods of eternal conquest is a subject that needs additional future investigation.[60]

Elsewhere and earlier in the ancient Near East, temples and palaces were supported by a system of set-aside production and landed estates directly controlled and managed by members of both institutions. Whether the temple in Palestine owned land that was used to support its activities is unclear, and the authors differ in their opinion about this. According to Mosaic custom, the temple and the Levite priests were not supposed to be given land beyond pastureland in the towns where they lived; instead the temple and its priestly personnel were to be supported by the tithes and offerings of the twelve tribes of Israel (Josh 13–21). Nevertheless, both Horsley (in volume 2 of this six-volume set) and Knight (in Chapter 7 of this volume) discuss the role the priests played, first, in consolidating the temple-state under the Persians as tax collectors and, second, in collecting tithes for the temple. This role continued

60. Finkelstein and Silberman, "Temple and Dynasty."

with modification during both the Hellenistic and Roman periods. During the first half of the first century CE the role of priests in the economy expanded to include using temple wealth to make loans to needy peasants, eventually forcing them into debt service (see Horsley's essay in the second volume of this series). Whether the priests did this as agents of the temple or as private individuals to improve their own economic well-being is unclear, but Josephus (*Ant.* 20.180–81, 206–7) claims that priests sent armed gangs to seize grain from village threshing floors, leaving people to starve (see Horsley's essay in volume 2 of this six-volume set).

How secular institutions were supported is another issue, which certainly varied depending on whether Israel and Judah were independent kingdoms or tribute-paying dependencies of another power. Boer[61] feels that palace estates took a while to develop across Palestine compared to other areas of the Near East, but they were present during the ninth century BCE when Israel existed as an independent kingdom. He likewise proposes that the labor working on palace estates would have been indentured labor. What would have happened to these estates after Israel and Judah were conquered is unclear but they certainly would have been incorporated as tax-paying lands into the estates or domains of ruling imperial powers. Kessler (Chapter 8 in this volume) makes the interesting observation that the palace probably did not derive a large percentage of its institutional support from landed estates because agricultural fertility was not an important aspect of royal ideology, as it was elsewhere in the Near East where estate production was a central component of the institutional economy. If so, the important question that this raises is what palace estates would have provided if they existed. If the goal was simply to provision the palace household and its attendant retainers with food provisions, then the amount of land under cultivation need not have been large. However, if the increase from land and herds had to supply all of the staple and luxury goods consumed by the palace, then it would have needed more extensive holdings than it probably had. How then might the palace economy have operated during the first millennium when Judah existed as an independent kingdom?

Michael Pearson has observed that the size of the kingdom was an important factor in shaping the orientation and structure of the institutional economy in ancient states.[62] Rulers of large territorial empires regularly drew the bulk of their income from taxation and the estates under institutional control. Small kingdoms like Israel and Judah had to adapt to their more limited

61. Boer, *Sacred Economy*, 114.
62. Pearson, "Merchants and States."

circumstances. According to Pearson, "small political units typically have to take much more interest, for better or worse, in overseas trade than do rulers with large peasant populations that can be taxed relatively easily."[63] England, Venice, the Netherlands, and ancient Palestine (with access to the Mediterranean) are examples of small states compared to China and India (states with large land-masses from which leaders could draw institutional support).

References in the Hebrew Bible to the activities of the independent kingdom under Solomon are clear statements about institutional commerce carried out under the auspices of the palace. Finkelstein and Silberman argue that the incorporation of Judah into the Assyrian global economy in the 730s BCE was a very important event in the history of the kingdom.[64] Moreover, many of the references to the glories of trade and commerce under Solomon may stem from this period. Solomon established a collaboration with Hiram, the king of the Phoenician city of Tyre, long known as another early and important small merchant kingdom. Likewise, Solomon is visited by the queen of Sheba, the prime incense-producing area of the Near East with trade links to India. In Chapter 4 of this volume, Boer and Petterson reject the notion that commerce was important to the institutional economy because of their Marxist orientation, and because high-value goods were the objects of trade. The important point is that trade in luxuries is how merchant kingdoms often financed armies and other palatial activities.

The list of commodities flowing through Palestine from trade are extensive and include silver, gold, iron, tin, copper, bronze, slaves, horses, mules, ivory, ebony, turquoise, purple textiles or dyes, embroidered textiles, linen, coral, rubies, honey, oil, wine, grain, wool, cassia, sweet cane, livery, herd animals of various kinds, spices, precious stones, finished garments, and carpets (Ezek 27:12–25). Hyperbole notwithstanding, this is a list of a market emporium. Palestine, like Phoenicia, was the gateway to the Mediterranean for many kingdoms in the Near East and therefore a natural crossroads of trade. Kessler (in Chapter 8 of this volume) is correct to argue that the king and the palace were active in international trade. It is very likely that a good deal of this commerce was managed either by palace traders or by independent merchants acting as the king's agents.

The organization of the institutional economy would have changed markedly once Israel and Judah were integrated as tributary provinces within the Assyrian and Persian states. In addition to continued obligations of tithes

63. Pearson, "Merchants and States," 69.
64. Finkelstein and Silberman, "Temple and Dynasty," 265.

and offerings to the temple, preconquest institutional demands would have been modified, and new resource levies would have been demanded and created by the imperial bureaucracy. Kessler (in Chapter 8 of this volume) points out that when Judah became an Assyrian vassal, agricultural production had to be intensified to pay their tribute levy. He also suggests that there were significant changes in the royal economy, which was reorganized and centralized to meet new tax demands. The distinction between taxation and tribute in this volume is an important one. The landscape of ancient taxation is a difficult one to traverse because of the many ways that taxes could be assessed, and because it is often difficult to distinguish between taxation, tribute, and forms of institutional rent. These differences are important because they imply different situational relationships between the payers and payees.

Taxes as clarified above are the enforced extraction of resources from producers after all inputs have been made from planting to harvest. While peasant farmers were heavily taxed in many ancient societies, this does not appear to have been the case in many early agrarian states. Instead, citizen-farmers often were lightly taxed in comparison to our modern taxpaying experience. In ancient Greece the agrarian tax was one-tenth of the harvest (a *dekatē*) between 550 and 527 BCE, which was reduced to one-twentieth of the harvest (the *eikostē*) under the sons of Peisistratos between 527 and 510 BCE, before being dropped entirely during the fifth and fourth centuries BCE when institutional income was available from other sources. In Ptolemaic Egypt tax rates on agricultural land ranged from a twenty-fifth and a twelfth to one-sixth of the harvest, depending on the quality of the land. Agricultural taxes in the Roman world ranged from 10 to 12 percent,[65] while the tax rates given in Hindu texts range from one-sixth to one-twelfth of the harvest yield. Other examples could be cited, but the picture is one of relatively light taxation of citizens compared to what often occurred after conquest by an external power.[66]

The administration of conquered lands and how their populations were exploited was highly varied. Tonia Sharlach argues that the tax/tribute level within the Neo-Assyrian empire (911–612 BCE) amounted to a 10 percent levy on the produce of the land.[67] The Persian emperor Darius is credited as one of the first kings to standardize the level of taxation on land across the twenty provinces of the Persian Empire, using a percentage of the land valuation based on crop type and yield. Even here, however, Darius was cognizant

65. Hopkins, "Taxes and Trade," 116.

66. Hirth, *Organization.*

67. Sharlach, *Provincial Taxation*, 167.

of the fragility of the domestic economy, and as a response, "after fixing the amount of taxes which his subjects were to pay, he sent for the leading men of the provinces, and asked them if the taxes were not perhaps heavy; and when the men said that the taxes were moderate, he ordered that each should pay only half as much."[68] Maybe this is just good historical propaganda, but it does seem to be the case that some rulers considered the effects of tax/tribute levies even on conquered provinces and how they would affect the ability to extract resources on a sustainable basis over the long run. It was this type of concern that Horsley (in volume 2 of this six-volume set) cites when Nehemiah forces nobles to restore houses and fields to the people from which they had been taken (see Neh 5:1–13), and when Herod the Great imports grain from Egypt to support households during times of famine.

If one views taxation and tribute in terms of exploiting resident farmers, then close attention needs to be paid to changes in land management techniques and income opportunities within institutional and estate settings. Here many organizational arrangements are possible. Temple or palace estates can be transformed into prebendal estates to support specific institutional administrators, or estate lands can be rented to free or indentured labor in return for a portion of the crop. It is here that not only the greatest surplus can be produced and mobilized within society, but also the highest percentages of crop extractions are found. As a case in point, there was a sharp difference in levies applied to taxed and rented land in Ptolemaic Egypt. As mentioned above agricultural land in Ptolemaic Egypt was taxed at a level from one-twenty-fifth to one-sixth of the harvest. When levies are examined according to *type of land and the specific land tenure arrangements*, Joseph Manning found that individuals renting land from the state paid a combined 50 percent rate on the harvest.[69] This is fully three times the highest one-sixth tax rate (16.67 percent) on farmers holding land privately or through usufruct tenure. When possible, renting land to private individuals and sharecroppers, much less cultivating it with debt laborers, would have been a highly profitable source for institutional income.

One other very important economic institution throughout the length and breadth of antiquity was the development of the marketplace. It is here that considerable confusion exists, and clarification is necessary because some scholars incorrectly associate the presence of marketplaces with the operation of a market economy. In a market economy, demand affects the price of goods and affects the decisions either to produce or not to produce goods and where there

68. Briant, *From Cyrus to Alexander*, 393.
69. Manning, *Land and Power*, 123.

are active markets in land, labor, and capital. This confluence of features did not occur in antiquity in part because of the time and distance between when goods were made and when they were sold. There were many different types of marketplaces throughout antiquity, and they occurred in societies at all levels of complexity ranging from egalitarian tribes to ancient states.[70] Fundamentally the marketplace enabled people to come together in a single locale to efficiently engage in exchange that otherwise occurred as separate interactions between trade partners and in down-the-line household interactions. The marketplace was a fundamental provisioning mechanism for households in many societies, and this function attests to its durability over time even in the face of political unrest and environmental distress. The fact that Nehemiah demanded a cessation of trade on the Sabbath (Neh 13), and that Jesus cast merchants (Matt 21:12–13) out of the Jerusalem temple indicates that markets were a long-standing feature of the Palestinian economy.[71]

Merchants and the emporia associated with them certainly were present across the Near East during the Bronze Age. Boer (in Chapter 3 of this volume) associates the origin of marketplaces with the use of coinage and as an arm of the state to provision armies. This is a misalignment of several different economic processes. The use of coinage certainly was instituted by state authorities and cities across the Mediterranean in order to require that business transactions within them be conducted in "coin of the realm." In the Greco-Roman world money changers often charged 5 percent for changing coins, and when cities stipulated that all changing be done with a specific company, it provided an opportunity for the collection of a state commission as a form of conversion tax.

Farmers could be required to pay their taxes in coin, and Keith Hopkins has argued that the payment of taxes in coin increased the level of trade within the Roman economy between 200 BCE and 200 CE.[72] That practice had two effects. First it minimized the institutional cost of converting grain to coinage or other resources, and second it mobilized grain and other produce from the domestic economy into broader circulation within society. But that does not mean that farmers would have sold their grain directly to individual consumers within a marketplace. Not only would this be cumbersome for the farmer, but

70. Garraty and Stark, *Archaeological Approaches*; Hirth "Finding the Mark." Hirth, *Organization*.

71. Fitzpatrick-McKinley, "Understanding Law" (Chapter 6 in this volume); and Horsley (in volume 2 in this six-volume set).

72. Hopkins, "Taxes and Trade."

grain flows would be very unpredictable for the consumers that needed them. When farmers paid their taxes in-kind, they did so at harvest time, usually at the threshing floor where state administrators could directly and accurately evaluate the percentage of the harvest to be paid. The threshing floor also would be the most logical and efficient place for farmers to sell their crops for coin. But who would have bought them? Not the state, because they would have wanted to avoid the conversion costs associated with in-kind tax payments. The answer, of course, are merchants, who would then be able to resell grain stocks in large or small quantities to the state, the military, or consumers who needed them in regional marketplaces. It was the practice of buying low at harvesttime and selling high throughout the year that contributed to the development of a bad reputation for merchants.

Conclusion

There is nothing simple about reconstructing ancient economy. An economy has many moving parts that operate independently to produce and distribute resources for different reasons at many different levels of society. The model used here to examine those different sectors was the domestic economy and the informal and formal sectors of the institutional economy. All three of these economic sectors needed resources to carry out their social and economic activities. The domestic economy consisted of households of various sizes and compositions that supported themselves. Self-sufficiency was their goal, and in addition to the food they produced for autoconsumption, they also exchanged goods with other households to establish interaction networks that were important for their maintenance and survival. Households overcame the limitations of small size through a range of informal institutions just as formal institutions knit the society together as a whole. Examples of all three levels of economic activity can be found in ancient Palestine.

Ancient economies were economically plastic, heterogenous in terms of their composition, and socially embedded in cultural systems where they developed. While some scholars have argued that the economy is a dimension of society that cannot be studied on its own terms,[73] no one would deny that if the economy came to a standstill, society as we know it would quickly fall apart. The economy is shaped by the values and needs of the societies where they develop; that is why it is defined here as a socially mediated form of interaction. But economies are also highly adaptive entities that can grow rapidly in unanticipated and sometimes deleterious ways through the actions of their

73. E.g., Polanyi, *Great Transformation.* Polanyi, "Economy"; Dalton, "Economic Theory."

members—for example, when the broader social system must make intentional adjustments to reduce debt, release food stores, redistribute land holdings, or reduce levels of taxation. The study of ancient economy is a fertile field for investigation, and this volume is a productive contribution to broadening our understanding of how it operated and developed in ancient Palestine.

Bibliography

Acheson, James. "Welcome to Nobel Country: A Review of Institutional Economics." In *Anthropology and Institutional Economics*, edited by James M. Acheson, 3–42. Monographs in Economic Anthropology 12. Lanham, MD: University Press of America, 1994.

Adams, Samuel L. *Social and Economic Life in Second Temple Judea*. Louisville: Westminster John Knox, 2014.

Allan, William. *The African Husbandman*. Edinburgh: Oliver & Boyd, 1965.

Anderson, Patricia, and Annelou L. van Gijn. "The Functional Riddle of 'Glossy' Canaanean Blades and the Near Eastern Threshing Sledge." *Journal of Mediterranean Archaeology* 17 (2004) 87–130.

Arnold, David. *Famine: Social Crisis and Historical Change*. New Perspectives on the Past. Oxford: Blackwell, 1988.

Ayyagaria, Meghana, et al. "Formal versus Informal Finance: Evidence from China." *Review of Financial Studies* 23.8 (2011) 3048–97.

Blakeslee, Donald. "The Origin and Spread of the Calumet Ceremony." *American Antiquity* 46 (1981) 759–68.

Blanton, Richard, et al. "A Dual-Processual Theory for the Evolution of Mesoamerican Civilization." *CA* 37 (1996) 1–14.

Blenkinsopp, Joseph. *Ezra–Nehemiah: A Commentary*. OTL. Philadelphia: Westminster, 1988.

Boer, Roland. *The Sacred Economy of Ancient Israel*. LAI. Louisville: Westminster John Knox, 2015.

Braudel, Fernand. *The Wheels of Commerce*. Translated by Siân Reynolds. Civilization & Capitalism 15th–18th Century 2. New York: Harper & Row, 1986.

Briant, Pierre. *From Cyrus to Alexander: A History of the Persian Empire*. Translated by Peter T. Daniels. Winona Lake, IN: Eisenbrauns, 2002.

Conklin, Harold. "An Ethnoecological Approach to Shifting Agriculture." In *Environment and Cultural Behavior*, edited by Andrew P. Vayda, 221–33. Texas Press Sourcebooks in Anthropology 8. American Museum Sourcebooks in Anthropology. Austin: University of Texas Press, 1969.

———. *Hanunóo Agriculture: A Report on an Integral System of Shifting Cultivation in the Philippines*. Food and Agriculture Organization Series on Shifting Cultivation Rome: Food and Agriculture Organization of the United Nations, 1957.

Cox, Nancy. *The Complete Tradesman: A Study of Retailing, 1550–1820*. The History of Retailing and Consumption. Aldershot, UK: Ashgate, 2000.

Dalton, George. "Aboriginal Economies in Stateless Societies." In *Exchange Systems in Prehistory*, edited by Timothy K. Earle and Jonathon E. Ericson, 191–212. Studies in Archeology. New York: Academic, 1977.

———. "Economic Theory and Primitive Society." *American Anthropologist* 63 (1961) 1–25.

Davies, Susanna. *Adaptable Livelihoods*. New York: St. Martin's, 1996.

Dietler, Michael, and Brian Hayden. *Feasts: Archaeological and Ethnographic Perspectives on Food, Politics, and Power*. Washington, DC: Smithsonian Institution Press, 2001.

Dong, Fengxia, Jing Lu, and Allen Featherstone. "Effects of Credit Constraints on Household Productivity in Rural China." *Agricultural Finance Review* 72 (2012) 402–15.

Donkin, R. A. *Agricultural Terracing in the Aboriginal New World*. Viking Fund Publications in Anthropology 56. Tucson: Published for the Wenner-Gren Foundation for Anthropological Research by the University of Arizona Press, 1979.

Durkheim, Émile. *The Division of Labor in Society*. New York: Macmillan, 1984 (originally published 1893).

Dyer, Christopher. *A Country Merchant, 1495–1520: Trading and Farming at the End of the Middle Ages*. Oxford: Oxford University Press, 2012.

Earle, Timothy. "Archaeology, Property, and Prehistory." *Annual Review of Anthropology* 29 (2000) 39–60.

———. *How Chiefs Come to Power: The Political Economy in Prehistory*. Stanford: Stanford University Press, 1997.

Erasmus, Charles. "Culture Structure and Process: The Occurrence and Disappearance of Reciprocal Farm Labor." *Southwestern Journal of Anthropology* 12 (1956) 444–69.

Fall, Patricia, et al. "Agricultural Intensification and the Secondary Products Revolution along the Jordan Rift." *Human Ecology* 30 (2002) 445–82.

Flannery, Kent, and Joyce Marcus. *The Creation of Inequality*. Cambridge: Harvard University Press, 2012.

Finkelstein, Israel, and Neil Asher Silberman. "Temple and Dynasty: Hezekiah, the Remaking of Judah and the Rise of the Pan-Israelite Ideology." *JSOT* 30 (2006) 259–85.

Firth, Raymond. "Capital, Saving, and Credit in Peasant Societies: A Viewpoint from Economic Anthropology." In *Capital, Saving, and Credit in Peasant Societies*, edited by Raymond Firth and B. S. Yamey, 15–34. Chicago: Aldine, 1964.

Fried, Morton. *The Evolution of Political Society*. Random House Studies in Anthropology 7. New York: Random House, 1967.

Friedman, Jonathan, and Michael Rowlands. *The Evolution of Social Systems*. Pittsburgh: University of Pittsburgh Press, 1978.

Gallant, Thomas. *Risk and Survival in Ancient Greece: Reconstructing the Rural Domestic Economy*. Stanford: Stanford University Press, 1991.

Garraty, Christopher P., and Barbara L. Stark. *Archaeological Approaches to Market Exchange in Ancient Societies*. Boulder: University Press of Colorado, 2010.

Geertz, Clifford. *Peddlers and Princes: Social Change and Economic Modernization in Two Indonesian Towns*. Chicago: University of Chicago Press, 1963.

Goody, Jack, and Stanley Jeyaraja Tambiah. *Bridewealth and Dowry*. Cambridge Papers in Social Anthropology. Cambridge: Cambridge University Press, 1973.

Gray, Robert. "Sonjo Bride-Price and the Question of African 'Wife Purchase.'" *American Anthropologist* 62 (1960) 34–57.

Hagstrum, Melissa. "The Goals of Domestic Autonomy among Highland Peruvian Farmer-Potters in Peasant Craft Specialization: Home Economics of Rural Craft Specialists." In *Research in Economic Anthropology* 20 (1999) 265–98.

———. "Household Production in Chaco Canyon." *American Antiquity* 66 (2001) 47–55.

Håkansson, Thomas, and Mats Widgren. "Labour and Landscapes: The Political Economy of Landesque Capital in Nineteenth Century Tanganyika." *Geografiska Annaler: Series B, Human Geography* 89 (2007) 233–48.

———, eds. *Landesque Capital: The Historical Ecology of Enduring Landscape Modifications.* New Frontiers in Historical Ecology 5. Walnut Creek, CA: Left Coast, 2014.

Halstead, Paul. "The Economy Has No Surplus: Economic Stability and Social Change among Early Farming Communities of Thessaly, Greece." In *Bad Year Economics,* edited by Paul Halstead and John O'Shea, 68–80. New Directions in Archaeology. Cambridge: Cambridge University Press, 1989.

Halstead, Paul, and John O'Shea, eds. *Bad Year Economics.* New Directions in Archaeology. Cambridge: Cambridge University Press, 1989.

Hands, Arthur. *Charities and Social Aid in Greece and Rome.* Aspects of Greek and Roman Life. Ithaca: Cornell University Press, 1968.

Harding, Thomas G. "Precolonial New Guinea Trade." *Ethnology* 33 (1994) 101–25.

———. *Voyagers of the Vitiaz Strait.* Monographs of the American Ethnological Society 44. Seattle: University of Washington Press, 1967.

Harris, Marvin. "The Economy Has No Surplus." *American Anthropologist* 61 (1959) 185–99.

Hayden, Brian. *The Power of Feasts: From Prehistory to the Present.* Cambridge: Cambridge University Press, 2014.

Heider, Karl. "Visiting Trade Institutions." *American Anthropologist* 71 (1969) 462–71.

Hirth, Kenneth G. *The Aztec Economic World: Merchants and Markets in Ancient Mesoamerica.* Cambridge: Cambridge University Press, 2016.

———. "Finding the Mark in the Marketplace: The Organization, Development and Archaeological Identification of Market Systems." In *Archaeological Approaches to Market Exchange in Ancient Societies,* edited by Christopher P. Garraty and Barbara L. Stark, 227–47. Boulder: University Press of Colorado, 2010.

———. *The Organization of Ancient Economies: A Global Perspective.* Cambridge: Cambridge University Press, 2020.

———. "Political Economy and Archaeology: Perspectives on Exchange and Production." *Journal of Archaeological Research* 4 (1996) 203–39.

Hirth, Kenneth, and Joanne Pillsbury. "Redistribution and Markets in Andean South America." *CA* 54 (2013) 642–47.

Hodder, Rupert. *Merchant Princes of the East.* Chichester, UK: Wiley, 1996.

Holleran, Claire. *Shopping in Ancient Rome: The Retail Trade in the Late Republic and the Principate.* Oxford: Oxford University Press, 2012.

Hopkins, Keith. "Taxes and Trade in the Roman Empire (200 BC–AD 400)." *JRS* 70 (1980) 101–25.

Izuho, Masami, and Wataru Hirose. "A Review of Archaeological Obsidian Studies on Hokkaido Island (Japan)." In *Crossing the Straits: Prehistoric Obsidian Exploitation in the North Pacific Rim,* edited by Yaroslav V. Kuzmin and Michael D. Glascock, 9–25. BAR International Series 2152. Oxford: Archaeopress, 2010.

Johnson, Allen, and Timothy Earle. *The Evolution of Human Societies.* Stanford: Stanford University Press, 1987.

Kardulias, Nick P., and Richard W. Yerkes. "Microwear and Metric Analysis of Threshing Sledge Flints from Greece and Cyprus." *Journal of Archaeological Science* 23 (1996) 657–66.

Khuri, Fuad I. "The Etiquette of Bargaining in the Middle East." *American Anthropologist* 70 (1968) 698–706.

Kozuh, Michael. *The Sacrificial Economy: Assessors, Contractors, and Thieves in the Management of Sacrificial Sheep at the Eanna Temple of Uruk (ca. 625–520 BC)*. Explorations in Ancient Near Eastern Civilizations 2. Winnona Lake, IN: Eisenbrauns, 2014.

Kumar, Chandra. "Credit Rationing and the Economics of Informal Lending." PhD diss, Cornell University, 2009.

Kuzmin, Yaroslav, and Andrei Ptashinsky. "Obsidian Provenance Studies on Kamchatka Peninsula (Far Eastern Russia): 2003–9 Results." In *Crossing the Straits: Prehistoric Obsidian Exploitation in the North Pacific Rim*, edited by Yaroslav V. Kuzmin and Michael D. Glascock, 89–120. BAR International Series 2152. Oxford: Archaeopress, 2010.

Langlands, Alexander. *Cræft: An Inquiry into the Origins and True Meaning of Traditional Crafts*. New York: Norton, 2017.

Lazerson, Mark. "Factory or Putting-Out? Knitting Networks in Modena." In *The Embedded Firm: On the Socioeconomics of Industrial Networks*, edited by Gernot Grabher, 203–26. London: Routledge, 1993.

———. "Putting-Out Production in Modena." In *Explorations in Economic Sociology*, edited by Richard Swedberg, 403–28. New York: Russell Sage Foundation, 1993.

Littlefield, Alice, and Larry T. Reynolds. "The Putting-Out System: Transitional Form or Recurrent Feature of Capitalist Production?" *Social Science Journal* 27 (1990) 359–72.

Malinowski, Bronislaw. *Argonauts of the Western Pacific*. Studies in Economics and Political Science 65. London: Routledge & Kegan Paul, 1922.

———. "Kula: The Circulating Exchange of Valuables in the Archipelagoes of Eastern New Guinea." In *Tribal and Peasant Economies*, edited by George Dalton, 171–84. Texas Press Sourcebooks in Anthropology 2. American Museum Sourcebooks in Anthropology. New York: American Museum of Natural History, 1967.

Manning, J. G. *Land and Power in Ptolemaic Egypt: The Structure of Land Tenure*. Cambridge: Cambridge University Press, 2003.

Messer, Ellen. "Seasonality in Food Systems: An Anthropological Perspective on Household Food Security." In *Seasonal Variability in Third World Agriculture*, edited by David E. Sahn, 151–75. Baltimore: Johns Hopkins University Press, 1989.

Mintz, Sidney. "The Employment of Capital by Market Women in Haiti." In *Capital, Saving, and Credit in Peasant Societies*, edited by Raymond Firth and B. S. Yamey, 256–86. Chicago: Aldine, 1964.

Netting, Robert McC. *Balancing on an Alp: Ecological Change and Continuity in a Swiss Mountain Community*. Cambridge: Cambridge University Press, 1981.

———. "Population, Permanent Agriculture and Polities: Unpacking the Evolutionary Portmanteau." In *The Evolution of Political Systems*, edited by Steadman Upham, 21–61. School of American Research Advanced Seminar Series. Cambridge: Cambridge University Press, 1990.

———. *Smallholders, Householders: Farm Families and the Ecology of Intensive, Sustainable Agriculture*. Stanford: Stanford University Press, 1993.

North, Douglass C. "Institutions and the Performance of Economies over Time." In *Handbook of New Institutional Economics*, edited by Claude Menard and Mary M. Shirley, 9–30. Dordrecht: Springer, 2008.

————. "The New Institutional Economics and Third World Development." In *The New Institutional Economics and Third World Development*, edited by John Harriss et al., 17–26. London: Routledge, 1995.

Oka, Rahul, and Chapurukha Kusimba. "The Archaeology of Trading Systems, Part I: Towards a New Trade Synthesis." *Journal of Archaeological Research* 16 (2008) 339–95.

O'Shea, John. "The Role of Wild Resources in Small-Scale Agricultural Systems: Tales from the Lakes and the Plains. In *Bad Year Economics*, edited by Paul Halstead and John O'Shea, 57–67. New Directions in Archaeology. Cambridge: Cambridge University Press,1989.

Pearlman, David. "Threshing Sledges in the East Mediterranean: Ethnoarchaeology with Chert Knappers and Dhoukanes in Cyprus." MA thesis, University of Minnesota, 1985.

Pearson, Michael. "Merchants and States." In *The Political Economy of Merchant Empires*, edited by James D. Tracy, 41–116. Studies in Comparative Early Modern History. Cambridge: Cambridge University Press, 1991.

Polanyi, Karl. "The Economy as Instituted Process." In *Trade and Market in the Early Empires*, edited by Karl Polanyi et al, 243–70. Glencoe, IL: Free Press, 1957.

————. *The Great Transformation: The Political and Economic Origins of Our Time*. Boston: Beacon, 1944.

Popkin, Samuel L. *The Rational Peasant. The Political Economy of Rural Society in Vietnam*. Berkeley: University of California Press, 1979.

Renfrew, Colin, et al. "Obsidian and Early Cultural Contact in the Near East." *Proceedings of the Prehistoric Society* 32 (1966) 30–72.

Robbins, Lionel *An Essay on the Nature & Significance of Economic Science*. 2nd ed., revised and extended. London: Macmillan, 1935.

Rosen, Steven. "Early Multi-Resource Nomadism: Excavations at the Camel Site in the Central Negev." *Antiquity* 77 (2003) 749–60.

Sahlins, Marshall. *Stone Age Economics*. Chicago: Aldine, 1972.

Sandstrom, Alan. "Ritual Economy among the Nahua of Northern Veracruz, Mexico." In *Dimensions of Ritual Economy*, edited by E. Christian Wells and Patricia A. McAnany, 93–119. Research in Economic Anthropology 27. Bradford, UK: Emerald Group, 2008.

Scelza, Brooke A., and Joan B. Silk. "Fosterage as a System of Dispersed Cooperative Breeding." *Human Nature* 25 (2014) 448–64.

Schloen, J. David. *The House of the Father as Fact and Symbol: Patrimonialism in Ugarit and the Ancient Near East*. Studies in the Archaeology and History of the Levant 2. Leiden: Brill, 2001.

Scott, James C. *The Moral Economy of the Peasant*. New Haven: Yale University Press, 1976.

Sharlach, Tonia. *Provincial Taxation and the Ur III State*. Cuneiform Monographs 26, Leiden: Brill, 2004.

Silver, Morris. *Economic Structures of the Ancient Near East*. Totwa, NJ: Barnes & Noble, 1985.

Smith, Adam. *An Inquiry Into the Nature and Causes of the Wealth of Nations*. Edinburgh: Thomas Nelson and Peter Brown, 1827.

Stanish, Charles. *Ancient Andean Political Economy*. Austin: University of Texas Press, 1992.

Steward, Julian H. *Basin Plateau Aboriginal Sociopolitical Groups*. Smithsonian Institution. Bureau of American Ethnology Bulletin 120. Washington, DC: US Government Printing Office, 1938.

Sundström, Lars. *The Exchange Economy of Pre-Colonial Tropical Africa*. Studia Ethnographica Upsaliensia 24. New York: St. Martin's, 1974.

——. *Penny Capitalism: A Guatemalan Indian Economy*. Publications of the Smithsonian Institution Institute of Social Anthropology 16. Washington, DC: US Government Printing Office, 1953. Washington, DC: Government Printing Office, 1953.

Tax, Sol. *Penny Capitalism: A Guatemalan Indian Economy*. Smithsonian Institution Institute of Social Anthropology Publication 16. Washington, DC: Government Printing Office, 1953.

Thaler, Richard H. *Misbehaving: The Making of Behavioral Economics*. New York: Norton, 2015.

Trigger, Bruce G. *Understanding Early Civilizations: A Comparative Study*. Cambridge: Cambridge University Press, 2003.

Turvey, Calum, and Rong Kong. "Informal Lending amongst Friends and Relatives." *China Economic Review* 21 (2010) 544–56.

Veyne, Paul. *Bread and Circuses: Historical Sociology and Political Pluralism*. Translated by Brian Pearce. London: Penguin, 1990.

White, Randall. "Systems of Personal Ornamentation in the Early Upper Palaeolithic: Methodological Challenges and New Observations." In *Rethinking the Human Revolution: New Behavioural and Biological Perspectives on the Origin and Dispersal of Modern Humans*, edited by Paul Mellars et al., 287–302. MacDonald Institute Monographs. Cambridge: MacDonald Institute for Archaeological Research, 2007.

Wiessner, Polly. "Hxaro: A Regional System of Reciprocity for Reducing Risk among the !Kung San." PhD diss., University of Michigan, 1977. Ann Arbor: University Microfilms, 1997.

Wood, Raymond. "Plains Trade in Prehistoric and Protohistoric Intertribal Relations." In *Anthropology on the Great Plains*, edited by W. Raymond Wood and Margot Liberty, 98–109. Lincoln: University of Nebraska Press, 1980.

Zuiderhoec, Arjan. *The Politics of Munificence in the Roman Empire: Citizens, Elites and Benefactors in Asia Minor*. Greek Culture in the Roman World. Cambridge: University Press, 2009.

3. Production and Allocation in Ancient Southwest Asian Economics

Roland Boer

A reconstruction of the economies of ancient Southwest Asia involves a subtle interplay between data and theory.[1] Theoretically, I draw on two key aspects. The first is a distinction between economic practices of allocation and extraction, while the second develops the categories of institutional forms, regimes, and modes of production.[2] Let me say a little more about each.

Allocation and Extraction

Allocation and reallocation designate the practice in which labor, land, and equipment are allocated to various members of agricultural communities on the basis of capability and need. So also is the produce—of animals and plants—allocated among the village community, often in complex patterns of need, obligation, and reciprocity. In this light, allocation is a survival strategy for those who face continual challenges to such survival. This includes putting aside small surpluses for the ever-present threat of a bad year due to drought, flood, or pestilence. By contrast, extraction involves the appropriation of labor and produce by those who do not work directly in production. In short, they live off the labor of others. On this matter, a further distinction applies: exploitation and expropriation. *Exploitation* means the extraction of surplus from what one possesses or controls, while *expropriation* means the extraction

1. I prefer the terminology of ancient Southwest Asia, since this is its actual location in the Eurasian landmass.

2. This study draws upon and develops further the main points of Boer, *Sacred Economy*.

44

of this surplus from what is possessed by another (plunder is the most obvious form). Usually, allocation and extraction cannot be completely separated from one another, for within allocatory systems some extraction is found, and extraction systems seek surpluses from both allocatory forms and other patterns of extraction (for example, an imperial predator may appropriate the surplus from a local system of extraction).

I draw this methodological frame from the Marxist-inspired *régulation* theory,[3] adapted for ancient economies. The building blocks of any economic system are institutional forms. These are not institutions understood in the usual sense, although there is some fruitful interaction with institutional economics.[4] Instead, they designate the core functional components of an economic system—components that are both autonomous and connected with one another in changing patterns. For the economies of ancient Southwest Asia, these institutional forms are subsistence survival, kinship-household, estates, and tribute-exchange. I will examine each form in more detail below; suffice to point out here that one finds from time to time efforts to make one institutional form the determining feature of ancient economies. Thus, proposals have been made that the household was the key to such economies, in terms of the communal or domestic mode of production; or patronage becomes a patrimonial system (even though patronage is an aspect of kinship-household); or tribute produces a tributary economy; or, as one might expect, trade is seen as the basis of economic activity. Such moves make the mistake of the false universal. Each was important, but only in relation to the other institutional forms. Indeed, these connections lead to the second-level category: a regime, which is a particular constellation of all of the institutional forms, with one dominating the others. A regime marks a period of relative stability, the reasons for which need to be established.

This approach is in marked contrast to the neoclassical economic assumption that stability is the norm and crisis the exception that must be explained. Instead, crisis was the norm and stability the exception. As a specific arrangement of institutional forms, a regime entails tensions and compromises between them. The crucial binding factor here is a mode of *régulation*, a specific set of ideological, institutional (in the usual sense), and behavioral norms that are both assumed and enforced. Pierre Bourdieu's *habitus* may be used to describe such a mode of *régulation*. Only when we have accounted for the

---

3. See especially Boyer and Saillard, eds., *Régulation Theory*; Jessop and Sum, *Beyond the Regulation Approach*.

4. Villeval, "Régulation Theory."

institutional forms, the regimes, and the modes of *régulation* can we speak of an overarching mode of production.[5]

Subsistence Survival

The core institutional form was what I call subsistence survival. It pertained to the majority of ancient Southwest Asia's small population, which was engaged in the main economic activity of agriculture—understood in terms of both animal husbandry and crop growing.

The beginnings of subsistence survival appear many thousands of years earlier, during what V. Gordon Childe called the "Neolithic Revolution."[6] It was a long process indeed, but it entailed a significant transformation in modes of production, from hunter-gatherer existence to agriculture.[7] The transformation entailed the symbiotic—and mutual—domestication and genetic shifts in grains and animals (human and nonhuman). Archaeologists now date the process from the beginning of the Holocene era (c. 9,500 BCE), noting that it took place in distinct regions of the world, albeit with differing tempos.[8] Human beings tended to settle in villages (although seminomadism was constitutive of such a life), social forms changed, and techniques of production were creatively

5. Readers may have noticed that I do not use one of the more usual approaches to ancient economies, whether world-systems theory (derived from Wallerstein), Weberian approaches (most notably through Karl Polanyi and Moses Finley), or neoclassical economic theory, especially in its "economics imperialist" mode that came into its own after 1989 and supposed overcoming of communism. In brief, an "economics imperialist" approach is based on neoclassical theory, taking it through a process of reductionism: to the rational and self-interested individual as the basic analytic unit, to a "market" without social basis, and to a "market" devoid of history. In other words, it is individualizing, desocializing, and dehistoricizing. The next step is that with such a reduction this redefined neoclassical economics then engages in colonizing these and every other area of the social sciences and humanities, including ancient history. See especially Fine and Milonakis, *From Economics Imperialism to Freakonomics*; and Milonakis and Fine, *From Political Economy to Economics*. For further discussion of these approaches, their shortcomings, and what I do draw from them, see Boer, *Sacred Economy*. Further, in this study, I do not deal with mode of *régulation*, since this topic will appear in "Economic Relationships Found in the Bible" (this volume).

6. Childe, *Man Makes Himself*, 59–86. A revolution may take millennia, as was the case here.

7. This is not to say that hunter-gatherer existence disappeared, for it (with its inherent contradictions) existed alongside and was eventually absorbed within agricultural and tribal economies—as is the case with earlier modes of production.

8. See especially Zeder, "Origins of Agriculture in the Ancient Near East." The process took place—with various animals and crops—mostly autonomously in major areas of the world at distinct times and at different speeds: Afro-Eurasia, Australia–Papua New Guinea, the Pacific and the Americas. See further, albeit with some qualifications, Christian, *Maps of Time*, 207–44; Smith, *Emergence of Agriculture*.

transformed. This situation also meant a new array of diseases that could develop due to the proximity of human and other animal bodies, which diseases require for their life cycles.

Domestication of plants entailed the tasks of planting, weeding, and harvesting, which meant that they lost—through favored treatment—genetic contact with other similar plants.[9] Genetic and morphological change meant that the plants in question became dependent on human beings. The results were thinner husks surrounding larger ("naked") seeds, which were clustered together and attached to the stem with stronger and thicker stalks. The advantages are many: germinating earlier, staying on the stalk longer and not scattering as easily, ripening over a longer period and producing larger yields. Without the pressing need to reproduce, the luxury of care meant that the plants in question could become larger and fatter. The main crops so transformed in ancient Southwest Asia were emmer wheat, einkorn wheat, and barley, as well as legumes such as lentils, peas, and chickpeas. Not to be forgotten are the genetic shifts in olive trees and grapevines, whose main task in life became the provisioning of human beings.

In this part of the world, sheep and goats became the herd staples. They slowly mutated from the wild versions,[10] so that milk and usable fibers came from their bodies at human instigation.[11] Selective feeding, controlled breeding, and restricted movement also meant their bodies became smaller than their wild cousins. Somewhat later, a select few of the heavy and resource-depleting bovines (descended from the auroch) were deployed for traction, while later still and only in areas with sufficient water pigs appear. Even so, sheep and goats were the core animals, due to their versatility in producing fibers, meat, and milk, and their relatively minimal requirements for fodder and water. So transformed were the animals that they could no longer survive without human beings. Reciprocally, human beings found themselves in a similar situation.

As these long processes were underway, the institutional form of subsistence survival came into its own, with sedentary and nomadic features woven

9. Soil types also played a role, and knowledge of the best types developed through trial and error, and through fertilization. For useful introductions, see Bridges, *World Soils*; Legros, *Major Soil Groups*, 180–205, 265–90.

10. The dog, derived from the wolf, preceded sheep and goats, but dogs—mostly—function rather differently.

11. Lactation became perpetual due to daily milking. The genetic transformation of sheep (descended from the mouflon, or *Ovis gmelini*) entailed that eventually the fine inner layer of wool dominated, and the coarse and stiff fur of the outer layer diminished. This process was assisted by a shift from plucking to shearing, which encouraged new growth of the fine wool. See Sherratt, "Plough and Pastoralism," 282.

together.[12] Since the nature of subsistence survival is largely "aceramic," leaving minimal archaeological and recorded data, we need to draw from the relatively new fields of archaeobotany and archaeozoology.[13] In relation to the palaeobotanical evidence provided by archaeobotany, the range of crops mentioned above was still grown but also included bitter vetch, figs, dates, and nuts.[14] This approach may be described as a risk-averse and tried method of polyculture.[15] Food was eaten fresh, preserved, baked, and—when pots began to be used—cooked. Before the resultant stews made food easier on teeth and stomach, evidence indicates significant wearing of teeth from chewing on coarse grains. I add that the production of alcohol—what may loosely be called beer—was a central factor in human collective living. The earliest evidence indicates that the bakery and brewery were one and the same structure, with the same vessels used for both (since yeast remained in them and was not yet extracted as a distinct substance). Of ancient crops, about 60 percent were of barley, and of the barley crop up to 40 percent was used for the ancient brew—šēkār in Hebrew (Lev 10:9; Deut 29:6; Prov 20:1).

Archaeozoology reveals that sheep and goats were the key, with a 2:1 ratio of sheep and goats.[16] Both species are versatile in what they produce, but also in their survival ability. Goats are extraordinary, able to eat the most surprising items and to regulate metabolism when faced with food and water shortages.[17]

12. Rather than clearly separated, as is often assumed. The variations were many, ranging between the ideal poles of full sedentarism and full nomadism.

13. We should also keep in mind historical evidence. Subsistence survival is found in the earliest human settlements, through to medieval Europe, seventeenth-century North America, pre-1873 Japan, and twentieth-century Russia, Greece, the Maghreb, and Iraq. It was a feature of agriculture in pre-Ottoman and Ottoman periods, and twentieth-century Greater Syria, including the Levant. Granott, Land System; Hopkins, Highlands of Canaan, 257–58; Roberts, Landscapes of Settlement, 15–37; Wilkinson, Archaeological Landscapes; Fischbach, State, Society and Land, 38–41; Guillaume, Land, Credit and Crisis, 28–42.

14. Hald, Thousand Years, 44–121.

15. Much later, in the first millennium BCE, grafting appeared, probably from eastern Asia. Not only did it enable the spread of olive cultivation, but it was also deployed with apple, plum, pistachio, pear, and the sweet and sour varieties of cherry. From more eastern parts, this practice spread into the Mediterranean. Zohary, Hopf, and Weiss, Domestication.

16. Archaeozoology deal with animal bones after human consumption, taking account of the passage in time from the initial gnawed bone tossed to a dog to its appearance in the laboratory. For a sample of key literature, see Redding, "Theoretical Determinations"; Hesse and Wapnish, Animal Bone Archaeology; Wapnish and Hesse, "Archaeozoology"; O'Connor, Archaeology; Sasson, Animal Husbandry.

17. Goats are able to survive with the loss of 30 percent in body weight (double any other animal). After water shortage, the effects of which they limit through regulated sweating and defecation, they can replenish quickly, drinking up to 40 percent of body weight in one session.

Relative to goats, sheep are less versatile, but they eat regenerating grass (which goats strangely avoid), and they deliver more proteins and fats. Like goats, they can walk far from water sources in search of pasture. Thus, it makes sense to have more sheep than goats. But the question remains: Why have both species when one would do the job? The main reason is disease or another calamity. If disease devastated one of the two species, the other species would survive. Further, goats and sheep are enthusiastic breeders, so a herd can be restored in a few seasons. Under a subsistence survival mode, bone analysis shows that the herds were culled regularly to keep the animals healthy and the herd at an optimal size. Males were culled more regularly, since females were the key to breeding and milk provision. Apart from wool and milk from living animals, one used every part of a dead animal, rather than choosing delicate morsels and disposing of the remainder (as is characteristic of luxury consumption and indeed commercial breeding).[18]

As for pigs, their use was periodic and patchy, becoming relatively widespread only in the Greco-Roman era.[19] The reason is that pigs are not overly useful for subsistence survival. They may produce meat, but one struggles to obtain milk and wool. They are also fond of drinking relatively large amounts of water and cope badly with temperature extremes. It should be no surprise that they appear in well-watered areas (such as Egypt).[20] Even so, the pig's consumption of resources pales by comparison with the cow. A cow needs approximately fifty liters (13.2 gallons)of water per day, more in hot weather, while a sheep or a goat needs two to three liters (0.5–0.75 gallons)—meaning that cows can walk no more than sixteen kilometers, or 10 miles, from water sources. Few were the cows found in villages, and they tended to die of old age since they were used for traction, especially plowing and hauling loads. Obviously, this required members of a village to share bovines for such purposes.[21]

---

18. The consistent metaphorization of goats and sheep in the Hebrew Bible and New Testament is not a surprise: Lev 17:7; Num 27:17; 1 Sam 16:11, 19; 17:34; 2 Sam 5:2; 7:8; 1 Kgs 22:17; 2 Chr 11:15; 18:16; Pss 23; 44:11, 22; 74:1; 78:52, 70–72; 95:7; 100:3; Isa 1:11; 13:14, 21; 34:6, 14; 40:11; 53:6–7; Jer 12:3; 23:1; 50:6; Ezek 34:2–16; Mic 2:12; Matt 7:15; 9:36; 10:6, 16; 12:11–12; 15:24; 18:12–14; 25:31–46; 26:31; Mark 6:34; 14:27; Luke 15:1–7, 29; 17:7; John 10:1–18, 26–27; 21:15–19; Acts 8:32; Rom 8:36; Heb 9:11–14, 19; 10:4; 11:37; 13:20; 1 Pet 2:25.

19. Hesse, "Pig Lovers": Hesse and Wapnish, "Archaeozoological Perspective," 468–70.

20. Brewer, "Hunting," 441–43.

21. Sasson estimates that a village of 100 people would need three hundred sheep and goats, but only twelve bovines. Thus, they were highly prized, with specific laws concerning bovines (Exod 21:28–36). Sasson, *Animal Husbandry*, 56.

An inescapable feature of subsistence survival was its social determination. Since I address this topic in more detail in the next section, here I focus on the social organization of agriculture. Instead of "private" fields and plots, the key was a system of field shares, determined by what Soviet-era Russian scholars call the village commune (*mir* or *obshchina*), and what others describe as *musha'* farming.[22] By "field share" I mean a social unit that includes labor and land rather than land alone. Spatially, the shares tended to be noncontiguous and relatively long, so as to ensure an even spread of different types of soil. These field shares underwent periodic reallocation—every one to five years—within a village or even a collection of villages. In light of the need to spread risk, to optimize labor, soil conservation, and the consistency of crops, and to take account of changing patterns of household ability and needs, the field shares were reallocated by means of lots, village councils, or elders. And the produce of the shares was also reallocated among households. Other common projects required slightly different approaches, such as tending grapevines, olive groves, and fruit orchards, or producing bread and alcoholic beverages. In these cases, labor was shared, as also with the herds of sheep and goats, which were grazed on common ground shared with other villages.[23]

To sum up, the three crucial features of subsistence survival were diversity, security, and optimal use. Diversity appears in the range of crops, as also in the animal species and the use of all animal parts across all ages. Diversity also provides security, since failure in one part of the herd or crop was not a disaster for the whole.[24] Optimal usage—rather than maximal usage for the sake of commercial gain—ensured longer-term survival: pasture, water, and soil were not used until exhaustion but always underutilized for the sake of future use. This optimal approach also influenced human and animal populations, which were usually kept below carrying capacity. Each of these practices also ensured small surpluses for the bad year that might be a season away.[25] This institutional

22. The literature on such farming is immense, but see the following material that is relevant for the period under consideration: Bergheim, "Land Tenure"; Khalidi, *Land Tenure*; Nadan, "Colonial Misunderstanding"; Nadan, *Palestinian Peasant*; Firestone, "Land–Equalizing"; Schäbler, "Practicing Musha"; for full bibliography, see Excursus 7 in Boer, *Sacred Economy*.

23. Noteworthy here are the myriad traces of village paths, trails, and tracks, required for walking to and between the field shares and other villages. The spatial production is quite unique, which may appear fragmentary but actually constituted complex units of land shares, pastures, vines and fruit trees, without clearly demarcated boundaries. Wilkinson, "The Tell," 56–57; Wilkinson, *Archaeological Landscapes*; Casana, "Structural Transformations."

24. Binford, *Constructing Frames of Reference*, 193; Wharton, "Risk."

25. Hayden, "On Territoriality"; Redding, "General Explanation"; Redding, "Subsistence

form was adaptable and constantly reconfigured in light of prevailing and often difficult circumstances. These tried techniques have proved remarkably resilient and widespread, with human beings reverting to them even today in "times of trouble."

Before we rush to assume some form of "primitive communism," I need to address two matters. First, the challenges faced by subsistence survival were not negligible. The problems were many: increased labor because of new technologies such as the plow;[26] new diseases and plagues as the result of collective living in well-watered and fertile areas—not to mention the attendant refuse (and absence of toilets)[27] or the increasingly temperate climate; the effects of droughts and famines on less mobile populations; more limited diets and physical problems from repetitive agricultural tasks and from carrying heavy loads; and, finally, limited life expectancy (between twenty-five and thirty years), with almost half of children dying before maturity.[28] In the face of these challenges, subsistence survival had to be adaptive and creative.

The second matter to be addressed concerns the issue of internal exploitation within subsistence survival. While there may have been a functional leveling of labor between members of village communities (all hands were needed for the myriad tasks required), subsistence survival also witnessed economic differentiation. In order to understand how this worked, I draw on Friedrich Engels' influential distinction between small, middle, and big peasants.[29] While smallholding peasants tilled land that was often just enough for self-sufficiency, they were also under constant pressure to provide labor for others and faced consistent encroachments on their land. Middle peasants walked a fine line between aspiring to become big peasants and slipping into small-peasant status. By contrast, big peasants exploited small peasants and less fortunate middle

Security."

26. Hopkins, *Highlands of Canaan*, 38–41.

27. Osteoarchaeological research indicates the widespread effects of malaria, as well as gastrointestinal diseases, brucellosis (from infected animal products such as goat's milk), typhus, typhoid, dysentery, tuberculosis, and plague. For slightly later evidence, see Grmek, *Diseases*, 86–89; Sallares, *Malaria and Rome*.

28. We should not be surprised that some *affluent* foragers preferred to appropriate only a few features of subsistence survival agriculture, but not to adopt it completely. Christian, *Maps of Time*, 223–29.

29. Engels, "Peasant Question." Engels drew on first–hand research in the countryside of France, while also relying on material from Russia and Ireland. His arguments deeply influenced the situation in the Soviet Union, where the communists focused on relieving the exploitation of small and even middle peasants. For an insightful development of Engels' categories in the Greco-Roman era, see Ste. Croix, *Class Struggle*, 210–11.

peasants. Typical exploitation included demands for labor or land tenure, and at times debt slavery. Engels stresses that the categories are never hard and fast, since the types of production appear in mixed proportions in different parts. In some areas one finds more big peasants, while in others—especially where the soil is poor—small peasants predominate but must be immensely creative in finding ways to survive. The main point I wish to draw from Engels is that even within subsistence survival one finds patterns of exploitation in terms of productive capacity and wealth, but that peasants are impressively creative in their strategies of survival.

These patterns of internal exploitation created a perpetual tension between the necessarily communal nature of subsistence survival (for an individual would not last long on his or her own) and the aggrandizing agenda of big peasants. For example, while the village communities may allocate field shares, the big peasant would work hard to ensure greater field shares for himself. (I use that pronoun deliberately.) Or if the village headman was an "elected" position, the big peasant would seek to ensure that he was elected. Here too we find patterns of patronage, which often ran along kinship lines—especially in light of the fact that most residents in a village were related to one another—but could also cut across such lines if the big peasant met resistance. However, the underlying reality was that village communities tended to tolerate big peasants as long as they did not threaten the survival of the village. This reality forced big peasants to present themselves as beneficial to the village community, which would be accepted as long as it matched actions.

Kinship-Household

I have spent some time with subsistence survival, since it was the core institutional form that is so often overlooked in studies of ancient economies. The same cannot be said for what may be called kinship-household.[30] While kinship refers to the human dimension, the more recent preference for household studies risks a range of static assumptions. These are based on the fixedness of archaeological remains, let alone the apparent "given" that a "household"

---

30. Apart from a spate of kinship studies spanning many years, the focus has shifted in the last three decades to households. Studies of households stem from the influential article by Wilk and Rathje, "Household Archaeology." Many are the studies of ancient Southwest Asia inspired by this shift, running through into the Greco-Roman era: Neyrey, "Managing the Household"; Osiek and Balch, *Families*; Saller, "*Pater Familias*"; Saller, "Women, Slaves"; Saller, "Household and Gender"; Meyers, "Material Remains"; Meyers, *Households and Holiness*; Moxnes, *Putting Jesus*; Baker, "Imagined Households"; Bodel and Olyan, eds., *Household and Family*; Sivertsev, "Household Economy"; Yasur et al., eds., *Household Archaeology*; Berlin, "Household Judaism."

is a fixed structure, with its walls, roofs and doors. This tendency has led to some questionable approaches that attempt to determine "family" size, if not populations, on the basis of the assumed capacity of archaeologically recovered remains of dwellings.[31] In response, I would like to emphasize the sheer flexibility of such households, drawing my inspiration from Henri Lefebvre's "rhythmanalysis."[32]

The malleability of kinship should by now be obvious, manifested in the way genealogies were constantly reshaped to include "outsiders" for whatever reason (destruction of a neighboring village by a marauding band or through disease), all in the name of the continuity of tradition. In terms of built structures, I stress the rhythms and flows. Living organisms and inanimate objects constantly moved in and out of such structures, which varied from simple one-room constructions to those with two levels. Animals were kept in close proximity, often coming inside and sharing the space with human beings overnight. Animal parts were cooked outside in common areas, with the remains tossed onto piles for dogs to gnaw. Given that a "room of one's own" is a remarkably recent development in human history, the spaces produced and used invariably involved multiple bodies, awake or asleep. These spaces were constantly reproduced for multiple purposes. This may be illustrated by the difficulty of discerning what have been called "cult corners," which may have been a partition, niche, platform, bench, or plastered surface.[33] The ostensible purpose was for ritual observance, but the space was redeployed for many other purposes, whether temporary food storage, tying up an animal, putting a child to rest, and so on. The tendency to locate such "corners" in doorways or passages adds to the flexible reproduction of space. Even the built structures, themselves, reveal the malleability of space. While products of stone, clay and fired pottery last longer, appearing in the archaeological record, constructions made of mud, straw, branches and skins do not. Even if they are not torn down or packed by people on the move, they soon break down into their constituent ingredients when human beings are not present.

This flexibility also pertained to the labor, equipment, and produce in village communities—which were typically of 75–150 people.[34] Repair of a

---

31. While this method is called a "density coefficient," the other approach for population estimates focuses on a supposed required calorie intake (roughly two thousand per day) in relation to product area and density.

32. Lefebvre, Rhythmanalysis; Lefebvre, Éléments de rythmanalyse.

33. Hitchcock, "Cult Corners."

34. Knight, Law, Power, and Justice, 122–23.

structure, the use of traction animals for plowing, breastfeeding, weaving, pottery, woodcutting, hunting, fishing, sowing and harvest, alcohol and olive oil
production—these and more required multiple skills and shared labor. Where
possible, many tasks were undertaken by either gender (although this was more
of a challenge with wet nursing),[35] for farmers of both sexes were by definition
multi–skilled. Furthermore, survival needs meant that the animal and plant
products were reallocated within the village. Those whom I identified earlier as
big peasants would seek to ensure that their "allocation" was larger than others,'
but even this tendency had its limits, for it had to be seen at least as benefiting the whole village. As for governance, the evidence is admittedly vague since
few records survive. It seems to have functioned in forms of village assemblies,
councils of elders and headmen—structures that continued even in town dis-
tricts.[36] These bodies administered a range of tasks: reallocation of field shares;
management of common orchards and grazing land; administration of customary law; and responding to external pressures such as taxation, military threat,
crop shortages, disease, and famine.

Finally, we may also locate the patterns of patronage within the framework of kinship-household.[37] Culturally, the patriarchal clan heads assumed
and were usually given deference and respect. In this case, patronage was part of
the workings of kinship-household (which was no means based on an anachronistic sense of equality). At another level, the big peasant would also assume
the role of patron, based on the fiction that the relations between him and his
clients were reciprocal. But the big peasant's interests could also run counter
to kinship lines, attracting under his wing "everyone who was in distress, and
everyone who was in debt, and everyone who was discontented [mar–nepeš]"
(1 Sam 22:2). In this account, the future king David becomes a patron or "chief"
(šar—1 Sam 22:2; 2 Sam 2:13, 17, 30–31) to a group of clients who had fallen
out with the structures of kinship-household and its patterns of customary
law (compare Abram in Gen 14, who remains within such structures). The
much-discussed pattern of honor and shame finds its proper location in such
a group. Rather than a vague "cultural" norm of ancient Southwest Asian and

35. Concerning the multiple tasks of women, see Peskowitz, *Spinning Fantasies*, 193 n.
19.

36. On ancient evidence, see Jankowska, "Communal Self-Government," 274–76; Diakonoff, "Structure of Near Eastern Society"; Heltzer, *Rural Community*, 75–83. On later
evidence concerning the Hellenistic and Roman eras, see Ste. Croix, *Class Struggle*, 221–22.

37. Although patronage is by means a dominant form, useful information may be
gleaned from Schloen, *House of the Father*; Simkins, "Patronage"; Lemche, "From Patronage
Society."

Mediterranean society,[38] honor-shame is the preserve of the obscenely rich and gangsters. Notably, David runs a protection racket for a gang of looters, who "wandered wherever they could go" (1 Sam 23:13).

Estates

A third institution form was the estate. Primarily extractive, estates were typically established by temple and palace, often in conjunction with each other. Their purpose was to supply the nonproducers with the necessities and luxuries of life to which they had become accustomed.[39] Estates first arose in riverine environments, such as Egypt and lower Mesopotamia, where the water sources required greater levels of central management for irrigation and flood management. In areas such as upper Mesopotamia and the Levant, where agriculture relies on rainfall patterns, estates took a little longer to appear. In the former, estates arose under the direction of temples, which were later absorbed by the palace. In the latter, they tended to appear as part of efforts by the palace (which already controlled temples).

The estates were managed in two main ways, although these often overlapped. In some cases, such as the temple of Baba (Bau) from third-millennium BCE Lagash or the third dynasty of Ur, estates were managed directly by the temple. In other cases, such as Old Babylonia of Hammurabi or in the Neo-Assyrian Empire, land and its usufruct was tenured out to individuals and groups. Tenants had to provide one-third to one-half of the produce to the palace, were responsible for equipment, and had to farm diligently. Labor for the estates was secured by various means—whether laborers were war captives, deportees, refugees, debtors, or workers under some other compulsion. Given the chronic labor shortage in the ancient world (and life expectancy of no more than thirty), any means would do. On the estates workers might have been indentured, slaves or tenant farmers (another layer of tenure). On the more highly organized estates, such as at Ur III, teams of farmers, fishers, craft workers, shepherds, barge haulers, and construction workers are identified, and the daily rations are meted out.[40]

38. Hobbs, "Reflections on Honor"; Crook, "Honor, Shame."

39. I draw here especially from Diakonoff, "On the Structure"; Diakonoff, *Structure*; Diakonoff, "General Outline"; Diakonoff, "City-States"; Diakonoff, "Syria"; Liverani, "Communautés de village"; Liverani, "Ville et campagne"; Liverani, "Economy of Ugaritic."

40. We should not be seduced by the sources, which overwhelmingly deal with estate management and tend to give the impression that the estates were vast and widespread. Very few were relatively large, such as the estates connected with the Eanna temple in Uruk, or in Ur III, but most of the records reveal an average of about thirty laborers, some having only

I add here a brief observation concerning slavery. It is preferable to see indentured labor and debt slavery as largely the same phenomenon, although I prefer to use the first term, *indentured labor*. Occasionally captives from war became slaves, in the sense that someone or some group had lifelong possession and control over another's life. However, the reality was that nearly all estate labor was indentured and thereby unfree. The living conditions for different types of laborers differed little. Despite occasional proposals to the contrary,[41] slavery as such was not dominant; since it was not the primary form of producing surplus, the types of physical coercion, in terms of personnel and weapons technology, were not sufficient for a predominant slave economy, and there was not an ideological framework that made slavery a primary feature.

The question of labor raises the issue of how estate workers related to subsistence laborers. A significant degree of interchange took place, ranging from those indentured to work full time on the estates to those who did so periodically, whether for corvée labor on specific tasks or during peak seasons. Indeed, a major form of taxation of village communes was precisely in terms of this type of labor, for which the community as a whole was responsible. At the same time, this pattern reveals the internal contradiction of the estate system. Labor was—in the opinion of the ruling class—necessary on the estates, and they did their best to find whatever way to draw as many laborers as possible onto the estates, to lengthen and make permanent periodic indenture, and thereby to expand the land under cultivation (see Isa 5:8–10 and Mic 2:1–2). The "returns" from estates were much higher than the customary 10 percent levied (where possible) on village communities. So rulers and their hangers-on had little interest in the viability of subsistence-survival agriculture. Obviously, this situation led to periodic collapse of the estate system, as we will soon see.

Tribute-Exchange

The final institutional form is what may be called tribute-exchange. The linkage between tribute and exchange is deliberate, since the patterns of tribute-tax and exchange were intimately connected through the actions of the state and its functionaries. In this section, I address three issues: the nature of plunder (in terms of tribute and tax), markets, and the roles of merchants, who were usually also landlords and tax agents.

A common distinction would have it that taxation is what a state does to its citizens, and tribute is what it exacts from other states under its sway. One

---

two or three. Liverani, "Economy of Ugaritic."

41. Mendelsohn, *Slavery*; Dandamaev, *Slavery*.

is internal and the other external. A further distinction applies in terms of the overt or covert presence of violence. If violence is used in an obvious fashion— armed thugs in the middle of the night—we tend to call it plunder. Instead of seeing these practices—tax, tribute, and plunder—as distinct, I suggest that they are part of a continuum. The reasons are two: first, violence is always present, in terms of its covert threat within the structures of a state or in terms of the actual use of violence in specific situations; second, the distinction between citizens of a state and foreigners is problematic in the ancient world. Despite the grandiose claims of aspiring despots,[42] the boundaries of their realms were always vague and shifting. Thus, the statements concerning vast territories sanctioned by the gods (Lev 25:23), and about the delivery of justice, peace, and well-being (1 Kgs 4:20; 5:9–14 [4:29–34 ET]) should be seen as consummate political fiction.[43] Without the complex mechanisms for managing territories and borders between states (immigration, customs, police, judiciary, citizenship, and infrastructure in terms of water and transport), ancient states had to rely on intermittent bands of soldiers and tax collectors for haphazard enforcement. Only the Persians came close with their efforts at administration, and they appeared quite late in the piece. But the Persian Empire lasted barely two centuries, for the various gradations of plunder produce a system that is inherently unstable. The goods to be plundered do not appear overnight. When raiding a neighbor and making off with its painstakingly acquired treasures (usually stored in temples), one cannot simply return the next year and hope to find that all the loot has magically reappeared. Or when taxing villages, the authorities in question need to be extremely careful in order to ensure that the viability of the rural population is not undermined. Tax levels would—ideally—need to be minimal, since the preferred subsistence survival form of existence leaves little room to move. Surpluses were generated not for the sake of filling someone else's coffers, but for the bad season that always threatened. The problem is that ideal and carefully calibrated approaches to tax-tribute were beyond most, if not all, ancient states. Apart from the temptation to squeeze peasants, these states did not have the administrative wherewithal to carry it out.

As for the question of markets, which were intimately connected with the various types of plunder, the key is to recalibrate our understanding of "markets." Under the influence of neoclassical economics, too many have come to assume that "the market" (without any qualifier) is primarily a profit-making mechanism. This means that whenever a market appears, it is inherently

42. Yoffee, *Myths*, 160.
43. Steinkeller, "On Rulers," 177–78; Briant, *Cyrus to Alexander*, 50–58.

capitalist. The effect is to render all of human history in terms of gradations of capitalism. The ancients may have been a little less adept at such practices, yet they were "partly capitalist."[44] But let us stop for a moment and ask whether this is actually the case. It turns out that most markets throughout human history have not been capitalist markets—for we need to remember that an ideal "market" does not exist, but only particular manifestations of markets.

To explain: local markets existed throughout ancient Southwest Asia, for the purpose of exchanging local goods not readily available in a particular village. Given the friction of distance, these subsistence markets tended to function between villages within view of one another (two to four kilometers apart), exchanging food items, pottery, and tools. By contrast, in the first millennium BCE, a new type of market arose and spread across ancient Southwest Asia. As Graeber argues,[45] these markets were intimately connected with the invention of coinage, which happened at around the same time in different parts of the world and using different methods (Lydia, India, and China). Soon enough, a ruler or advisor hit on a novel idea to solve a seemingly intractable logistical problem: how to provision armies on the move. Thus far, it had taken as many personnel as the army itself to ensure it was fed, housed, and kept in reasonable fighting form. The new plan was momentous: pay the soldiers in coin and demand taxes from the people in coin. How would the people get hold of the coins? Sell their agricultural produce to the soldiers, along with whatever else—above and below the belt—that the soldiers needed. Now the rural laborers had the coins that the local monarch required for taxes, should the tax collector and his band of thugs appear. The types of markets that arose were extensions of the local, rural markets I mentioned earlier. But now they spread throughout areas where the new approach to paying soldiers and tax gathering were implemented. We might call these ventures "tax markets" to highlight their specific role; they arose as an effort to solve a specific logistical problem. They were never a perfect logistical mechanism, for villagers would do their best to avoid the tax gatherer, and soldiers continued to pillage as they had already done for millennia. But my point is that these markets arose as an attempted solution to a logistical problem. Indeed, it could be argued that most markets throughout human history have been logistical exercises, in this case as a by-product of a state's needs.

44. Algaze, *Ancient Mesopotamia*, 42; see also Ekholm and Friedman, "'Capital,'" 41. Even the widespread use of Polanyi's distinction between "embedded" and "disembedded" markets assumes this sense of "the market."

45. Graeber, *Debt*, 149–50.

The question remains: what about the profit motive, especially if we are to believe Adam Smith's metaphysical claim that human nature involves a basic desire to "truck, barter, and exchange one thing for another"?[46] The short answer is that profit was a secondary phenomenon in these tax markets. The long answer requires further elaboration.

To begin with, the vast majority of long-distance exchange was for exotic preciosities—the high cost of which justified the risks and costs of acquisition—that the ruling class felt was appropriate and for the sake of impressing others of the same ilk. Here we find ivory, apes, and peacocks (1 Kgs 10:22), if not precious stones, fine alcohol, expensive clothes, elephants, monkeys, bulls' heads, and hippopotamus parts.[47] Further, who was given the task of acquiring such goods? They are commonly called merchants, but it is instructive to consider the terminology used for these figures. First Kings 10:28–29 uses the term *sōḥar* (root *sḥr*), which includes within its semantic field the sense of going about and around, if not scurrying, let alone an enchanter or sorcerer. It draws near to *rōkēl* (participle of *rkl*), which appears alongside *sḥr* in Ezek 27:12–25 (see also Gen 23:16; 2 Chr 9:14; Neh 3:31–32; 13:20; Prov 31:14; Song 3:6; Isa 23:2–3; Ezek 17:4; 27:3, 22–23, 36; 38:13; Nah 3:16), and bears the sense not merely of running about, but also of a slanderer. Add a third term for "merchant," *Kĕna ʿan* or *Kĕna ʾănî* (Canaan or Canaanite), and we have the added meanings of lowly (*kn ʾ*) and becoming low, or lowly (Isa 23:8; Ezek 16:29; 17:4; Hos 12:8 (7 ET); Zeph 1:11; 14:21; Prov 31:24). The outcome is a distinctly unflattering picture of the aforesaid merchant, who may best be described as a "hustler" or as a "groveling busybody." Necessary for acquiring the exotic goods so desired by the ruling class, they were simultaneously despised and constantly under suspicion. If Ezek 27–28 is not enough to reveal this perception (it is a prophetic condemnation of such activity), then let me add an example outside biblical material. In the thirteenth century, the king of Ugarit wrote to Hatusili III, king of Hatti, complaining. "The men of the city of Ura, the merchants, are a heavy burden upon the land of your subject." The reason: these meddlesome merchants acquire houses and fields and force people into debt bondage

---

46. Smith, *Wealth of Nations*, 1.2.1. The history of this argument is long and complicated. Smith appears at a crucial turning point, when intense debates over human nature and the attendant economic behavior made the transition from explicit engagement with biblical narratives concerning Adam and Eve to ostensibly "secular" concerns. Theorists of the rapidly spreading capitalist mode of production needed slogans to characterize human nature in pro-capitalist terms. Smith was up to the challenge. See further Boer and Petterson, *Idols of Nations*.

47. Milevski, *Early Bronze Age*, 146–63.

to work on them. Hattusili replies: the merchants must return home and stop harassing people, let alone appropriating houses and fields (CTH 93).[48] Indeed, the Akkadian term for such a person is *tamkāru* (*dam-gàr*, cognate with Hebrew *mkr*), signalling not merely a merchant, but one who is engaged in debt slavery. The selling in question involves "selling" and thereby "betraying" children and family members. It should be no surprise that they never formed a distinct subclass, perhaps a "middle class," to the point of being excluded from the run of everyday life, if not separated from the rest in a type of economic apartheid.[49]

As the final few examples make clear, these groveling busybodies in question were rarely if ever purely engaged in such dubious practices. They were also in the business of managing estates as landlords, to whom the palace would tenure out such estates, as well as being debt-collectors and tax-tribute collectors. It should be no surprise that they were held in low esteem. That they should make money as part of their activities—as a byproduct of the processes—only added to the opprobrium.

Three Regimes

To sum up the reconstruction thus far, I have proposed four institutional forms: subsistence survival, kinship-household, estates, and tribute-exchange. These are of course abstractions from everyday economic life, especially in the way they were never entirely distinct from one another. In fact, the four institutional forms were perpetually combined in different formations that may be called—following the terminology of *régulation* theory—regimes. As mentioned earlier, regimes designate periods of relative stability in the context of perpetual economic disruption. In this final section, I will outline the three main regimes of ancient Southwest Asia, in which the late and marginal "little" kingdoms of the southern Levant flashed briefly in the first millennium BCE before being absorbed into the larger empire nearby. The regimes may be called the subsistence regime, the palatine regime, and the regime of plunder. While the first was primarily allocative, the other two were extractive. However, the key is that in each regime we may find all four of the institutional forms, even if in terms of what the regime in question sought to counter. Thus, the subsistence regime sought to negate the effects of the estates and tribute-exchange, while these two drew upon the human and material resources of subsistence-survival and

---

48. CTH 93. Beckman, ed., *Hittite Diplomatic Texts*, 177. For further examples, see EA 8, PRU, IV, 17.229: Moran, ed. and trans., *Amarna Letters*, 12–13; Heltzer, *Rural Community*, 63; Alster, "He Who Pays"; Jursa, "Debts and Indebtedness," 204–5.

49. Giorgadze, "Hittite Kingdom," 268–69.

kinship-household, but were also geared to overcome their resistance.

The Subsistence Regime

Under a subsistence regime, the institutional forms of subsistence-survival and kinship-household were dominant, while the other two forms were subordinate, if not absent (or rather, present as a perpetual threat to be avoided). This regime dominated in areas outside the sway of larger powers, or at least in marginal zones where enforcement was intermittent and haphazard. Above all, it dominated during periods of what are usually called "crisis" and "collapse"—most notably towards the end of the third millennium BCE when "the Kingdom of Sumer and Akkad(e)" (Ur III) comes to a close, the "dark age" of the sixteenth and early fifteenth centuries, and then the centuries-long period at the turn of the first millennium, which affected the Mediterranean world even longer than ancient Southwest Asia. Stemming from Herodotus, the narrative of periodic "collapse" is difficult to shake in histories of the ancient world.

The crucial question is, "collapse" for whom? If one thinks of states, empires, and their small ruling classes (no more than 2 percent of the population), then it certainly was a collapse. The fleeting experience of power disappeared, as did the estates upon which they relied for the "necessities" of life. Their cities, palaces, and temples were deserted, if not reduced to rubble. The biblical book of Lamentations is the most obvious example of literature that presents such a scenario, as does the telling observation by one as Rib-Hadda in the Amarna Letters: "I am afraid the peasantry will strike me down."[50] But if one considers the perspective of the rural laborers in the village communities, the situation was quite different. These periods were celebrated; since they did not have to pay onerous taxes to a gang of armed men, able hands were not subjected to indentured labor on the palatine estates, and they could focus on what they knew best, subsistence-survival agriculture. As Judg 17:6 indicates, "In those days there was no king in Israel; all the people did what was right in their own eyes" (see also Judg 18:1; 19:1; 21:25; 1 Kgs 22:17; 2 Chr 18:16). Reading against the grain of the text's ideological perspective, this verse may be seen as a desired situation for the majority of people located in the countryside.[51]

While events sometimes unfolded around them without warning, there is enough evidence to suggest that rural laborers took active part in the process of destroying the centers of extractive economic power. The Habiru of the

50. EA 77; in Moran, trans. and ed., *Amarna Letters*, 148.
51. Jobling, "Feminism."

Amarna Letters were a constant attraction for disgruntled farmers, who would either disappear and join the Habiru full time or become a Habiru by night and a villager by day.[52] The appeal of the Habiru was strong, as we find in this rallying cry by ʿAbdi-Aširta: "Let us drive out the mayors from the country that the entire country be joined to the ʿApiru, . . . to the entire country. Then will (our) sons and daughters be at peace forever. Should even so the king come out, the entire country will be against him, and what will he do to us?"[53] If I add that the people often characterized in the records as barbaric and dangerous nomads, with their marauding and threatening of the powers that be (in the eyes of those powers), actually included disaffected peasants, then the number of people ready to hasten the demise of a local despot and his hangers-on grows. Such groups were ready indeed to provide welcome assistance in destruction and demolition. Their annual patterns of migration "could be transformed into aggressive campaigns if the power of the centralized state was weak."[54]

I conclude with two observations. First, a rarely acknowledged fact is that usable inventions often emerged during such periods. For example, during the sixteenth-century "dark age" the combination of horse and chariot appears, while at the end of the second millennium iron technology spread. Perhaps even more surprising—a little further afield—is that the alphabet was invented during the latter period. How can this be? Was not the alphabet invented by the Phoenicians, from whom the Greeks later adopted it? Not quite, for the Phoenicians used what is called an *abjad* (the word is drawn from the first letters of the Arabic script and their assumed order), in which the characters represent consonants. By contrast, in an alphabet the characters represent consonants and vowels.[55] This the Greeks invented during their "dark age," which ran well into the first millennium BCE.

52. "Habiru" (*Apiru*) is a specific name from the Amarna letters, but it designates anyone who has slipped away from the burdens of estate life, or any group that has felt the pressure of a close power center (with its demands for taxation in labor and in produce). The deeper the economic crisis, the more the ranks of the Habiru swelled. They established self-governing communities and occasionally entered the military service of local monarchs if it served their interest, yet their underlying motivation remained opposition to royal rule, estates, and tribute. The term's semantic field includes the denotative exile, outlaw, and refugee, to the connotative hostile, enemy, and rascal. See Liverani, *Myth and Politics*, 102–3.

53. EA 74; in Moran, ed. and trans., *Amarna Letters*, 143; see also Diakonoff, "Syria," 195; Liverani, *Israel's History*, 27–28.

54. Kozyreva, "Old Babylonian," 99.

55. Daniels, "Study of Writing Systems," 4.

The second observation addresses when the subsistence regime is to be found. I have mentioned that this regime predominated during notable periods of what are often called "collapse" and "crisis," but it appears throughout the four millennia of ancient Near Eastern history, running from Uruk to the end of the Persian Empire. In whatever zone, away from the periodic sway of powers, the subsistence regime can be found—not least in the area of the southern Levant. In this corner of ancient Southwest Asia, it is worth noting that the fluorescence of what became—briefly—ancient Israel and Judah took place during the two or three centuries at the turn of the first millennium and not so much when the little kingdoms were established. During this time relative stability was achieved, settlements took place in the Judean highlands through the use of new technologies (lime cisterns, terracing, and iron tools), and resistance to an extractive regime could be organized against efforts to subordinate highland settlements. Even late in the piece, when a regime of plunder was being instituted under Ezra and Nehemiah, the resistance of the "peoples of the land" shows its face once again.

The Palatine Regime

As the name suggests, the palatine regime saw the dominance of the extractive institutional form of estates. The primary contradiction (to gloss Mao) was with subsistence survival, while tribute-exchange was a secondary feature. This regime characterized most of the economic history of ancient Southwest Asia, beginning with the rise of Uruk and running through some three millennia until late in the first millennium BCE. On its way, we find Akkad(e), Ur III, Assyria, and Babylon—to name but a few of the more well-known formations. This is a stunning stretch of human history, covering about half of the period of human civilization in this part of the world. Whole modes of production have risen and fallen in far shorter time periods (capitalism, for instance, is about half a millennium old). But we must keep in mind that time frames were longer in the earlier phases of human economic activity. For instance, the preceding agricultural or "Neolithic Revolution"[56] began in the tenth millennium BCE and unfolded over the next six millennia or so.

Despite its apparent longevity, the palatine regime was inherently unstable. As I indicated above, the temple-palace insistence on estates to provision itself usually had little concern for the viability of subsistence-survival

56. See Childe, *Man Makes Himself.*

agriculture, let alone their kinship-household structures. Given the chronic shortage of labor, the estates—administered directly by palace or temple or by landlords—dragooned labor in whatever possible way. It should be no surprise that consistent peasant resistance was the norm, manifested in everyday acts of foot-dragging, noncompliance, leaving crops unharvested, or simply absconding.[57] So palatine regimes often came to abrupt ends—not merely due to defeat at the hands of an invading army or two. For some reason, the ruling classes in question seemed not to be able to learn the lesson, so they tried over and again to reestablish estate systems, until at last all avenues were exhausted by the end of the second millennium BCE and the centuries-long regime of subsistence survival gained the upper hand. By the ninth century BCE a new extractive regime had taken its place.

This is the point when ancient Israel appears on the scene, a rather late and marginal arrival. Yet the economic regime it attempted to institute was anachronistic: it sought a palatine regime in a time (first millennium) when they had become secondary concerns. The archaeological evidence from the southern Levant is ambiguous, although this has not prevented some from imagining a powerful state with multiple estates.[58] Powerful it was not, but it does seem to have attempted to introduce a palatine regime, as the limited evidence of the *lmlk* ("to/for the king") seals of the eighth or seventh centuries and the Samaria ostraca from roughly the same period suggest.[59] Indications of town enlargement, building construction redolent of state power, water and storage systems, and the direction of goods toward those towns also point in this direction.[60] To this we may add—with some caution—the mentions in the biblical text of indentured labor, whether periodic or permanent (1 Kgs 4:6; 5:27–30 [13–16 ET]; 9:15–21), royal administrators (4:7–19), tens of thousands of horses and their stalls (5:6 [4:26 ET]), the vast supply of food to the palace (5:2–3 [4:22–23 ET]), and the temple itself with its almost endless animal sacrifices (1 Kgs 6–8). Caution is needed with the biblical material, for it also imagines Solomon as some form of imperial potentate, on par with the Neo-Assyrian or Persian emperors. The catch is that these empires deployed the rather different regime of plunder, while the Israelites used a rather modest

57. Yee, "Recovering"; Scott, *Weapons*, 106–9.

58. Faust has tried to construct such a picture, suggesting palatine storehouses for grain and wine, olive presses for palace consumption, centers for wine production, and estates on the periphery of the Judean highlands. Faust, "Household Economies," 267–69.

59. *Lmlk* is a Hebrew seal imprint commonly found on jars, meaning "to/for the king." On the *lmlk* seals, see especially Grabbe, *Ancient Israel*, 168, 180–82.

60. For a survey of the archaeological material, see Nam, *Portrayals*, 104–31.

palatine regime. This anachronism may be read as both a sign of the marginal economic status of the southern Levant, but also as a literary signal of the contradictory situation in which ancient Israel found itself as a palatine regime in the wider context of a regime of plunder.

The Regime of Plunder

This final regime arose as a response to the centuries-long dominance of the subsistence regime, which ran from about 1200 to 900 BCE in most of ancient Southwest Asia (and even longer in the Mediterranean, where it persisted until the eighth century BCE). We may speak of the constitutive resistance of the subsistence regime. I draw the terminology of constitutive resistance from Antonio Negri and his collaborators, who argue not that resistance responds to oppressive power but rather that power constantly struggles to find new ways to respond to constitutive resistance: "Even though common use of the term might suggest the opposite—that resistance is a response or reaction—*resistance is primary with respect to power*."[61] Oppressive power and extractive economic forces must perpetually find new modes of trying to contain this constitutive resistance. This means that both the palatine and plunder regimes, in all their instability, were efforts to overcome and control the resistance of subsistence survival.

Secondarily, the regime of plunder may also be seen as an economic response to the shortcomings of the palatine regime. The difference between the two may be cast in terms of the distinction between exploitation and expropriation. As mentioned earlier, exploitation designates the extraction of products from what is under one's immediate control (in this case, estates), while expropriation is the extraction of goods from what is not one's immediate possession (plunder). But I must add a caveat: the regime of plunder also involved—especially under the Persians—significant elements of exploitation. Let me put it this way: the Neo-Assyrians operated primarily through expropriation, plundering their way across ancient Southwest Asia, while the Persians blended both expropriation (having learned much from the Neo-Assyrians) and exploitation in their refined regime of plunder.

The Neo-Assyrians were hardwired for plunder at economic and ideological levels. Although they attempted some forms of more stable production in the immediate hinterland through resettlement of deportees,[62] their

---

61. Hardt and Negri, *Multitude*, 64 (italics original).

62. Wilkinson, "Late Assyrian Settlement"; Wilkinson and Barbanes, "Settlement

default approach was to ransack. The economic requirements were significant, with large armies, significant rebuilding in the capital and regional centers, administrators—all in the context of a perpetual shortage of labor. Religious ideologues played a significant role, presenting a world in which Assyria was surrounded by numerous enemies keen to destroy the valiant few. So the gods declared war, and the Assyrian king was the "staff of their anger" to bring order to the world. Bustenay Oded notes that "To reject this model of centralized universal empire would have meant violation of the world order; introduction of chaos; offence against the gods and rebellion against the 'great king.'"[63] No matter how much terror the Assyrians were able to inspire (2 Kgs 19:17–18; Isa 10:5–7; 36–37), such an approach is riven with a profound contradiction: one can plunder only so much. Eventually, a limit is reached, whether in terms of impenetrable mountains, a stronger enemy, or the absence of the nonrenewable resource of plunder. These problems mounted quickly, threatening the whole economic and ideological construction. Almost as soon as Neo-Assyria became the dominant power in the seventh century BCE, it crashed.

At the same time, the Neo-Assyrians left a lasting impression. The relative size and grandeur of the empire became a source of imperial "aspiration." The methods of conquest, using steel and new military tactics, enabled a whole new type of conquest, which subsequent states eagerly copied and refined. The idea that any state worthy of greatness would engage in plunder became even more their raison d'être.[64] The Persians in particular took these lessons to heart. They could be as brutal as the Neo-Assyrians, if not more so. But they also realized that the threat of force rather than its constant use was perhaps even more powerful. This persistence presence of covert violence enabled a significant modification of the Neo-Assyrian model: the development of arguably the most sophisticated administrative model ever seen in the ancient world (although it still had significant limits). Throughout what became a relatively vast empire, the Persians busily organized the regions into provinces, with a complex web of local governance, judiciary, and taxation. Given the size of the empire, it had far greater and more diverse resources available, but it was also able to rely on the smaller "returns" from taxation and tribute, without immediately destroying its tax "base." Ideologically, the Persians adopted Zoroastrianism, which was geared towards unity in diversity. This henotheism

Patterns"; Wilkinson et al., "Landscape and Settlement."

63. Oded, *War*, 185.

64. Liverani, *Prestige and Interest*, 135–43.

with its acknowledged pantheon of lesser beings peculiarly suited a regime with Persia as its center, but with cultural and religious diversity across the empire.[65]

The most crucial innovation by the Persians was to deploy the logistical possibilities enabled by coinage. As I mentioned earlier, demanding taxes and tribute in coin meant that markets developed to supply at first soldiers on the move. But once its benefits were realized, the use of such markets spread to many other areas of the imperial administration. Clearly, these tax or administrative markets were a product of the imperial state, a logistical exercise that enabled an empire of this size to function. Yet even with all these refinements, the system remained unstable. It may be very well to apply a relatively moderate form of taxation and tribute, managed through tax markets, but the temptation was always there to demand more taxes than viable. Although the question remains: what constitutes viability? If farmers engaged in subsistence-survival agriculture developed surpluses for the bad season that could be only a few months away, selling such surpluses on markets created obvious risks. And if they shifted to maximal rather than optimal use of the land to meet their tax requirements, the dangers were exacerbated. Despite all its relative sophistication, the Persian Empire lasted no more than two centuries. Its fragility was exposed by a small but tightly disciplined army under Alexander of Macedon.

Conclusion

To sum up, of the four institutional forms, those of subsistence-survival and kinship-household constituted the core of economic activity in the ancient Near East and thereby in the southern Levant. They provided the driving force of what I have called the subsistence regime, which continued in various ways—at times dominant for centuries, and other times persisting in more marginal areas—for some four millennia. It was also the constitutive resistance, based on allocative methods, which the other two institutional forms constantly sought to overcome. Thus, in the palatine regime, the form of estates was dominant, although its inherent instability meant that it crashed regularly, only to lead to new efforts to establish this regime. By contrast, the extractive regime of plunder sought a new way to overcome the subsistence regime. Through plunder (Neo-Assyrians) and the refinements of tribute-exchange through the use of tax markets (Persians), a whole new regime came into being in the first millennium. In various ways, it was to last beyond the Persians, under the Sassanids further east, but also under the Greeks and Romans for a time. Eventually, the Greco-Roman era modified the regime into a rather different structure, but that is another story that is addressed in the second section of this volume.

65. Briant, *From Cyrus to Alexander*, 76–78.

Throughout these wider economic dynamics, ancient Israel and Judah tried to find a place. They flourished briefly, but the little kingdoms were already anachronistic in economic terms, for they attempted to install a palatine regime when such a regime was already past. Soon enough, they were conquered and absorbed into the wider regime of plunder.

Bibliography

Algaze, Guillermo. *Ancient Mesopotamia at the Dawn of Civilization: The Evolution of an Urban Landscape*. Chicago: University of Chicago Press, 2008.

Alster, Bendt. "He Who Pays with Valid Money: On the Status of Merchants in Early Mesopotamia." In *Tablettes et images aux pays de Sumer et d'Akkad: Mélanges offerts à Monsieur H. Limet*, edited by Önhan Tunca and Danielle Deheselle, 1–6. Mémoires - A.P.H.A. Liege: University of Liege, 1996.

Baker, Cynthia. "Imagined Households." In *Religion and Society in Roman Palestine: Old Questions, New Approaches*, edited by Douglas Edwards, 113–28. New York: Routledge, 2004.

Beckman, Gary, ed. *Hittite Diplomatic Texts*. 2nd ed. WAW 7. Atlanta: Scholars, 1999.

Bergheim, Samuel. "Land Tenure in Palestine." *PEQ* 26 (1894) 191–99.

Berlin, Andrea. "Household Judaism." In *Galilee in the Late Second Temple and Mishnaic Period*, edited by David Fiensy and James Strange, 1:208–15. 2 vols. Minneapolis: Fortress, 2014.

Binford, Lewis R. *Constructing Frames of Reference: An Analytical Method for Archaeological Theory Building Using Hunter-Gatherer and Environmental Data Sets*. Berkeley: University of California Press, 2001.

Blum, Jerome. *The End of the Old Order in Rural Europe*. Princeton: Princeton University Press, 1978.

Bodel, John, and Saul Olyan, eds. *Household and Family Religion in Antiquity: Contextual and Comparative Perspectives*. Ancient World—Comparative Histories. Malden, MA: Blackwell, 2008.

Boer, Roland. *The Sacred Economy of Ancient Israel*. LAI. Louisville: Westminster John Knox, 2015.

Boer, Roland, and Christina Petterson. *Idols of Nations: Biblical Myth at the Origins of Capitalism*. Philadelphia: Fortress, 2014.

Boyer, Robert, and Yves Saillard, eds. *Régulation Theory: The State of the Art*. Translated by Carolyn Shread. London: Routledge, 2002 [French orig., 1995].

Brewer, Douglas. "Hunting, Animal Husbandry and Diet in Ancient Egypt." In *A History of the Animal World in the Ancient Near East*, edited by Billie Jean Collins, 427–56. HdO 64. Leiden: Brill, 2002.

Briant, Pierre. *From Cyrus to Alexander: A History of the Persian Empire*. Translated by Peter T. Daniels. Winona Lake, IN: Eisenbrauns, 2002.

Bridges, E. M. *World Soils*. 3rd ed. Cambridge: Cambridge University Press, 1997.

Casana, Jesse. "Structural Transformations in Settlement Systems of the Northern Levant." *AJA* 112 (2007) 195–221.

Childe, V. Gordon. *Man Makes Himself*. New York: Mentor, 1951 [first published in 1936].

Christian, David. *Maps of Time: An Introduction to Big History*. Berkeley: University of California Press, 2011 [first published in 2004].

Crook, Zeba. "Honor, Shame, and Social Status Revisited." *JBL* 128, 3 (2009) 591–611.

Dandamaev, Muhammad. *Slavery in Babylonia: From Nabopolassar to Alexander the Great (626–331 BC)*. Translated by Victoria A. Powell. Edited by Marvin A. Powell and David B. Weisberg. DeKalb: Northern Illinois University Press, 2009.

Daniels, Peter T. "The Study of Writing Systems." In *The World's Writing Systems*, edited by Peter T. Daniels and William Bright, 3–17. New York: Oxford University Press, 1996.

Diakonoff, Igor M. "The City-States of Sumer." In *Early Antiquity*, edited by Igor M. Diakonoff and Philip L. Kohl, 67–83. Translated by Alexander Kirjanov. Chicago: University of Chicago Press, 1991.

———, ed. *Early Antiquity*. Translated by Alexander Kirjanov. Chicago: University of Chicago Press, 1991.

———. "General Outline of the First Period of the History of the Ancient World and the Problem of the Ways of Development." In *Early Antiquity*, edited by Igor M. Diakonoff and Philip L. Kohl, 27–66. Translated by Alexander Kirjanov. Chicago: University of Chicago Press, 1991.

———. "On the Structure of Old Babylonian Society." In *Beiträge zur sozialen Struktur des alten Vorderasien*, edited by Horst Klengel, 15–31. Translated by G. M. Sergheyev. Schriften zur Geschichte und Kultur des alten Orients 1. Berlin: Akademie, 1971.

———. "The Structure of Near Eastern Society before the Middle of the Second Millennium B.C." *Oikumene* 3 (1982) 7–100.

———. *Structure of Society and State in Early Dynastic Sumer*. Monographs of the Ancient Near East 1/3. Los Angeles: Undena, 1974.

———. "Syria, Phoenicia, and Palestine in the Third and Second Millennia B.C." In *Early Antiquity*, edited by Igor M. Diakonoff and Philip L. Kohl, 286–308. Translated by Alexander Kirjanov. Chicago: University of Chicago Press, 1991.

Ekholm, Kajsa, and Jonathan Friedman. "'Capital' Imperialism and Exploitation in Ancient World Systems." In *Power and Propaganda: A Symposium on Ancient Empires*, edited by Mogens Trolle Larsen, 41–58. Mesopotamia 7. Copenhagen: Akedemisk, 1979.

Engels, Friedrich. "The Peasant Question in France and Germany." In *Karl Marx and Frederick Engels: Collected Works*, 27:481–502. 50 vols. Moscow: Progress, 1990 [first published in 1894].

Faust, Avraham. "Household Economies in the Kingdoms of Israel and Judah." In *Household Archaeology in Ancient Israel and Beyond*, edited by Assaf Yasur-Landau et al., 255–73. Culture and History of the Ancient Near East 50. Leiden: Brill, 2011.

Fine, Ben, and Dimitris Milonakis. *From Economics Imperialism to Freakonomics: The Shifting Boundaries between Economics and Other Social Sciences*. Economics as Social Theory 31. London: Routledge, 2009.

Firestone, Ya'akov. "The Land-Equalizing Mushā' Village." In *Ottoman Palestine, 1800–1914: Studies in Economic and Social History*, edited by Gad G. Gilbar, 91–130. Leiden: Brill, 1990.

Fischbach, Michael R. *State, Society and Land in Jordan*. Social, Economic, and Political Studies of the Middle East and Asia 75. Leiden: Brill, 2000.

Giorgadze, G. G. "The Hittite Kingdom." In *Early Antiquity*, edited by Igor M. Diakonoff and Philip L. Kohl, 266–85. Translated by Alexander Kirjanov. Chicago: University of Chicago Press, 1991.

Grabbe, Lester L. *Ancient Israel: What Do We Know and How Do We Know It?* London: T. & T. Clark, 2007.

Graeber, David. *Debt: The First 5,000 Years*. Brooklyn, NY: Melville House, 2011.

Granott, Abraham. *The Land System of Palestine: History and Structure*. London: Eyre & Spottiswood, 1952.

Grmek, Mirko D. *Diseases in the Ancient Greek World*. Translated by Mireille Muellner and Leonard Muellner. Baltimore: Johns Hopkins University Press, 1989.

Guillaume, Philippe. *Land, Credit and Crisis: Agrarian Finance in the Hebrew Bible*. Bible World. Sheffield: Equinox, 2012.

Hald, Mette Marie. *A Thousand Years of Farming: Late Chalcolithic Agricultural Practices at Tell Brak in Northern Mesopotamia*. BAR International Series 1880. Oxford: Archaeopress, 2008.

Hardt, Michael, and Antonio Negri. *Multitude: War and Democracy in the Age of Empire*. New York: Penguin, 2004.

Hayden, Brian. "On Territoriality and Sedentism." *Current Anthropology* 41 (2000) 109–12.

Heltzer, Michael. *The Rural Community in Ancient Ugarit*. Wiesbaden: Reichert, 1976.

Hesse, Brian. "Pig Lovers and Pig Haters: Patterns of Palestinian Pork Production." *Journal of Ethnobiology* 10 (1990) 195–225.

Hesse, Brian, and Paula Wapnish. *Animal Bone Archaeology from Objectives to Analysis*. Manuals on Archeology 5. Washington DC: Taraxacum, 1985.

———. "An Archaeozoological Perspective on the Cultural Use of Mammals in the Levant." In *A History of the Animal World in the Ancient Near East*, edited by Billie Jean Collins, 457–91. HdO 64. Leiden: Brill, 2002.

Hitchcock, Louise A. "Cult Corners in the Aegean and the Levant." In *Household Archaeology in Ancient Israel and Beyond*, edited by Assaf Yasur-Landau et al., 321–45. CHANE 50. Leiden: Brill, 2011.

Hobbs, T. Raymond. "Reflections on Honor, Shame, and Covenant Relations." *JBL* 116 (1997) 501–3.

Hopkins, David. *The Highlands of Canaan: Agricultural Life in the Early Highlands*. SWBA 3. Sheffield: Almond, 1985.

Jankowska, Ninel B. "Communal Self-Government and the King of the State of Arrapha." *JESHO* 12 (1969) 233–82.

Jessop, Bob, and Ngai-Ling Sum. *Beyond the Regulation Approach: Putting Capitalist Economies in Their Place*. Cheltenham, UK: Elgar, 2006.

Jobling, David. "Feminism and 'Mode of Production' in Ancient Israel: Search for a Method." In *The Bible and the Politics of Exegesis: Essays in Honor of Norman K. Gottwald on His Sixty-Fifth Birthday*, edited by David Jobling et al., 239–51. Cleveland: Pilgrim, 1991.

Jursa, Michael. "Debts and Indebtedness in the Neo-Babylonian Period: Evidence from Institutional Archives." In *Debt and Economic Renewal in the Ancient Near East*, edited by Michael Hudson and Marc van de Mieroop, 197–220. International Scholars Conference on Ancient Near Eastern Economies 3. Bethesda, MD: CDL, 2002.

Khalidi, Tarif, ed. *Land Tenure and Social Transformation in the Middle East*. Beirut: American University of Beirut, 1984.

Knight, Douglas A. *Law, Power, and Justice in Ancient Israel*. LAI. Louisville: Westminster John Knox, 2011.

Kozyreva, Nelly V. "The Old Babylonian Period of Mesopotamian History." In *Early Antiquity*, edited by Igor M. Diakonoff and Philip L. Kohl, 98–123. Translated by Alexander Kirjanov. Chicago: University of Chicago Press, 1991.

Lefebvre, Henri. *Éléments de rythmanalyse*. Explorations et découvertes en terres humaines. Paris: Syllepse, 1992.

————. *Rhythmanalysis: Space, Time and Everyday Life*. Translated by Stuart Elden and Gerald Moore. Athlone Contemporary European Thinkers. London: Continuum, 2004.

Legros, Jean-Paul. *Major Soil Groups of the World: Ecology, Genesis, Properties and Classification*. Translated by V. A. K. Sarma. Boca Raton, FL: CRC, 2012.

Lemche, Niels Peter. "From Patronage Society to Patronage Society." In *The Origins of the Ancient Israelite States*, edited by Volkmar Fritz and Philip Davies, 106–20. JSOTSup 228. Sheffield: Sheffield Academic, 1996.

Liverani, Mario. "Communautés de village et palais royal dans la Syrie du IIème millénaire." *JESHO* 18 (1975) 146–64.

————. "Economy of Ugaritic Royal Farms." In *Production and Consumption in the Ancient Near East: A Collection of Essays*, edited by Carlo Zaccagnini, 127–68. Budapest: Le Chaire D'egyptologie de L'universite Eotvos Lorand de Budapest, 1989.

————. *Israel's History and the History of Israel*. Translated by Chiara Peri and Philip Davies. Bible World. London: Equinox, 2005.

————. *Myth and Politics in Ancient Near Eastern Historiography*. Edited and introduced by Zainab Bahrani and Marc Van De Mieroop. Studies in Egyptology and the Ancient Near East. London: Equinox, 2004.

————. *Prestige and Interest: International Relations in the Near East ca. 1600–1100 B.C.* History of the Ancient Near East: Studies 1. Padua: Sargon, 1990.

————. "Ville et campagne dans le royaume d'Ugarit: Essai d'analyse economique." In *Societies and Languages of the Ancient Near East: Studies in Honour of I. M. Diakonoff*, edited by Muhammad Dandamaev, et al., 250–58. Warminster, UK: Aris & Phillips, 1982.

Mendelsohn, Isaac. *Slavery in the Ancient Near East: A Comparative Study of Slavery in Babylonia, Assyria, Syria, and Palestine from the Middle of the Third Millennium to the End of the First Millennium*. 1949. Reprint, Westport, CT: Greenwood, 1978.

Meyers, Carol. *Households and Holiness: The Religious Culture of Israelite Women*. Facets. Minneapolis: Fortress, 2005.

————. "Material Remains and Social Relations: Women's Culture in Agrarian Household of the Iron Age." In *Symbiosis, Symbolism, and the Power of the Past: Canaan, Ancient Israel, and Their Neighbors from the Late Bronze Age through Roman Palaestina*, edited by William G. Dever and Seymour Gitin, 425–44. Winona Lake, IN: Eisenbrauns, 2003.

Milevski, Ianir. *Early Bronze Age Goods Exchange in the Southern Levant: A Marxist Perspective*. Approaches to Anthropological Archaeology. London: Equinox, 2011.

Milonakis, Dimitris, and Ben Fine. *From Political Economy to Economics: Method, the Social and the Historical in the Evolution of Economic Theory*. Economics as Social Theory 30. London: Routledge, 2009.

Moran, William L., ed. and trans. *The Amarna Letters*. Baltimore: Johns Hopkins University Press, 1992.

Moxnes, Halvor. *Putting Jesus in His Place: A Radical Vision of Household and Kingdom*. Louisville: Westminster John Knox, 2003.

Nadan, Amos. "Colonial Misunderstanding of an Efficient Peasant Institution." *JESHO* 46 (2003) 320–54.

————. *The Palestinian Peasant Economy under the Mandate: A Story of Colonial Bungling*. Harvard Middle Eastern Monographs 37. Cambridge: Harvard University Press, 2006.

Nam, Roger S. *Portrayals of Economic Exchange in the Book of Kings*. BibIntSer 112. Leiden: Brill, 2012.

Neyrey, Jerome H. "Managing the Household: Paul as Paterfamilias of the Christian Household Group in Corinth." In *Modelling Early Christianity: Social-Scientific Studies of the New Testament in Its Context*, edited by Philip F. Esler, 208–18. London: Routledge, 1995.

O'Connor, Terry. *The Archaeology of Animal Bones*. Stroud, UK: Sutton, 2000.

Oded, Bustenay. *War, Peace and Empire: Justifications for War in Assyrian Royal Inscriptions*. Wiesbaden: Reicher, 1992.

Osiek, Carolyn, and David Balch L. *Families in the New Testament World: Households and House Churches*. The Family, Religion, and Culture. Louisville: Westminster John Knox, 1997.

Peskowitz, Miriam B. *Spinning Fantasies: Rabbis, Gender and History*. Contraversions 9. Berkeley: University of California Press, 1997.

Redding, Richard W. "A General Explanation of Subsistence Change: From Hunting and Gathering to Food Production." *Journal of Anthropological Archaeology* 7 (1988) 56–97.

———. "Subsistence Security as a Selective Pressure Favoring Increasing Cultural Complexity." *Bulletin on Sumerian Agriculture* 7 (1993) 77–98.

———. "Theoretical Determinations of a Herder's Decisions: Modeling Variation in the Sheep/Goat Ratio." In *Animals and Archaeology*. Vol. 3, *Early Herders and Their Flocks*, edited by Juliet Clutton-Brock and Caroline Grigson, 223–41. Oxford: British Archaeology Reports, 1984.

Roberts, Brian K. *Landscapes of Settlement: Prehistory to the Present*. London: Routledge, 1996.

Sallares, Robert. *Malaria and Rome: A History of Malaria in Ancient Italy*. Oxford: Oxford University Press, 2002.

Saller, Richard. "Household and Gender." In *The Cambridge Economic History of the Greco-Roman World*, edited by Walter Scheidel et al., 87–112. Cambridge: Cambridge University Press, 2007.

———. "*Pater Familias, Mater Familias*, and the Gendered Semantics of the Roman Household." *Classical Philology* 94 (1999) 182–97.

———. "Women, Slaves, and the Economy of the Roman Household." In *Early Christian Families in Context: An Interdisciplinary Dialogue*, edited by David L. Balch and Carolyn Osiek, 185–204. Religion, Marriage, and Family Series. Grand Rapids: Eerdmans, 2003.

Sasson, Aharon. *Animal Husbandry in Ancient Israel: A Zooarchaeological Perspective on Livestock Exploitation, Herd Management and Economic Strategies*. Approaches to Anthropological Archaeology. London: Equinox, 2010.

Schäbler, Birgit. "Practicing Musha': Common Lands and the Common Good in Southern Syria under the Ottomans and the French (1812–1942)." In *Rights to Access, Rights to Surplus: New Approaches to Land in the Middle East*, edited by Roger Owen, 241–309. Cambridge: Harvard University Press, 2000.

Schloen, J. David. *The House of the Father as Fact and Symbol: Patrimonialism in Ugarit and the Ancient Near East*. Studies in the Archaeology and History of the Levant 2. Winona Lake, IN: Eisenbrauns, 2001.

Scott, James C. *Weapons of the Weak: Everyday Forms of Peasant Resistance*. New Haven: Yale University Press, 1985.

Sherratt, Andrew B. "Plough and Pastoralism: Aspects of the Secondary Products Revolution." In *Pattern of the Past*, edited by Ian Hodder et al., 261–306. Oxford: Oxford University Press, 1981.

Simkins, Ronald A. "Patronage and the Political Economy of Ancient Israel." *Semeia* 87 (1999) 123–44.

Sivertsev, Alexei. "The Household Economy." In *The Oxford Handbook of Jewish Daily Life in Roman Palestine*, edited by Catherine Hezser, 229–45. Oxford Handbooks in Classics and Ancient History. Oxford: Oxford University Press, 2010.

Smith, Adam. *An Inquiry into the Nature and Causes of the Wealth of Nations*. The Glasgow Edition of the Works and Correspondence of Adam Smith 2. Oxford: Oxford University Press, 1979 [first published in 1776].

Smith, Bruce D. *The Emergence of Agriculture*. Scientific American Library Series 54. New York: Scientific American Library, distributed by W. H. Freeman, 1994.

Ste. Croix, G. E. M. de. *The Class Struggle in the Ancient Greek World: From the Archaic Age to the Arab Conquests*. London: Duckworth, 1981.

Steinkeller, Piotr. "On Rulers, Priests, and Sacred Marriage: Tracing the Evolution of Early Sumerian Kingship." In *Priests and Officials in the Ancient Near East: Papers of the Second Colloquium on the Ancient Near East—The City and Its Life, Held at the Middle Eastern Culture Center in Japan (Mitaka, Tokyo), March 22–24, 1996*, edited by Kasuko Watanabe, 103–37. Heidelberg: Winter, 1999.

Villeval, Marie-Claire. "Régulation Theory among Theories of Institutions." In *Régulation Theory: The State of the Art*, edited by Robert Boyer and Yves Saillard, 291–98. Translated by Carolyn Shread. London: Routledge, 2002 [French ed., 1995].

Wapnish, Paula, and Brian Hesse. "Archaeozoology." In *Near Eastern Archaeology: A Reader*, edited by Suzanne Richard, 17–26. Winona Lake, IN: Eisenbrauns, 2003.

Wharton, Clifton. "Risk, Uncertainty, and the Subsistence Farmer: Technological Innovation and the Resistance to Change in the Context of Survival." In *Studies in Economic Anthropology*, vol. 7, edited by George Dalton, 152–80. Washington, DC: American Anthropological Association, 1971.

Wilk, Richard, and William Rathje. "Household Archaeology." *American Behavioral Scientist* 25 (1982) 617–39.

Wilkinson, Tony. *Archaeological Landscapes of the Near East*. Tucson: University of Arizona Press, 2003.

———. "Late Assyrian Settlement Geography in Upper Mesopotamia." In *Neo-Assyrian Geography*, edited by Mario Liverani, 139–60. Quaderni di geografia storica 5. Rome: Università di Roma, 1995.

———. "The Tell: Social Archaeology and Territorial Space." In *The Development of Pre-State Communities in the Ancient Near East*, edited by Dianne Bolger and Louise C. Maguire, 55–62. Themes from the Ancient Near East BANEA Publication Series 2. Oxford: Oxbow, 2010.

Wilkinson, Tony, and Eleanor Barbanes. "Settlement Patterns in the Syrian Jazira during the Iron Age." In *Essays on Syria in the Iron Age*, edited by Guy Bunnens, 397–422. ANESSup 7. Leuven: Peeters, 2000.

Wilkinson, Tony, et al. "Landscape and Settlement in the Neo-Assyrian Empire." *BASOR* 340 (2005) 23–56.

Wolf, Eric R. *Peasants*. Foundations of Modern Anthropology Series. Englwood Cliffs, NJ: Prentice-Hall, 1965.

Yasur-Landau, Assaf, et al., eds. *Household Archaeology in Ancient Israel and Beyond.* Culture and History of the Ancient Near East 50. Leiden: Brill, 2011.

Yee, Gale A. "Recovering Marginalized Groups in Ancient Israel: Methodological Considerations." In *To Break Every Yoke: Essays in Honor of Marvin L. Chaney,* edited by Robert B. Coote and Norman K. Gottwald, 10–27. SWBA 2nd ser., 3. Sheffield: Sheffield Phoenix, 2007.

Yoffee, Norman. *Myths of the Archaic State: Evolution of the Earliest Cities, States and Civilizations.* Cambridge: Cambridge University Press, 2005.

Zeder, Melinda A. "The Origins of Agriculture in the Ancient Near East." *CA* 52 (2011) 221–35.

Zohary, Daniel, et al. *Domestication of Plants in the Old World.* 4th ed. Oxford: Oxford University Press, 2012.

4. Economic Relationships Found in the Worlds of the Bible

ROLAND BOER AND CHRISTINA PETTERSON

This study focuses on specific biblical texts that concern economic relationships in ancient Near East and the Greco-Roman world. It will soon become clear that we need to avoid the assumption that "economics" solely concerns trade and commerce. Instead, the primary economic activity for more than 90 percent of the populations of the ancient Near East and the Greco-Roman world was agriculture, which included both crop growing and animal husbandry.

We have selected three topics from the Hebrew Bible and two from the New Testament. The first concerns the narrative tension between Joseph and Moses, a literary manifestation of an economic tension between subsistence-survival agriculture and estate systems. This is followed by an analysis of exchange in texts concerning Solomon and Tyre, and then comes a discussion of specific practices associated with transactions over land—often but erroneously regarded as "private property." The New Testament examples concern Gospel parables of rapacious landlords and demonized peasants and tenants, and the much-debated question of slavery in Paul's few writings.

Throughout, we assume three layers of economic activity derived from *Régulation* economic theory: (1) the building blocks of institutional forms, which coalesce at different times into (2) regimes. These regimes provide relative stability over a period of time, but they are inherently unstable, eventually giving way to another regime. Finally, the aggregate of regimes forms (3) a mode of production. In what follows, from the Hebrew Bible we analyze texts concerning three regimes, each of them dominated by one institutional form: a subsistence regime (dominated by subsistence survival), a palatine regime (dominated by estates), and a regime of plunder (dominated by patterns of tribute and exchange). From the New Testament we analyze two texts concerned with the colonial and slave regimes (with the *polis-chōra* relationship in la Greek and Roman colonies dominating in the first text, and slavery dominating in the second). Although we are unable to go into detail here,[1] this timeline provides a sense of how the regimes related to one another.[2]

Economic Timeline

Uruk	Akkad(e)	Ur III	Old Assyria & Babylon	Neo-Assyria, Neo-Babylonia, Persia *(Israel)
Palatine regime				Regime of plunder
←————————————[*SR]————————→ [*SR]————→[*SR]←				————————————→
vs. Subsistence regime				vs. Subsistence regime
4000 BCE	**3000**	**2000**		**1000** **0**
				*(Israel: SR vs. brief palatine)

* SR: prolonged dominance of subsistence regime

Further, we operate with two methodological positions. First, a regime's relative stability is enabled by a mode of *régulation*,[3] which we understand as a set of behavioral patterns and institutions that enable and challenge the ideological reproduction of a given regime. This takes place in three domains: (1) constraint (laws and rules) and compromises, (2) patterns of behavior and assumptions, and (3) the methods by which these are socially reinforced and undermined. A mode of *régulation* need not be religious, but in the context of the Bible, the primary nature of such a mode was deeply and inescapably religious. Further, during periods of relative stability, a mode of *régulation* provides the necessary social and ideological glue to enhance such stability. Yet, during times of turbulent change, modes of *régulation* become plural, exploring ways to challenge the problematic status quo, attempting to find ways through to a new consensus. Additionally, as part of a mode of *régulation*, texts relate to their contexts in mediated and unexpected ways, attempting to resolve socioeconomic tensions in the production of their stories, poetry, myths, and song. Neither windows onto reality nor expressions of the ideologies of the various

1. See further Boer, *Sacred Economy*. Boer and Petterson, *Time of Troubles*. The examples used in this text are drawn from these works, as well as from Roland Boer, "Economic Politics."

2. Boer, *Sacred Economy*, 194.

3. Boyer and Saillard, "Summary of *Régulation* Theory," 41; Jessop and Ling Sum, *Beyond the Regulation Approach*, 42. Lipietz, "Accumulation."

groups that purportedly produced them, texts have indirect and contradictory connections with the socioeconomic context to which they respond.

Joseph and Moses

The first exhibit concerns the struggle between Joseph and Moses (Gen 41 to Exod 15). *Joseph?*, you might ask. Is not the fight to the death between Pharaoh and Moses? The text attempts to exchange the protagonists, suggesting that the new pharaoh did not know Joseph and thus began to oppress the Israelites (Exod 1:8). Instead of charging the text with subtly redirecting the reader's gaze, we prefer to see this as one of the many mediations of the basic conflict in the text.[4] To draw out this conflict, we focus on four features: the opposition between estate and subsistence regimes itself; the insertion of geographic or spatial distance between the opposed regimes, now in terms of Egypt and Canaan; the pattern of traversing that distance; and the depth of rupture required to break the stranglehold of the estates.

First, Joseph clearly establishes a hyperestate system—a central feature of the palatine regime—once he achieves recognition and then power in Egypt.[5] Gen 41 tells the fabulous story in which Joseph is first called from prison to interpret the pharaoh's double-dream. Indeed, the fat cows of the dream (Gen 41:1–8) already signal the tone of the narrative. Overfattened cows were a distinct marker of relative affluence and power, and one can well imagine the idle rich dreaming about them. By contrast, the small number of bovines in rural villages were normally used not for consumption but for traction, since they consume vast amounts of water and fodder.[6] Having successfully interpreted the dream, Joseph is promptly appointed as the overseer of not one estate among many, but of a hyperestate that is the land of Egypt itself (Gen 41:33–45).[7] Joseph does what any estate manager would do if given free rein: he gathers up all the grain so that the people have nothing left for themselves

---

4. As observed earlier, we tend to analyze the tensions within a text as indirect and mediated representations of socioeconomic tensions. That said, it is sometimes possible to identify a dominant ideological position, which then reveals its internal tensions in unexpected ways. Thus, the account of paradise in Gen 2–3 or its reframed version in the Song of Songs assumes the normality of estates and the palatine system. The same could be said of the account of Joseph and Moses, except that the text attempts to valorize both by shifting the blame to the unnamed pharaoh.

5. On estates as an institutional form, as well as subsistence—survival and their perpetual economic tensions, see Boer, "Aspects" (this volume).

6. Brewer, "Hunting," 434–38. For the *fatted calf* as a symbol of power and excess, see 1 Sam 28:24; 1 Kgs 1:9, 19, 25; 15:17; Jer 46:21; Amos 5:22.

7. Skinner, *Critical and Exegetical Commentary on Genesis*, 501–2.

and have to come to him for sustenance (Gen 41:46–49, 53–57). Yet produce is only half of the story, for the key lies with labor; and the best estate labor is indentured labor. So, later in the story (Gen 47:13–26), Joseph manipulates the situation so that people are forced to sell their bodies into slavery.

The text says less concerning the opposition to the estate system (Gen 46:8–27), although the clan of Jacob may be seen as the textual presence of the village community—central to the subsistence regime. The clan of "keepers of livestock" numbers seventy persons. Although this is an ideal number (marking fullness), that does not equate with the genealogical list (Gen 46:8–27); it also marks—if we include women and children—the normal range of a village-commune. Clan and village-commune were usually coterminous, as suggested by Judg 6:24; 8:32; 2 Sam 14:7; Jer 3:14.[8] Their apparent seminomadism was very much part of village existence, as was the tendency for nomadic groups to settle periodically. Both pastoral nomadism and sedentary agriculture were variations, with many overlaps, on the resilient patterns of subsistence survival.

The tale has already provided one instance of exacerbation (Joseph's mega-estate), but another follows. Instead of the tension between estates and subsistence agriculture taking place within close proximity, this tension is stretched out, as it were, with each end pushed as far apart as possible—among other peoples and in other places (Canaan versus Egypt). The distance is emphasized by two features: the physical amount of text that concerns this spatial separation (Gen 41–50) and the constant but onerous travel between the two places. Narrative distance emphasizes the economic gulf between estates and village communities.

Distance traveled leads to the third point: co-option of labor for the estates. Ostensibly, the story concerns clan squabbles and a grand reconciliation, but it also enables the securing of labor. This co-option begins with hostage-taking (Gen 42:18–25) and then includes the "surety" of other family members (43:8–10), the fear that all the brothers will become slaves (43:18), and whatever trick it takes—the golden cup—to secure their labor (44:10–13, 18–34). From the perspective of the village community, someone indentured for estate labor seemed to be "no more" (Gen 42:6). Yet, this is only the beginning, for eventually Joseph manages to indenture his whole family into the estate system (already foreshadowed in Gen 44:16–17 and given divine approval in 45:4–14; 46:1–4).[9] Upon arrival in Egypt, they become indentured laborers, keepers of

8. Jankowska, "Communal"; Schloen, *House of the Father*, 155–65; Liverani, *Israel's History*, 21–22.

9. Some are seduced by the divine approval of Joseph while others note the negative

BOER AND PETTERSON—ECONOMIC RELATIONSHIPS

the landlord's livestock (Gen 47:1–6). Joseph—and not the new pharaoh—has indentured the labor of his own clan. The text hints that Joseph and the oppressive pharaoh become one, for the name of the territory where Jacob's clan is settled is Rameses (47:11), the same name connected with slave labor and storage facilities in Exod 1:11.[10]

While the various metaphorical items of the story—golden cups, foreign places, hostages, and then enslavement—indicate the convoluted strategies used to co-opt labor for the estates, they also indicate the constituent resistance of village communities to co-option. Despotic power and its system of estates are not at the center of the narrative; rather, that power must constantly adapt to find new ways to commandeer the labor so desperately needed for the estates. This brings us to the final point of the narrative: the depth of the rupture required to break the hold of the estate system. Exod 1–15 may be read as a massive story of breaking with the estates and their indentured labor. The story attempts to shift the blame not only onto a cruel pharaoh (see above) but also onto the increasingly oppressive labor conditions (Exod 1:8—22; 2:23–25; 5:10–21). Would Joseph's labor conditions have been any different? Yet, the key is the amount of effort required to break away from the estate system. In this legendary tale, the effort takes the form not of sporadic violence (Exod 2:11—15) but of the drawn-out account of the divinely ordained plagues (Exod 5:1—12:36). It becomes even tougher since God hardens Pharaoh's heart time and again. Then we have not only violence against the firstborn of the Egyptians, but also the drowning of Pharaoh's horses and charioteers in the sea (Exod 13:17—15:21). This violence marks not merely the rupture between the powerful and the powerless but also the sheer eagerness with which people would seek the destruction of despots and their centers and symbols of power.

The twenty-five chapters that cover the transition between Genesis and Exodus may then be seen as tale in which the struggle between estates and village communities—and thus between palatine and subsistence regimes— leaves its traces on one of the most significant accounts in the Hebrew Bible. These traces have been mediated and metaphorized in terms of clan struggles, exotic places, foreign despots, and miraculous escapes. But let us close this section with another signal of the depth of the tension we have been tracing. When Jacob hears that Joseph is alive and powerful in Egypt, the text reads, "He was stunned; he could not believe them" (Gen 45:26). We suggest that

tone, albeit for other reasons. Kim, "Reading the Joseph Story"; Stone, "Joseph in the Likeness of Adam."

10. Brodie, *Genesis as Dialogue*, 397.

Jacob expresses surprise, not that Joseph is alive, but that the traitor is managing a mega-estate.

Solomon and Tyre

The previous section concerned literary mediations of the tensions between subsistence and palatine regimes (dominated by subsistence-survival and estate institutional forms)—the main regimes of some three millennia of economic history, from the rise of Uruk in the fourth millennium to the early first millennium BCE. The texts in the present section deal with exchange, which is often described as "commercial" exchange. Under the Persians in particular, such exchange became relatively widespread, as they deployed markets and coinage to deal with logistical (usually military) problems over a somewhat vast empire. Indeed, the Persians had refined a regime already established by the Neo-Assyrians, which we have termed a regime of plunder, in which tribute-exchange was dominant. But why connect exchange with plunder? The first step involves making a distinction between polite internal plunder (commonly known as taxation) and brute external plunder. Both are forms of extracting goods and wealth from others. The second step concerns the rise of markets, which were developed for the double purpose of taxation and military logistics. With the invention of coinage and its adoption by rulers (especially the Persians in this part of the world),[11] it became apparent that the strange new items with abstract value attached to them could be deployed for military provisioning. Instead of using as many people to provision an army as those in the army itself, rulers hit on the idea of paying soldiers in coin and simultaneously demanding taxes in coin. How could agricultural laborers acquire coins? By selling produce and goods to the soldiers in question.[12] Thus, the first widespread markets were determined by state concerns of logistics and tax, with profit clearly a secondary phenomenon.

Given this context, it is surprising that representations of exchange, let alone entrepreneurial merchants, are quite rare in the Hebrew Bible. Two are notable: Solomon and Tyre, in 1 Kgs 10 and Ezek 27–28. In 1 Kgs 10:22, Solomon appears as the quintessential merchant-king, who brings prosperity by engaging in trade: "For the king had a fleet of ships of Tarshish at sea with the fleet of Hiram. Once every three years the fleet of ships of Tarshish used

11. Coinage was invented at roughly the same time in Lydia, India, and China, with different technologies and no apparent contact.

12. Even in this situation, however, old practices of customary price rather than the vagaries of supply and demand dominated.

to come bringing gold, silver, ivory, apes, and peacocks." Two items are worth noting. First, these ships "used to come" (*bw'*) every three years. No exporting and importing take place here, for the ships bring items to Solomon and his court. Their function is to acquire items, but what items? Valuable metals (gold and silver), expensive ornamental material (ivory), and exotic animals (apes and peacocks, or perhaps rare fowl).[13] No mention is made of bulk goods, such as grains, meats, dairy products, or vegetables. Instead, acquisition and preciosities are the key elements of an ideal image, projecting a picture of how an Israelite empire might have appeared. It is clearly drawn from the realities of actual empires, whether Neo-Assyrian, Neo-Babylonian, or Persian, each of them providing an ideal to which the "little kingdoms" might aspire.[14]

The crucial distinction is between exchange in bulk and in preciosities: trade in bulk has small profit margins and requires cheap transport and complex logistics; by contrast, the exchange of a small amount of nonessential preciosities with high value (tangible and intangible) takes place when they are difficult to acquire due to high risks, prohibitively expensive transport, and limited logistics. While bulk trade is for the whole population, preciosities are for those who can afford it—the small ruling class. It follows that in precapitalist societies, bulk exchange is marginal, decentered, and local, while exchange in preciosities may take place over greater distances, for it requires minimal and sporadic interaction.[15] The only form of bulk acquisition was for feeding palace and estate, a command economy that operated by means of estates and taxation. Occasionally, in a preciosity-poor region, some bulk goods might be sent to a neighboring little kingdom for the sake of acquiring preciosities.

To return to the text, within the wider context of 1 Kgs 10:22 the focus remains consistent: a concern with acquiring preciosities. In one year, the gold that "came to" Solomon was a mythical 666 talents, which were made into shields, cups, and other vessels. It was used to overlay an ivory throne. So much gold was available that silver was counted nothing. Not short on hyperbole, our anonymous author (or authors) says this about Solomon's throne: "Nothing like it was ever made in any kingdom" (1 Kgs 10:20). The queen of Sheba too arrives, riding camels laden with spices, gold, and precious stones.[16] As she un-

13. For comparable and much longer lists, see EA 14, 22, 25; Moran, ed. and trans., *Amarna Letters*, 27–37, 51–61, 72–84. See also Nam, *Portrayals*, 70–73.

14. Many were the minor potentates who attempted to emulate the Assyrians and the Great (Persian) King. Briant, *From Cyrus to Alexander*, 172, 201–2; Long, *1 Kings*, 75–76.

15. On the distinction between preciosities and bulk, see Wallerstein, *Modern World-System*; Chase-Dunn and Hall, *Rise and Demise*, 52–54, 204, 248.

16. Finkelstein and Mazar, *Quest*, 215, imagine the queen of Sheba as Solomon's "trading

loads these exotic items, she is overwhelmed by Solomon's wealth and wisdom, which surpass any report she has heard. To add to the influx, an appended couple of verses (1 Kgs 10:11–12) include Hiram of Tyre, who brings from Ophir yet more precious stones and the rare almug wood, which is used for temple and palace building, and for lyres and harps for the singers.

The important feature of these stories is what may be called the idea of exchange, the purpose of which is to acquire goods. All of these preciosities travel in one direction: to Solomon (see also 1 Kgs 4:20—5:6 [ET 4:20–26]). Even within the "commercial" Persian Empire, the emphasis was thoroughly centripetal, in which tribute and trade merge into one.[17] There is little sense of exporting goods, let alone two-way exchange; a favorable balance of trade; or the weighing of risks, outlays, losses, returns, and investment. Nor is there any presence of the brisk trade in bulk agricultural goods. This applies just as much to the "men of the road and the to-and-fro of the busybodies" ('anšê haṭṭārîm ûmisḥar hārokĕlîm) of 1 Kgs 10:15. Even in the Greek world and its phase of colonization, the prime function of trade was the acquisition of goods one did not have to be paid for by whatever means were available—mines, plunder, or the necessary evil of merchants.[18] Wallerstein's observation may well read as commentary on this text concerning Solomon: the acquisition of preciosities "depended on the political indulgence and economic possibilities of the truly wealthy."[19]

Let us consider another text, 1 Kgs 10:28–29:

> Solomon's import of horses was from Egypt and Kue, and the king's traders received them from Kue at a price. A chariot could be imported from Egypt for six hundred shekels of silver, and a horse for one hundred fifty; so through the king's traders they were exported to all the kings of the Hittites and the kings of Aram.

This translation comes from the NRSV, which has conveniently turned the text into the image of a fully-fledged and profit-driven market economy.[20]

---

partner,'" "undoubtedly" reflecting the presence of the "lucrative Arabian trade."

17. Briant, *Cyrus to Alexander*, 201.

18. Ste. Croix, *Athenian*, 349–70. Evidence from ports such as the Piraeus or those of Egypt indicates that ships paid a flat tax for entering and leaving a port. If one was concerned to ensure a balance of trade in favor of exports, one would hardly tax ships *leaving* port. Briant, *Cyrus to Alexander*, 385.

19. Wallerstein, *Modern World-System*, 20.

20. Some follow suit, such as by speaking of a *global economy*: Bright, *History of Israel*, 216–17. Our analysis draws on Petterson, "King Solomon and the Global Economy."

It is instructive to consider the text without a neoclassical economic frame. A better translation is:

And horses went out [*yṣ'*] for Solomon which were from Egypt and Kue [or linen; *miqwēh*]; the king's busybodies [*sḥr*] acquired [*lqḥ*] them from Kue at a price. And a chariot came up [*'lh*] and went out [*yṣ'*] from Egypt for six hundred shekels of silver, and a horse for one hundred and fifty; so for all the kings of the Hittites and the kings of Aram they brought them out [*yṣ'*] by their hand.

The terms used indicate a rather different impression. What the NRSV translates as "export" is simply "go out" (*yṣ'*), and the subject is either horse or chariot and not an entrepreneurial Solomon; "import" is actually "acquire" or "get" (*lqḥ*). As for *soḥar* (*sḥr*) and *rôkēl* (*rkl*), their semantic fields indicate that "busybody" or even "hustler" captures the sense best, or perhaps "groveling busybody."[21] In this light, a different picture emerges: instead of a commercial enterprise for profit, it is a rather lucrative task given to despised and busybody merchants, who acquire horses for Solomon, as well as for the kings of the Hittites and of Aram. In this legendary tale, they needed horses and chariots, and someone was prepared to get them. That these busybodies would have been rewarded handsomely goes without saying.

To sum up, the texts concerning Solomon's exchange or "trade" have the consistent themes of acquisition rather than trade for profit; the overwhelming concern has to do with preciosities and with the denigration of merchants. And we have suggested that a better term for such "merchants" is "middlemen," or indeed "grovelers"—outsiders responsible for acquiring preciosities for the political indulgence of a small ruling class.

A third text remains, which is often used to depict commercial exchange in the ancient world:

Tarshish scurried [*sḥr*] about with you due to your massive piles of riches; silver, iron, tin, and lead they gave [*ntn*] for your forsaken wares ['*zb*]. Javan, Tubal, and Meshech trafficked [*rkl*] with you; they gave human beings and vessels of bronze for your barren cargo ['*rb*].[22] Beth-togarmah gave for your forsaken wares horses, war horses, and mules. The Rhodians swarmed [*rkl*] about you; many coastlands became your own busybodies

21. See the full discussion of these two terms in Chapter 3 of this volume.

22. The semantic field of '*rb* includes "exchange," "become dark," and "arid, barren, or sterile." It is also the name for Arabia. In its substantive form, "barren cargo" expresses these associations.

[*shr*]; they brought you in payment ivory tusks and ebony. Aram scurried [*shr*] about with you because of your many shady dealings (*'sh*); they gave for your forsaken wares turquoise, purple, embroidered work, fine linen, coral, and rubies. Judah and the land of Israel swarmed [*rkl*] over you; they gave for your barren cargo wheat from Minnith, millet, honey, oil, and balm. Damascus scurried [*shr*] about with you due to your many shady dealings—because of your piles of riches of every kind—wine of Helbon, and white wool. Vedan and Javan from Uzal gave for your forsaken wares wrought iron; cassia and sweet cane were for your barren cargo. Dedan swarmed [*rkl*] about you for saddlecloths for riding. Arabia and all the princes of Kedar were your favored busybodies [*shr*] in lambs, rams, and goats; in these they scurried [*shr*] about with you. The busybodies [*rkl*] of Sheba and Raamah swarmed [*rkl*] over you; they gave for your forsaken wares the best of all kinds of spices, and all precious stones, and gold. Haran, Canneh, Eden, the busybodies [*rkl*] of Sheba, Asshur, and Chilmad swarmed [*rkl*] over you. These swarmed [*rkl*] over you for choice garments, for clothes of blue and embroidered work, and for carpets of colored material, bound with cords and made secure; in these they swarmed [*rkl*] about you. The ships of Tarshish sailed for you with your barren cargo. (Ezek 27:12–25, AT)

The initial impression is the predominance of preciosities, but a closer look reveals the wheat, millet, and honey supplied by Judah and Israel, and the lambs, rams, and goats from Arabia and the princes of Kedar. Thus, Tyre acquires goods from the two main areas of agriculture—basic crops and products from sheep and goats. Before we conclude that enterprising and profit-minded farmers have finally made an appearance,[23] note that the text does not mention farmers or peasants. Instead, given the nature of exchange between the "little kingdoms" of the ancient world, these transactions took place between the courts. For preciosity-poor minor potentates, the payment of grains and animals—acquired through taxation—was a necessary evil in the pursuit of preciosities. On this matter it is worth noting that despite all his supposed wealth, Solomon gives Hiram of Tyre both wheat and twenty towns in Galilee (1 Kgs 5:11; 9:11–13).[24] But when Hiram comes to view the towns, he finds them entirely useless.[25]

---

23. Odell, *Ezekiel*, 349–50.

24. Nam, *Portrayals*, 126.

25. Seibert argues that the material functions as a subtle critique, especially in light of Deut 17:14–20. Seibert, *Subversive Scribes*, 174–80.

More significant is the emphasis of the Isaiah passage and its genre. In terms of emphasis, items flow into Tyre in centripetal fashion;[26] the lists are swamped by preciosities; the city's status is exceptional or anomalous—note especially the trafficking in human beings. It is a little kingdom that embodies the status of the middleman or busybody noted earlier. In terms of genre, not only is it a literary word picture, full of the obligatory literary license,[27] but it is above all a prophetic condemnation of Tyre.[28] The town is thoroughly denigrated for precisely what is does: accumulate wealth through the dirty business of exchange. This text is part of the wider image of the glittering ship of Tyre, decked out in all the finery acquired from here and there. That ship is about to come to grief: "By your great wisdom in trade / you have increased your wealth, / and your heart has become proud in your wealth" (Ezek 28:5).

This disdain of middlemen or busybodies appears throughout the prophetic literature, where they become a byword for all that is unsavory, taking all that is best and hoarding it (Isa 23:2–3, 8, 17; Ezek 17:3–4; 38:13; Hos 12:8–9 [ET 7–8]; Nah 3:16; Zeph 1:11; Zech 14:21; see also Neh 13:20). The mark of the busybody, the balances, is also condemned (Hos 12:8; Zeph 1:11; see also Lev 19:36; Deut 25:13; Amos 8:5–6; Mic 6:11; Prov 16:11; 20:10, 23).[29] Above all, these texts critique the activity of these merchants, who also happened to be tax collectors, usurers, and landlords for, like Tyre, they "prostitute" themselves "with all the kingdoms of the world on the face of the earth" (Isa 23:17).

The Question of Property in Land

The third item has to do with a fascinating group of materials concerning the transferal of what many have called "private" or "inviolable" property, inevitably of land. These include Abraham's acquisition of the field of Machpelah in Gen 23; Jacob and the issue of land for an altar in Gen 33:19–20; stipulations regarding inheritance, redemption, and jubilees in Lev 25 and 27; Boaz's acquisition from Naomi of both land and woman in Ruth 4; David and the threshing floor of Araunah in 2 Sam 24:18–25 (see 1 Chr 21:1—22:1); Ahab and Naboth's vineyard in 1 Kgs 21; Jeremiah and the field of his cousin Hanamel in

26. Launderville, *Spirit and Reason*, 162–63, 170–71.

27. Many are seduced by the word *image* as describing a commercial trade network: Liverani, *Israel's History*, 170. Launderville, *Spirit and Reason*, 162–63; Diakonoff, "Naval Power."

28. Launderville, *Spirit and Reason*, 150; Renz, *Rhetorical Function*, 95–96.

29. Law 94 in Hammurabi's code also condemns false weights in lending or receiving money.

Jer 32:6–15; and various texts in the Psalms and Prophets that concern inheritance. The underlying issue of how land is represented is pertinent to all of the regimes that appear in the economic context of the Hebrew Bible: subsistence, palatine, and plunder. But how should we understand the question of land and its transfer? Our assumption in dealing with these texts is expressed best by Steinkeller: the category of private property in interpreting the relation to land in ancient economies is "useless, confusing and harmful."[30] This is not least because the legal-cum-economic category of private property was first invented by the Romans—in response to slavery—in the late second century BCE.[31] Before this time one cannot legitimately speak of private property without a serious anachronism. Of course, this raises the question as to how we interpret the texts we have mentioned.

Let us begin with some terminological clarification. Three main terms that have been assumed to refer to some form of private property are *'ăhuzzâ*, *nahălâ* and *helqat haśśādeh*.[32] To begin with, *'ăhuzzâ* comes from the same root as the word for "tenure": *'hz* means "to hold" or "seize." It is clearly not "property," as the lexica would have us believe. Thus, Abraham seeks to acquire some land, as a burial "tenure" (*'ăhuzzat qeber*, Gen 23:4, 9, 20),[33] from the "Hittite" clan of Ephron so that his own clan may have a place to bury their dead. There is no suggestion that the Hittites cease to be the overlords, even though the burial tenure passes on to Abraham's sons. Similarly, Hamor's granting of *'ăhuzzâ* to Jacob's sons in Gen 34:10 permits them tenure in and thereby usufruct—the legal right to use the products of—the land.

Often paralleled with *'ăhuzzâ* is *nahălâ*. The standard meaning given is inviolable and inalienable property.[34] Yet the focus of the root *nhl* concerns not the

30. Steinkeller, "Land-Tenure," 296. See also Steinkeller, "Towards a Definition," 93; Brinkman, "Land Tenure," 74; Godelier, *Mental*, 86; Deist, *Material Culture*, 143–44; Guillaume, *Land*, 10–12. Of the many who continue to assert the existence of private property in land we cite a representative sample: Bright, *History of Israel*, 81; de Geus, "Agrarian Communities"; Dever, *What Did the Biblical Writers Know?*, 239; Matthews, "Physical Space"; Houston, "Was There a Social Crisis," 134; Levine, "Farewell"; Pastor, *Land and Economy*, 1; Thompson, *Historicity*, 211, 295–96.

31. For a full presentation of this historical point, see Boer and Petterson, *Time of Troubles*.

32. The discussion of these terms is indebted, with some modification, to Guillaume *Land*, 18–21.

33. Here the lexica are a little confusing, suggesting both "possession" and "property." Clines, ed., *Dictionary*, 1:187. Koehler et al., *Lexicon*, 32—err even more with "landed property."

34. Koehler et al., *Lexicon*, 687; Clines, ed., *Dictionary*, 5:659. In his rather loose studies, Borowski too sees *'ăhuzzâ* and *nahălâ* as synonyms and defines them as inherited private

object itself but the process of transition or passing over. Thus, it means to "take possession" (*qal* verb form), "allocate" (*piel* verb form), and "give" (*hiphil* verb form), all with the association of inheritance. That is, it designates the acquisition (*qal* verb form) of something that is allocated or given (*piel* and *hiphil* verb forms). All of which means that *ăḥuzzâ* and *naḥălâ* are not synonymous: the former designates tenure, while the latter means the way such tenure is acquired.

The third term is *ḥelqat haśśādeh* ("allocated field"), more often functioning as a metaphor (Gen 33:19–20; Ruth 4:3; 2 Sam 14:30–31; 2 Kgs 9:21, 25; Jer 12:10; Amos 4:7; cf. the verb *ḥlq*, "apportion," in Jer 37:12). This is a share of land usage between members of village communities and not, as it is so often rendered, a field or plot of land. Why not? In contrast to a field or even a farm, which is surveyed, measured, and demarcated from neighbors, a land share is a moveable strip or strips of land that are constantly reallocated on the basis of usufruct and labor.[35] Or rather, it is a reallocation of usufruct and labor rather than land; for this reason, it is better to speak of an allotment of land usage. In this light, it is possible to understand the various references to "boundary" or "landmark" (Deut 19:14; 27:17; Prov 22:28; 23:10; Job 24:2; Hos 5:10),[36] to "the lot [*gôral*] of their [*naḥălâ*]" (Josh 14:2 AT; see also 18:2–10),[37] as well as to the "measuring rope" (*ḥebel*), the semantic field of which actually includes an "allotted portion" of land (Deut 3:4, 13–14; 32:9; Amos 7:17; Mic 2:5; Zeph 2:6–7; Zech 2:5 [2:1 ET]; Pss 16:6; 78:55; 105:11). These are the means for measuring and demarcating strips of reallocated land usage in relation to one another.

What are the implications for the texts we mentioned earlier? Rather than reflections of real life, these engage in processes of metaphorization, in response to social and economic conditions and in ways that are unexpected and indirect. Frameworks, too, are crucial for understanding the function of

---

property within the context of the clan. Borowski, *Agriculture*, 22; Borowski, *Daily Life*, 26. Deist has a curious twist, noting all the terms mentioned here, even recognizing the process of allotment, but then assuming that they become inalienable property. Deist, *Material Culture*, 143–44.

35. A consistent thread of some awareness of this approach to agriculture may be found among biblical commentators, albeit with more or less specificity. Alt, *Kleine Schriften*, 3:348–72; Henrey, "Land Tenure"; Kohler, "Gemeinderschaft und Familiengut"; Elliger, "Allotment"; Chaney, "Ancient Palestinian Peasant Movements," 64–65; Kaufman, "Reconstruction," 280; Lemche, *Early Israel*, 196–98; Endor, *Social Structure*, 141–60.

36. Among others, Wright and Matthews mistakenly assume that they refer to markers of personal property in land. Wright, *God's People*, 70; Matthews, "Physical Space," 5.

37. The hypothesis that this was a once-and-for-all allotment of land (narratively speaking) that was subsequently inalienable misses the function of the terminology. Sweeney, *I and II Kings*, 249; Deist, *Material Culture*, 145. By contrast, Kitz explores the implications of the allocation by lot. Kitz, "Undivided Inheritance."

these texts. To begin with genre, the four texts mentioned earlier (Gen 23; 33:19–20; Lev 25 and 27; Ruth 4) are part of a complex political myth running from Genesis to Joshua at least. This means the texts cannot be read as direct reflections of everyday life, for they form part of the metaphorical structure of myth. Overlapping with this mythic genre is the cultic focus of three of the texts, Gen 33:19–29, 2 Sam 24:18–25, and 1 Chr 21:18–22. The transfer of some land is here clearly not a matter of private property, but the designation of some collective, tribal land by a patriarch or a king for an altar.

Further, these texts metaphorize collective relations to land and inheritance, especially the means and relative ease with which it changes possession. In each case the collective dominates: explicitly in terms of named clan members, implicitly in terms of the paterfamilias (Abraham and Jacob). Or the collective is marked by the sign of Yhwh. Jacob's altar, the acquisition of Araunah's/Ornan's threshing floor, and the instructions regarding what should be done with items dedicated to Yhwh (Lev 27), may all be read as collective ownership at a higher degree. This assumption is summed up in Lev 25:23: "The land is not to be sold [timmākēr] in perpetuity, for the land is for me [lî ha'areṣ]; for you are strangers and sojourners with me" (AT).[38] This is the metaphor par excellence for collective relations with the land, precisely within the context of the founding political myth. Given that Yhwh is the "God of Israel," anything that is Yhwh's is thereby the people's as a whole—a necessarily imaginary community. At this level is Yhwh the land's overlord; everyone else is merely a tenant on the land, and that tenancy is conditional.[39] Within this fictive framework, usufruct of the land is contingent upon observing the commandments. If the people do so, they will enjoy the vines and olive trees planted by others (Deut 6:11; Josh 24:13); if not, others will make the most of the houses and vineyards they have constructed (Amos 5:11; Zeph 1:13).

Genre and metaphorizing of collective relations and usufruct—these overlapping features frame the texts we mentioned earlier. In this context, the texts evince the following features: utopian and dystopian images; processes of transfer, or rather the contingent relation between land and human beings; the collective nature of such contingency; and the prime concern with usufruct. On the first point, the Psalms and prophetic literature present both dire and ideal images of allocatory life (characteristic of subsistence regimes). On the positive side, Ps 16:6 indicates that a blessed and bountiful time is when the measuring rope (ḥebel)

---

38. In Babylonian terminology, makkūr designates the claim that the gods "own" the land. Van der Spek, "Land Ownership," 190–92.

39. Guillaume, Land, 10, 17–18.

falls favorably, providing a good *naḥălâ*, while Ps 105:11 speaks of the land of Canaan as a whole being subject to the measuring rope of a *naḥălâ*. Similarly, but in a more warlike setting, in Ps 78:55 enemies may be scattered so that the land may be measured out "by a rope for a portion" (*běḥebel naḥălâ*).[40] But the warlike setting may become more negative, for YHWH may inflict punishment so there is an absence of casting the measuring rope by lot (Mic 2:5). Or indeed, as Amos 7:17 (see also Zech 2:5 [ET 2:1]) suggests, that someone else will come and turn women into prostitutes, kill sons and daughters, and apportion the land by means of a measuring rope (*běḥebel těḥulāq*). This process of metaphorization is not, simplistically, a reflection of real practices of daily life but rather a construction of a mythical image of ideal existence in an allocatory framework, which may become unstuck due to the disfavor of YHWH. The precise function of this negative image is to reinforce the idealization of an allocatory form of economic life, with the bucolic village-commune as its basis.

As for contingent processes of transfer, the contortions of Num 27 and the various "laws" of redemption (*g'l*) in Lev 25:25–55 concern the means by which items are passed around within the clan. In other words, an individual's relation with any piece of land is highly contingent. So also Jeremiah's parable[41] of the "redemption" (*haggě'ullâ*, Jer 32:7, 8) of the piece of land of his relative Hanamel features an internal shift within a clan. The land itself is a side issue, for the parable obsesses over the process. However, the utopian nature of the text reveals itself with the delightful absurdity of Jer 32:15: "For thus says YHWH of hosts, the God of Israel: houses and fields and vineyards shall again be acquired [*yiqqānû*] in this land." Rather than a "free market" of buying and selling private property, people freely reallocate according to kinship lines.

The folktale in Ruth 4 tells of a comparable shifting sideways—for Boaz is a "kinsman" (Ruth 3:2). Here a characteristic feature of folktale and myth appears once again, exploring the edges and transgressions of acceptable norms, in part to assert the importance of those customary norms. This text also mentions two of the terms we mentioned earlier. The matter at hand concerns the *naḥălâ* of Elimelech (Ruth 4:5, 10). Given the emphasis of this term on a flexible, even alternative, process rather than object transferred, the whole text of Ruth 4:1–12 is a quaint tale of that process of transfer: a meeting at the gate, ritual words, a sandal passed over, some trickery in acquiring three shares rather

40. Enemy prisoners themselves may be forced to lie down and then be measured off with a rope, designating those to be killed and those to be spared (2 Sam 8:2).

41. Holladay enthuses that it is "the most detailed description of the transfer of property to be found in the OT." Holladay, *Jeremiah* 2, 214. By contrast, Carroll's focus on its fictional and prophetic role is a telling counter. Carroll, *Jeremiah*, 2:618–23.

than one. Further, the land in question is *ḥelqat haśśādeh*, a share of land that would be regularly reallocated in the village-commune (Ruth 4:3)[42] That the focus of the land share is usufruct becomes clear when Ruth is acquired (*qnh*) and thereby the children that follow. Produce counts, whether of the land, animals, or indeed women.

The issues of usufruct and the boundaries of acceptable transfer of *naḥălâ* come to the fore in the story of Naboth's vineyard. Ahab seeks to extend his estate with a piece of land in order to grow some vegetables (1 Kgs 21:3).[43] As with Ruth 4, the term *naḥălâ* appears: Naboth abruptly replies to Ahab's approach, "Yhwh forbid that I should give you the inheritance of my fathers [*naḥălat 'ăbōtay*]" (1 Kgs 21:3; see also v. 4). And as with Ruth, the issue is the process of transfer rather than any notion of inalienable property.[44] A gruesome tale follows, without Ruth's quaint air. On the surface, it may appear that Jezebel's scheming seeks to overturn the inalienable nature of inheritance, only to be condemned by Elijah. However, a careful consideration of the text reveals that Naboth has refused the king's prerogative to take over tenure, even with a generous alternative, that Jezebel acts in terms of the king's power to do so, and that Elijah condemns Ahab not for violating Naboth's *naḥălâ*, but for his death (1 Kgs 21:19). In other words, the story deals clearly with usufruct and the transfer of tenure, whether this takes place by fair means or foul.[45]

Thus, these texts must be seen in terms of myth (whether utopian or dystopian), collective engagements, usufruct, and a concern with the process of transfer rather than the object itself. Instead of buying and selling of private property in land, we find a metaphorization of the edges and transgressions of inheritance transferal, of the intricacies of kinship, of what an ideal or baleful world might look like.

Parables in Landlord Eyes

With the fourth collection of texts, we move to the New Testament, dealing with nothing less than the parables. We are interested in particular in the troublesome parables in which God appears—sanctioned by the words of Jesus—as

---

42. In this light one may understand Jer 37:12, where Jeremiah leaves Jerusalem to "apportion" (*ḥlq*) land in Benjamin. Guillaume, *Land*, 45–46.

43. That it is a field share is indicated by 2 Kgs 9:21, for it is the specific allotment of Naboth where Jehu meets Joram. The story has been read as "proof" of private property in land in ancient Israel. Silver, *Prophets*, 74.

44. Contra Sweeney, *I and II Kings*, 249; Cronauer, *Stories*, 127–28.

45. Contra Walsh, 1 *Kings*, 319; deVries, 1 *Kings*, 257.

an exploiting landlord. The economic context is a colonial regime, characteristic of the lands conquered in the eastern Mediterranean by the Greeks under Alexander and then by the Romans. The pertinent feature of this regime was the colonial modulation of the *polis-chōra* relation, in which the *polis* became the colonial presence and the *chōra* the colonized territory that had to supply local and more distant *poleis* (Roman included). The small ruling class—including landlords—tended to be based in the *poleis*, although they also had a good number of exploited laborers and peasants.

In relation to the parables, the question arises: are they told from a ruling-class, landlord, and *polis* perspective, or are they told from the viewpoint of "peasant life"?[46] Many would side with the latter, but the problem is that instead of the "families of peasants, fishermen, or day workers" we find instead a "significant number of individuals who belong to the elite families: rulers or aristocrats, who lived in big mansions, had servants to perform different tasks and owned large amounts of land."[47] Many are the explanations given for such a disjunction. Guijarro suggests that stories of peasant families would not have appealed to Jesus' listeners. And Moxnes opines that even though the parables are located in elite households, their perspective is from "below," with "neither the implied author nor the audience sharing the social location of the characters in the story."[48]

This tenet is difficult to hold. Let us take the parable of the wicked tenants in Mark 12:1–12 (also Matt 21:33–46 and Luke 20:9–19). This parable produces myriad problems for interpreters who want to use the parables for a social justice agenda. The difficulty is ultimately a theological one, as Schottroff indicates:

> The matter-of-fact interpretation of the vineyard owner as God, which rules in the interpretative tradition with only a few exceptions, must be fundamentally called into question if we take the social-historical analysis of the text seriously. The owner of the vineyard acts like an opponent of God; he does the opposite of what the God of the Torah and the Lord's Prayer desires and does.[49]

The problem is the allegorical interpretation, which equates God with the owner of the vineyard, the violence perpetrated, and also the ensuing

---

46. Dodd, *Parables*, 21.
47. Guijarro, "Family," 48.
48. Moxnes, *Putting Jesus in His Place*, 43–44.
49. Schottroff, *Parables*, 17.

dismissal of the Jewish people as the heirs of the vineyard. Schottroff attempts to counter this allegory by means of her nondualist parable theory, attempting to emphasize the lives of ordinary people instead of treating them as signifiers for a theological meaning.[50] Thus Schottroff suggests that the tenants reflect "the economic hopelessness of the increasingly poor agrarian population and their hatred for their new master"—so much so that "in this parable we hear how indebtedness turns those burdened with it into violent people filled with hatred."[51] A problem remains: the perspective of the parable, which is clearly that of the slave-owning landlord rather than the tenants. The landlord is presented as the one who performed all the labor in establishing the vineyard and was only claiming that to which he was entitled. The tenants attempt to appropriate this through violence and murder.[52]

It is instructive to consider Schottroff's analyses of individual parables to see which ones she finds unacceptable (she has an excellent eye for the socioeconomic inequalities, and therefore refuses to see God as complicit in these structures). Any parable that depicts God as a slave-owner, landowner, or king is regarded by Schottroff not as an analogy, but as an antithetical parable, which intends to present the listeners with the difference between God's kingdom and the current situation. Examples include the parable of the unforgiving servant (Matt 18:23–36), the laborers in the vineyard (Matt 20:1–16), the wedding banquet (Matt 22:1–13), and the slave parables in Luke (12:35–38; 17:3–10; and 19:11–27).[53]

Schottroff follows Herzog in seeing the parables as expressions of class conflict. Thus, they must both read against the grain of the parable to detach God from the rich slave-owner. While Herzog detaches the parables from their later Gospel interpretations,[54] Schottroff keeps them in their respective literary contexts, which means that she needs other arguments to support her antithetical readings. The main interpretive tactic she uses is her translation of *homoioun* and *homoios* as "compare" rather than "equate," because "compare" includes the possibility of seeing difference in the comparison rather than similitude. Schottroff and Herzog thus want to isolate God from the ongoing

50. Schottroff, *Parables*, 2. See the methodological sections in part 2, 81–113.

51. Schottroff, *Parables*, 17.

52. Mark's version is the harshest, which Matthew and Luke both attempt to ameliorate. The later versions are favored by scholars attempting an interpretation which presents God in a more flattering way. For example, see Bailey, *Jesus*, 410–26.

53. The parable of the weeds among the wheat, with God as a slave-owner, is passed by with only a brief mention of its eschatological significance. Schottroff, *Parables*, 207.

54. Herzog, *Parables*.

class conflict of which the texts are a product—or at least in Herzog's case to enlist Jesus (and thereby God) in a version of guerilla warfare against the ruling class. Our point is that class conflict is already represented from a certain class' viewpoint: that of the ruling class or the landlords, a perspective from which peasant resistance is depicted as self-serving rebellion.[55] We can reconstruct, flesh out, and read from below all we like, but the text simply does not recognize the viewpoint from below as valid.

Thus, the information on the conditions of production and the socioeconomic history of the land, which provide a reading from below, comes not from the New Testament material, but rather from historical studies of Roman Palestine and Egypt, which suggests that the New Testament texts represent more the *polis*-based perspective of the ruling class rather than the common people. As in archaeological excavations, the lower classes are present in the texts only as traces. Given this feigned rural dress of the parables, we suggest that rather than coming from the mouth of Jesus, they originate in the *polis*.

Slavery

The final topic concerns slavery, which constituted a significant regime alongside the colonial regime. Obviously, slavery dominated this regime, but we are interested here in the "slave-relation," which operated at social, intellectual, psychic, and textual levels.[56] As slavery became integral to economic activity, it influenced the modes of human social interaction. Such interaction became mediated through slaves, but the key is that mediation itself became a wider norm within human consciousness and thereby the literature, linguistic forms, and even religions produced at the time. Such was the saturation that slaves need no longer be actually present, for mediation itself became central to the way people thought and behaved. In this section, we focus on the first, and arguably most important, Christian ideologue, Paul, after which we examine the slave-relation in the Gospels.

It would be self-deception if one failed to see that Jesus of Nazareth, the apostles, and the church, both in its formative period and its later development, accepted the dominant system of labor of the time, including the slave structure, without hesitation or any expressed reluctance.[57] Further, the overwhelming tendency of biblical studies is to focus on household slavery, which is

55. As an instructive parallel, see the example of Ernst Bloch's reading of the sons of Korah (Numbers 16) in Boer, *Political Myth*, 20–21.

56. Martin, *Slavery as Salvation*.

57. Westermann, *Slave Systems*, 150.

unsurprising given that this is also the major focus of the New Testament. The problem is that such a focus misses the prevalence of rural slavery on the estates and in agricultural production. Instead, the slaves in the parables either belong to a wealthy household or work for an absentee landlord.

With this in mind, let us turn to Paul, whose letters are full of slave metaphors. Above all, there is the letter to Philemon concerning the slave Onesimus. In order to understand this letter, we draw on the work of Ulrike Roth, which shows how this letter may function as a productive starting point for early Christian attitudes toward slavery.[58] Roth's argument is that Onesimus was a contribution as human chattel to the *koinōnia*, and that Paul was a co-owner of Onesimus. She argues this point through attention to the letter's communication strategies, through analysis of the term *koinonia* and its practices of pooled ownership of various resources, through attention to Paul's display of mastery, and through an analysis of the parallel universe of Pauline Christianity, which brings the contradiction between Christian brotherhood and the economic system of slavery to the fore. Roth concludes:

> whilst slavery, like citizenship, was irrelevant in the new world order, it was the order of the "old" world, which acknowledged slavery, that allowed Paul a double coup: in his dealings with Philemon and Onesimus, Paul embraces the order of both this world and the next, creating parallel universes that, with regard to slavery, could only have been understood by non-Christians (and probably by some fellow Christians) as an expression of a complete and unreserved acceptance of the slave system.[59]

We would like to address a number of significant points resulting from Roth's article. The first concerns Paul as a slaveholder. Based on a dual reading of *koinōnia* as both a practical association of pooling resources for a specific goal, as well as Paul's spin into a community of believers (*koinōia tēs pisteōs*), Roth argues that Paul is consciously mingling the two layers in order to assert his authority and undergird his demand for Onesimus. Based on the contractual arrangements inherent in *koinōnia*, to which Paul refers several times, he is challenging Philemon to honor the agreements in this arrangement. The precise issue is Onesimus, who if he was a contribution by Philemon to the *koinōnia*, would make Paul the de jure part-owner of Onesimus. This situation accords with the agreement entailed in the nature of the *koinōnia*, where material contributions become common property. Slaves, as chattel, would have been part

58. Roth, "Paul and Slavery."
59. Roth, "Paul, Philemon, and Onesimus," 128.

of this contractual arrangement. Roth notes that a similar arrangement could be argued for the relation between Paul and Epaphroditus in Philippi.[60] She argues that there are two particular points in the letter that reinforce the master-slave relation between Paul and Onesimus. The first is Paul's readiness to take on possible debts, which shows him thinking as a slave master and acknowledging his legal responsibilities to Philemon.[61] The second is the presentation of Onesimus as Paul's agent—the physical extension of Paul, who is to be received by Philemon both in the flesh and in the Lord, thereby reinforcing Onesimus' status as a "thing," a sentient tool or the hands of Paul's mind, but also "of the old world."[62] This brings us to the second item of interest to take from Roth's article, namely, the idea of slave as a thing, used as a slave, within the church.

Scholarship on slavery and Christianity has come a long way since William Westermann's naïve assertion that the early Christians regarded slaves as human personalities instead of *things* as in Roman law.[63] In particular, the work of Glancy and Harrill has broken much new ground.[64] Another provocative example is Marchal's analysis of Onesimus as a sexual vessel. Yet, another step remains, which many scholars have been reluctant to acknowledge: the use of slave labor within congregations. These scholars attempt to insert a buffer against such a possibility in various ways: seeing Paul's perspective as *aligning* comfortably with that of the slave-owners,[65] seeing Paul's possible interaction with slaves when accepting the hospitality of slaveholders,[66] using qualifiers when mentioning Paul and slave ownership ("as though"),[67] perhaps even regarding Onesimus as a runaway slave—since this avoids the notion put forward by Knox, Winter, and Roth, that Onesimus was sent by Philemon to

60. Roth, "Paul, Philemon, and Onesimus," 120–21, and note 70.

61. Roth, "Paul, Philemon, and Onesimus," 123–24.

62. Roth, "Paul, Philemon, and Onesimus," 122.

63. Westermann, *Slave Systems*. See the helpful but already dated survey by Byron, "Paul and the Background of Slavery." But see Osiek and Balch, *Families*. Here they state that "the human dignity of slaves was recognized by their acceptance into the community, without calling into question the mention of slavery itself" (188).

64. Glancy, *Slavery in Early Christianity*; Glancy, *Slavery as Moral Problem*; Harrill, *Manumission*; Harrill, *Slaves*.

65. Marchal, "Usefulness."

66. Glancy, *Slavery in Early Christianity*, 45. See also Barclay, "Paul." Barclay states that the slave context that would be most familiar to Paul would have been "that of slaves living in the urban homes of their masters" (165), followed by a number of examples from Paul's letters and their references, for instance, to Chloe's people in 1 Cor 1:11.

67. For "as though he himself was the owner of Onesimus" see Arzt-Grabner, *Philemon*, 246. For scare quotes ("elsewhere, the epistle maintains the claim that Onesimus 'belongs' to the apostle"), see Frilingos, "'For My Child.'"

assist Paul, which would make Paul someone who directly benefited from slave labor. It seems that most follow, whether explicitly or implicitly, Byron's assessment of the status quo: "As appalling as the notion of slavery is in any society, the fact remains that, in the context of the New Testament, slavery did take on some positive aspects. This is not to suggest, of course, that Paul was a supporter of slavery. But he and other New Testament authors were able to find something that was of 'redeeming' value for their theology."[68]

Following Roth, we follow the grain of the text: slaves were used in the service of Christianity. We mean not only that Paul would have benefited from someone's slave in someone's house, but that the various congregations made use of slave labor, as was the case with Onesimus and Epaphroditus. For example, the reference to Chloe's house in 1 Cor 1:11 suggests for Barclay "probably . . . the presence of slaves in the homes of some of his converts,"[69] and Osiek and Balch, following Theissen, acknowledge the possible presence of "'slaves or dependent workers'" in Chloe's home.[70] Both Glancy and Nasrallah go a little further and suggest that the message to Paul was conveyed by Chloe's slaves,[71] but without coming to the obvious conclusion that early Christianity exploited slaves as a matter of course—as did the rest of society.

In her conclusion, Roth follows and expands upon Barclay's point that the hospitality offered in the first house churches is unimaginable without slaves.[72] Roth points out that missionary activity could not have been carried out without the work of slaves (see also Acts 8:1–5, where Paul works with Aquila and Priscilla until Silas and Timothy arrive in Corinth).[73] While most commentators assume that Timothy and Silas bring funds, which enables Paul to concentrate on preaching,[74] the text says nothing about bringing anything. This opens up the possibility that Timothy and Silas work to support Paul, enabling him to preach full time. This is emphasized by the order, or command (*entolē*),[75] issued by Paul to Silas and Timothy to join him as soon as possible (Acts 17:15).

68. Byron, "Paul and the Background of Slavery."

69. Barclay, "Paul and the Background of Slavery," 165.

70. Osiek and Balch, *Families*, 99. The reference is to Theissen, *Social Setting*, 93.

71. Glancy, *Slavery in Early Christianity*, 49; Nasrallah, "Bought with a Price," 64n45.

72. Barclay, "Paul."

73. Petterson, *Acts of Empire*, 65–67.

74. Bruce speaks of Timothy and Silas bringing "supplies." Bruce, *Acts*, 344. See also Marshall, *Acts*, 293–94, 452; Witherington, *Acts*, 448–49.

75. Translations and commentaries usually translate *entolē* as "instructions," which softens the force of the word and assumes that they are *coworkers*, not subservient to Paul.

Another place where Paul's use of slaves appears is in his letters, where he (and his disputed alter ego) steps in, indicating that he himself is now writing:[76]

I, Paul, write this greeting with my own hand. (1 Cor 16:21)

I, Paul, write this greeting with my own hand. This is the mark in every letter of mine; it is the way I write. (2 Thess 3:17)

See what large letters I make when I am writing in my own hand! (Gal 6:11)

So if you consider me your partner, welcome him as you would welcome me. If he has wronged you in any way, or owes you anything, charge that to my account. I, Paul, am writing this with my own hand: I will repay it. I say nothing about your owing me even your own self. (Phlm 1:17–19)

I, Paul, write this greeting with my own hand. Remember my chains. Grace be with you. (Col 4:18)

We also have the example in Rom 16:22, where Tertius (a typical slave name, suggesting the possibility of a Primus and Secundus also under Paul's *potestas*), inscribes himself: "I Tertius, the writer of this letter, greet you in the Lord."[77] Elsewhere, Roth pursues the topic of "Christian slavery,"[78] situating "Paul's use of slave labor in the wider context of the exploitation of slaves in the Roman Empire."[79] In terms of the economics of missionary success, "slave exploitation was a systematic [and, we would add, systemic] feature behind Christianity's early success."[80] Beginning with Meggitt's contention that full labor and ministry were incompatible within Paul's modus operandi,[81] and taking into account the efforts at staying connected with various communities, Roth concludes that the "demand for slaves to undertake some of the leg-work—in a literal sense—emerges as very real," of which Onesimus and

76. Petterson, *Acts of Empire*, 2–3.
77. For indications of Tertius as a slave name see Solin, *Die stadtrömischen Sklavennamen*, 152–53.
78. Roth, "Paul and Slavery."
79. Roth, "Paul and Slavery," 156.
80. Roth, "Paul and Slavery," 170.
81. Meggitt, *Paul*, 76. However, it must be said that Meggitt's overall thesis, on the poverty of Paul and his communities, falls under what Roth astutely calls the "pauperising approach" to early Christians' social standing, which functions to minimize the possibility of implication in slavery and exploitation (which she also notes is not a given). Roth, "Paul and Slavery," 164.

Epaphroditus are suitable examples.[82] The travels and epistles (from *epistellō*, of course) that made the Pauline mission such a success were unthinkable with A line of questioning, which we cannot pursue out slave labor. Here we find offers of accommodation, financial and in-kind travel subventions, and courier services, as examples of slave-based services which slave-owners may offer Paul. We add the possibility of Paul's own co-owned slaves assisting him on travels, as the above example from Acts shows.[83]

All of this brings us to the contradiction between slave ownership in the early congregations and the ideology of equality espoused by Paul in his epistles (as noted by many).[84] If it is clear that the early Christian communities exploited slave labor in their missionary activity, then the issue becomes slightly more acute, needing an effort at a solution. Here we draw on the theory of an imaginary resolution of a real contradiction, first proposed by Lévi-Strauss and then elaborated by Fredric Jameson in an Althusserian framework.[85] In short, an irresolvable social and indeed economic contradiction often generates an attempt at resolution at an ideological level. Obviously, such a resolution cannot deal with the real social contradiction, so it reveals, through its very tensions and problems, the irresolvable nature of the problem.

In this light, we propose that Paul's use of metaphorical slavery is a desperate and brilliant attempt at working to resolve the actual contradiction at an ideological level. It consists quite simply in making everyone slaves, figuratively speaking, while maintaining, supporting, and benefiting from the fundamental inequality of this economic structure in daily life: as Roth says, Paul has his cake and eats it too.[86] The contradiction is not expressed in these terms, but relies rather on a difference between this world and the next, flesh and spirit, death and resurrection, and so on, which revolve around the fundamental problem of the early Christians caught between this world and the next.[87] This means that the metaphor does not simply arise from everyday life[88] but

82. Roth, "Paul and Slavery," 171.

83. More research needs to be done. A line of questioning, which we cannot pursue here, would be the passive verbs in the texts, since they may conceal the metaphorization of slave labor (e.g., Mark 12:1; Acts 8:28; 1 Cor 1:11).

84. Barclay mentions "the central tension in the present status of Onesimus as both slave and brother to Philemon." Barclay, "Paul," 183.

85. Lévi-Strauss, *Tristes Tropiques*; Jameson, *Political Unconscious*; Althusser, *Lenin and Philosophy*.

86. Roth, "Paul, Philemon, and Onesimus," 124.

87. Boer, *In the Vale of Tears*, 179–98.

88. As Glancy seems to suggest in her characterization of slavery as "fertile ground for

emerges as an ideological effort to deal with an actual and pressing problem. It also indicates the inability to resolve this problem in practice.[89]

This metaphor of slavery took on a life of its own, wresting itself free from the problems that gave rise to it. One place in which the metaphor comes out quite clearly is in the parables of Jesus that deal with slaves and God as the slaveholder. As we mentioned earlier, Schottroff takes particular exception to the parables that present God as a slaveholder and argues that these must be seen as antithetical parables, pointing to the difference between the slaveholder and God. Crucial to her argument is the dubious move of translating *homoioun* and *homoios* as "compare" rather than "equate," since this translation loosens the connection between God and the slaveholder in these parables. Schottroff also insists heavily on nonallegorical interpretations of the various parables, because she wants to use the exploitative and violent content of the parables to signify the actual socioeconomic context and to separate a given parable from the kingdom of God.

However, many of the parables do contain the "keys" to their own interpretation, either through an extensive one-by-one exposition of the various elements, such as in the parable of the sower (Mark 4:2–20; Matt 13:1–23; and Luke 8:4–15) or as in the weeds in the field (Matt 13:36–43) or as in the formula *homoiuon/homoios estin* (Matt 7:24–27 and Luke 6:46–49). We wonder whether the existence of the allegorical key to the parables displays the contradictions of class struggle, in that the agricultural imagery is used to explain something else. However, the allegorical reading (broadly defined) was in Dodd's analysis set out in terminology much closer to that of Paul than that of Jesus.[90] This he understood to mean that Mark 4:11–12 ("And he said to them, 'To you has been given the secret of the kingdom of God, but for those outside, everything comes in parables; in order that 'they may indeed look, but not perceive, and may indeed listen, but not understand; so that they may not turn again and be forgiven'") indicates that this is a piece of apostolic teaching. Both Dodd's and Schottroff's rejections of the allegorical method are founded in their refusals to acknowledge anti-Judaism in Jesus' teaching; both see this facilitated and encouraged by the allegorical method and its inside-outside structure.[91] However understandable such an ideological position might be,

---

generating metaphorical language." Glancy, "Slavery," 457.

89. Contra Turner, "Christian Life."

90. Dodd, *Parables*, 14.

91. Their motivations have different foundations. Over against Schottroff's liberative reading, Dodd's concern is more historically motivated, in his keenness to keep the original

it also seems to close down some interpretative options that we are keen to pursue—not so much in relation to the question of insiders and outsiders, but rather in relation to what the abstraction itself indicates.

This allegorical key, which is also present in Matthew and Luke, undergirds the dual nature of the material in question and, along with *homoiuon/ homoios estin*, encourages an allegorical reading. In this light, we suggest that the use of parables in the Gospels is an expression of the abstraction identified in Paul's writings, specifically in his attempt to overcome the contradiction between the use of slaves within the church and the equality of its members.

To go further, Christian metaphors of slavery include both negative and positive connotations: "The Christian can be termed both a slave of Christ and a freed person of Christ."[92] Crucial in this designation is not the positive or the negative valence, but the characterization of the Christian as a slave, one way or another.[93] This is not only the case in Paul and later uses thereof, but also in Jesus' parables, such as in Luke 16:13, which concerns a slave not being able to serve two masters. Here God and wealth are personified as masters, which means that the listener is interpellated as a slave. Further, in the various parables where God is characterized as slaveholder, the slaves are either obedient or disobedient, and are rewarded or punished accordingly—all of which provides the listener with a choice between being an obedient or a disobedient *slave*. Finally, Paul's instruction to become slaves to one another through love (Gal 5:13) echoes Jesus' pronouncement in Mark that whoever wants to be first shall become everyone's slave, following Jesus' own example.[94] We would see this the other way around: Mark's saying is an attempt to resolve an unresolved tension in Paul's letters.

Let us now add the question of private property, which the Romans first developed as a legal-economic category in response to the pervasive reality of slavery. Here we face a contradiction: Jesus at times argues against property, while in no way criticizing the institution of slavery, which he uses as a way to get theological points across. The problem is that there is a very close connection between property and slavery, so it would be possible to see the criticism of property as a criticism also of slavery. At the same time, we want to take our argument in a different direction and point out that the question of property in the Gospels is not without its problems. On the one hand, we note the various

Jesus apart from the primitive church. Dodd, *Parables*, 14–15.

    92. Glancy, "Slavery," 457–58.
    93. See also Meeks, *Moral World*, 157, 169.
    94. Glancy, "Slavery," 459.

sayings about camels and eyes of needles (Matt 19:23–24; Mark 10:23–25; Luke 18:24–25), as well as the parable of the rich fool (Luke 12:13–21). Yet, we also have the parables in which God is apparently cast as a king or slaveholder, to the point of being in charge of substantial property, as we find in the parable of the faithful or the unfaithful slave (Matt 24:45–51; Luke 12:41–48), or in the parable of the talents (Matt 25:14–30). A particularly interesting example is the chapter in Luke containing three parables that illustrate repentance. Two of them concern property as metaphors for sinners, namely, the lost sheep (Luke 15:1–7) and the lost coin (Luke 15:8–10). Both parables equate the repentance of a sinner with the finding of something lost. The third is the parable of the prodigal son (Luke 15:11–32), whose father owns a large slave-run property. In all three cases, God is the property owner who rejoices in the return of what is lost.

On the basis of these examples, we propose that the Gospels propagate the slave ethos, or, in our terminology, the slave-relation to the listener—continuing the metaphorical tradition springing from Paul's attempt to overcome the profound tension between slave exploitation and equality. In doing so, the Gospels are not really advocating an alternative society in regard to slavery, but remain within the parameters of the status quo. The odd rich person—who sells off property, gives it to the poor, and joins Jesus—does not change the dynamics of slaves and slave owners. Instead, he contributes to the endurance of the slave-relation.

Luke 17:7–10 best sums up the slave-relation, namely, the extension of the slave ethos to everyone, in submission to God:

> Who among you would say to your slave who has just come in from plowing or tending sheep in the field, "Come here at once and take your place at the table"? Would you not rather say to him, "Prepare supper for me, put on your apron and serve me while I eat and drink; later you may eat and drink"? Do you thank the slave for doing what was commanded? So you also, when you have done all that you were ordered to do, say, "We are worthless slaves; we have done only what we ought to have done!"

We have traced this ideological form back to the contradiction between ideology and practice in Paul's thinking, out of which the metaphorization of slavery arose as an imaginary effort at resolution. Slavery continued well after Constantine, and Christianity's contribution to slavery seems to be more one of undergirding the system with an ideology that actually strengthened it, in the sense that the servile attitude was imbued as something desirable. This is what we designate the slave-relation.

Conclusion

In this survey of key biblical texts concerning economic relations in the Bible, we have ranged over the struggles between estates and subsistence survival (Joseph and Moses), the despised presence of tribute-exchange (Solomon and Tyre), the complex question of private property, the troublesome nature of parables that present the perspective of the ruling class, and the many levels of the slave-relation, from Paul to the Gospels. In light of our economic framework, we have sought to challenge conventional interpretations and read the texts in slightly different ways, all the way from Joseph as a landlord to the persistence of slavery as an unchallenged feature, not only in Paul's usage of slaves, but also in their assumed role in the Gospels. Throughout, it became clear that the Bible—as an exhibit of a mode of *régulation*—offers not so much a reflection of actual economic relations, but rather a complex mediation, or indeed metaphorization, of economic realities—in unexpected ways.

Bibliography

Alt, Albrecht. *Kleine Schriften zur Geschichte des Volkes Israel.* Vol. 3. Edited by Martin Noth. Munich: Beck, 1959.

Althusser, Louis. *Lenin and Philosophy, and Other Essays.* Translated by Ben Brewster. Modern Reader. New York: Monthly Review, 1971.

Arzt-Grabner, Peter. *Philemon.* Papyrologische Kommentare zum Neuen Testament. Göttingen: Vandenhoeck & Ruprecht, 2003.

Bailey, Kenneth E. *Jesus through Middle Eastern Eyes: Cultural Studies in the Gospels.* Downers Grove, IL: IVP Academic, 2008.

Barclay, John M. G. "Paul, Philemon and the Dilemma of Christian Slave-Ownership." *NTS* 37 (2009) 161–86.

Bendor, Shunya. *The Social Structure of Ancient Israel: The Institution of the Family (Beit 'Ab) from the Settlement to the End of the Monarchy.* Jerusalem Biblical Studies 7. Jerusalem: Simor, 1996.

Boer, Roland. "The Economic Politics of Biblical Narrative." In *The Oxford Handbook of Biblical Narrative,* edited by Danna Nolan Fewell, 529–39. Oxford Handbooks. New York: Oxford University Press, 2016.

———. *In the Vale of Tears: On Marxism and Theology V.* Historical Materialism Book Series 52. Leiden: Brill, 2013.

———. *Political Myth: On the Use and Abuse of Biblical Themes.* New Slant. Durham, NC: Duke University Press, 2009.

———. *The Sacred Economy of Ancient Israel.* LAI. Louisville: Westminster John Knox, 2015.

Boer, Roland, and Christina Petterson. *Time of Troubles: A New Economic Framework for Early Christianity.* Minneapolis: Fortress, 2017.

Borowski, Oded. *Agriculture in Iron Age Israel*. Winona Lake, IN: Eisenbrauns, 1987.
———. *Daily Life in Biblical Times*. ABS 5. Leiden: Brill, 2003.
Boyer, Robert, and Yves Saillard. "A Summary of *Régulation* Theory." In *Régulation Theory: The State of the Art*, edited by Robert Boyer and Yves Saillard, 36–44. London: Routledge, 2002 [French orig., 1995].
Brewer, Douglas. "Hunting, Animal Husbandry and Diet in Ancient Egypt." In *A History of the Animal World in the Ancient Near East*, edited by Billie Jean Collins, 427–56. HdO 64. Leiden: Brill, 2002.
Briant, Pierre. *From Cyrus to Alexander: A History of the Persian Empire*. Translated by Peter T. Daniels. Winona Lake, IN: Eisenbrauns, 2002.
Bright, John. *A History of Israel*. 3rd ed. Philadelphia: Westminster, 1980.
Brinkman, Carl. "Land Tenure." In *Encyclopedia of the Social Sciences*, edited by Edwin R. A. Seligman, vol. 6–7, 73–76. 15 vols. New York: Macmillan, 1933.
Brodie, Thomas L. *Genesis as Dialogue: A Literary, Historical & Theological Commentary*. Oxford: Oxford University Press, 2001.
Bruce, F. F. *The Acts of the Apostles: The Greek Text with Introduction and Commentary*. 2nd ed. London: Tyndale, 1952.
Byron, John. "Paul and the Background of Slavery: The *Status Quaestionis* in New Testament Scholarship." *CurBR* 3.1 (2004) 62–72.
Carroll, Robert. *Jeremiah*. Vol. 2. Reprint, Sheffield: Sheffield Phoenix, 2006.
Chaney, Marvin L. "Ancient Palestinian Peasant Movements and the Formation of Premonarchic Israel." In *Palestine In Transition: The Emergence of Ancient Israel*, edited by David Noel Freedman and David Frank Graf, 39–90. SWBA 2. Sheffield: Almond, 1983.
Chase-Dunn, Christopher, and Thomas D. Hall. *Rise and Demise: Comparing World-Systems*. New Perspectives in Sociology. Boulder, CO: Westview, 1997.
Clines, David J. A., ed. *The Dictionary of Classical Hebrew*. 9 vols. Sheffield: Sheffield Academic, 1993–2012.
———, ed. *The Dictionary of Classical Hebrew*. Vol. 5. Sheffield: Sheffield Academic, 2003.
Cronauer, Patrick T. *The Stories about Naboth the Jezreelite: A Source, Composition and Redaction Investigation of 1 Kings 21 and Passages in 2 Kings 9*. LHBOTS 424. New York: T. & T. Clark, 2005.
De Geus, Cornelis. H. J. "Agrarian Communities in Biblical Times: 12th to 10th Centuries BCE." In *Rural Communities, Second Part = Receuils Jean Bodin IV*, 203–37. Paris: Dessain et Tolra, 1983.
Deist, Ferdinand E. *The Material Culture of the Bible: An Introduction*. BibSem 70. Sheffield: Sheffield Academic, 2000.
Dever, William G. *What Did the Biblical Writers Know and When Did They Know It? What Archaeology Can Tell Us about the Reality of Ancient Israel*. Grand Rapids: Eerdmans, 2001.
DeVries, Simon J. *1 Kings*. WBC 12. Waco: Word Books, 1985.
Diakonoff, Igor M. "The Naval Power and Trade of Tyre." *IEJ* 42 (1992) 168–93.
Dodd, C. H. *The Parables of the Kingdom*. Rev. ed. London: Collins, 1961.
Elliger, Karl. "Allotment." In *The Interpreter's Dictionary of the Bible*, edited by George Arthur Buttrick, 85–86. Nashville: Abingdon, 1962.
Finkelstein, Israel, and Amihai Mazar. *The Quest for the Historical Israel: Debating Archaeology and the History of Early Israel*. Edited by Brian B. Schmidt. ABS 17. Atlanta: SBL, 2007.

Frilingos, Chris. "'For My Child, Onesimus': Paul and Domestic Power in Philemon." *JBL* 119 (2000) 91–104.

Glancy, Jennifer A. "Slavery and the Rise of Christianity." In *The Cambridge World History of Slavery*, vol. 1, edited by Keith Bradley and Paul Cartledge, 456–81. Cambridge: Cambridge University Press, 2011.

———. *Slavery as Moral Problem: In the Early Church and Today*. Facets. Minneapolis: Fortress, 2011.

———. *Slavery in Early Christianity*. 2002. Reprint, Minneapolis: Fortress, 2006.

Godelier, Maurice. *The Mental and the Material: Thought, Economy and Society*. Translated by Martin Thom. London: Verso, 1986 [1984].

Guijarro, Santiago. "The Family in First-Century Galilee." In *Early Christian Families: Family as Social Reality and Metaphor*, edited by Halvor Moxnes, 42–65. London: Routledge, 1997.

Guillaume, Philippe. *Land, Credit and Crisis: Agrarian Finance in the Hebrew Bible*. Bible World. Sheffield: Equinox, 2012.

Harrill, J. Albert. *The Manumission of Slaves in Early Christianity*. HUT 32. Tübingen: Mohr Siebeck, 1995.

———. *Slaves in the New Testament: Literary, Social and Moral Dimensions*. Minneapolis: Fortress, 2006.

Henrey, K. H. "Land Tenure in the Old Testament." *PEQ* 86 (1954) 5–15.

Herzog, William R., II. *Parables as Subversive Speech: Jesus as Pedagogue of the Oppressed*. Louisville: Westminster John Knox, 1994.

Holladay, William L. *Jeremiah 2: A Commentary on the Book of the Prophet Jeremiah Chapters 26–52*. Hermeneia. Minneapolis: Fortress, 1989.

Houston, Walter. "Was There a Social Crisis in the Eighth Century?" In *In Search of Pre-Exilic Israel*, edited by John Day, 130–49. JSOTSup 406. London: T. & T. Clark, 2004.

Jameson, Fredric. *The Political Unconscious: Narrative as a Socially Symbolic Act*. Ithaca: Cornell University Press, 1981.

Jankowska, Ninel B. "Communal Self-Government and the King of the State of Arrapha." *JESHO* 12 (1969) 233–82.

Jessop, Bob, and Ngai-Ling Sum. *Beyond the Regulation Approach: Putting Capitalist Economies in Their Place*. Cheltenham, UK: Elgar, 2006.

Kaufman, Stephen A. "A Reconstruction of the Social Welfare System of Ancient Israel." In *In the Shelter of Elyon: Essays on Ancient Palestinian Life and Literature in Honour of G. W. Ahlstrom*, edited by W. Boyd Barrick and John R. Spencer, 277–86. JSOTSup 31. Sheffield: JSOT Press, 1984.

Kim, Hyun Chul Paul. "Reading the Joseph Story (Genesis 37–50) as a Diaspora Narrative." *CBQ* 75 (2010) 219–38.

Kitz, Anne M. "Undivided Inheritance and Lot Casting in the Book of Joshua." *JBL* 119 (2000) 601–18.

Koehler, Ludwig, et al. *The Hebrew and Aramaic Lexicon of the Old Testament*. 2 vols. Translated and edited under supervision of M. E. J. Richardson. Leiden: Brill, 2001.

Kohler, Josef. "Gemeinderschaft und Familiengut im israelitischen Recht." *Zeitschrift für Vergleichende Rechtswissenschaft* 17 (1959) 217–22.

Launderville, Dale F. *Spirit and Reason: The Embodied Character of Ezekiel's Symbolic Thinking*. Waco: Baylor University Press, 2007.

Lemche, Niels Peter. *Early Israel: Anthropological and Historical Studies on the Israelite Society before the Monarchy*. Translated by Frederick H. Cryer. VTSup 37. Leiden: Brill, 1985.

Lévi-Strauss, Claude. *Tristes Tropiques*. Translated by John Weightman and Doreen Weightman. Picador Classics. London: Pan, 1989.

Levine, Baruch A. "Farewell to the Ancient Near East: Evaluating Biblical References to Ownership of Land." In *Privatization in the Ancient Near East and Classical World* edited by Michael Hudson and Baruch A. Levine, 223–46. Peabody Museum Bulletin 5. Cambridge, MA: Peabody Museum of Archaeology and Ethnology, 1996.

Lipietz, Alain. "Accumulation, Crises, and Ways Out: Some Methodological Reflections on the Concept of 'Regulation.'" *International Journal of Political Economy* 18/2 (1988) 10–43.

Liverani, Mario. *Israel's History and the History of Israel*. Translated by Chiara Peri and Philip Davies. Bible World. London: Equinox, 2005.

Long, Burke O. *1 Kings, with an Introduction to Historical Literature*. FOTL 9. Grand Rapids: Eerdmans, 1984.

Marchal, Joseph A. "The Usefulness of an Onesimus: The Sexual Use of Slaves in Paul's Letter to Philemon." *JBL* 130 (2011) 749–70.

Marshall, I. Howard. *Acts of the Apostles: An Introduction and Commentary*. TNTC. Grand Rapids: Eerdmans, 1982.

Martin, Dale. *Slavery as Salvation: The Metaphor of Slavery in Pauline Christianity*. New Haven: Yale University Press, 1990.

Matthews, Victor H. "Physical Space, Imagined Space, and 'Lived Space' in Ancient Israel." *BTB* 33 (2003) 12–20.

Meeks, Wayne A. *The Moral World of the First Christians*. LEC 6. Philadelphia: Westminster, 1986.

Meggitt, Justin J. *Paul, Poverty and Survival*. SNTW. Edinburgh: T. & T. Clark, 1998.

Moran, William L., ed. and trans. *The Amarna Letters*. Baltimore: Johns Hopkins University Press, 1992.

Moxnes, Halvor. *Putting Jesus in His Place: A Radical Vision of Household and Kingdom*. Louisville: Westminster John Knox, 2003.

Nam, Roger. *Portrayals of Economic Exchange in the Book of Kings*. BibInt 112. Leiden: Brill, 2012.

Nasrallah, Laura Salah. "'You were Bought with a Price': Freedpersons and Things in 1 Corinthians." In *Corinth in Contrast: Studies in Inequality*, edited by Stephen J. Friesen, Sarah A. James and Daniel N. Schowalter, 54–73. NovTSup 155. Leiden: Brill, 2014.

Odell, Margaret S. *Ezekiel*. Smith & Helwys Bible Commentary. Macon, GA: Smith & Helwys, 2005.

Osiek, Carolyn, and David L. Balch. *Families in the New Testament World: Households and House Churches*. Family, Religion, and Culture. Louisville: Westminster John Knox, 1997.

Pastor, Jack. *Land and Economy in Ancient Palestine*. London: Routledge, 1997.

Pervo, Richard. *Acts: A Commentary*. Hermeneia. Minneapolis: Fortress, 2009.

Petterson, Christina. *Acts of Empire: The Acts of the Apostles and Imperial Ideology*. Critical Theology and Biblical Studies. Eugene, OR: Cascade Books, 2012.

———. "King Solomon and the Global Economy." Paper presented at the Society of Biblical Literature (SBL) annual meeting in San Francisco, November 19–22, 2011.

Renz, Thomas. *The Rhetorical Function of the Book of Ezekiel*. VTSup 76. Leiden: Brill, 1999.

Roth, Ulrike. "Paul and Slavery: Economic Perspectives." In *Paul and Economics: A Handbook*, edited by Thomas R. Blanton IV and Raymond Pickett, 155–82. Minneapolis: Fortress, 2017.

————. "Paul, Philemon, and Onesimus." *ZNW* 105 (2014) 102–30.

Schloen, J. David. *The House of the Father as Fact and Symbol: Patrimonialism in Ugarit and the Ancient Near East*. Studies in the Archaeology and History of the Levant 2. Winona Lake, IN: Eisenbrauns, 2001.

Schottroff, Luise. *The Parables of Jesus*. Translated by Linda Maloney. Minneapolis: Fortress, 2006.

Seibert, Eric A. *Subversive Scribes and the Solomonic Narrative: A Rereading of 1 Kings 1–11*. LHBOTS 436. London: T. & T. Clark, 2006.

Silver, Morris. *Prophets and Markets: The Political Economy of Ancient Israel*. Social Dimensions of Economics. Boston: Kluwer-Nijhoff, 1983.

Skinner, John. *A Critical and Exegetical Commentary on Genesis*. ICC. Edinburgh: T. & T. Clark, 1910.

Solin, Heikki. *Die stadtrömischen Sklavennamen: Ein Namenbuch. Barbarische Namen, Indices*. Forschungen zur antiken Sklaverei. 2. Stuttgart: Steiner, 1996.

Ste. Croix, G. E. M. de. *Athenian Democratic Origins, and Other Essays*, edited by David Harvey and Robert Parker with the assistance of Peter Thonemann. Oxford: Oxford University Press, 2004.

Steinkeller, Piotr. "Land-Tenure Conditions in Third-Millennium Babylonia: The Problem of Regional Variation." In *Urbanization and Land Ownership in the Ancient Near East*, edited by Michael Hudson and Baruch A. Levine, 289–329. Peabody Museum Bulletin 7. Cambridge, MA: Peabody Museum of Archaeology and Ethnology, Harvard University, 1999.

————. "Towards a Definition of Private Economic Activity in Third Millennium Babylonia." In *Commerce and Monetary Systems in the Ancient World: Means of Transmission and Cultural Interaction*, edited by Robert Rollinger and Christoph Ulf, 91–111. Melammu Symposium 5. Wiesbaden: Steiner, 2004.

Stone, Timothy. "Joseph in the Likeness of Adam: Narrative Echoes of the Fall." In *Genesis and Christian Theology*, edited by Nathan MacDonald et al., 63–73. Grand Rapids: Eerdmans, 2012.

Sweeney, Marvin A. *I and II Kings: A Commentary*. OTL. Louisville: Westminster John Knox, 2007.

Theissen, Gerd. *The Social Setting of Pauline Christianity: Essays on Corinth*. Edited and translated with an introduction by John Howard Schütz. Edinburgh: T. & T. Clark, 1982.

Thompson, Thomas L. *The Historicity of the Patriarchal Narratives: The Quest for the Historical Abraham*. BZAW 133. Berlin: de Gruyter, 1974. Reprint, Harrisburg: Trinity International, 2002.

Turner, Geoffrey. "'The Christian Life as Slavery: Paul's Subversive Metaphor." *HeyJ* 54 (2013) 1–12.

Van der Spek, Robartus J. "Land Ownership in Babylonian Cuneiform Documents." In *Legal Documents of the Hellenistic World*, edited by Markham J. Geller and Hedwig Maehler, 173–245. London: Warburg Institute, University of London, 1995.

Wallerstein, Immanuel. *The Modern World-System I: Capitalist Agriculture and the Origins of the European World-Economy in the Sixteenth Century, with a New Prologue*. Studies in Social Discontinuity. Berkeley: University of California Press, 2015 [1974].

Walsh, Jerome T. *1 Kings*. Berit Olam. Collegeville, MN: Liturgical, 1996.

Westermann, William. *The Slave Systems of Greek and Roman Antiquity*. Memoirs of the American Philosophical Society 40. Philadelphia: American Philosophical Society, 1955.

Witherington, Ben, III. *The Acts of the Apostles: A Socio-Rhetorical Commentary.* Grand Rapids: Eerdmans, 1998.

Wright, Christopher J. H. *God's People in God's Land: Family, Land, and Property in the Old Testament.* Grand Rapids: Eerdmans, 1990.

5. Women and Economics in Ancient Israel and Judah

Cynthia Shafer-Elliott

Introduction

The phrase "Nevertheless, She Persisted" became a sort of feminist rallying cry after an incident in February 2017 involving Democratic Massachusetts senator Elizabeth Warren. The episode concerned Alabama senator Jeff Sessions, who was (then) President Trump's nomination of US attorney general. During Sessions' confirmation hearing, Warren read an opposition letter penned in 1986 by Coretta Scott King, who herself was writing at that time in opposition to Sessions' appointment as a federal judge. Republican Senate Majority Leader Mitch McConnell interrupted Warren, stating that she was violating Senate Rule 19, which states that Senators cannot "directly or indirectly, by any form of words impute to another Senator or to other Senators any conduct or motive unworthy or unbecoming a Senator."[1] The Senate then voted along party lines to silence Senator Warren for the rest of the thirty-hour hearing; however, Democratic senator Jeff Merkley of Oregon subsequently read the letter from Coretta Scott King without objection.[2] After being silenced by her fellow senators, Warren read King's letter in its entirety outside the Senate chamber, which was live streamed on Facebook. Speaking of the incident later, McConnell stated, "Senator Warren was giving a lengthy speech. She had

1. Reilly, "Why," para 6.
2. Campuzano, "Jeff Merkley Reads," para 1.

appeared to violate the rule. She was warned. She was given an explanation. *Nevertheless she persisted.*[3]

McConnell's description of Warren's actions, "Nevertheless she persisted," was immediately appropriated by feminists (and others) and used in hashtags and memes to refer to any strong women who refuse to be silenced.[4] Furthermore, the phrase has taken on a larger meaning to refer more broadly to women's persistence whether it be in daily life or in breaking barriers, despite being silenced or ignored.[5] Molly Murphy MacGregor, the executive director and cofounder of the National Women's History Project, stated that "'Nevertheless, She Persisted' is really about every woman who really had to use her tenacity and courage to accomplish whatever she set out to accomplish. It's universal . . . You think about our mothers and grandmothers—they've been persisting for a very long time."[6]

Indeed, not only is the persistence of women global but it is also timeless. It is in this manner that I will use the phrase "Nevertheless She Persisted" as a way to characterize the ancient Israelite and Judahite woman—a woman who persisted, who used her intelligence and skill to help her household survive and possibly thrive. This chapter will focus on the significant impact Israelite and Judahite women had on their local economies, how their economic environments affected their lives, and how women's voices may be found within Hebrew Scriptures that deal with the economic realities of the ancient world.

The Social World

The social world of the average ancient Israelite and Judahite woman was centered on kinship. A good illustration of this is as a series of concentric circles: the nucleus is the household and is often referred to as the bet ʾav ("house of the father," Gen 46:31[7]) and more rarely as bêt ʾēm ("house of the mother," Gen 24:28). Several households, or bâttîm ʾab (plural of bet ʾav), made up the next kinship circle—a mišpaḥah, meaning clan or extended family. It is thought that rural villages were often occupied by one or more mišpaḥōt (plural of mišpaḥah), as found in Exod 6:14, 25 and Num 1:2. Several clans, or mišpaḥōt, claiming a common ancestor made up a tribe (šebet or matteh) and lived within the boundaries of the tribe's traditional geographical territory (Gen 49:28;

3. Reilly, "Why," para 7.
4. The National Women's History Alliance, "2018," para 3
5. Victor, ""Nevertheless, She Persisted," para 10.
6. Reilly, "Why," para 3.
7. All biblical references are taken from the NRSV, unless stated otherwise.

Num 1:16). One could argue that once it is established and fully formed, the monarchy, or *mamlakah*, was the final and largest circle in the kinship structure (1 Sam 24:20).[8] Israelite and Judahite kinship was patrilineal meaning membership was predominately based on the male line, which affected other aspects of their society and economy, such as descent and inheritance. Simply put, in ancient Israel and Judah a person was always viewed in light of their kinship group, not as an individual. The communal nature of ancient Israelite/Judahite society is often difficult for those of us in the modern West to fully grasp, but it is imperative for a more authentic perception of the world of the Hebrew Bible, especially as we attempt to understand the role women played in the economy of ancient Israel and Judah.

The *bet 'av* or household was the nucleus of everyday life for the average ancient Israelite/Judahite woman; consequently, we must shift our attention to the house and the household in order to better understand her world. The term *household* is preferred by sociologists over the term *family* because it is more comprehensive of what this nuclear unit consisted of. A family is defined by kinship, descent, and marriage, which in Israel and Judah could include but was not limited to the matriarch and patriarch, their unmarried children, their married sons and grandsons and their families, secondary wives, and any unmarried or widowed female patrilineal family members. A household, on the other hand, is defined by coresidence and coworking;[9] this could include slaves, guests, or hired seasonal workers. In ancient Israel and Judah, a household would consist of a family and also those who lived and/or worked in the household but were not related to the family. An example of an Israelite household can be seen in Judges 17–21, where the household of Micah the Ephraimite includes Micah (the patriarch), his widowed mother, his sons, and more than likely their families (17:2, 18:22) living in several dwellings surrounded by a boundary wall (18:14–16, 22). The household grows when Micah hires a young Levite (who isn't related to the family) to serve as the household priest (17:10–12).

The social residence pattern practiced in ancient Israel and Judah was patrilocal, which is when a married couple resides with or near the husband's *bet 'av* or household. When a son reaches maturity, he remains in his father's household; when his marriage has been arranged by his parents, he brings his wife to live in his *bet 'av*. A daughter, on the other hand, remains in her father's *bet 'av* until her marriage has been arranged (usually shortly after puberty), at

---

8. Backfish and Shafer-Elliott, *Old Testament Theology*, forthcoming; Meyers, "Procreation," 574–76; Shafer-Elliott, "All in the Family," 34.

9. Wilk and Rathje, "Household Archaeology," 618, 620.

which time she moves into her husband's *bet 'av*. The typical Israelite/Judahite marriage was endogamous, which is the custom of marrying within the limits of one's local community, clan, or tribe (the opposite is exogamy, which is the custom of marrying outside the limits). In the Hebrew Bible, it is common to see marriages between extended families, with the woman going to live with her husband's *bet 'av* (Gen 24; Gen 29:9–19, 2 Chr 11:18).[10]

Many confuse patrilineal kinship structure and patrilocal residence patterns with patriarchy and thus assume that Israel/Judah were patriarchal societies. Patriarchy is a society, system, or group in which men dominate women and have the power and authority. Viewing Israel/Judah as a patriarchal society may ring true to a certain extent, especially from our current (hopefully) egalitarian context; however, Carol Meyers,[11] Aubrey Baadsgaard,[12] and others have recently argued that the social-science model of heterarchy should be used to more accurately describe the social structure of ancient Israel and Judah. Heterarchy (from *heteros* or "the other," and *archein*, meaning "to rule")[13] can be defined as:

A form of management or rule in which any unit can govern or be governed by others, depending on circumstances, and, hence, no one unit dominates the rest. Authority within a heterarchy is distributed. A heterarchy possesses a flexible structure made up of interdependent units, and the relationships between those units are characterized by multiple intricate linkages that create circular paths rather than hierarchical ones. Heterarchies are best described as networks of actors—each of which may be made up of one or more hierarchies—that are variously ranked according to different metrics.[14]

Indeed, the Hebrew Bible and other sources including archaeology, ancient Near Eastern texts, iconography, and ethnoarchaeology, all testify that the social structure of ancient Near Eastern societies was anything but clean and simple. Using the umbrella term of *patriarchy* does not reflect the ebb and flow of ancient Israelite/Judahite society particularly within a domestic context. Certainly, Israel and Judah were patrilocal and patrilineal, but it's not clear that the term *patriarchy* as an all-encompassing word paints an accurate picture of the social world of

10. Gen 29:9–19 is included as an example of endogamy, but not of patrilocality since Jacob lives with his wife's family—also called *matrilocality*.

11. Meyers, "Hierarchy or Heterarchy?"; Meyers, "Was Ancient Israel a Patriarchal Society?," 27.

12. Baadsgaard, "Taste."

13. Miura, "Heterarchy."

14. Miura, "Heterarchy."

ancient Israel and Judah. Alternatively, the term *heterarchy* discourages us from oversimplifying, sanitizing, or romanticizing the social world of ancient Israel; rather, it allows us to see the various social units as involved in multiple vertical and lateral relationships.[15] *Heterarchy* seems to best describe the social structure of Israel/Judah, particularly on a domestic level, which allows the average, ancient Israelite/Judahite woman to be more visible to us.

The Household Economy

The household lived and worked in a typical house that was popular throughout the Iron Age (ca. 1200–586 BCE): a flat-roofed, rectangular, two-story building consisting of usually three to four long rooms on the first floor separated by pillars made of wood or stone, with a broad room in the back running perpendicular to the long rooms. The bottom floor of the house was used for activities related to the household economy and possibly for sheltering the household animals. The second floor was where the household members would sleep and conduct some light household chores. A forecourt (often called a courtyard)[16] is regularly found at the front of such dwellings and is thought to have been an outdoor communal space for conducting household tasks during the dry season (from roughly May to October). The house and its forecourt were just as much a work space as a living space and were utilitarian in nature.

Ancient Israelites and Judahites were agropastoralists (i.e., the growing of crops and the raising of livestock was their primary means of economic activity), with the majority living in rural villages, hamlets, and farmsteads and the minority living in more urban environments, like fortified settlements or walled "cities." Regardless of what type of settlement they lived in, the household was the dominant economic unit that functioned more or less on a subsistence level. A *subsistance* economy is one that produces just enough for the household to survive: they are self-providing; measure wealth in terms of natural resources; rely on hunting, herding, and cultivation for food; and utilize the natural environment and reproduction for their survival. The household economy ranged in levels of subsistence but was always agrarian/pastoral in nature.[17]

---

15. Meyers, "Hierarchy or Heterarchy?," 250–51.

16. There is much discussion as to whether the typical Iron Age house had an indoor courtyard or not. See the following: Faust and Bunimovitz, "Four Room House"; Hardin, *Lahav II*; Kempinski and Reich, *Architecture of Ancient Israel*; Schloen, *House of the Father*; Shiloh. "Four-Room House"; Shiloh "Elements"; Stager and King, *Life in Biblical Israel*; Yasur-Landau et al., *Household Archaeology*.

17. For an in-depth treatment of subsistence economics see Roland Boer's "Production and Allocation," in this volume.

Subsistence-level economies were often in "crisis" of one form or another; however, it was the household economy that was the most resilient part of the Israelite/Judahite social structure—while empires and kingdoms may be rising and falling, the average people were always working the land.[18]

In their landmark paper on household archaeology, Richard Wilk and William Rathje observe four basic functions that households perform on a daily basis, which then of course influences the household economy: first is production or "human activity that procures resources or increases their value"; distribution is second and includes "the process of moving resources from producers to consumers and could include the consumption of resources"; third, transmission, which is "a special form of distribution that involves transferring rights, roles, land, and property between generations"; and finally reproduction that can be summed up as "the rearing and socializing of children."[19] While these categories are helpful, we must be mindful that numerous variables influenced if and how these household categories actually operated in any given society. Some of these variables include the type of society, its environment, social strata, and phase of cultural evolution as well as whether the household is complemented, replaced, or competing with other social groups (such as lineages, villages, monarchies, and so forth.).[20]

The excavation of Iron Age houses in ancient Israel and Judah clearly show that households were performing daily tasks related to production, distribution, transmission, and reproduction. For example, the current phase of excavations at Tell Halif, an Iron Age II (ca. 985–700 BCE)[21] site in southern Israel has specifically focused on Halif's domestic architecture and areas of activity through the use of household archaeology. In the A8 house, an installation with a large grinding slab was found in one of the side long-rooms with numerous fragmented storage jars near it. This, along with the microsamples taken, clearly illustrate that the grinding of grain occurred in this area. An oven with dark patches of ash, a fragmented cooking pot, charcoal, bones, and lithics were also found in the next long-room along with nineteen loom weights and

18. Boer, *Sacred Economy*, 80.

19. Wilk and Rathje, "Household Archaeology," 622, 624, 627, 630.

20. Wilk and Rathje, "Household Archaeology," 621.

21. While the Iron Age II is roughly ca. 985–700 BCE, the stratigraphy for Halif during this time period is as follows: Stratum VID, 900–850 BCE; Stratum VIC, 850–800 BCE; Stratum VIB, 800–700 BCE, which was destroyed by the Neo-Assyrian campaign into Judah in 701 BCE; then rebuilt (albeit poorly) Stratum VIA 700–680 BCE, with a gap in occupation from 680 to 500 BCE. See Hardin, *Households*, 91, table 4.1. The A8 house was part of Stratum VI B in roughly the eighth century BCE.

three loom weight fragments. The artifacts found and their spatial relationship to one another and the house imply that activities related to food preparation and weaving both occurred in this room.[22]

Household Roles

Subsistence-level societies like ancient Israel and Judah were concerned with survival—survival in the here and now, and into the future. One could say that a preoccupation with survival left very little room for inflexible gender roles; that a certain "all hands on deck" mentality pervaded the *bet 'av*, if not the wider ancient Israelite/Judahite society. However, Carol Meyers notes that there does seem to be some duties that were dominated by one sex or the other, and that they were determined, at least in part, more by biological factors than by gen- der roles.[23] She classifies these as roles related to protection, procreation, and production.[24]

Protection was under the purview of the household males, in particular the patriarch. This can be illustrated through the custom of hospitality, where the ap- pearance of a stranger could be a potential threat and a competitor for resources (Gen 19).[25] The fertility of the household land, animals, and people were essential to survival; consequently, procreation by its members was imperative to the future of the household. Procreation was clearly within the female realm since their lives were dominated by their reproductive roles and concerns, such as menstruation, conception, birth, lactation, and weaning. Furthermore, the matriarch supervised the reproductive status of the other women in the household. For example, in Gen 16, when Sarah (the matriarch of the household) is unable to conceive, she arranges for her maidservant Hagar to serve as a surrogate.[26]

While it does seem that specific roles within the household were domi- nated by certain members, all household members, regardless of sex, age, or any other differential, were responsible for the production factor. As was mentioned

22. Shafer-Elliott, "Putting One's House," 9–10, 12–14.

23. "The distinction between sex and gender differentiates sex (the anatomy of an indi- vidual's reproductive system, and secondary sex characteristics) from gender, which can refer to either social roles based on the sex of the person (gender role) or personal identification of one's own gender based on an internal awareness (gender identity). In some circumstances, an individual's assigned sex and gender do not align, and the person may be transgender, non-binary, or gender-nonconforming." https://courses.lumenlearning.com/culturalanthropology/chapter/sex-and-gender- distinction/

24. Meyers, "Procreation," 574–76.

25. Matthews and Benjamin, *Social World*, 9–11.

26. Meyers, "Procreation," 574.

earlier, within household studies *production* is defined as "human activity that procures resources or increases their value";[27] production, therefore, is the basis for the entire household economy. As subsistence-level agropastoralists, ancient Israelite/Judahite men, women, and children were preoccupied with living off of the often inhospitable land and producing various goods from their fields, orchards, gardens, and animals, such as pottery, fabric, weapons and tools, and various foodstuffs. Just as the fertility of the members was of utmost importance to the survival of the household, so was the fertility of the household land and animals. The daily activities that household members engaged in were centered on various production-related tasks during certain times of year, such as planting and harvest, requiring all able members of the household to contribute. Although when the majority of men were off to war, household women were required to bear the full burden of production.

Women and the Household Economy

Within subsistence-level households, social-scientific research shows that the average ratio of female-to-male contribution is 2:3, demonstrating that women contributed 40 percent of the household labor.[28] Societies with this level of a somewhat even division of household labor further illustrate that gender roles were a luxury that very few subsistence-level household economies could afford.[29] The importance of women to the household economy in ancient Israel/Judah is exemplified in Lev 27. Often viewed as an appendix to the book, chapter 27 focuses in general on the pledges or vows that funded the sanctuary/temple; more precisely, this section attends to the following questions: How does an Israelite make a vow or dedication? How is the value of said vow/dedication determined? And is there an acceptable monetary substitute for the vow/dedication? These questions are answered by dividing the vow, it's value, and monetary equivalents into age and gender categories (see figure 1.1).

5.1. Leviticus 27 Monetary Equivalents for Vows Based on Age and Gender[30]

Age	Male	Female
1 month–5 years old	5 shekels of silver	3 shekels of silver
5–20 years old	20 shekels of silver	10 shekels of silver

27. Wilk and Rathje, "Household Archaeology," 622.
28. Meyers, "Procreation," 574–76;
29. Meyers, "Procreation," 574–76.
30. Meyers, "Procreation," 585.

Age	Male	Female
20–60 years old	50 shekels of silver	30 shekels of silver
60+ years old	15 shekels of silver	10 shekels of silver

In the above table (Figure 5.1), one can see that in each age category, males have a higher value than females. Traditionally, this value has been interpreted as depicting a person's worth, further indicating the so-called patriarchal culture of ancient Israel/Judah. However, if this list is reconsidered through social-scientific approaches, another, more informed picture emerges. The monetary value listed in Lev 27 registers *the production capacity* of a person at various stages of life and how it relates to the sanctuary, not their individual worth.[31]

As can be seen in Figure 5.1, the lowest economic-productivity age group is the youngest, one month to five years old (Lev 27:6), with males at five shekels of silver, and females at three. The low production value of this age group regardless of sex illustrates the high infant mortality rate, and that those who do survive contribute little to the household economy. In the next age group, five to twenty years old (Lev 27:6), the economic value for women is ten shekels, while men are twenty (Lev 27:5). The reality of this age group is that women become engaged in their reproductive roles that affect how much they are able to contribute to the household economy. The twenty- to sixty-year-old age group demonstrates that both males and females are at their peak production capacity at fifty shekels (men) or thirty shekels (women). As one can see, the production capacity for women increases as their reproductive role declines. The final age category is sixty years or older with the production capacity of men at fifteen shekels and women at ten (Lev 27:7). It is during this time that men's household economic capacity declines sharply, compared to the minimal decrease for women: men decline from fifty shekels to fifteen, while women decline from thirty to ten. Possible reasons for this drastic decrease include the intense physical demand on people (but especially men) between twenty and sixty, not to mention high mortality rates in times of war. Lev 27 demonstrates the production capacity of men and women throughout various stages of their life—not their worth as men or women. This further supports the notion that all members of the household (men, women, old, young) were essential to the household economy and indeed to the very survival of the household.[32]

31. Lipka, "B'chukotai"; Meyers, "B'chukotai," 780; Meyers, "Procreation," 582–86. For more on other theories, see: Jacob Milgrom, *Leviticus* 23–27, 2368–80.

32. Lipka, "B'chukotai," 773–75; Meyers, "B'chukotai," 780; Meyers, "Procreation," 582–86.

Women as Household Managers

As was mentioned earlier, women in the five- to twenty-year-old category, as seen in Lev 27:6, have an economic value of ten shekels, while men of the same ages are valued at twenty (Lev 27:5). The reality of this age group is that women become engaged in their reproductive role (soon after puberty and then marriage) that would affect how much they are able to contribute to the household economy. Even though the production factor was the basis for the household economy, the demands of women's reproductive role impacted their daily contributions, including often necessitating that their daily household activities be conducted within or near the dwelling.[33] Consequently, many of the tasks that could be done at the household often fell under the female domain—and none more than the task of preparation. Preparation is an element of production that focuses on transforming ingredients and foodstuffs into edible food.[34] It has been estimated that ancient Israelite/Judahite women spent ten hours a day (at minimum) engaged in domestic labor, with a significant amount of time spent preparing one thing—bread.[35] Another estimation is that the ancient Israelites/Judahites obtained 50 percent of their daily caloric intake from cereals, primarily types of barley and wheat.[36] The reliance on bread by the Israelites/Judahites can also be seen in the Hebrew word *lechem*, which literally means "bread," but is metanymous with food. In order to be transformed into edible food, grain must go through an involved process including parching or soaking, milling or grinding, and heating and/or leavening—with the end results being either porridge or gruel and, of course, bread.[37] It would take about an hour to prepare one and three-quarters of a pound of flour and that the daily per capita consumption of flour would have been slightly more than one pound per adult. A household consisting of two adults and four children, therefore, would require about four pounds of flour, which calculates to two or more hours a day to prepare enough flour.[38] Archaeological excavations of Iron Age houses in Israel and Judah demonstrate that ovens are usually found in a centralized location both indoors and outside in the forecourt. Centralized ovens enabled the female members of the household to perform other tasks as they prepared food, and allowed for the sharing of resources such as the oven

33. Meyers, "Procreation," 574.
34. Shafer-Elliott, *Food in Ancient Judah*, 23.
35. Meyers, "Family in Early Israel," 25–27.
36. Borowski, *Daily Life*, 66; Meyers, "Having Their Space," 14.
37. Borowski, *Daily Life*, 66; Meyers, "Having Their Space," 14.
38. Meyers, *Rediscovering Eve*, 110.

itself and its fuel. Additionally, the sharing of a centralized oven encouraged social relations and cohesion within the group (Lev 26:26).[39]

Seeing that bread was essential to the daily survival of the household, we can infer that the task of preparing the grain into bread was one of great importance; furthermore, we can further deduce that those who performed the tasks of preparing bread were highly skilled and vital to the survival of the household. Textual, archaeological, and ethnographic evidence all indicates that it was the women of the household who were responsible for the preparation of food, including daily bread. For instance, archaeologist Christine Hastorf aggregated data from numerous ethnographic and archaeological research projects related to food preparation. She notes that "In cross-cultural studies of 185 societies, women completed most food preparation and cooking tasks, performing *more than 80 percent* of these tasks in any one group."[40] Furthermore, "the only [food-related] tasks that men tended to dominate in were hunting, butchering, generating fire, and farming (plowing).[41]" To put it simply, women have been and continue to be responsible for the majority of domestic food-related tasks. The preparation of food, like many household tasks, was time-consuming, physically demanding, and technologically sophisticated; furthermore, these tasks required high levels of skill and knowledge.[42] Christine Hastorf notes that it is "through these acts [of food preparation that] women acquire their own place and enablement, with their productive contributions being linked especially to familial prestige and position as well as training the next generations in these useful skills."[43] As senior experts, Israelite and Judahite women would pass on their knowledge to the next generation.

The women who managed and performed these tasks, therefore, were essential to the household economy; however, it was the matriarch of the household who oversaw the management of the household including the manufacture of various goods such as baskets, cloth, pottery, soap, and tools; but one of her most important roles included having authority over one of the major aspects of production: the preparation, storage, distribution, and consumption of food. It was the matriarch who decided what produce and how much of it was to be stored, prepared as a meal, or produced into other foodstuffs (such as beer,

---

39. Baadsgaard, "Taste," esp. 42; Ebeling, *Women's Lives*, 32–33; Meyers, "Engendering"; Meyers, "Family in Early Israel," 25; Shafer-Elliott, "Economics."

40. Hastorf, *Social Archaeology*, 183 (italics added).

41. Hastorf, *Social Archaeology*, 183.

42. Meyers, *Rediscovering Eve*, 135.

43. Hastorf, *Social Archaeology*, 183.

wine, oil, parched grain, and dried fruit), as well as who was going to perform these tasks and when. In other words, the matriarch controlled the food, including who ate, when, what, and how much. Authority over the household food is a powerful position—one that is regularly overlooked.

There are a few examples from the Hebrew Bible of women having control over the household food. In 1 Sam 25, Nabal has insulted the soon-to-be-king David. Abigail attempts to neutralize the delicate situation her husband has put them in by sending household food to David—enough for a (royal?) feast: two hundred loaves, two skins of wine, five sheep ready dressed, five measures of parched grain, one hundred clusters of raisins, and two hundred cakes of figs. The nameless woman of Shuman in 2 Kgs 4:8–10 not only determines to provide the prophet Elijah with a meal when he is in the area, but also has a small, furnished room on the roof of their house built for him to use whenever he is there. But perhaps the best example of the authority of the matriarch as the household manager can be seen in the woman of strength in Prov 31: "She is like the ships of the merchant, she brings her food from far away. She rises while it is still night and provides food for her household and tasks for her servant girls . . . She looks well to the ways of her household and does not eat the bread of idleness" (vv. 14–15, 27). While some may argue that this example shows an elite woman, we can still glean what types of daily activities the matriarch could have overseen.

The matriarch's management of the household foodways goes much further than who eats and when. She also would have been heavily involved in the "gastropolitics" of the household. Gastropolitics, or the politics of food, is generally characterized as "the political discourse that encircles all things linked to eating and invokes the charged meanings underlying all culinary events."[44] There are diverse and powerful meanings interconnected with food. Food is intimately involved with establishing, maintaining, legitimating, reinforcing, and even deconstructing household manners, customs, and traditions, including various issues related to authority, identity, power, and gender.[45] For example, how the first Passover meal was to be conducted is given in Exod 12:

> Tell the whole congregation of Israel that on the tenth of this month they are to take a lamb for each family, a lamb for each household. If a household is too small for a whole lamb, it shall join its closest neighbor in obtaining one; the lamb shall be divided in proportion to the number of people who eat of it . . . They shall take some of the blood and put it on

44. Hastorf, *Social Archaeology*, 182; Appadurai, "Gastro-Politics," 495.
45. Hamilakis, "Food Technologies," 40.

the two doorposts and the lintel of the houses in which they eat it. They shall eat the lamb that same night; they shall eat it roasted over the fire with unleavened bread and bitter herbs. Do not eat any of it raw or boiled in water, but roasted over the fire, with its head, legs, and inner organs. You shall let none of it remain until the morning; anything that remains until the morning you shall burn . . . You shall observe this rite as a perpetual ordinance for you and your children. When you come to the land that the Lord will give you, as he has promised, you shall keep this observance. And when your children ask you, 'What do you mean by this observance?' you shall say, 'It is the Passover sacrifice to the LORD, for he passed over the houses of the Israelites in Egypt, when he struck down the Egyptians but spared our houses.'" (Exod 12:3–4, 7–9, 24–27a)

The regulations for the Passover meal are centered on the household's observation of the festive meal; furthermore, the regulations are accompanied by the mandate for households to share the reasons for and meaning behind the meal. Those who hold the power over the household food thus also have influence over the "charged meanings" underlying food and meals. The household meal is not only a time to transmit acceptable cultural norms, such as table manners, but it is also a time to reinforce the household's identity such as why certain foods are acceptable and others are not, or why we celebrate certain holidays. Certainly, the matriarch's role as manager of the household foodways was essential not only to the physical survival of the household but also to the survival of the household's accepted social and cultural norms.

Women as Religious Leaders

When studying the religion of ancient Israel, we must keep in mind that what we think of as the common religious practices found within the Hebrew Bible (i.e., one god, worshiped in Jerusalem, led by a certain class of men) is what may be called *official* or *centralized* religion. Conversely, those religious practices that did not conform to the accepted ritual system are labeled *popular religion*, or as religious practices that are not endorsed or are unregulated. This dualistic compartmentalization of such a complex subject does not reflect the reality of the diverse religious cultures and practices of ancient Israel and Judah, which can be found in both the Hebrew Bible and archaeology.[46] Since our aim is to recognize the economic contribution of women, we must first recognize the correlation between women's roles and women's status in Israelite society in general and their place in religious ritual in particular.

46. Stravrakopoulou, "'Popular' Religion," 37, 38, 50.

Phyllis A. Bird writes that there were three essential understandings of women's "nature and duty" that greatly impacted and restricted her sphere of activity (spatially, temporally, and functionally) and her place in the Israelite cultus.[47] These three elements were (1) women's periodic impurity during reproductive years; (2) the legal authority of fathers, husbands, or brothers over women, which can be labeled as legal subordination, and subsequent subordination in the public sphere; and (3) women's imperative role in the survival of the household both in production and reproduction.[48] In what follows, I will address the ancient Israelite woman's role as a religious leader primarily within the household since this seems to be the arena where she was most free to exercise religious leadership.

In the ancient Near East, the world was viewed through a "spiritual" lens. It was thought that there were deities overseeing just about every aspect of life, and appeasing them so that they bring blessings and not chaos was of utmost importance. The rituals performed to appease the gods, along with the agricultural calendar, dominated cultic activity not only on the official stage of the shrine or temple, but also in the household. Excavations of Iron Age houses in Israel and Judah provide evidence that households were performing cultic rituals on a regular, if not daily, basis. Some objects are clearly related to cultic ritual, like incense burners, amulets, and zoomorphic or anthropomorphic figurines; other objects, such as juglets and food-serving utensils, appear utilitarian and were likely used in a number of scenarios. It is thought that some houses contained their own (portable) shrines (often called *model shrines*); other shrines were stationary, taking up a room or part of a room in the dwelling[49]; still other shrines were benches or niches (sometimes called *cult*

47. Phyllis Bird uses the term *cultus* to mean "the organized, usually public, aspects of religious life centered in a temple, shrine, or other sacred site, maintained by a priesthood and/or other specialized offices and roles, and finding expression in sacrifices, offerings, teaching and oracular pronouncement, feasts, fasts, and other ceremonies and ritual actions." Bird, *Missing Persons*, 84n12. This definition, as Bird continues to point out, encompasses what the authors/redactors of the Hebrew Bible chose to recognize and does not include what has been learned about Israelite religion from extrabiblical texts and archaeology. This definition should be broadened to include the religious rituals conducted in local household and village contexts. These rituals, as we will see, are often the same as the public cultus but are also more diverse.

48. Bird, *Missing Persons*, 88.

49. See my analysis of Room 2 in the F7 house at Tell Halif: Shafer-Elliott, "Role of Household," 202–13.

corners); in reality few cult corners have been found, which could demonstrate that these were features of more elite households.[50]

Food played a significant role in household religious activities, including feasts at yearly, monthly, and weekly regular events as well as special occasions usually related to life-cycle milestones, such as birth, circumcision, and marriage. Sacrifices were conducted at these events, with the sacrifice being part of the festive meal only after the choice parts were offered to the household deities. Archaeological excavations at Tell Halif, Israel, uncovered a neighborhood of Iron Age houses, with clear evidence of both religious and feasting activities found in Room 2 of the F7 house, indicating that religious domestic feasting occurred here.[51]

Within the Hebrew Bible there are a few examples of religious domestic feasting. For example, in Jer 7:18, the prophet condemns Judahite households for offering sacrifices at home to deities other than YHWH: "The children gather wood, the fathers kindle fire, and the women knead dough, to make cakes for the queen of heaven; and they pour out drink offerings to other gods, to provoke me to anger." Jeremiah's disapproval is about the worship of deities other than YHWH, not that it occurred at home or was led by the patriarch and matriarch. In fact, Carol Meyers argues that sacrifices and religious feasting originated in the household, with sanctuaries modeling their own after the household.[52] Other instances of religious domestic feasting include Job 1:4 where Job's children take turns hosting the feast days in their homes, as well as Deut 14:22–27, which instructs the household regarding the offering of their tithe: if the tithe of grain, wine, oil, and firstlings of the herd and flock cannot be consumed at the location God chooses (presumably Jerusalem) because the distance is too far, then they are to sell the tithe offerings and "spend the money for whatever you wish—oxen, sheep, wine, strong drink, or whatever you desire. And you shall eat there in the presence of the LORD your God, you and your household rejoicing together" (Deut 14:26). As was discussed earlier, women carried out the household food-preparation tasks, and we can surmise that this would include those meals related to the cultic and celebratory feasts.

50. Meyers, *Rediscovering Eve*, 149; Shafer-Elliott, Cynthia, "Role of the Household," 207–8. For a detailed classification and analysis of household ritual objects see Albertz and Schmitt, *Family*, 59–75; and appendix A.

51. Shafer-Elliott, "Role of Household," 202–13; Hardin, *Lahav II*, 96, 124, 128–29, 131, 133–43.

52. Meyers, *Rediscovering Eve*, 165.

Women as Healthcare Professionals

The household was also the primary place for dealing with health issues. Again, because people in the ancient Near East viewed everything through a spiritual lens, it was thought that health problems were caused by a person's misdeeds or if a deity was displeased in some way. Consequently, remedies included prayer and incantations, and medical activities were also considered religious activities.[53] Household treatments typically involved substances that were ingested, inhaled, or directly applied to wounds. These substances were made from nearly one hundred different types of plants native to the land of Israel, many of which were the same plants used for cooking. For instance, hyssop was used to add flavor to food but could also be used as a laxative (Ps 51:7).[54] Both balm and oils are mentioned in the Hebrew Bible as types of remedies (Jer 8:22; 46:11; 51:6; Isa 1:6). As preparers of the household food, women were well acquainted with the culinary and medicinal properties of various plants. In fact, the Hebrew Bible refers to women as herbalists, a point that can be seen in a mistranslation often made of 1 Sam 8:13. Samuel warns the Israelites that a king "will take your daughters to be perfumers and cooks and bakers." The word *raqqāḥāh* is translated here as "perfumer"; however, the word more broadly can be defined as *ointment maker* and refers to medicinal, culinary, or aesthetic uses of plants and to ointments that were regularly produced by household women who had great skill in their craft.[55] Women as nurses caring for the sick and dying are also portrayed in the Hebrew Bible (2 Sam 13:5; 1 Kgs 1:2; 2 Kgs 4:18–30).

There is one category of a woman's economic impact that straddles both her role as a healthcare worker and her role as a religious leader—that is her reproductive role.[56] In a subsistence-level society with low birth rates (a survival rate of about 50 percent)[57], and with short life spans (especially for women), one can imagine how seriously the life and death risks in each stage of the life cycle were taken, and how these risks impacted the survival of the household. Women gained knowledge and expertise in the area of midwifery—so much so that some (usually mature) women were even considered professional midwives (Gen 35:17, 38:28; Exod 1:15–21). The imperative nature of the female reproductive role and women's concerns regarding all things surrounding this

---

53. Meyers, *Rediscovering Eve*, 151.

54. Zohary, *Plants of the Bible*, 183; Meyers, *Rediscovering Eve*, 152.

55. Meyers, *Rediscovering Eve*, 152; Bird, *Missing Persons*, 95n37.

56. Meyers, *Households and Holiness*, 15–16.

57. Meyers, *Rediscovering Eve*, 99.

role made them uniquely qualified to oversee the household healthcare and thus to contribute greatly to the household economy.

Women's Religious Vows and Economics

Within the Hebrew Bible, vows are made in relation to asking something of the deity and vowing to provide some sort of "gift" in return—but only if the deity follows through. In Num 6:2ff and Num 30:3–15, we see that men and women acting with their own agency made binding vows to Yhwh. Deut 23:21 and Eccl 5:4 warn that once a vow is made, it cannot be undone and fulfilling it in a timely manner is crucial; furthermore, not only are these vows religious in nature, but they also have the potential for huge economic ramifications.[58] Num 30:3–15 specifically addresses vows made by women, which could indicate that vows were particularly popular among them.[59] The stipulations in this passage demonstrate that if a vow offered by woman brings about vocal disapproval by her father (vv. 3–5; if she still lives in his *bet 'av*) or her husband (vv. 6–15; living within her husband's *bet 'av*), then the vow can be annulled; however, if a vow is made by a divorced or widowed woman, then she must fulfill it (v. 9). A likely scenario resulting (in part) in the codification of this law might have arisen because women (more so married women than single women) did not possess much of their own property. A married woman received a wedding gift (*zêbed*, sometimes translated as "dowry") from her father that served as "insurance" in case of bad times to come, namely, widowhood.[60] It is unclear if a woman could make a withdrawal on her dowry for any reason; consequently, in order to fulfill her vow, she would have to appeal to her husband, who likely was uninformed of the vow until it came time to redeem it.[61]

If, however, a woman (and men less so) was unable to fulfill her vow (through help from her father or husband or by other means), there was, in some circles, another acceptable way of defraying the costs of redeeming a vow—prostitution. Deuteronomy 23:17–18 addresses the act of prostitution as a means to fulfilling a vow, and that this was a known occurrence: "You shall not bring the fee of a prostitute or the wages of a male prostitute into the house of the LORD your God in payment for any vow" (v. 18). Furthermore, in Prov 7 Lady Folly's husband is on a long journey and has their money with him. Today she had to offer sacrifices and pay her vows, and in order to be able to do so

58. Van der Toorn, *From Her Cradle*, 97–99.

59. Van der Toorn, *From Her Cradle*, 97.

60. Matthews and Benjamin, *Social World of Ancient Israel*, 14.

61. Van der Toorn, *From Her Cradle*, 98.

she dresses like a prostitute, looking to meet a young man (vv. 10, 14–15, 20). Not only was the paying of vows to the temple with money from prostitution a known and tolerated practice, but the money was used by temple personnel to pay for the production of divine images (Isa 23:17–18; Mic 1:7). Karel van der Toorn suggests that "Until the Deuteronomic reform it [prostitution to fulfill vows] seems to have been tolerated by the official religion, which preferred the resulting votif gifts over an ethical rigorism."[62] Apparently, women who made religious vows but did not have the immediate resources to fulfill them when the time came had to rely on their other "skills."

Conclusion

This chapter has covered the various ways ancient Israelite and Judahite women contributed to their local economies, how their economic environments affected their lives, and how the Hebrew Bible may reflect the economic realities for women—particularly average women and their everyday lives. As can be seen, the importance of women's economic contributions in ancient Israel and Judah was immense. In a world where survival was the name of the game, ancient Israelite and Judahite women did *persist*, using their intelligence and skill to help their households survive and hopefully thrive. Indeed, "Nevertheless, She Persisted" is a recognition of female endurance that is unbounded by time and distance.

Bibliography

Albertz, Rainer, and Rüdiger Schmitt. *Family and Household Religion in Ancient Israel and the Levant*. Winona Lake, IN: Eisenbrauns, 2012.

Appadurai, Arjun. "Gastro-Politics in Hindu South Asia." *American Ethnologist* 8 (1981) 494–511.

Baadsgaard, Aubrey. "A Taste of Women's Sociality: Cooking as Cooperative Labor in Iron Age Syro-Palestine." In *The World of Women in the Ancient and Classical Near East*, edited by Beth Alpert-Nakhai, 13–44 Newcastle: Cambridge Scholars, 2008.

Backfish, Elizabeth P., and Cynthia Shafer-Elliott. *Old Testament Theology in Its Cultural Context: Theology from the Ground Up*. Grand Rapids: Baker Academic, forthcoming.

Bird, Phyllis A. *Missing Persons and Mistaken Identities: Women and Gender in Ancient Israel*. OBT. Minneapolis: Fortress, 1997.

Boer, Roland. *The Sacred Economy of Ancient Israel*. LAI. Louisville: Westminster John Knox, 2015.

Borowski, Oded. *Daily Life in Biblical Times*. ABS 5. Atlanta: SBL, 2003.

Campuzano, Eder. "Jeff Merkley Reads Coretta Scott King's Letter about Jeff Sessions on Senate Floor." Politics. *Oregonian*, February 7, 2017. https://www.oregonlive.

---

62. Van der Toorn, *From Her Cradle*, 101.

com/politics/2017/02/jeff_merkley_reads_coretta_scott_king_letter_about_jeff_sessions.html/.

Ebeling, Jennie R. *Women's Lives in Biblical Times*. London: T. & T. Clark, 2010.

Faust Avraham, and Shlomo Bunimovitz. "The Four Room House: Embodying Iron Age Israelite Society." *NEA* 66.1 (2003) 22–31.

Hamilakis, Yannis. "Food Technologies/Technologies of the Body: The Social Context of Wine and Oil Production and Consumption in Bronze Age Crete." *World Archaeology* 31 (1999) 38–54.

Hardin, James W. *Lahav II: Households and the Use of Domestic Space at Iron II Tell Halif: An Archaeology of Destruction*. Reports of the Lahav Research Project at Tell Halif, Israel Series 2. Winona Lake, IN: Eisenbrauns, 2010.

Hastorf, Christine Anne. *The Social Archaeology of Food: Thinking about Eating from Prehistory to the Present*. Cambridge: Cambridge University Press, 2017.

Kempinski, Aharon, and Ronny Reich, eds. *The Architecture of Ancient Israel: From the Prehistoric to the Persian Periods*. Jerusalem: Israel Exploration Society, 1992.

Lipka, Hilary. "B'chukotai." In *The Torah: A Women's Commentary*, edited by Tamara Cohn Eskenazi, 773–75. New York: Union for Reformed Judaism, 2008.

Lumen Learning. "Sex and Gender Distinction." Cultural Anthropology. https://courses.lumenlearning.com/culturalanthropology/chapter/sex-and-gender-distinction/.

Matthews Victor H., and Don C. Benjamin. *Social World of Ancient Israel: 1250–587 BCE*. Grand Rapids: Baker Academic, 1993.

Meyers Carol. "B'chukotai (Leviticus 26:3—27:34)." In *The Torah: A Woman's Commentary*, edited by Tamara Eskenazi and Andrea Weiss, 774–80. New York: Union for Reform Judaism Press, 2008.

———. "Engendering Syro-Palestinian Archaeology: Reasons and Resources." *NEA* 66 (2003) 185–97.

———. "The Family in Early Israel." In *Families in Ancient Israel*, edited by Leo G. Perdue, 1–47. Family, Religion, and Culture Series. Louisville: Westminster John Knox, 1997.

———. "Having Their Space and Eating There Too: Bread Production and Female Power in Ancient Israelite Households." *Nashim: A Journal of Jewish Women's Studies & Gender Issues* 5 (2002) 14–44.

———. "Hierarchy or Heterarchy? Archaeology and the Theorizing of Israelite Society." In *Confronting the Past: Archaeological and Historical Essays on Ancient Israel in Honor of William G. Dever*, edited by Seymour Gitin et al., 245–54. Winona Lake, IN: Eisenbrauns, 2006.

———. *Households and Holiness: The Religious Culture of Israelite Women*. Facets. Minneapolis: Fortress, 2005.

———. "Procreation, Production, and Protection: Male-Female Balance in Early Israel." *JAAR* 51 (1983) 569–93.

———. *Rediscovering Eve: Ancient Israelite Women in Context*. Oxford: Oxford University Press, 2013.

———. "Was Ancient Israel a Patriarchal Society?" *JBL* 133 (2014) 8–27.

Milgrom, Jacob. *Leviticus 1–16: A New Translation with Introduction and Commentary*. Anchor Bible 3. New Haven: Yale University Press, 1991.

———. *Leviticus 23–27: A New Translation with Introduction and Commentary*. Anchor Bible 3B. New Haven: Yale University Press, 1991.

Miura, Satoshi. "Heterarchy." In *Encyclopedia Britannica* (2014). https://www.britannica.com/topic/heterarchy/.

National Women's History Alliance. "2018 Theme and Honorees." https://nationalwomenshistoryalliance.org/2018-theme-honorees/#

Reilly, Katie. "Why 'Nevertheless, She Persisted' Is the Theme for This Year's Women's History Month." *Time*, March 1, 2018. https://time.com/5175901/elizabeth-warren-nevertheless-she-persisted-meaning/

Schloen, J. David. *The House of the Father as Fact and Symbol: Patrimonialism in Ugarit and the Ancient Near East*. Studies in the Archaeology and History of the Levant 2. Winona Lake, IN: Eisenbrauns, 2001.

Shafer-Elliott, Cynthia. "All in the Family: Ancient Israelite Families in Context." In *Mishpachah: The Jewish Family in Tradition and in Transition*, edited by Leonard Greenspoon, 33–43. Studies in Jewish Civilization Series. West Lafayette, IN: Purdue University Press, 2016.

———. "Economics—Hebrew Bible." In *The Oxford Encyclopedia of the Bible and Gender Studies*, edited by Julia O'Brien, 1:119–25. 2 vols. Oxford Encyclopedias of the Bible. New York: Oxford University Press.

———. *Food in Ancient Judah: Domestic Cooking in the Time of the Hebrew Bible*. Bible World. Sheffield: Equinox, 2013.

———. "Putting One's House in Order: Household Archaeology at Tell Halif, Israel." In *The Hunt for Ancient Israel: Essays in Honour of Diana V. Edelman* edited by Cynthia Shafer-Elliott et al. Sheffield: Equinox, 2021.

———. "The Role of the Household in Religious Feasting." In *Feasting in the Archaeology and Texts of the Bible and the Ancient Near East*, edited by Peter Altmann and Janling Fu, 199–221. Winona Lake, IN: Eisenbrauns, 2014.

Shiloh, Yigal. "Elements in the Development of Town Planning in the Israelite City." *IEJ* 28 (1978) 36–51.

———. "The Four-Room House: Its Situation and Function in the Israelite City." *IEJ* 20 (1970) 180–90.

Stager, Lawrence E., and Philip J. King. *Life in Biblical Israel*. LAI. Louisville: Westminster John Knox, 2001.

Stravrakopoulou, Francesca. "'Popular' Religion and 'Official' Religion: Practice, Perception, Portrayal." In *Religious Diversity in Ancient Israel and Judah*, edited by Francesca Stavrakopoulou and John Barton, 37–58. London: T. & T. Clark, 2010.

Toorn, Karel van der. "Female Prostitution in Payment of Vows in Ancient Israel." *JBL* 108 (1989) 193–205.

———. *From Her Cradle to Her Grave: The Role of Religion in the Life of the Israelite and Babylonian Woman*. Translated by Sara J. Denning-Bolle. BibSem 23. Sheffield: JSOT Press, 1994.

Victor, Daniel. "'Nevertheless, She Persisted': How Senate's Silencing of Warren Became a Meme." *New York Times*, February 8, 2017. https://www.nytimes.com/2017/02/08/us/politics/elizabeth-warren-republicans-facebook-twitter.html/.

Wilk, Richard R., and William L. Rathje. "Household Archaeology." *American Behavioral Scientist* 25 (1982) 617–39.

Yasur-Landau, Assaf, et al., eds. *Household Archaeology in Ancient Israel and Beyond*. CHANE 50. Leiden: Brill, 2011.

Zohary, Michael. *Plants of the Bible*. Cambridge: Cambridge University Press, 1982.

6. Understanding Law in Ancient Near Eastern Context

ANNE FITZPATRICK-MCKINLEY

It would be unwise to begin any investigation of economics in biblical law without first taking account of a number of issues. The problem of dating of the legal texts has been discussed since the early and vital work of Julius Wellhausen (1844–1918) and has a direct bearing on how modern readers understand the function and place of these laws in Israel's life. Since Wellhausen's investigations, we can no longer be confident that any of the laws date to the period before the establishment of the monarchy in the tenth century BCE, or even to the period of the monarchy. Wellhausen famously declared, "the law is later than the prophets,"[1] thereby undoing the very foundations of the previous understanding of Israelite society as a society that, from the time of its formation in the wilderness after the flight from slavery in Egypt, aspired towards self-regulation on the basis of the biblical law codes.

The function of the law codes presents another problem. Even if they could be dated to the premonarchic or monarchic period, did they function as a source of legal decision in ancient Israel and Judah's daily life, or was it not until much later times—even as late as the rabbinic period—that they came to serve as a source of legislation? The problem of determining whether the so-called economic laws—and of course all of the biblical laws—were applied in everyday life and legal practice is compounded by a lack of evidence of day-to-day legal practice and of how any laws might have been enforced, and by a dearth of legal documents from everyday life in the kingdoms of Israel and Judah. If the

1. Wellhausen, *Prolegomena*, 3.

law codes formed the basis of legal decision-making, then they ought to be reflected in legal contracts. Unfortunately, evidence of legal contracts from Israel and Judah is lacking. Indeed, as shall be revealed, our evidence of Judeans using written law comes not from Israel or Judah but from Judean communities in Babylonia and Egypt in the sixth to fourth centuries BCE. The economic laws applied by these communities in these settings are not biblical laws, however, but local legal customs and practices.

Finally, and perhaps most importantly, modern readers will need to take account of their modern preconceptions with the function of law codes and ask whether they may be projecting their own ideas about law and its place in the socioeconomic life of the societies that produce it (viz., codes provide an authoritative source for judges to apply in courts) onto the world of the ancient Israelites and Judeans.[2] What kind of worldview informed biblical law? Since the evidence examined here will demonstrate that there is no evidence of the practical application of the biblical laws in daily economic life, alternative functions for these laws will be explored. In particular, the possibility that they functioned in an ever-changing and shifting liturgical context will be explored.

The Problem of Dating the Codes

To understand any text from the ancient world, it seems obvious to begin with the time of composition and then to trace the subsequent interpretation, preservation, and copying of the text. So, for example, the Babylonian myth of creation, the Enuma Elish, can be traced from the time of its composition in the second millennium BCE to its preservation and interpretation in Seleucid-ruled Babylonia, in the late first millennium BCE. The Code of Hammurabi dates to c. 1800 BCE but was copied and preserved for centuries afterward in various locations throughout Mesopotamia. In the case of biblical law, it has not been possible to trace its development in the same way, for we do not possess any versions of the codes, or even fragments of the codes, that can be dated earlier than the third century BCE, when we find the biblical law codes preserved by the community that produced the Dead Sea Scrolls. The second-century BCE

2. Many biblical scholars have assumed that ancient Israel must have had a written code: Weingreen, for example, argued that a developing society needs a written law and that a corpus of law was developed in Israel during the monarchic period (Weingreen, *From Bible to Mishna*). However, as we shall see, oral law is likely to have been more important in Israel and in ancient Mesopotamian and Mediterranean societies in general. Oral codes also function in some modern societies and are often misunderstood by scholars as a result of a bias in favor of written codes and their functions (see discussion in Goody, *Logic of Writing and the Organization of Society*.

Letter of Aristeas, produced by Judeans resident in Ptolemaic-ruled Egypt, also refers to the Torah (i.e., the law), discussing its translation from Hebrew to Greek.[3] While no specific biblical laws or codes are cited in this Letter, the text assumes that the Hebrew Torah is a vital part of Jewish self-understanding, and like the biblical traditions, the account ties the Torah to the exodus experience. Nonetheless, the Letter of Aristeas never discusses the application of Torah in daily life, not even in general terms, but focuses instead on the miraculous nature of the Greek translation and the preservation of that translation in the great library of the Ptolemaic kings in Alexandria in Egypt.[4] What might this tell us about the ancient Jews' understanding of the function and purpose of biblical law? This question will be examined below.

Law Codes and Ezra and Nehemiah

Working backwards from these datable references and datable copies of biblical law from approximately the third century BCE, we arrive at the time of the great reforms of Ezra and Nehemiah of the fifth century BCE, when some groups of the Babylonian diaspora settlements are purported to have returned to Judah with the permission of the Persian king (Ezra 1). In both the books of Ezra and Nehemiah, the stories of these returnee leaders center on the law, but to varying degrees: Nehemiah demands an end to the practice of Judahites taking foreign wives and demands the observance of the Sabbath—in particular the cessation of trade on the Sabbath (Neh 13) as well as economic reforms concerning mortgages and debts (Neh 5). Most scholars have assumed that Nehemiah's reforms were based on the biblical codes, which in the absence of good leadership (Jerusalem was under the influence of Samarian and Ammonite forces, according to Nehemiah) were neglected by the Judahites resident in Yehud.[5] As argued below, however, it is not clear that Nehemiah is directly appealing to any written code.

---

3. The Letter of Aristeas is not of course a letter. It is a literary text that recounts a story of the translation of the Torah from Hebrew to Greek and is ideological in intent. Its intended audience has been much discussed: was it aimed at Greeks, Egyptians, Jews in general, or Jews who doubted the value of the Greek version of the Torah. There is no doubt that it is a Jewish composition and not the work of the Greek librarian Aristeas.

4. For a general introduction to the Letter of Aristeas, see Collins, *Between Athens and Jerusalem*, 97–103.

5. For example, Albertz, "Purity Strategies."

If Nehemiah demonstrates a strong concern for the law within a mission primarily aimed at restoring the walls of Jerusalem (Neh 2:5),[6] Ezra's reforms are entirely centered on the demand that the people observe the laws of the biblical codes: They are to hear as the law is recited to them, to listen as it is explained by the Levites (Neh 8:8), to rejoice in it and to celebrate it, and to put it into practice, which seems to involve the commitment not just to hearing it and understanding it but also to celebrating the Feast of Booths, which the text understands to be a regulation of the law in question (Neh 8:14). The people seal a solemn covenant in which they agree not to engage in foreign marriages so that they may remain separate from the people of the land, to refrain from trade on the Sabbath, to observe the law of the Sabbatical Year, and to observe the offerings for the temple, the firstfruits, and tithes for the Levites (Neh 10:28–39). What can these passages, so clearly set by their authors in the Persian period, tell us about the development of biblical law?

Here again, however, the nature of our evidence defies the attempt to construct a neat chronology of the development of biblical law. Setting aside the complex and vexed question of whether these two figures, Ezra and Nehemiah, ever in fact existed,[7] under a close examination of the texts it becomes apparent that the narratives about the reconstitution of the community as the covenant people are far from clear when it comes to the questions of the nature and function of the law. Nehemiah's relationship to the law is a bit like that of the prophets of the eighth century: he seems to assume aspects of it (for example, keeping the Sabbath, taking loans without interest) but at the same time never refers directly to specific regulations.[8] Instead, Nehemiah appeals to the Law of Moses in general terms.

Nehemiah 13:1 opens with mention of the reading of the "book of Moses" in the hearing of the people, but when it comes to Nehemiah's appeal for a cessation of trade on the Sabbath a few verses later (Neh 13:10–22), there is no reference to a Mosaic law on the Sabbath (cf. Exod 20:8; Lev 23:3); instead there is a harsh reminder to the people of the wrath YHWH had shown

6. Nehemiah's mission was probably based on an imperial order to establish a troop (*birta*) in Jerusalem on behalf of the Persian government. His so-called legal mission or legal reform, which centered on his economic reform and on the themes of intermarriage and Sabbath observance (which some have seen as part of an economic reform), should be understood within the wider context of his imperial mission. I have elsewhere argued that Nehemiah's attention to the law was not required by his Persian masters, but represents what might be termed a "cultural coloring" which, as a YHWH devotee returning from the Babylonian communities, he brought to his mission (Fitzpatrick-McKinley, *Empire*).

7. See the discussion in Fitzpatrick-McKinley, "Ezra, Nehemiah."

8. As Wellhausen long ago noted (see footnote 1, above.)

to Jerusalem because the ancestors of the current generation had profaned the Sabbath (Neh 13:18). Again, in Neh 5, where he attempts to put an end to the taking of interest on loans and the seizure of land by creditors of the poor, he appeals only to the "fear of YHWH" and never specifically to the laws of the biblical codes, even though, just as in the case of the Sabbath law, he would have found there justification for his banning of the taking of interest if the Torah as we know it had been available to him (see Exod 22:25; Lev 25:36; Neh 5:9, 15). This seems strange, given that Nehemiah struggled to convince the people of Jerusalem to observe his teaching to the extent that he was compelled to force it upon them (Neh 13:25). Why, if he possessed the biblical codes as we know them and understood them as sources for legislating the daily lives of Judeans, did Nehemiah not appeal to the Torah directly? Surely such an appeal would only have strengthened his case.

Furthermore, even though Nehemiah's rulings on debt slavery, interest, and intermarriage echo biblical laws (and also echo aspects of Ezra's teaching on the same issues: Ezra 9; 10), there is no precise agreement between any of these accounts on what specific laws—on intermarriage for example—should be applied. There is no agreement as to which specific nations Israelites are prohibited from marrying: The three nations with whom Nehemiah prohibits marriage are the Ammonites, the Moabites, and the Ashdodites (Neh 13:23). Does the foundation of his rulings lie in the biblical codes? Nowhere do these three nations appear together in the Torah as unsuitable for marriage with Israelites, and nowhere else in the Bible, including of course in the law codes, is marriage with Ashdodites prohibited.[9] Not only is a justification for Nehemiah's teaching in the biblical codes nowhere to be found, but many non-legal biblical traditions do not recognize marriage, even of Israel's leaders to foreign women, as problematic (see further below).

Ezra, who probably came to Jerusalem sometime after Nehemiah (although this is far from clear),[10] demands that the people learn and study the Torah, and he appoints the Levites to teach a people who are apparently entirely ignorant in matters of the law (Neh 8:1–8), but Ezra never tells us what law he is referring to: what scholars now distinguish as the Deuteronomic Code, the Exodus codes, the Levitical code, or something else entirely. He refers instead rather more generally, like his counterpart Nehemiah, to the book or Law of Moses, and in Neh 9:34 to "your [i.e. God's] law . . . your commandments," or "the Law of God" which was

9. For possible explanation of Nehemiah's choice of nations with whom Israelites must not marry, see Fitzpatrick-McKinley, *Empire*, 217–51.

10. Grabbe, *Ezra–Nehemiah*, 141–54.

given by Moses, the servant of God" (Neh 10:28). What either might have meant by the law or the book of Moses? Attempts at its identification are thwarted by the fact that neither the teaching of Nehemiah nor that of Ezra reflects these laws in any precise way (if the law is understood to be that of the various pentateuchal codes). Nonetheless, Mosaic authority (and not specific Mosaic laws) seems to be the unifying factor, even though it is largely in the background in the Nehemiah story (Neh 13:1). As will be presented below, that fact of Mosaic authority is not insignificant when it comes to exploring the possible functions of the biblical codes for ancient Israelites and Judeans.

When it comes to historical questions, the figure of Ezra has presented even more problems than Nehemiah, with many scholars arguing that Ezra is a late literary construct of the Hellenistic and not the Persian period.[11] It is impossible to be certain whether the person Ezra existed or not, but I would argue that until there is evidence to the contrary, Ezra should be regarded as a figure (historical or literary) whose ideals about law belong within late Persian- and early Hellenistic-period Yehud, perhaps sometime in the second half of the fifth century or the early fourth century BCE. Unlike his counterpart Nehemiah, whose primary mission was to repair the walls of Jerusalem,[12] Ezra is virtually exclusively concerned with the law. In fact, he makes the people listen to its recitation as part of their renewal of the covenant (Neh 8), and the recitation and explanation of the law is firmly embedded by the authors of the Ezra material in the vital act of remembering YHWH's salvation of Israel (Neh 9:6ff). The importance of this idea of communal recitation of the Torah and its embeddedness on occasions when Israel remembers YHWH's salvation will be returned to later in this chapter.

11. As early as Torrey, the question of Ezra's historicity has been raised (*Composition and Historical Value*, 56–59). The work of Noth and Crüsemann followed. These also concluded that the Ezra material is likely to have been compiled later than the Persian period and serves therefore neither as a historically reliable narrative from which we might reconstruct a history of the Persian period, nor of course as an account of Ezra's legal reforms (Noth, *The History of Israel*, 330; Crüsemann, *Torah*, 339). Most pessimistic has been Lebram, who argued that the Ezra narrative was produced after 180 BCE by an anti-Hasmonean group (Lebram, "Die Traditionsgeschichte der Esragestalt"). See also Grabbe, for a discussion of the problem of the reliability of the account of Ezra's legal reforms (Grabbe, *Ezra–Nehemiah*, 188). Others such as Pakkala and Fried have been more optimistic about the possibility that Ezra was a historical figure who carried out some kind of legal reform (Pakkala, *Ezra the Scribe*; 48–49; 73–74, 236–43; Fried, "You Shall Appoint Judges," 65–72). Ezra was very important in traditions from the third century on, most likely because of his association with Torah; for fuller discussion see Fitzpatrick-McKinley, "Ezra, Nehemiah."

12. For the distinction between Nehemiah as an imperial appointee whose task was to restore the wall so that Jerusalem could serve as a fortress (*birta*) for Persian troops and Ezra's mission see Fitzpatrick-McKinley, *Empire*, 177–94.

Law Codes and the Deuteronomistic History

What of the period before the destruction of the temple by the Babylonians in 586 BCE, the period of the monarchy? Most scholars assume that Nehemiah and Ezra were reviving earlier traditions from a time when Israel regarded the biblical laws as sources for everyday regulating of their lives on issues having to do with slavery, inheritance, loans and interest, Sabbath, provision for the Levites, and divorce. Yet the evidence is far from clear. Apart from the famous account of the finding of the book of the Law in the temple by scribes in the time of the King Josiah (2 Kgs 22–23), the law does not seem to feature very often in the account of the kings of Israel and Judah and how these governed their kingdoms. Nowhere do kings implement a biblical code, and nowhere are they said to have lived by it.

While there are some references to the king's observance of the *miṣwot* (commandments), these do not seem to have been related to everyday legal proceedings but rather to worshiping Yhwh alone. When the king is instructed to read from a copy of the law in Deut 17, it is so that he will learn "fear of the Lord," "keeping the law and the statutes," but no reference is made to him ensuring that they become the foundation of legal decisions made by him or by judges. In 1 Sam 12:13–16, the prophet Samuel warns of the dangers of kingship as an institution, dangers that can only be deflected through the king's and the people's obedience to the "commandment of the Lord." The text implies that this involves worshiping Yhwh and fearing Yhwh rather than adhering to the regulations of a law book. In 1 Kgs 3, King Solomon is instructed to "keep my statutes and commandments," and here again there is no indication that this means living in accordance with a law code. In fact, following the dream in which Solomon hears these words spoken by Yhwh, he goes to Jerusalem and offers burnt offerings, implying perhaps that this is what was understood by Yhwh's instruction to "keep my statutes and commandments" (1 Kgs 3:15). In 1 Kgs 8:58, following Solomon's prayer, Solomon refers to the ordinances and commandments given to the fathers. What follows is a cultic ceremony where Solomon and the people offer sacrifice. In 1 Kgs 11, where Yhwh rebukes Solomon for "turn[ing] away from [him]" to worship other gods, he refers to Solomon's failure to keep the covenant and "my statutes," but it is clear that what the text understands by failing to keep the statues relates to Solomon's worship of other gods, not to his failure to observe or implement a code based on these statutes (1 Kgs 11:9–11, 33).

In all cases, the statutes and the ordinances that the king is accused of neglecting—though the terms appear to imply specific laws—seem to have been related to the requirement for the sole worship of YHWH and are therefore cultic rather than legal in their orientation. Even in passages where the Deuteronomistic historians are chiding an individual king for social and economic injustices, there is a noticeable absence of any appeal by the writers to the law. Take, for example, 2 Sam 11–12, the account of David's coveting of Uriah the Hittite's wife and his murder of Uriah so that he could have Bathsheba. The prophetic voice in the story, in this case that of Nathan, never appeals to any biblical law such as the regulation about coveting another man's wife (Exod 20:17) or even to the fundamental prohibition of murder. Instead the prophet uses the vehicle of a self-condemnatory parable through which he forces David to confront his injustice.[13]

By contrast, two accounts of kingship in the Deuteronomic material center on a text referred to as "the book of the law": the aforementioned story of the finding of the lawbook in 2 Kgs 22–23, and the well-known law of the king (Deut 17:14–20). The latter calls upon the king to read from the book of the law at all times; the former tells how an ancient lawbook that had been deposited in the foundations of the temple would provide the inspiration for King Josiah's reform. Note however, that in neither case does the lawbook seem to have provided a source of legislation; instead, it had a ritual function, which will will be explored below.[14]

Law Codes and the Prophets

A popular assumption is that the eighth-century prophets, Amos, Hosea, Micah and First Isaiah, preached on the basis of their view that the laws of the biblical codes should form the basis of Israel's life, in particular that the ideals of the codes—social and economic inclusion and protection of the poor—should govern the conduct of all parts of Israelite society, including of the king and upper classes. However, as Wellhausen long ago noted, nowhere do the

13. Similarly, in 2 Kgs 4:1–7, we hear the story of a recently widowed woman and her oppression at the hands of a creditor who has seized her two sons as slaves because she cannot repay the interest. She pleads with Elisha, who rather than appealing to the law prohibiting such action by creditors in Exod 22:21 (and 25), performs a miracle that enables the widow to repay the creditor and have her sons restored. No legal redress is sought in spite of the regulations in relation to this issue in the Exodus code.

14. See pp. 139–45 below.

prophets appeal to the law.[15] His explanation was that the law is later than the prophets. But this cannot be known because the precise or even approximate dating of texts that Wellhausen had argued for can no longer be regarded as certain. What can be stated, however, is that the economic ideals of the eighth-century prophets overlap in a general way with the regulations of the biblical codes: Thus Amos 5:12–13 and 8:4–6 express in a general sense the tone of the legal codes of Exodus, Leviticus, and Deuteronomy, treating the same themes of care for the poor and the sojourner, provision for those who do not have access to a livelihood,[16] impartiality in legal cases, and cheating in exchange through false weights and measures (cf. Amos 8:5).

However, while there is no contradiction between the ideals towards which Amos urges Israel to live and the ideals of the biblical laws relating to care for the poor in society, neither is there a direct correlation. For example, although he deals with debt slavery, Amos does not deal with the question of the Sabbatical and Jubilee Years, which would demand the freeing of Hebrew slaves. The fact that the prophets never appeal to biblical laws remains an anomaly for any understanding that would argue that the laws formed the basis of Israel's economic life; for if they did, why would these eighth-century social reformers who raged against economic injustice not have appealed to the legislation that prohibited the very practices against which they raged: the taking of interest from a fellow Hebrew (Exod 22:25); the coveting of another man's property (Exod 20:17); the taking of a poor man's cloak (Exod 22:27), partiality in judgment (Exod 23:3); and the taking of bribes by judges (Exod 23:6–8)? At the heart of the prophets' teaching lies, in my view, the fundamental belief in order in the creation, manifested in the Creator's ordering and dividing the natural world but also in the ideas of *mišpaṭ* and *ṣedeqah*—justice and righteousness—which demand humanity's ethical behavior as a crucial aspect of created order. This is most vividly portrayed in the verses where the cry of Amos against the distortion of justice to wormwood is followed by a hymn to the Creator (5:7–9; see also Jer 22:13–17). The foundation of Amos' social ethic in a creation theology is nicely summarized in the following passage:

> Do horses run on rocky crags?
> Does one plough the sea with oxen?

15. See note 1 above.

16. For example, Amos 8:6 criticizes Israelites for failing to leave behind the refuse of the wheat so that the poor who had no livelihood could collect it. This is discussed also in Deut 24:19.

> But you have turned justice into poison
> and the fruit of righteousness into wormwood. (Amos 6:12)

The reverse of justice and righteousness is *hamas* and *šod*—violence (including ethical violence) and destruction. If left to prevail due to Israel's neglect of socioeconomic justice, *hamas* and *šod* can break in upon creation and restore the precreation chaos, the day of the LORD so dreaded by Amos (Amos 5:18). Nowhere, however—in spite of their care for the poor, their criticism of debt slavery (Amos 8:6) and other general overlaps with the economic concerns of the law codes—do any of the prophetic traditions of the eighth century appeal directly to the laws in those codes, even though the prophetic teachings would have found full support in the legislation of the Levitical and Deuteronomic codes that warn the Israelite of oppressing the very same groups that Amos seeks to protect. How is this to be explained? Either Wellhausen is correct that the law came later than the prophets, or alternatively, the law codes may have been preserved separately from the kinds of teaching seen in Amos: that is to say, teaching that was designed to challenge Israel to alter its behavior.

This last point marks an important difference between the functions of the prophetic texts and the law codes as we find these described in the Bible itself. The prophets sought to bring about social change in the present, whereas the codes were recited at moments when Israel remembered YHWH's saving acts; they were preserved, studied, and recited during feast days, but so far as the biblical narratives indicate, they did not provide a sourcebook for judges who would seek to implement them in their daily judgments of legal cases.

Understanding Law Codes in Their Ancient Contexts

Modern readers tend to think in terms of the so-called biblical law codes as having a function with which they are not that familiar, a function different from our modern ideas of law. As Jackson suggested some time ago, the biblical codes functioned as a part of Israel's ritual life.[17] For some time, they may have remained the preserve of scribes and priests who maintained them in the temples. That possibility would explain the mixing of cultic laws on purity and sacrifices, ritual laws on how Israel is to preserve its identity when it enters the land, and everyday mundane law: The case of an ox falling into a pit in Exod 21:33–34, for example, would seem out of place in a pericope (Exod 19–24) so

---

17. Jackson, "Ideas of the Law." For a discussion of Jackson's model see Fitzpatrick-McKinley, *Transformation of Torah*, 99–102.

concerned with regulations for maintaining Israel's status as the covenant people (the Ten Commandments of Exod 20) as well as with purity and the cult when Israel enters the promised land. Exod 20 ends with instructions about the altar (vv. 24–26) before in Exod 21 a long list of mundane cases is introduced. While the appearance of such mundane cases within a pericope so concerned with preservation of Israel's special status and with worship and cultic regulations (Exod 19–24) might seem odd from our modern perspective, it might not have been considered so by ancient Israelite scribes, who might well have included examples from contract law as the texts evolved.[18] Indeed, this incorporation of contract law into texts largely concerned with royal propaganda and cultic matters has been observed as a feature of some Mesopotamian codes.[19]

That ancient Israelites and Judeans thought of the biblical law codes as having a ritual function is evident in the passage introducing Josiah's reform, where it is clear that the lawbook has been stored for ritual purposes, probably buried in the building foundations, and in the fact that its finding prompts not a social or economic reform but a cultic reform (2 Kgs 23:4–20). The burying of texts in building foundations for ritual purposes and their rediscovery in later times by priests and scribes in the employ of the royal court is a familiar *topos* in Mesopotamian literature, and like the story of Josiah, in Mesopotamia, the discovery of a long-buried text was frequently followed by a cultic reform of some kind.[20]

The understanding of the law codes as serving a ritual function is also evident in the law of the king, where the ideal king writes a copy of the law and reads from it in order to ensure the continuation of his rule and the well-being of Israel (Deut 17:19–20). There is no indication that the king was to set about implementing the laws in everyday life whereby they would become a source for judges judging cases or for royal officials enforcing them. Again, this contrasts sharply with prophetic writing such as Amos, where the point is to bring about

18. In Mesopotamia case laws were originally stored in libraries on tablets which often contain only one case law or one contract but eventually some of these were copied onto larger tablets. That similar developments took place in Israel seems a reasonable suggestion.

19. See discussion in Fitzpatrick-McKinley, *Transformation of Torah*, 96–98. Halbe has argued for a development of biblical law, in particular the Book of the Covenant, from a sacral basis towards a process which gradually came to incorporate profane law (Halbe, *Die Privilegrecht Jahwes Ex. 34.10–26.* Otto has argued for development in the opposite direction, from a foundation of profane law towards a process that saw the incorporation of sacral law (Otto, *Wandel der Rechtsgeschichte Israel*. In my view, it is simply not possible to be certain which material came first; furthermore, the mixing of sacral law and laws for everyday dealings was very common in ancient codes.

20. For some examples, see Fitzpatrick-McKinley, *Representations of Assyria* (forthcoming), chapter 1.

immediate and radical change in Israelites' economic activities in a way that will protect the poor and those who cannot fend for themselves.

For those who would argue that the laws were part of Israel's ritual life rather than a source for legislation to be applied in everyday cases of legal dispute, the problem of the prophets' silence on laws and law codes, and Nehemiah's and Ezra's reference to Mosaic authority in general rather than to specific laws, even where specific laws could only have strengthened their authority, recedes considerably, as addressed later in this chapter.

Finally, by way of completing this brief historical survey, it should be noted that all biblical traditions regard the biblical codes as having been revealed to Moses before the entry into the land.[21] Traditionally, the codes were thought to have been received by Moses as the people marched through the wilderness following their salvation from bondage, and were to be preserved and guarded by the priests descended from Aaron, the brother of Moses. While the story of the Exodus event and Moses stories have been interrogated by biblical scholars in search of a historical event without yielding much by way of historical certainty, the importance of Israel's remembrance of this event and its link to regulations received by Moses on Sinai is testified to throughout most of the biblical and postbiblical traditions. Yet, as already noted, our earliest written version of the biblical laws date to the third century BCE, and coupled with the absence of evidence for everyday legal practices in Israelite and Judean societies, it therefore becomes difficult to establish anything about the economic regulations of the law codes or their place and function in Israelite society prior to this.

For the purposes of the present discussion, readers are faced with trying to understand something about economic laws, which it is often assumed played some role in Israel's and Judaism's formative history—viz., during the premonarchic, monarchic, and Persian periods—without any reliable evidence about the historical moment when the legal texts in the Pentateuch were written down or about. It also must be considered whether or when they may have functioned as a source of legislation that governed the lives of ancient Israelites and Judeans.

The Function of Law Codes in the Ancient Near East and Israel

Within the context of the ancient Near Eastern world, there is nothing anomalous about the view that Israel's law codes did not provide the basis for the

---

21. Indeed, as later communities developed new regulations, they traced these back to the same historic moment on Mount Sinai and to the figure of Moses; see, for example, the book of Jubilees, the Temple Scroll of the communities behind the Dead Sea Scrolls, and of course the rabbinic writings.

society's legal practice. After all, Hammurabi would claim that his codes—revealed to him, "the King of Justice," by the god Marduk—were designed to prevent "the strong from oppressing the weak."[22] Yet Babylonian contract law having to do with precisely the issues addressed in Hammurabi's code shows no evidence of any of Hammurabi's laws being applied to everyday situations relating to slavery, debts, or other economic situations where the wealthy were in a position to exploit the poor. Even though the form of the code (the uninterrupted succession of conditional propositions introduced by "if" and formed of a protasis and apodosis) is often regarded as an exclusive characteristic of law codes, Jean Bottéro has noted its use in the Mesopotamian "scientific list" genre more generally. In fact, it is found in scientific, mathematical, and medical treatises as well. Bottéro describes the Code of Hammurabi as a list of judgments compiled, not to initiate real social and legal change, but rather as a list intended to demonstrate the ideals of nobility and equity.[23] He rightly notes the importance of the prologue and epilogue to understanding the function of the Code. This must be borne in mind when dealing with the biblical codes as well, which stand within a very specific narrative framework that serves as a kind of prologue and epilogue: that of the story of Israel's escape from Egypt and its arrival at the borders of the promised land (Exod 19–23).

Hammurabi was not the only Near Eastern king to declare the justness of his reign by reference to a legal code sanctioned by the gods, and in like manner—and sometimes perhaps in deliberate imitation of the great Hammurabi—various kings marked the beginning of their reign by claiming that they brought with them justice and order.[24] While numerous other ancient Near Eastern rulers would usher in their reigns by reference to social and economic justice and care for the poor and marginalized, for the most part there is no evidence that in reality these rulers were doing anything but conforming to local economic practices that would of necessity contravene the ideals of social justice propounded in the codes.[25] Thus, slavery was rife, with slaves being regarded as property and the slave trade being open to all kinds of abuses such as the theft of persons; the taking of interest on loans was often unregulated,

22. The epilogue to the Code of Hammurabi proclaims: "Let any oppressed man who has a cause come into the presence of the statue of me, the king of justice, And then read carefully my inscribed stela, and give heed to my precious words, and may my stela make the case clear to him; may he understand his cause" (CH Epilogue xxv, 3–17 [*ANET*, 155–78]).

23. Bottéro, "Le 'Code' de Ḥammu-rabi," 444; and note Finkelstein's description of the ancient Mesopotamian codes in Finkelstein, "Ammisaduqa's Edict," 103.

24. Many copies of Hammurabi's code circulated for centuries.

25. See Fitzpatrick-McKinley, *Transformation of Torah*, for discussion.

especially in rural communities at some remove from the reach of the authorities of the great cities; weights and measures, it seems, were sometimes rigged;
debt slavery was a constant factor; families lost patrimonial lands as a result of
drought, crop failure, famine, debt, and poverty; and society was by and large
highly stratified. It seems clear that the ancient Mesopotamian codes represented ideals of justice usually associated with a king and his patron gods, rather
than serving judges as sources of legal decision. It is widely acknowledged that
the use of written contracts preceded the use of written codes as a source of
legislation in antiquity.[26] Nonetheless, such written contracts may have been
relatively rare in more rural settings and among the poorer elements of society;
and in these primarily oral societies, including in Israel and Judah, oral custom—with the swearing of oaths no doubt playing an important role—likely
served as the basis for regulating daily economic disputes having to do with
issues such as land boundaries, slavery, inheritance, and loans.[27]

Oral law can function very effectively and, indeed, may raise fewer difficulties than systems based on written codes, since oral traditions are more
flexible and adaptable.[28] Elders and local judges would likely have had some
function here and are referred to a number of times in the biblical texts, but
never as enforcing the written codes of the Bible or as basing their rulings on
them. Deut 16:18–20 appears to provide instructions for judges:

> You shall appoint judges and officials throughout your tribes, in all your
> towns that the LORD your God is giving you, and they shall render just
> decisions for the people. You must not distort justice; you must not show
> partiality; and you must not accept bribes, for a bribe blinds the eyes of the
> wise and subverts the cause of those who are in the right. Justice, and only
> justice, you shall pursue, so that you may live and occupy the land that the
> LORD your God is giving you.

26. See Fitzpatrick-McKinley, *Empire*, 278–79.

27. For an extensive discussion, see Fitzpatrick-McKinley, *Transformation of Torah*,
92–93. See also the discussion in Bottéro, "Le «Code» de Ḫammu-rabi." See also 1 Kgs
8:31–32, which demonstrates how seriously oaths were regarded. They were watched over
by the gods, and hence punishment for breach of an oath would be delivered by the gods: "If
someone sins against a neighbor and is given an oath to swear, and comes and swears before
your altar in this house, then hear in heaven, and act, and judge your servants, condemning
the guilty by bringing their conduct on their own head, and vindicating the righteous by
rewarding them according to their righteousness." In other words, swearing an oath was a
serious undertaking, and the consequence of its breach was the risk of divine wrath.

28. For discussion see Goody, *Logic of Writing*.

Second Chronicles 19:5–7, at least a century later than the previous text and widely regarded as a text from the late Persian or Hellenistic period, is similar in tone:

> Be careful what you do: you are there as judges, to please not man but the LORD, who is with you when you pass judgment. Let the dread of the LORD be upon you, then; take care what you do, for the LORD our God will not tolerate injustice, partiality or bribery. (2 Chr 19:6–7)[29]

Note the general tone of the instructions to these judges. Nowhere are they instructed to enforce law on the basis of a written code; rather they are to do justice and avoid corruption. Presumably these are the values that are to underlie their decision-making, which is to be based on precedent preserved in oral tradition and custom, and perhaps to a lesser extent, given the nature of Israelite society as primarily oral, on written contract.

Examination of the evidence for the actual implementation of biblical laws reveals that the notion that these were at the heart of everyday practices of ancient Judeans and Israelites is somewhat problematic. As in Mesopotamian and, indeed, ancient Greek contexts, oral law, supplemented in some cases by written contracts that do not refer to any legal codes, played an important role.[30] Admittedly, evidence of contract law is limited; but where evidence is found, the indication is that the Israelites in question in the territory of Judah operated without any sense that they ought to be observing the laws prescribed in the Bible. The Yabneh Yam letter presents us with a rare glimpse of a legal case from Judah preserved in writing: A man complains that his cloak has been taken, and he appeals for its return because it had been taken over a misunderstanding.[31] What is striking is that the victim nowhere bases his appeal on pentatechual law where his case was specifically legislated: "You shall not take your neighbor's cloak in pledge for it is his only covering" (Exod 22:26–27; Deut 24:12–13). Note that even here in the written laws there is an absence of any legal sanction: In other words, this is more like moral instruction than law. The consequence of taking a poor man's cloak is not legal but moral: YHWH will hear his cry because YHWH is compassionate.[32] Without a sanction, the law could not have been applied by a judge. The same applies to most of the

29. Fitzpatrick-McKinley, *Transformation of the Torah*, 87.
30. See further Fitzpatrick-McKinley, *Transformation of Torah*, 93.
31. For the text see Donner and Röllig, *Kanaanäische*, 36.
32. The economically privileged in Israelite society are accused by Amos of "lying down beside every altar upon garments taken in pledge" (Amos 2:8) testament to the abhorrent nature of an act that would leave a person without his or her covering overnight.

regulations of the biblical codes that provide instruction on dealing with the disadvantaged and poor in society: They are not to be oppressed, cheated, charged interest on loans, or kept waiting for their wages (Deut 24:14–15); they are not to have their case perverted by a judge's acceptance of a bribe from someone who can afford it, because YHWH is compassionate and will hear the cry of the poor (for example, Exod 22:21–27; 23:3; 6–7; Deut 24:10–13; Lev 19:35). No legal sanction is prescribed, making any real application of the laws in court impossible.

Nonetheless, it is made clear that the Israelite who acts justly can expect YHWH to witness his righteousness (Deut 24:13). An indication of the kind of punishment that ancient Israelites might have expected to suffer if they failed to follow the moral instruction to act justly as this was defined in the teachings of the biblical codes may be found in Deut 27, in a list of curses for covenant break-ers: "Cursed be anyone who deprives an alien, an orphan, or a widow of justice." All the people shall say, 'Amen'" (Deut 27:19). This of course is not a legal sanction enforceable in courts or by judges but a curse brought about by YHWH.

There is a dearth of evidence of contract law from Israel and Judah, and of course no evidence of oral proceedings on which the discussion can be based, at least when it comes to the lives of Israelites and Judeans in the land. But it should be noted that the same situation can be observed when it comes to Hammurabi's famous code: Babylonian contract laws, of which there are far more examples than from Judah and Israel, nowhere references it, and it would appear that the Code of Hammurabi was not a source of practical law for daily life. Instead, it served to justify the reign of a king and was most likely used in a ritual setting—copied, preserved, recited on festival days that celebrated a king, and perhaps publicly displayed in order to associate the king with ideals of divine justice.[33]

In terms of the function of law codes, something similar to this ritual function is indicated by the Deuteronomic writers. In Deut 27:2, Moses and the elders command the people to set up large stones in the land and to engrave them with the commandments. The setting up of the stones at the moment when the people arrive at the promised land is accompanied by the setting up of an altar to YHWH, and here the ritual function of law is in clear view.

---

33. The point is strengthened by the fact that when a king issued a royal edict relating to an economic issue, the effect of the edict could be seen in economic and legal documents that followed the new rules of the edict. For discussion see Westbrook "Cuneiform Lawcodes," 215, and see also the discussion in Jackson, "Ideas of the Law."

In Deut 17:14–20, at a crucial turning point before Israel arrives in the promised land, instructions for the ideal king who will be the only king acceptable to YHWH are given:

> When you have come into the land that the LORD your God is giving you, and have taken possession of it and settled in it, and you say, "I will set a king over me, like all the nations that are around me" . . . When he has taken the throne of his kingdom, he shall have a copy of this law written for him in the presence of the levitical priests. It shall remain with him and he shall read in it all the days of his life, so that he may learn to fear the LORD his God, diligently observing all the words of this law and these statutes. (Deut 17:14–19)

The ideal king makes for himself a copy of the book of the law from which he must read daily. The purpose of this is that he may continue long in his reign, and also that it will prevent him from setting himself above his brethren (Deut 17:20). The preservation and recitation of the law serves as a guarantor of the king's and the people's well-being. Absent in the account is what modern readers might most expect—viz., any sense that the king is to enforce the law—and nowhere is it pointed out that he must implement the law throughout Israelite society or provide it to judges as a source for legal decision. Of course, in reality, a king who spends his days reading from a lawbook is not going to govern very well and is not going to deal with the realities of Israel's historical environment: constant threats from neighboring nations and from the great Mesopotamian and, subsequently, Hellenistic empires. The representation of the king preserved here as one who sits and studies the law is then an ideal.

The presence of the Levites on the occasion when the king copies the law and reads from it should not be overlooked, and this points again to the liturgical function of the biblical codes. Of course, the idea that the Levites would have such power over the king is historically highly improbable; the text has to be considered as an idealized account of kingship from the point of view of those who witnessed its end c. 586 BCE. Its perspective is Deuteronomic; hence the centrality of the Levitical priesthood who throughout the Deuteronomistic History are charged with the duty of teaching and preserving the law, but who in reality may often have suffered marginalization.[34]

---

34. Their marginalization is hinted at in a number of places and it is clear from Neh 13:10–14 that Nehemiah returns to Jerusalem to discover that they have been neglected. Ezek 44 takes a negative stance towards the Levites, while the book of Malachi seems to insist on their centrality (for example, Mal 2:4–10). For discussion of the Levites and their periodic marginalization, see Boccaccini, *Roots of Rabbinic Judaism*, 43–110.

Finally, Deut 6:4–9 clearly indicates the function of the laws and Israel's responsibility in relation to them: They are to be kept "in your heart"; Israelites are to "recite them to [their] children"; they are to "talk about them" in all of their day-to-day activities, to "bind them as a sign on their hand," to "write them on the doorposts of [their] house and on [their] gates." The law serves as a sign and its recitation commemorates the salvation of Israel by YHWH:

> When your children ask you in time to come, "What is the meaning of the decrees and the statutes and the ordinances that the LORD our God has commanded you?" Then you shall say to your children, "We were pharaoh's slaves in Egypt, and the LORD brought us out of Egypt . . . in order to bring us in, to give us the land that he promised on oath to our ancestors. Then the Lord commanded us to observe all these statutes, to fear the LORD our God, . . . If we diligently observe this entire commandment before the LORD our God, as he has commanded us, we will be in the right. (Deut 6:20–25)

Here, then, is the purpose of the laws: to commemorate the exodus and celebrate coming into the land. They are to be taught, recited, and remembered. This is what is required by "doing them," and in all of this celebration and remembering of the law, the poor among the people must be included; even the slaves and servants must be released from their labor in order to participate in the celebrations (Deut 26:11–15), and also to be included is the sojourner (Deut 26:11, 13).

Thus, the biblical writers do not point to the importance of regulating daily practices on the basis of the biblical laws, but are rather more concerned with the constant recitation of the law. There is then no evidence that the laws formed the basis of Israel's economic life during the monarchic, premonarchic, or postmonarchic periods. This is not to say, of course, that it did not form the basis of an ideal economic practice and ethic, as shown in section 5 below.

Biblical Economic Laws in the Diaspora

Moving outside the land to the Judean diaspora communities that are now visible to us in the 'Al Yahudah archive from Persian-period Babylonia, which contains documents relating to the lives of individuals bearing Judean names who are resident in a settlement not far from Babylon, again there is evidence that Judeans (if they are correctly identified as such) were living their daily lives without any reference to the biblical regulations.[35] The deported Judeans of

35. For an overview of this community see Pearce, "New Evidence."

Babylonia were not, as some scholars have imagined them, a somewhat conservative, religiously pious group living in isolation from the rest of the population in preparation for a return to Judah.[36] The inscriptions reveal them to have been a group regarded by the Babylonian and later by the Persian governments of the region as skilled soldiers. Like their counterparts in Elephantine in Egypt, they served as soldiers in return for land usufruct and likely also for some, in return for payment of a wage. In Babylonia they appear to have been occupied mainly as archers, and the land they were granted to cultivate was state-owned land, referred to as *the Bowland*.[37]

The Judean soldiers and their families lived in units, a fact that reflected not their desire to remain apart from non-Judeans but the service they gave first to the Babylonian and then to the Persian governments, both of which organized work units along ethnic lines.[38] Living among them were Babylonian and later Persian-Babylonian officials who organized their service to the government and managed their payment of taxes from the land they cultivated.[39]

The organization of the Judeans as a unit within a settlement should not surprise us too much since the Babylonian and Persian officials would surely not have permitted groups to live in isolation in any way that would have taken away from the value they could give to the government. What is surprising— given what scholars have assumed about Babylonian Judean communities for some time—is that affairs to do with family matters such as marriage and inheritance were governed not by biblical law but by local Babylonian practices. Once again, as has been seen to be the case in Judah itself, it would appear that biblical law did not form the foundation of day-to-day legal proceedings. If the Judean-Babylonians preserved the biblical codes, and it is likely that they did, then they must have preserved them for a different purpose.[40] Of course,

36. As Albertz seems to assume (Albertz, "Purity Strategies").

37. Tablet 15. Abraham, "Reconstruction."

38. See the discussion in Fitzpatrick-McKinley, "Preserving the Cult of YHWH"; and Uchitel, "Foreign Workers." The organization of work units on ethnic lines is evident in the Persepolis Fortification Tablets. Such organization, which allowed people of similar culture, lifestyle, and language to work together, was no doubt for practical reasons. Some groups may have been known to have particular skills—plastering, irrigation techniques—while others may have had no special skills.

39. Most of the commanders of military units will have been Babylonian and later Persian, although commanders of subunits of the troop could have been of various ethnic origins (for discussion see Fitzpatrick-McKinley, "Preserving the Cult of YHWH," 381–82, footnote 24. On Persian commanders and diverse ethnic units of soldiers see also Dusinberre, *Empire*, 90.

40. There is in fact no proof that these Judean communities preserved the biblical laws, but it is difficult to explain the ongoing life of the Babylonian communities and the

it is not surprising that soldiers serving in Babylonia had to observe local laws, but it is not clear that this was as a result of the insistence of the governments under which they served. There are indications that the Judean communities (and others such as Egyptians and Carians) working for Babylonia and later Persia were not always of lower social standing, a fact that can be gleaned from the rations assigned to some of them and from the titles held by others: *saknû* (foreman) and *rábu* (headman, used of an Egyptian). In addition, Egyptians working for the Persians were permitted their own assembly and it seems likely that some Judean communities may also have enjoyed this privilege.

In spite of the possibility that some Judeans had certain rights, the laws that governed the lives of Judean-Babylonians who feature in the 'Al Yahudah archive in areas such as marriage, divorce, inheritance, and interest on loans are Babylonian laws. Judeans in these Babylonian settlements marry non-Judeans. Furthermore, a document from the fifth year of Darius reveals Judeans conforming to Babylonian marriage laws and not to biblical laws. Specific Babylonian practices can be seen to lie behind some of the practices of these Judeans; for example, specific dowry laws and punishments for adulterous wives of lower socioeconomic standing lie behind the legal cases involving Judeans in two marriage documents.[41]

It was not only in the area of marriage that Judeans in Babylon used Babylonian legal customs: In matters to do with inheritance, slavery, and property transfer, Judeans also conformed to Babylonian customs and not to biblical law, even though all of these areas are legislated for in the biblical codes.[42] Not only is there evidence that the biblical laws were not implemented, many of the laws used by Judeans in Babylonia contravened biblical law, as Magdalene and Wunsch have noted.[43] Seven documents from the 'Al Yahudah archive witness Judeans sorting out problems having to do with slaves, some of whom appear to have been fellow Judeans. The practice behind a document involving a slave woman (likely a Judean) is that of antichresis—interest accruing can be offset

---

eventual emergence of the Babylonian Talmud from these communities without allowing for their having valued and preserved the law. There is evidence that military units serving the Babylonians and the Persians away from their homelands were permitted to observe their ancestral cults (for discussion of the evidence see Fitzpatrick-McKinley, "Preserving the Cult of YHWH").

41. For a detailed discussion of these two documents (BM 68921/BMA no.26 [BM 65149]) see Abraham, "West Semitic and Judean Brides," 198–219.

42. For a discussion of Judeans implementing Babylonian legal custom in relation to these areas see Magdalene and Wunsch, "Slavery," 113–34.

43. Magdalene and Wunsch, "Slavery."

by the labor of a slave provided to the creditor. The practice is visible also in another document from 'Al Yahudah in which a Judean female slave is being rented out to a Judean man by her Judean owner.[44] The practice is directly prohibited in Lev 25:39–40, and it can be noted, too, that there is no reference to any provision for the slaves to be exempt from work on the Sabbath or released in the Jubilee Year, as Exod 21:2 and Deut 5:15 would require.[45]

Another document of Judean slave owners in Babylonia resolves the case of a dispute between two groups of Judean brothers over the inheritance of two slaves—one Judean, the other likely not. What is striking about this case is that no differentiation is made between the two slaves even though one is Judean and the other not, again in contravention of the biblical laws on slavery that prescribe a time limit for a Hebrew's period of slavery (Exod 21:2; Lev 25:40–41). Nor again is there any reference to a servant's right to rest on the Sabbath or to the Sabbatical Year regulations for release of slaves (Lev 25:41; Deut 5:15).

Viewed from the perspective that the biblical laws must have formed the foundation of day-to-day legal practice for ancient Israelites and Judeans, the absence of any reference to biblical law, and indeed the contravention of this law, is most surprising; in particular, since so many scholars these days believe that the laws took their final written and authoritative form in the Babylonian communities after initial circulation and growth within the kingdoms of Israel and Judah.[46] If the codes were developed in the Babylonian communities by priests and scribes who had been deported there and by subsequent generations, then they may have been developed in scribal schools,[47] and judging by the evidence of the legal rulings from the 'Al Yahudah archive, they had little to do with the lives of the Judeans of Babylonia when it came to everyday economic matters. The laws that they applied in everyday life were traditional Babylonian laws as evident in the cases just discussed. This should not surprise us, since the daily

44. The document is IMMP 5 and can be found in Magdalene and Wunsch, "Slavery," 120.

45. See Fitzpatrick-McKinley, *Empire*, 276–77; and see Magdalene and Wunsch, "Slavery," 120–22.

46. Mullen, *Ethnic Myths*; Berquist, *Judaism in Persia's Shadow*.

47. The existence of a scribal school in any of the Babylonian settlements would have blended well into the cultural context of Babylonia during the period. One does not need to imagine a sophisticated institution with a purpose-built library as would have existed among the Babylonian elites and citizens. A meeting of scribes within a household would have sufficed, and no doubt the background of the Babylonian cities stimulated their interest in recording, reflecting upon, and editing their traditions.

issues that required legal decisions would have related to their lives as soldiers in the employ of the Babylonian and later Persian governments.[48]

In spite of having certain rights, it is quite possible that the Judeans regulated their family affairs on the basis of local customs because they did not yet regard the biblical codes as a source of legislation. In other words, the biblical codes remained embedded in their literary and liturgical contexts. They governed the relationship between YHWH and his people, which required not their daily implementation but their recitation of feast days and festivals. As yet there was no requirement for Judeans to govern their daily lives and their economic dealings on the basis of biblical law. The biblical codes reflect a different world to that in which the Judean Babylonians lived: an ideal world where Israel comes into the promised land as the covenant people to be ruled by a king selected by YHWH, and in which Israelites live apart from the people of the land: a world which, even in the land, never really existed.[49]

In Elephantine, a settlement on the Nile River not far from the Egyptian border with Kush (Ethiopia), hundreds of papyri testify to the daily lives of another group of Judean soldiers in the employ of the Persians between the sixth and fourth centuries BCE.[50] Once again, these documents from daily life, like their counterparts in the 'Al Yahudah archive, witness the Judeans in Egypt practicing local legal customs when it comes to issues such as marriage, divorce, inheritance, and the taking of loans at interest. Like their Babylonian counterparts, they are intermarrying and resolving disputes by reference to local laws.[51]

48. On the lives of these Judean soldiers see Fitzpatrick-McKinley, "Preserving the Cult of YHWH."

49. For full discussion see Fitzpatrick-McKinley, "Production of Literature."

50. On this community see Porten, *Archives from Elephantine.* There has been some discussion about the ethnic origins of this community with suggestions that they were Aramean, Judean, and Israelite or a combination of these. See discussion in Fitzpatrick-McKinley, "Preserving the Cult of YHWH," especially 399 n. 103 and n. 108 for bibliography. There are likely to have been other communities of Judean soldiers in Egypt. We know of one dating to the Ptolemaic period (and possibly earlier) from Edfu. Jeremiah refers to Judeans at Migdol, Memphis, Pathros, and Tahpanhes (Jer 44:1). These may have been military since there is evidence for Judeans serving the Saite pharaohs before they served the Persian and Ptolemaic rulers of Egypt (for discussion see Fitzpatrick-McKinley, "Preserving the Cult of YHWH"). Jeremiah criticizes what appear to be Judean-Egyptian communities for worshipping the "Queen of Heaven" (Jer 44:17) but never for failing to implement biblical law.

51. The legal practices behind the papyri have been intensely interrogated with a view to determining what legal codes informed them. Greenfield has concluded that the law was "Jewish," and that the Elephantine Jews practiced a Judaism that in other places did not emerge until much later (Greenfield, "Aramaic Studies and the Bible"). Greenfield's arguments do not stand up well against the observation of others that the legal practices of the Judeans at Elephantine show clear Egyptian, Assyrian, and Babylonian influences. (For

There are examples of Judean women marrying Egyptian men (TAD B2.6) and of Judean men marrying Egyptian women; a Judean temple official is married to an Egyptian woman (TAD B3.3). A Judean woman named Mibtahiah had inheritance rights and could take the initiative in divorcing her husband. Judean women could own houses and slaves and could bequeath them to their children (TAD B2.8, 10–11). Judean women can be seen to use local Egyptian legal custom to solve problems relating to their inheritance and marriages. Indeed, biblical law would not have permitted a woman to take such steps.[52] There is evidence of a Hebrew taking interest on loans made to another Hebrew, again in direct contravention of the biblical prescriptions (TAD B3.1; Exod 22:25; Lev 25:36–37; Deut 23:24). On many fronts then, the notion that the biblical codes formed the basis of practice of everyday Judeans at Elephantine is challenged.[53]

Yet it is clear that certain practices prescribed in the codes were followed. Passover in some form was observed, and an ostracon from Elephantine seems to imply that someone is worried that a *Yahô* (YHWH) worshiper will not turn up to meet a boat carrying produce because it is the Sabbath:

> Meet the boat tomorrow on Sabbath lest they (the vegetables) get spoiled. By the life of Yahô, if not I shall take your life.[54]

Other ostraca from Elephantine—CG44, CG 186—also refer to the Sabbath, and the name Shabbethai—the occurrence of which is taken by Porten to indicate Sabbath observance—occurs four times.[55] Thus, while the Elephantine YHWH worshipers conformed in some respects to the requirements of the biblical codes, there is no indication that they understood the law codes to be the basis of daily practices when it came to resolving economic disputes. Instead, like their counterparts in Babylonia, they applied local laws.

Egyptian influences, see Botta, *Aramaic and Egyptian Traditions*; for Assyrian and Babylonian influences, see Muffs, *Studies*, 179–90.)

52. This fact led Modrzejewski to conclude that the female community at Elephantine may have enjoyed more legal rights than their counterparts in Judah (Modrzejewski, *Jews of Egypt*, 35–36).

53. For a detailed discussion of the absence of biblical law in the Elephantine legal papyri and discussion of the Egyptian systems applied see Botta, *Aramaic and Egyptian Legal Traditions*, 19–32. For the suggestion that the influence was Assyrian law see Yaron, *Introduction*, 99–100.

54. For the ostracon and discussion of it see Porten, *Archives from Elephantine*, 127.

55. Porten, *Archives from Elephantine*, 127. See also the discussion in Porten, "Religion of the Jews."

But both of these communities were diaspora communities settled out-side the land, and it would be tempting to conclude that it was their residence outside the land that required them to observe laws other than the biblical laws. Why would the Babylonian and Persian governments have permitted them to use their indigenous codes? Might the Judeans in Judah have observed the bib-lical codes in this same period? The picture in the land of Judah itself between the sixth and fourth centuries, however, is far from clear.

Did the Community in Yehud in the Fifth to Fourth Centuries BCE Observe Biblical Law?

Roughly contemporaneous with the fifth-century Judean communities of sol-diers at Elephantine and at 'Al Yahudah are the aforementioned missions of Ezra and Nehemiah to Jerusalem (Ezra 7–10; Neh 1–13). Ezra and Nehemiah, of course, were returnees from the Babylonian communities, and one might have assumed that they appealed to the community in Jerusalem and Yehud to adopt their diasporan practice of living by biblical law, as Albertz has argued.[56] This would seem a reasonable conclusion since both the Babylonian accounts and the biblical accounts of the exile from Jerusalem recount how the upper classes and the scribes and priests were deported to Babylonia. It would not be surprising, then, if these groups preserved and copied the traditions of the covenant code. Indeed, many scholars have assumed that as the guardians of the national cultic traditions of the Jerusalem temple, these upper-class, ed-ucated Judeans, resettled in Babylonia, did just this.[57] However, evidence al-ready examined from the 'Al Yahudah archive challenges the view that among the Babylonian communities the biblical codes served as a source for everyday judgments.

If the Judeans in Babylonian territories preserved the written codes of the Bible (which the author believes to be the case), they preserved them for religious purposes, probably copying them, preserving them, reciting them, and teaching them to trainee scribes, just as their Babylonian scribal counterparts would have done with the treasured literary traditions of Babylon.[58] In spite of the value that may have been attached to the law codes,[59] they were not a

56. Albertz argued that Nehemiah wanted to bring "a Diaspora shaped concept of Juda-ism" to Yehud (Albertz, "Purity Strategies," 203).

57. For example, Mullen, *Ethnic Myths*, 328–31; and Smith-Christopher, *Religion of the Landless*, 5–11.

58. Goody has argued that the primary function of early law codes was educational (Goody, *Logic of Writing*, 135).

59. In fact, we do not have evidence of the role the law codes played, other than to say

source on the basis of which the Judean Babylonian elders, judges, and community leaders made legal decisions.[60] This is evident in the number of documents where Judeans lived by the local Babylonian legal practices.

What of their fellow Judeans in Yehud and the returnee leaders Ezra and Nehemiah? Examination of the account in Neh 8–9 reveals the problems that Ezra encounters. It was not simply a matter of reminding the people of the ancestral law that lay at the heart of the covenant between Israel and YHWH, and that had guaranteed their deliverance from Egypt and their settlement in the promised land. Ezra in fact seems to be introducing the laws to the people for the first time. He appoints Levites to teach the law to a community that, it would seem, does not know the law (Neh 8:8; cf. Ezra 10:1–3).

The task of the returnee leader Nehemiah is no easier, and instead of finding a community of Judeans anxious to renew their commitment to the law, Nehemiah resorts to force. When it comes to economic laws, to the legislation on slavery and debts and mortgages, the question is raised as to whether the regulations in Neh 5 indicate that the returnee Nehemiah was taking the opportunity to enforce biblical laws, since, in Judah, he was no longer subject to Babylonian legal practices. Again, the answer is complex, and the economic changes that Nehemiah initiates in Neh 5 do not correspond in any precise way to biblical legislation in the codes, although they do echo it in a general way. Thus, for example, as already noted, Neh 5:7 seems to agree with the regulation of taking interest from a fellow Israelite found in Lev 25:36, Exod 22:25, and Deut 23:24, but he does not appeal specifically to any of these, nor indeed in Neh 5 even to Mosaic authority in general. Neither does he appeal to the law for the release of Hebrew slaves in Exod 21:2–11 or in Deut 15:1–18. Overall, Nehemiah never appeals to Mosaic laws as he struggles to implement his economic reforms in Neh 5; instead, he appeals in a general way to the "fear of the LORD" (Neh 5:9, 15). It should be noted, too, that the basis of Nehemiah's economic reform is never said to be biblical law; rather, the reforms are prompted by the cry of the people from economic oppression by the wealthier (Neh 5:7 refers to the "nobles and leaders of Jerusalem"), and many of those who

they were not a source of everyday legal decisions. I assume that they played a central role in the communal life on the basis that for the following centuries they did so, and one of the most important and formative Jewish texts came out of the Babylonian communities, albeit centuries later.

60. Babylonian authorities permitted members of resettled communities who served the government to have their own leaders—called saknû or rábu. There would also have been a Babylonian overseer. The practice seems to have been continued by the Persians. On leadership in these communities see discussion in Fitzpatrick-McKinley, Empire, 270–72.

were oppressing the poor appear to have come from among Nehemiah's own men (Neh 5:10). Presumably these were men who had accompanied him from Babylonia to assist in his establishment of the fort in Jerusalem on behalf of the Persian government. Indeed, the economic crisis behind Nehemiah's reform may have arisen as a result of Nehemiah's imperial mission to repair the walls and establish troops in a fort in Jerusalem. The troops and the fort would have to be maintained by the local population, as was normal Persian practice, thereby bringing new economic burdens on the people of Yehud.[61] It was perhaps as a result of these new pressures that the people had been forced to mortgage their fields, vineyards, and houses.[62]

Ezra and Nehemiah are distraught at the practice of intermarriage, and Ezra goes as far as to demand that foreign wives and the children of these marriages be set aside (Ezra 10:3). A number of scholars have identified the primary issue here as economic—it concerned the inheritance of land.[63] But Ezra does not refer to this. According to the account, the people are moved to repentance and renew the covenant, setting aside their foreign wives and the offspring of these marriages on the basis of their recognition that they have failed to keep the covenant with YHWH (Ezra 10:3); but nowhere in the Bible is there legislation for forced divorce. Evidence from the ensuing centuries indicates that marriage between Jews and non-Jews continued for centuries and was not really problematized again until the rabbinic period.[64] Moreover, the period prior to Ezra and Nehemiah's teaching is characterized by the Deuteronomistic historians and by the authors of Chronicles as a period when ancient Israelites—even Moses himself—married foreign women. Moses, to whom Ezra attributes the prohibition of intermarriage (insofar as Ezra refers to his teaching as "the Law of Moses"), was married to a Kushite, Joseph to an Egyptian who was the daughter of an Egyptian priest (Gen 41:45). Indeed, in Num 12:7–9, YHWH rebukes Aaron and Miriam for criticizing Moses' marriage to an Egyptian.[65] The Chronicler's history in general, widely regarded as postdating Ezra and Nehemiah, provides a genealogy of Judah that includes

---

61. For discussion see Fitzpatrick-McKinley, "Preserving the Cult of YHWH."

62. For full discussion see Fitzpatrick-McKinley, *Empire*, 238–42.

63. Hoglund, "Achaemenid Context," 67.

64. Hayes, "Intermarriage and Impurity"; Hayes, *Gentile Impurities and Jewish Identities*.

65. For a discussion of intermarriage in the various biblical traditions and in particular on the place of foreign women see Gaines, *Music in the Old Bones*. See also the excellent discussion in Knoppers, who notes the anomalies of the biblical sources (Knoppers, "Intermarriage," 15–30).

Canaanites and Moabites,[66] precisely the groups with whom Nehemiah bans marriage (Neh 13). The book of Ruth recounts the story of a Moabitess who was married to an Israelite, and its theme has been identified as openness to foreigners who show goodwill to Israel and who worship YHWH.[67]

At the same time, in spite of the evidence that Judeans happily intermarried in contravention of Ezra and Nehemiah's teaching, and that in Babylonia and Egypt they observed laws on inheritance, divorce, loans, and slavery that contravened biblical law, there is evidence that they treasured the law, celebrated it on various feast days, preserved it, translated it, and recited it.

What happened to the laws of Ezra, then? If the laws were not applied, what was their function? Should it just be assumed that they were not applied because they had not yet been written down? This is not likely the case; and the evidence of the references to the laws in second-century BCE texts such as the Letter of Aristeas, some of the earlier scrolls from the Dead Sea Scrolls communities, and the book of Ecclesiasticus make this very doubtful, since all of these traditions refer to the biblical law as something ancient and established. Indeed, even the Greek writer Hecataeus, whose work is dated to c. 300 BCE, notes the importance of the laws to the Jews.[68]

If Ezra really did bring back the law from Babylonia, how was it regarded if it was not adhered to as the basis for daily life? Furthermore, to what laws was Ezra referring? What does he mean when he refers to the "law of Moses"? He never says, and the matter is not clear. What can be noted, however, is that his laws on forced divorce of foreign wives and on the specification of prohibited nations are nowhere found in precise duplication in any of the biblical codes; so, for example, Ezra 9:1–2 lists nations outlawed in Deuteronomy (7:1–3), but adds others (only Ammonites and Moabites are mentioned in Deut 23:3–4). Neither are the regulations demanded by Nehemiah found in precise form in the biblical law codes, and where he might have found a foundation for

66. For discussion see Knoppers, "Intermarriage," 29.

67. Hubbard, *Book of Ruth*, 41. In Ruth, Boaz wishes to carry out a legal transaction at the gates of the city (Ruth 4). The text implies that all those involved were familiar with the legal procedure and took its results for granted, yet no text is cited or referred to. Indeed, some scholars have noted the discrepancies between Ruth 4 and the biblical laws on the Levirate and Goel institutions of the biblical codes (Westbrook, *Property*, 3). For these discrepancies see Leggett, *Levirate and Goel*, 176–78.

68. Hecataeus reports of Moses that he "picked out the men of most refinement and with the greatest ability to head the entire people, appointed them priests ... and entrusted to them the guardianship of the laws and customs." Hecataeus is cited by the later author Diodorus Siculus 40.3.1–7. It is noteworthy that among Greek writers the Jews are known for their attachment to their laws.

his reforms—for example, in relation to loans and interest, and care for the Levites—he makes no direct appeal to biblical codes (Neh 5). All of this likely indicates that during the sixth to fourth centuries, ancient Judeans knew about the idea of Mosaic authority—that is to say, they knew that certain regulations could be ascribed with such authority—but they did not seem to have had an authoritative version of these.[69] The evidence of other Torah traditions from the period confirms this.

In Jubilees, which is dated to late in the second century BCE, the revelation to Moses of Mount Sinai is delivered by angels of the divine presence and includes laws not found in the pentateuchal codes. In the Temple Scroll from the community of the Dead Sea Scrolls, YHWH speaks in the first person and delivers laws not found in the pentateuchal codes.[70] This seems to prohibit us from speaking of a closed and finalized body of law that was understood to have divine authority, and it must be concluded that Torah was still fluid and developing during the centuries prior to the rabbinic movement. It was not regarded as a source of regulations by which to decide cases to do with slavery, inheritance, loans, and interest either in Judah or in the diasporan communities. Cases to do with everyday economic issues were decided on the basis of whatever custom and practice prevailed in the region. Biblical law, in spite of its concern with apparent everyday matters, was regarded by ancient Judeans as something other than a law code that had as its primary purpose the provision of regulations to be applied by judges.

Remember the Law to Remember Your God: The Function of the Biblical Codes in Israelite and Judean Life

But what use are laws that are never applied; who might have preserved them, and for what purpose? Again, the ancient Near Eastern practice of writing and preserving legal codes that were not to be implemented in daily practice—but rather served to express ideals of justice—may provide an answer. It is arguable that the biblical laws first took shape within the context of the religious cult, and more specifically within the context of Israel's traditions of remembering, and particularly of reciting, its past.

The laws dealing with poverty, inheritance, debt slavery, and other economic issues are, after all, embedded in larger units that are primarily concerned with cultic and sacrificial issues: matters to do with how to approach

69. Najman refers to the idea of a Mosaic authority without there being any closed or fixed canon of biblical law (Najman, "Interpretation as Primordial Writing").

70. As Horsley observes (*Scribes*, 190).

YHWH, ritual purity, observance of festivals, and the offering of sacrifices. As will be addressed below, it is notable that the laws are recited on occasions related to YHWH's salvific action towards Israel. In other words, looking for evidence of Israel consulting its lawbooks as sources for everyday rulings on economic issues is misguided. The laws were far more important than that; they lay at the very heart of Israel's self-understanding—a self-understanding expressed not by the implementation of these laws in everyday legal situations such as inheritance, divorce, slavery, and the sale of property, but by the recitation of these laws by the community at key moments in the liturgical year. The key to understanding this function, and indeed the ethos behind the texts, lies in the position of the laws within the larger narrative frameworks.

Reading Biblical Law Codes in Their Narrative Frameworks

Consider for example the position of the account of the giving of the law to Israel in the wider narrative framework in which it occurs: it is positioned between the story of the exodus and instructions on the building of the tabernacle once Israel has reached the promised land (Exod 19–31). In Deuteronomy, it lies between the account of the end of Moses' career and the arrival of the people at the borders of the promised land (Deut 12–26). Here are key moments in Israel's history when YHWH has intervened to save Israel and to choose Israel for a special possession, to be "a kingdom of priests and a holy nation" (Exod 19:6). It is in a moment of danger and despair—when Israel is in the wilderness—that Moses receives the law on Mount Sinai. He brings it down to the people, sets it before them, and reads it to them. The people respond in awe and fear and Moses returns to the mountain to receive further instruction. The main theme of the account is not legal prescriptions and how they are to be applied and implemented, but YHWH's holiness and the need to fear the deity's presence. The instructions relate more to cultic purity than to anything else (Exod 19:12–15). When YHWH speaks to the people through Moses in Exod 20:21–26, the theme of worship of YHWH and of no other gods besides YHWH dominates. This is followed nonetheless in Exod 21 and 22 by specific ordinances that seem to relate directly to the socioeconomic life of Israel, but are mixed with regulations for its cultic life.[71]

71. It is also widely acknowledged that some of these laws received on Sinai find verbatim parallels in Babylonian codes (the law of the goring ox is the most famous example and occurs in the Code of Hammurabi and the Laws of Esnunna). It is difficult to explain this, but we should probably think of an evolving tradition of law rather than a fixed body of law,

FITZPATRICK-MCKINLEY—UNDERSTANDING LAW

The laws however, in many cases, and in spite of their noncultic orientation, are not really laws, because they would be impossible to implement, lacking, as they do in many cases, any legal sanction or instruction for restoration and reparation.[72] Many of the laws are moral instruction, not legislation proper (in the sense of sources for judges); for example, Exod 23:1–8 prescribes the right thing to do rather than laying out legal and potentially enforceable consequences for making a false report, bearing false witness, showing partiality to a poor man, and not assisting a neighbor. From a legal perspective, definition of the crime and proceedings for punishment and reparation would be required, but only Yhwh's watchful eye over the Israelites' behavior stands as a warning to those who fail to live by these moral instructions. Even in the two aforementioned texts where instructions to appoint judges are given (Deut 16:18–20; 2 Chr 19:5–7), the judges are not told on what basis they are to judge; rather, they are instructed to judge in a just and compassionate way: not to take bribes, not to show partiality, to do justice so that they may live long in the land which Yhwh has given them.

Not only do modern readers frequently find themselves dealing with moral instruction where they might expect to find specific economic laws, but the justification for laws apparently designed to promote inclusion of the marginalized in society—the widow, the orphan, the *ger* (resident alien)—are expounded as a consequence of Israel's own historical experience: for you yourselves were strangers in Egypt (Exod 22:21); you were slaves, you were hungry, without a homeland, lost in the wilderness, you knew hunger, you knew oppression. For example, Lev 25:35 instructs that no one shall exact interest on a loan from his brother (viz., a fellow Israelite). There is no precise definition of the instruction that might aid a judge in the application of Lev 25:35, nor is there a legal sanction that a judge might enforce. Instead, the ruling is followed by Yhwh's firm declaration: "I am the Lord your God, who brought you forth out of the land of Egypt" (Lev 25:38). The regulation, among many others, resembles moral instruction more than legal prescription. Hence Yhwh will wreak his revenge on those who oppress the poor, but there was no social implementation of antipoverty laws demanded. In Exod 22:25, the theme of loans at interest is treated again, and creditors are instructed that they must not exact interest from the poor among Yhwh's people. But what is the legal

---

and some of the provisions will have been added by scribes who knew Babylonian laws. They did not need to be resident in Babylonia for influence to have taken place, as there was a wide circulation of scribal traditions in the region (as testified by the library of the Assyrian king Assurbanipal).

72. For discussion see Fitzpatrick-McKinley, *Transformation of Torah*.

sanction for not charging interest? There is none—only YHWH's warning that he will hear the cry of the poor because he is compassionate.

It is in the context of ritual or cultic experiences that these laws are to be invoked and recited by the community, and it is at these moments that the laws serve their function of promoting social justice and inclusion in a way that appears to have been separate from the daily practices of law; these laws were based instead on oral custom, the swearing of oaths, and the likely occasional use of written contracts. Remember your slavery in Egypt, and when you celebrate your deliverance, you shall include in these celebrations, and particularly at meals, those among you who are less fortunate, because you yourselves were once less fortunate: this was the message of the biblical law codes. Occasions for the recitation of these memories include various festivals, some of which may date to very early times. Deut 26:5–11 presents a short account of Israel's salvation from Egypt before some regulations are introduced:

> A wandering Aramean was my ancestor; he went down into Egypt and lived there as an alien, few in number, and there he became a great nation, mighty and populous. When the Egyptians treated us harshly and afflicted us, . . . we cried to the LORD, the God of our ancestors . . . The LORD brought us out of Egypt . . . and gave us this land, a land flowing with milk and honey. So now I bring the first of the fruit of the ground . . . Then you, together with the Levites and the aliens who reside among you, shall celebrate with all the bounty that the LORD your God has given to you and to your house.

The passage occurs between a section instructing Israelites how to celebrate the Feast of Firstfuits when they come into the land (Deut 26:1–4) and a section that continues with further instruction on who must be included in such celebrations: the poor among you, the fatherless and the widow, the Levite and the sojourner (Deut 26:11–14). The chapter ends with instructions to obey the statutes and the ordinances (Deut 26:16–19). What the text implies, however, is that the commandments relate precisely to the preceding section in Deut 26:12–15, where Israelites fulfill YHWH's command when they give from the tithe to the Levite, the fatherless, the widow, and the sojourner, and when they remember the exodus, celebrate the Feast of Firstfruits, and, most importantly, include the poor and disadvantaged in this feast. Why this must be done is crucially and directly rooted in Israel's own historical experience in Egypt (Deut 26:6).

Deuteronomy chapter 26 belongs in the Covenant Law pericope of Deut 12–26, where Moses gives the people the laws to live by in the land. Chapter 12 opens the pericope with directions for worship that are a central part of the covenant. The pericope ends in 26:16–19 with the same theme of directions for worship for the covenant people, with the command to include the poor, the sojourner, and the Levite. ("For you yourselves were once strangers in Egypt," [Deut 16:12], is an oft-repeated explanation of the need for this command of inclusion.) Inclusion at festivals does not of course eliminate poverty or disadvantage over the longer term, nor on a daily basis will it alter the economic circumstances of the poorer members of Israelite society. It serves, however, to remind Israel of its past oppression in Egypt and to exercise an ethic of care for the poor among the people, just as YHWH had shown compassion to Israel in its bondage and landlessness.

The preceding argument indicates that when Ezra assembles the people to recite the law to them and have it explained by the Levites, he is faithfully representing the real function of biblical codes in ancient Israelite society as these were understood in the pentateuchal and Deuteronomistic traditions. The biblical codes belong within the context of the community's remembering of its salvific history with YHWH. Hence, the Ezra account includes a recitation of YHWH's salvific action towards Israel after the recitation of the law (Neh 9:6–38).

While modern readers might expect Ezra's recitation of the law to have been a reading of the Book of the Covenant or some other biblical code, what is heard is a recitation of Israel's past history with YHWH, from the time of the patriarchs until the return to Jerusalem in the Persian period, when the Israelites have come full circle: slaves again, but now in their own land (Neh 9:36). What Ezra has in mind when it comes to keeping the law seems to be remembering the past, in particular the instructions about remaining separate from the inhabitants of the land, and the rituals that are to accompany it. Hence, in Neh 9, the people's commitment to the covenant is symbolized by their observance of the Feast of Booths, which commemorates Israel's time in the wilderness, the very place where it received the law. Thus, biblical law belongs within the sacred, cultic context of Israel's remembering of YHWH's salvific history with his people.

Inclusion: Poverty, Inheritance, Property, and Slavery

If it is correct to assume that the premonarchic, monarchic, and postexilic periods do not witness Israelites and Judeans implementing the laws of the biblical codes in daily life, the codes nonetheless preserve views about poverty, inheritance, property, and slavery, as they project an ideal of economic justice for ancient Israel, the covenant people. At the heart of this project is not a real solution to economic inequality—the abolition of slavery or of poverty, for example—but the instruction to Israelites to show compassion in their economic dealings with those less fortunate. No legal sanction accompanies these instructions, as has been shown; rather, Israelites are reminded that YHWH watches over their dealings with the poor among his people and the sojourners in their midst. The inclusion of these impoverished groups in the communal celebrations of Israel's salvific history with YHWH was a key component of showing compassion and of acknowledging Israel's past salvation by the hand of YHWH. Why Israel, above all nations, is required by YHWH to show justice and compassion is articulated in Amos 3:1–2:

> Hear this word that the LORD has spoken against you, O people of Israel,
>   against the whole family which I brought up out of the land of Egypt:
> You only have I known of all the families of the earth;
>   therefore I will punish you for your iniquities.

In this passage, YHWH appears to be saying to Israel, Since I have known you, treated you well, and shown compassion towards you, I will punish you, because you should know better. This is the foundation of the ethic of social and economic justice found in the biblical codes. In Lev 25:55 one encounters a further articulation of why Israel ought to treat all slaves justly: "For to me the people of Israel are servants; they are my servants whom I brought forth out of the land of Egypt: I am the LORD your God."

Transitional Moments on the Way to Understanding the Torah as a Source of Legislation for Everyday Life

If the biblical laws were more a part of Israel's practice of remembering the salvific acts of YHWH, and the command to recite them with the inclusion of marginalized groups was part of those process of remembering, how did they later become the basis for ruling on daily matters (e.g., divorce, inheritance, slavery, the taking of interest on loans, and on how judges should deal with the poor)? To answer that question, evidently, an investigation of the rabbinic period would be key, and many historical factors will have been decisive (all of which lie outside the scope of the present discussion). Prior to the rabbinic period, such formative moments in this transition can be viewed in the biblical texts.

Jeremiah's Appeal to Law Codes

In Jer 34, a text dated towards the end of the kingdom of Judah (many scholars suggest a later Deuteronomistic hand here),[73] one encounters something that appears to be a royal edict, viz., a proclamation of a king intended to reform aspects of the existing legal practices. In Mesopotamia in general—while there is no evidence of the use of the codes such as the Code of Hammurabi as a source for judges—royal edicts are known to have effected legal practices, and this can be seen both in economic and in legal contracts from the years following the issue of an edict.[74] The account in Jeremiah is, in my view, the first time a biblical figure seeks to implement an aspect of biblical law (rather than an entire code). Prior to this, as already noted, biblical law was a commodity to be preserved by the priests, scribes, Levites, and other cultic officials, and to be copied, read, and recited by the king and people at festivals.

In Jer 34:8, King Zedekiah is recorded to have made a covenant with the people requiring that every Hebrew slave owner should set his fellow Hebrew slave, male and female, free. The story tells how this was effective, but only for a brief period, and the Hebrew slave owners repossessed those slaves they had emancipated. In the verses that follow, Yhwh's attention is drawn to the behavior of the people, and he connects Zedekiah's action of freeing the slaves (not connected, up to this point in the text) to the law of the Sabbatical Year, which appears in Exod 21:1–6 and also in the Deuteronomic and Levitical codes. Yhwh is enraged by the repossession of the slaves and through Jeremiah declares:

> Thus says the Lord, the God of Israel: I made a covenant with your fathers when I brought them out of the land of Egypt, out of the house of bondage saying: "At the end of six years each of you must set free the fellow Hebrew who has been sold to you and has served you six years; you must set him free from your service." (Jer 34:13–14)

Could this be, for the first time in the history of monarchy, an instance of a king seeking to implement a regulation from biblical law (Exod 21:1–6)? It should be noted that King Zedekiah *does not* refer to any law as the basis of his edict, nor *is there a reference* to its being the Sabbatical Year, when the requirement to release Hebrew slaves was to be implemented according to the biblical codes. It is rather in the verses that follow that the prophet Jeremiah places Zedekiah's

73. See Brueggemann, *Commentary on Jeremiah*.

74. For discussion of royal edicts see Westbrook, "Cuneiform Lawcodes," 215; Jackson, "Ideas of the Law"; and see Fitzpatrick-Mckinley, *Transformation of Torah*, 84–86.

freeing of slaves within the orbit of law by making reference to the Sabbatical Year (Jer 34:14). The law, which would have had serious economic consequences for slave owners—and indeed for the slaves, for where were they to go, and how were they to gain a livelihood?—failed to endure. When it does fail, it is the prophetic voice that draws our attention to the fact that this is in breach of a code that YHWH intended, not just as an ideal, and not just as something to be treasured and preserved in the cult as an aspect of Israel's expression of its relationship with YHWH, but to be actually implemented. From a practical point of view, its failure is not surprising.

This is the first time in the biblical narratives about monarchy that a law is represented as having influenced socioeconomic practice. In all other references to the kings and the law codes or to the book of the law, the king affected by the law (Josiah for example, see above) simply repents and turns his focus to the sole worship of YHWH. The Jeremiah story, in other words, might well present the first time when a leader in the Bible attempted to implement part of a code: to get society to conform to a legal instruction. But this is to be credited to Jeremiah and not to King Zedekiah, who at no point refers to the legal requirement of freeing Hebrew slaves in the Sabbatical Year, and who in reality may simply have issued an edict on slaves as part of a wider political strategy.

Ezra's reforms may recount another occasion, which goes a lot further than any other texts in its demands of the people.

Ezra's Appeal to Law Codes

While, as has been demonstrated, it is difficult to be certain about the historical circumstances surrounding the account of Ezra and his reforms, certain ideals are established in the text. While there is no evidence that Ezra's demand that the people live by the law was met—intermarriage, at the heart of his concerns, was not observed, for example—he seems to have been the first to attempt to take the recitation of the law out of its largely liturgical function and to demand that it form the basis of an Israelite's behavior in everyday life (Neh 8:8). The law was not just to be remembered and recited as Israel celebrated its salvation (from its exodus and its coming into the land), but the law was to form the basis of Israel's behavior around marriage regulations (Ezra 7:25–28). Hence, the ban on intermarriage was so important that those already married to non-Judeans were forced to put away their foreign wives and the offspring of these marriages (Ezra 10:3). Whether Ezra's demands of the people extended beyond intermarriage is not clear, and the narrative is very much focused

FITZPATRICK-MCKINLEY—UNDERSTANDING LAW 163

on this problem of intermarriage rather than on wider laws relating to issues such as slavery, debts, inheritance and other aspects of Israel's economic life. Nehemiah's reforms also appear to be rooted in the law, but as we have seen, in spite of his reference to Mosaic authority, the reforms in Neh 5 and his ruling on intermarriage and the Sabbath do not correspond in any precise way to the biblical codes in Exodus, Leviticus, and Deuteronomy.

After Ezra's and Nehemiah's attempted reforms, there is a gap in our knowledge. We lack evidence for the following centuries, and it is not until the Maccabean reforms that readers encounter again a community debating the place of the law in its life (1–2 Macc). The accounts point to a crisis among Judeans themselves. They are divided, it would seem, between those who believe that the law must be adhered to in every detail, and those who believe that adherence to the ancestral law is halting the progress of settling Jerusalem, which had won favor with the Greek Seleucid rulers. Some Jews wanted to seize the opportunity to have Jerusalem recognized as a *polis*—with all of the consequent advantages this could bring: citizenship, wealth, and political status—while other Jews focused less on Jerusalem's settlement and more on being "zealous for the law" (1 Macc 2:27). However, once again it is not clear what was meant by *Torah*, and it may be the case that the concern of the law-observing had to do with religious observances such as practicing circumcision, keeping of the Sabbath, and holding to dietary laws rather than keeping the economic laws of the biblical codes.[75]

What Laws Regulated the Economic Lives of Ancient Israelites and Judeans?

If the law, prior to the rabbinic movement, was primarily a part of Israel and Judah's communal celebrations of its salvific past with its God YHWH, and if the contents of the codes were more like moral instruction than laws that could be applied by judges and used as the basis of legal contracts, what laws regulated Israel's economic life? In the context of two diasporan communities examined here, this chapter has revealed that it was the local laws of the land that regulated issues such as marriage, divorce, inheritance, slavery, and loans and debts. Noneconomic aspects of the biblical laws, centered on religious observation, seem to have been observed by these groups, as indicated by the Sabbath ostracon from Elephantine and the evidence for the Judeans at Elephantine making burnt offerings at Passover.

75. A fuller discussion of the crisis reflected in 1 and 2 Maccabees lies outside the scope of the present study; for introduction and bibliography, see Grabbe, *Judaic Religion.*

In relation to the religious observances of the Babylonian communities behind the ʾAl Yahudah archive, it can only be said that in relation to economic matters, they observed local practice, but it is likely that they preserved the Torah as moral and cultic teaching. Their right to preserve and even to observe aspects of their indigenous law would likely have been recognized by the Babylonian and later Persian governments, and there are other examples of foreign soldiers in the employ of both of these governments doing so.[76] The fact that (as is now known) the Judean soldiers in Egypt were organized as a *politeuma* supports this view, and other instances of such military communities demonstrate that the Ptolemaic government permitted these communities to observe their indigenous customs.[77]

Unfortunately, as to Judeans in the land, there is little or no evidence in relation to what regulations governed their economic dealings. However, some educated assumptions can be made. First, that everyday disputes about property, inheritance, loans, and slaves were resolved by reference to oral customs. Within such an oral system, found throughout antiquity, the swearing of oaths will have played a central role. There is no reason to assume that the moral instructions of the various sections of the law codes that call for impartiality in judgment and care for the marginalized—particularly at festivals—would not have influenced individual Israelites; but real economic issues, impacts, and crises will likely have dominated. Thus, King Zedekiah's liberation of Hebrew slaves was soon reversed, probably as a result of economic realities. In all probability, the biblical laws do not legislate with the purpose of establishing an egalitarian society or even of eliminating poverty; rather they seek to ensure that the poor are not totally excluded. This is achieved when Israelites include the poor at key moments: at the Sabbath, Firstfruits, and other festivals, when Israel remembers its origins as landless slaves in Egypt. A similar type of social ethic informs the teaching of the eighth-century prophet Amos, who rages against injustice, appealing not to laws but to a general demand on the Israelite to be just, impartial, and inclusive.

76. For a detailed discussion see Fitzpatrick-McKinley, "Preserving the Cult of YHWH."

77. Until the finding of the Herakleopolis papyri, most scholars doubted that the Judean communities in Egypt were organized on the basis of a *politeuma*. This type of civic structure was permitted to military units of foreign soldiers serving the Ptolemaic government. The communities were permitted to observe their ancestral religions and even to have their own courts. There is sufficient evidence in relation to the Judean community at Herakleopolis to permit us to say that the Judeans there could use their own courts, and there is evidence that non-Judeans sometimes chose to have their cases heard there. For the papyri see Cowey and Maresch, *Urkunden des Politeuma der Juden von Herakleopolis (144/3–133/2 Vor Chr.)*, and for a general discussion see Fitzpatrick-McKinley, "Preserving the Cult of YHWH."

The laws, nonetheless, were Israel's treasured possession, and their eco-nomic ideals of inclusion and compassion prevailed, so that in m. Avot 1:2,[78] Simeon the Righteous proclaims:

On three things does the world stand:
On the Torah,
and on the Temple Service,
and on deeds of loving kindness.[79]

Conclusion

Thus, contrary to popular assumptions, Israel's laws were embedded in its religious life long before they legislated for its economic life, and were first called upon and recited within the celebration of its covenant relationship with YHWH. On a day-to-day basis, it would seem that economic issues having to do with slavery, divorce, and inheritance were dealt with on the basis of whatever practice was in play within a given period and environment. It is only much later, in the rabbinic period, that the laws come to be regarded as a source on the basis of which rulings could be made in the rabbinic courts. Thus, it can be concluded that the law of the land, embedded in oral custom and partly in written contract, was law for daily economic life. The law of the Torah, on the other hand, was the guarantor of Israel's covenant relationship only as long as the community celebrated the festivals in accordance with the legislation of the codes that required the celebration and its remembering of the community's salvific history with YHWH through a recitation of the laws. As has been shown, however, precisely what constituted law differed from tradition to tradition.

Bibliography

Abraham, Kathleen. "The Reconstruction of Jewish Communities in the Persian Empire: the 'Āl-Yahūdu Clay Tablets." In *Light and Shadows—The Catalog—The Story of Iran and the Jews*, edited by H. Segev and A. Schor, 264–68. Tel Aviv: Beit Hatsufot, 2011.
———. "West Semitic and Judean Brides in Cuneiform Sources from the Sixth Century BCE: New Evidence from a Marriage Contract from Āl-Yahudu." *AfO* (2005) 198–219.
Albertz, Rainer. "Purity Strategies and Political Interests in the Policy of Nehemiah." In *Confronting the Past: Archaeological and Historical Essays on Ancient Israel*, edited by Seymour Gitin et al., 199–206. Winona Lake, IN: Eisenbrauns, 2006.

---

78. This refers to the mishnaic tract Pirkei Avot (commonly known as *The Sayings of the Fathers* or *The Ethics of the Fathers*).

79. Pirkei Avot 1:2, trans. Neusner.

Berquist, Jon L. *Judaism in Persia's Shadow: A Social and Historical Approach*. 1995. Reprint, Eugene, OR: Wipf & Stock, 2003.

Boccaccini, Gabriel. *Roots of Rabbinic Judaism*. Grand Rapids: Eerdmans, 2002.

Botta, Alejandro. *The Aramaic and Egyptian Traditions at Elephantine: An Egyptological Approach*. LSTS. London: T. & T. Clark, 2009.

Bottéro, Jean. "Le «Code» de Hammu-rabi." *Annali della Scuola normale superiore di Pisa. Classe di Lettere e Filosofia* 12 (1982) 409–44.

Brueggemann, Walter. *A Commentary on Jeremiah: Exile and Homecoming*. Grand Rapids: Eerdmans, 1998.

Collins, John. *Between Athens and Jerusalem: Jewish Identity in the Hellenistic Diaspora*. 2nd ed. Grand Rapids: Eerdmans, 2000.

Cowey, James, and Klaus Maresch. *Urkunden des Politeuma der Juden von Herakleopolis (144/3–133/2 Vor Chr.)* Abhandlungen der Nordrhein-Westfälischen Akademie der Wissenschaften. Sonderreihe Papyrologica Coloniensia 29. Wiesbaden: Westdeutscher, 2001.

Crüsemann, Frank. *The Torah: Theology and Social History of Old Testament Law*. Translated by Alan Mahnke. Minneapolis: Fortress, 1996.

Donner, Herbert, and Walter Röllig. *Kanaanäische und aramäische Inschriften*. Vol. 1, *Texte*. 3 vols. Wiesbaden: Harrassowitz, 1962.

Dusinberre, Elspeth. *Empire, Authority, and Autonomy in Achaemenid Anatolia*. Cambridge: Cambridge University Press, 2013.

Finkelstein, Jacob J. "Ammisaduqa's Edict and the Babylonian Lawcodes." *JCS* 15 (1961) 19–104.

Fitzpatrick-McKinley, Anne. *Empire, Power and Indigenous Elites: A Case Study of the Nehemiah Memoir*. JSJSup 169. Leiden: Brill, 2017.

———. "Ezra, Nehemiah, and Some Early Greek Lawgivers." In *Rabbinic Law in Its Roman and Near Eastern Context*, edited by Catherine Hezser, 17–48. Tübingen: Mohr Siebeck, 2003.

———. "Preserving the Cult of Yhwh." In *Sibyls, Scripture and Scrolls: John Collins at Seventy*, edited by Joel Baden et al., 375–408. JSJSup 175/1–2. Leiden: Brill, 2017.

———. "The Production of Literature in Judean Military Colonies in Egypt." In *The Hunt for Ancient Israel: Essays in Honour of Diana V. Edelman*, edited by Ehud ben Zvi and Kristin Joachimsen, 407–35. London: Equinox, 2021.

———. *Representations of Assyria in the Literary Traditions of Its Subjects*. London: Equinox, forthcoming.

———. *The Transformation of Torah from Scribal Advice to Law*. JSOTSup 287. Sheffield: Sheffield Academic, 1999.

Fried, Lisbeth. "You Shall Appoint Judges: Ezra's Mission and the Rescript of Artaxerxes." In *Persia and Torah: The Theory of Imperial Authorization of the Pentateuch*, edited by James W. Watts, 63–90. SymSer 17. Atlanta: SBL, 2001.

Gaines, Janet Howe. *Music in the Old Bones: Jezebel through the Ages*. Carbondale: Southern Illinois University Press, 1999.

Grabbe, Lester L. *Ezra–Nehemiah*. OTR. London: Routledge, 1998.

———. *Judaic Religion in the Second Temple Period: Belief and Practice from the Exile to Yavneh*. London: Routledge, 2002.

Goody, Jack. *The Logic of Writing and the Organization of Society*. Studies in Literacy, the Family, Culture, and the State. Cambridge: Cambridge University Press, 1986.

Greenfield, Jonas. "Aramaic Studies and the Bible." In *Congress Volume: Vienna, 1980*, edited by John Emerton, 110–30. VTSup 32. Leiden: Brill, 1981.

Halbe, Jörn. *Die Privilegrecht Jahwes: Ex. 34, 10–26: Gestalt und Wesen, Herkunft und Wirken in vordeuteronomische Zeit*. FRLANT 114. Göttingen: Vandenhoeck & Ruprecht, 1975.

Hayes, Christine. *Gentile Impurities and Jewish Identities: Intermarriage and Conversion from the Bible to the Mishnah*. Oxford: Oxford University Press, 2002.

―――. "Intermarriage and Impurity in Ancient Jewish Sources." *HTR* 91 (1999) 3–36.

Hoglund, Kenneth. "The Achaemenid Context." In *The Persian Period*, edited by Philip R. Davies, 54–72. STS 1. JSOTSup. Sheffield: Sheffield Academic, 1991.

Horsley, Richard A. *Scribes, Visionaries and the Politics of Second Temple Judaism*. Louisville: Westminster John Knox 2007.

Hubbard, Robert L, Jr. *The Book of Ruth*. NICOT. Grand Rapids: Eerdmans, 1988.

Jackson, Bernard. "Ideas of the Law and Legal Administration: A Semiotic Approach," in *The World of Ancient Israel: Sociological, Anthropological and Political Perspectives*, edited by Ronald E. Clements, 185–202. Cambridge: Cambridge University Press, 1989.

Knoppers, Gary. "Intermarriage, Social Complexity, and Ethnic Diversity in the Genealogy of Judah." *JBL* 120 (2001) 15–30.

Lebram, Jürgen-Christian. "Die Traditionsgeschichte der Esragestalt und die Frage nach dem historischen Esra." In *Sources Structures and Synthesis: Proceedings of the Groningen 1983 Achaemenid History Workshop*, edited by Helen Sancisi-Weerdenburg, 103–38. Achaemenid History 1. Leiden: Instiuut vor het Nabije Oosten, 1987.

Leggett, Donald A. *The Levirate and Goel Institutions in the Old Testament*. Cherry Hill, NJ: Mack, 1974.

Magdalene, F. Rachel, and Cornilia Wunsch. "Slavery between Babylon and Judah: the Exilic Experience." In *Slaves and Households in the Near East*, edited by Laura Culbertson, 113–34. University of Chicago Oriental Institute Seminars 7. Chicago: University of Chicago Press, 2011.

Modrzejewski, Joseph. *The Jews of Egypt: From Rameses II to Emperor Hadrian*. Translated by Robert Cornman with a foreword by Shaye J. D. Cohen. Princeton: Princeton University Press, 1995.

Muffs, Yochanan. *Studies in the Aramaic Legal Papyri from Elephantine*. HdO 66. Leiden: Brill, 1969.

Mullen, E. Theodore. *Ethnic Myths and Pentateuchal Foundations: A New Approach to the Foundations of the Pentateuch*. SemeiaSt. Atlanta: Scholars, 1997.

Najman, Hindy. "Interpretation as Primordial Writing: Jubilees and its Authority Conferring Strategies." *JSJ* 30 (1999) 379–410.

Neusner, Jacob. *The Mishnah: A New Translation*. New Haven: Yale University Press, 1988.

Noth, Martin. *The History of Israel*. Translated by P. R. Ackroyd. 2nd ed., in rev. and corr. translation. London: SCM, 1960. Reprint, 1983.

Otto, Eckart. *Wandel der Rechtsgeschichte in der Gesellschaftgeschichte des Antiken Israel: Eine Rechtsgeschichte des "Bundesbuch" Ex. 20,22–23,13*. StudBib 3. Leiden: Brill, 1988.

Pakkala, Juha. *Ezra the Scribe: The Development of Ezra 7–10 and Nehemiah 8*. BZAW 347. Berlin: de Gruyter, 2004.

Pearce, Laurie. "New Evidence for Judeans in Babylonia." In *Judah and the Judeans in the Persian Period*, edited by Oded Lipschits and Manfred Oeming, 300–411. Winona Lake, IN: Eisenbrauns, 2006.

Porten, Bezalel. *Archives from Elephantine: The Life of an Ancient Jewish Military Colony.* Berkeley: University of California Press, 1968.

———. "The Religion of the Jews of Elephantine in Light of the Hermopolis Papyri." *JNES* 28 (1969) 116–21.

Smith-Christopher, Daniel. *The Religion of the Landless: The Social Context of the Babylonian Exile.* Bloomington, IN: Meyer-Stone, 1989. Reprint, Eugene, OR: Wipf & Stock, 2015.

Torrey, Charles C. *The Composition and Historical Value of Ezra–Nehemiah.* BZAW 2. Giessen: Ricker, 1896.

Uchitel, Alexander. "Foreign Workers in the Fortification Archive." In *Mésopotamie et Elam: Actes de XXXVIième rencontre assyriologique internationale, Gand 10–14 juillet 1985,* edited by L. De Meyer and H. Gasche, 127–35. Mesopotamian History and Environment: Occasional Publications 1. Ghent: University of Ghent, 1991.

Weingreen, Jacob. *From Bible to Mishna: The Continuity of Tradition.* Manchester: Manchester University Press, 1976.

Wellhausen, Julius. *Prolegomena to the History of Israel.* Translated by J. Sutherland Black and Allan Menzies. Edinburgh: Black, 1885.

Westbrook, Raymond. "Cuneiform Lawcodes and the Origins of Legislation." *ZA* 79 (1989) 201–22.

———. *Property and the Family in Biblical Law.* JSOTSup 113. Sheffield: JSOT Press, 1991.

Yaron, Reuven. *Introduction to the Law of the Aramaic Papyri.* Oxford: Clarendon, 1961.

7. Economics in Israelite Law

Douglas A. Knight

Introduction[1]

The subject of economics and law brings together two fields that are at once both discrete and intertwined. Each has its own long and complex history of study and analysis. Each is populated with professionals practicing their trade. Each is nurtured and taught by advanced institutions of learning. Each has classical foundations and continually evolving theoretical and critical traditions. Each makes headlines and influences national and local policy. Each affects the everyday affairs of communities and individuals.

Yet despite their distinct identities both economics and law are social constructs, and this common social basis links the two in essential ways. The economic dimensions of a society are played out in a legal context that regulates, limits, and defines the workings of the market, the status and deployment of capital, the relations between management and labor, the role of the state and other power agents, the affairs of the powerless and disenfranchised, and all aspects of investment and exchange at macro- and microlevels. For their part, laws are themselves not transcendent principles but explicit products of a given society to sanction or disallow specific forms of corporate and individual behavior. Inasmuch as both the economic and the legal spheres stem from the

1. This paper is based on an earlier version delivered at the session on Economics in the Biblical World, held at the annual meeting of the Society of Biblical Literature in Boston on 18 November 2017. I want to thank especially the two respondents, Gale Yee and Catherine Murphy, for their comments and suggestions, which I have sought to incorporate in this revision.

same society, they interact with each other as expressions of that culture and as reciprocal influences on or correctives of each other. These intricacies are present in small-scale communities as well as in highly complex societies, both in ancient and in modern times. In a word, neither law nor economics exists without the other.

This situation pertains for ancient Israel as it does for today. While the presence of laws in the Hebrew Bible may suggest to some readers a certain ethereal quality, these laws—to the extent they represent real, functioning laws—reflect the mundane, material world of social, political, and economic affairs. Yet to progress further in understanding this relationship between law and economics, it is first useful to distinguish between two phenomena: Israelite law and biblical law.[2]

Israelite law represents the legal systems that existed in ancient Israel. These laws were issued by those with the authority or power to enact regulations to protect interests, proscribe certain forms of behavior, stipulate the remedies or penalties attending to the breach of norms, and thus create or maintain a type of social order. No legislative body existed in ancient Israel to deliberate and issue such laws; the power to establish legal constraints rested in the hands of the monarch at the state level and with other leaders in tribal or village communities. These "living" laws did not need to be retained in archives or law libraries since they were known and enforced by those in power as long as these regulations remained relevant and useful.

On the other hand, *biblical law*, now found in the Hebrew Bible, resulted from the long process of producing the biblical text, which was effected not by legislators but by scribes, priests, and other influential or powerful persons. We have basically no evidence that the biblical laws actually functioned as community norms or were ever enforced. Some biblical narratives depict scenarios involving legal matters, such as the narrative of the daughters of Zelophehad (Num 27:1–11; 36:1–12) or the incident surrounding Naboth's vineyard (1 Kgs 21) or the adjudication of Achan's violation of the rules of holy war (Josh 7), but there is no hard evidence that the events in these stories ever occurred as described. Some of these laws may plausibly have been applied to real-life conflicts or behavior, but we have no grounds to assume a priori that they had actual legal power, certainly not across the broad expanse of Israel's population and history. Rather, the "laws" presented in the Hebrew Bible constitute literature, the product of a literary tradition. While the Israelite laws did not need to be written because they circulated in oral and traditional forms among

2. For more discussion see Knight, *Law, Power, and Justice*, 10–16.

the people, the biblical laws did not need to be applied since they had standing as a literary artifact. They fit into the trajectory of written lists of directives stretching from Sumerian and Babylonian times to Roman law. They could be referenced or invoked as norms by leaders familiar with them, but there is little ground for assuming that the larger population knew them enough to be guided by them in their daily lives. The biblical "laws" were more lawlike than they were actual laws: they are phrased as laws but could scarcely have functioned as the laws to which all the people were subjected. The reason for this conclusion rests in the very nature of Israelite society and the place of literacy in it, as the reader will presently see.

Socioeconomic Contexts in Ancient Israel

At least two distinguishable worlds existed in Israel from the Iron II period through the Persian period (ca. 900–331 BCE), and in similar state societies among its neighbors as well: the world of the powerful and wealthy and the world of the powerless and impoverished.[3] The vast majority, some 70 to 90 percent or more of the population of the southern Levant, was scattered throughout the countryside in countless small villages outside the urban settings. The villages averaged only 75–150 souls each, some even smaller. Their size could range from 0.25 acre to 2.5 acres (0.1–1.0 hectare). Such small settlements tended to be kinship-based and linked with nearby neighboring villages through family as well as economic ties. Taken together, they formed the bulk of the total population of Iron II Israel and Judah, estimated at 460,000 in the eighth century BCE.[4] The villagers' actual power in national politics and economics, however, fell far short of their numbers.

In striking contrast, though, was life in the Israelite cities. These urban centers, while economically and politically powerful, were not nearly as populous as their modern counterparts. Only the capital cities during monarchic times reached into the thousands, and the low thousands at that. Both Samaria and Jerusalem shortly before each fell may have attained only 12,000–13,000 inhabitants, many of those in Jerusalem living outside the city walls. The so-called royal cities (Megiddo, Hazor, Gezer, Dan) and the administrative cities (such as Beersheba) counted less than 1,000 inhabitants each. The surface size of these cities extended from 2.7 to 25 acres (1.1–10.0 hectares).[5] The

3. These two worlds are described in more detail in Knight, *Law, Power, and Justice*, 115–26 and 157–73, with documentation.

4. Broshi and Finkelstein, "Population," 54.

5. Broshi and Finkelstein, "Population," 48.

wealthier, more powerful class clustered in these walled cities, relatively small residential and political environments that they shared with their servants, bureaucrats, scribes, priests, attendants, and others who could make their lives easy, or at least easier. The cities were "containers of power," to use Anthony Giddens' phrase,[6] somewhat analogous to the modern phenomena of "gated communities." This assemblage of elite, wealthy, and powerful is ancient Israel's counterpart to the 1 percent in many of today's societies, which has recently been the focus of prominent movements and critiques.

There was one other type of city that varied from the capitals, royal cities, and administrative cities—the residential cities or towns. They were also relatively small in size with a population of some 500–1,250 inhabitants each and a space covering five to 12.5 acres (two to five hectares). They served primarily their regions' needs in trade and production, as well as grain storage and small-scale manufacturing. Unlike the other city types, these residential cities were normally not built by the central state authority for specific administrative or governmental purposes. Their role was more local or regional, and their inhabitants were largely artisans, peasants, and laborers.

The quality of life varied dramatically in these different environments. The villagers generally lived in a desperate, permanent state of risk and poverty. The fortunate among them had inherited a small plot of land to till, but many others were landless peasants, laborers, slaves, and other vulnerable persons. This majority population was subject to the vicissitudes of a subsistence economy, and their harsh life meant poor nourishment, health risks, exploitation by the more powerful, and few social institutions other than their own communities to offer protection. On the other hand, the small proportion of the general population that lived in the cities possessed most of the resources of the country, engaged in international trade, enjoyed luxury goods, owned slaves, resided in more spacious and better-appointed dwellings, had access to power, and benefited from better nourishment and healthcare—thus experiencing a more comfortable and less labor-intensive life than the lower classes. A middle class scarcely existed. Those who attended to the wealthy and powerful enjoyed some comfort and privilege (more than their rural counterparts but not as much as the elite), but they were subject to the whims of their patrons and did not constitute a relatively stable middle class.

These circumstances of living and work patterns had obvious implications for the production and retention of literature, including laws. While examples of written Hebrew in ancient Israel date as far back as the tenth century

6. Giddens, *Constitution of Society*, 195.

BCE, the mere existence of writing has virtually no bearing on the actual extent of literacy among the populace. Writing was, for the most part, a professional enterprise conducted for the benefit of the elites, as was also the case in other cultures of the time. Literacy at the advanced level needed for official documents, archives, legal contracts, literature, and the like was probably limited to not more than 1 to 2 percent of the population during the monarchic, exilic, and postexilic periods, and a somewhat wider dispersion among other sectors apparently did not occur until Hellenistic times. Even the royals and the elites themselves may not have been very literate; they had slaves and hired scribes to write and read for them.

The written materials leading to the production of our Hebrew Bible must thus be understood in light of this class-based, occupation-centered activity. Writing was largely an urban phenomenon, found in the palace, the temple, the bureaucratic offices, the commercial houses, and the educational settings. And here, in these urban settings and in one institutional context or the other, is where the texts—from first drafts to final redactions—emerged and were finally brought together into the biblical literature. The biblical laws belong to this literary process. Villagers, scarcely any of whom were likely to have been literate at a high level, did not have a hand in textual production, nor were they likely to have had the competence even to read what others had written. The customary laws that developed in village contexts were remembered and transmitted in oral form; they could be circulated and applied without reference to written documents. Village law was living law, not the records of governmental and temple archives or the texts of scribes, students, and judges.

Economic Model

These two primary spheres of social, political, and economic activity—the villages and the cities—were actually much more complex than they may appear on the surface. Within each is a plethora of other worlds: in the villages—different kinship groups, social divisions (e.g., men, women, children, the elderly), regional variations, trades or guilds, traditional powers (e.g., tribal or village leaders, heads of households); and in the cities—the royal house, governmental officials, professions (e.g., merchants, scribes), military, priests and temple personnel, slaves and laborers, representatives of other countries (during times of Israel's sovereignty they were emissaries from abroad, but during imperial times they were agents of the emperor).

Within the social and political worlds are various economic systems of production, exchange, and control. In his recent book, Roland Boer characterizes them in terms of two distinct economic patterns, allocative and extractive.[7] *Allocation* refers to the workers and their products mostly found in the villages and rural areas where subsistence survival predominated, dependence on family and kinfolk was essential, patronage was practiced, and agriculture and animal husbandry were the main modes of production. As described above regarding village culture in ancient Israel, the vast majority of the people lived under this pattern, allocating all their resources and labors to their survival needs. In contrast, *extraction* is a pattern in which persons who are themselves not the producers of the goods are able to extract the produce of others, whether by exploitation, taxation, seizure, plunder, or other manipulative or forceful means. Many of them resided in the cities as large landowners, merchants, lenders, government officials, temple personnel, and more. The palace and the temple survived by means of laying claim to the resources and yield of the general population. This asymmetry in power and wealth became even more severe when the country was colonized by foreign empires, from the Assyrians and Babylonians to the Persians, Hellenists, and Romans. The imperial center possessed the power to compel its colonies to send taxes, tributes, labor, soldiers, bureaucrats, and slaves as needed.

Boer elaborates the workings of the allocative and extractive patterns in what he refers to as three "regimes": the subsistence regime, the palatine regime, and the regime of plunder. According to him, the subsistence regime, the only one of the three that is allocative, was "the economic staple of ancient Southwest Asia, and especially the southern Levant."[8] The agricultural base kept the majority of the population alive, although it was tenuous due to climate fluctuations as well as the oppressive demands from centralized powers, domestic and foreign. Even in good times the minimal needs for survival from one harvest to the next could barely be met, and the people were unable to accumulate much if any surplus to carry over from one year to the next. The other two regimes were quick to extract as much as they could squeeze out of the vulnerable classes. The centralized state,[9] in the form of the monarchic government, utilized taxation, conscription, seizure of goods and land, and enslavement to line its coffers. Members of the upper class, generally based in the cities,

---

7. Boer, *Sacred Economy*. Other recent relevant studies, especially for the later periods of Neo-Babylonian and Persian rule, include Adams, *Social and Economic Life*; Pirngruber, *Economy*; Brueggemann, *Money*; and numerous other publications dealing with various aspects of the agrarian and imperial economies during Israel's history.

8. Boer, *Sacred Economy*, 2; see 53–109 for an in-depth discussion of the subsistence regime.

9. See Boer, *Sacred Economy*, 110–45, for more details.

pursued strategies of their own devising to enrich themselves at the expense
of the peasants, although they often did so in league with, or at least with the
consent and sanction of, the state powers. The third regime raised the stakes
from the national to the international level—the world of imperial powers.[10]
When the emperor exacted tribute from the colonies, of which Israel was one
for most of its history, all the subjugated people stood to suffer, though probably the lower classes more so than the upper since the latter could often avoid
the imperial demands by pressing the poor of the land to provide more from
their already limited produce and labor. An empire's extraction reached beyond
tribute, for it derived much gain also by capitalizing on its control of economic
exchange, credit, and resources. We will return again to the effects of such extractive activities on the humans who suffered from them.

A further word is due the religious establishment, which Boer rightly
discusses as part of the extractive regimes. Far from being exclusively institutions of religiosity, the temple and other cultic sites played an enormous role in
the economy of the country of Israel as also of the foreign empires.[11] Villages
and residential cities fostered the domestic cult primarily, while royal and administrative cities fed the national cult, the state-sanctioned and -supported
system with the centralized temple at its apex and a central priesthood to manage it. The biblical descriptions of the first temple in Jerusalem evoke an image
of lavish structures, paraphernalia, vestments, and appointments—surely an
idealized picture intended to convey an image of the grandeur of Solomon,
its putative builder, and the kingdom as a whole. Lacking archaeological cor-
roboration of that temple's existence, we have only the literary superlatives to
suggest opulence. In all likelihood, though, the actual temple during monarchic
times, similar to temples in many other kingdoms, commanded a dominant
position in the economy of the country due not only to the king's patronage
and permission but also to the shrewd strategies of the priests and other temple
personnel. Temples in other empires had enormous holdings in land, buildings, slaves, livestock, and precious objects, and they also figured prominently
in markets, banking, lending, and commerce. Temples were, in a word, much
more than houses of worship, just as many religious establishments today possess extensive investments in land and other commodities. They have a history
as active players in the economic scene, and many of their cultic laws seek to
regulate practices that affect their economic affairs.

10. See Boer, *Sacred Economy*, 146–92, for more discussion.
11. See details in Knight, *Law, Power, and Justice*, 236–40.

Ideological Criticism

The method of ideological criticism is especially useful to unearth the economic interests at play in the laws. The starting points lie precisely in the observations made above. First, there is a crucial difference between Israelite law and biblical law. Both are driven by ideologies, but the ideologies differ significantly in each case—the subsistence-oriented interests of the majority populace for the Israelite laws and, on the other hand, for the biblical laws the interests of the much smaller group of the established upper class. Second, the two overriding socioeconomic worlds contrast with each other—the village cultures based on kinfolk alliances and reflecting the majority of the country's poor population; and the urban settings dominated by the wealthy and powerful with the support of their slaves, laborers, bureaucrats, artisans, and others. Third, the economic systems, the allocative and the extractive, are at home in these settings: the allocative in the subsistence economy of the villages and the countryside; the extractive in the other primary contexts—the urban environments where wealth and privilege are in league with the monarch and the mechanisms of state; the imperial powers centered in distant lands but represented locally by governmental, commercial, and military personnel; and the cultic establishment, a subset of the state structure with formidable holdings in the economy of the country. All of these have distinct ideological leanings.

Laws, like literature in general, are socially constructed, which makes them subject to ideological criticism. The basic question posed by this method is not, What does the text mean?, but Whose text is it? Who has something at stake in the production and preservation of the text? Applied to both the Israelite laws and the biblical laws, the question sharpens in each case: Who benefits, and who does not? For example, if it is true that the unwritten, customary Israelite laws stemmed largely from and circulated among the non-reading public, the majority of whom were poor peasants living in villages and agricultural contexts, then their legal norms reflected their terms of life, as we will describe shortly. And on the other hand, if the biblical laws were produced mainly by urbanites controlling much of the country's power and privileges, then we can expect these laws to have advanced their special interests.

An important school of legal theory that flourished especially in the United States, Britain, France, and Germany in the 1970s and 1980s is known as *critical legal studies*, or CLS.[12] Its starting point is that all law is politics—that laws result from political processes and seek to preserve the political and

12. More description and literature references are found in Knight, *Law, Power, and Justice*, 58–66.

economic status quo. Laws are not innocent, and they are not heaven-sent. Laws typically reflect the power structures and protect the interests of those who produce them. It is often the case today just as it was in ancient times that these interests can be shrewdly concealed, and it takes a healthy dose of skepticism to uncover what may really be driving the laws. For example, just because a law seems to be aimed at helping the poor or the unprivileged, lurking in the background may be an ulterior motive—to strengthen the position of the privileged through the means of mollifying the poor, or even just by seeming to do so. In fact, some of the thinking that produced CLS emerged within the movements that highlighted endemic and systemic inequalities in modern societies on issues related to race, gender, and class, inequalities that were so deeply engrained in the structures of society that they survived long without being rooted out.

While CLS focuses especially on laws of the modern period, the principles are equally pertinent for ancient cultures. The differences lie predominantly in the varying character of the societies, which means that our application of these principles to Israelite and biblical laws needs to be attuned to the nature of ancient Israelite society. Politically and economically, ancient Israel had an agrarian, autocratic, and at times imperial system, and the influences of special interests, powers, and privileges must be discerned in that context. We can observe power maneuvers in our own context, and we need only to be alert to how they occurred in ancient settings as well. The fact that the Hebrew Bible is held as sacred by many today does not mean that it was insulated from such manipulations during its own production, though we can expect resistance in certain circles to this critical reading of the text.

Specific Legal Issues and Their Economic Dimensions

With the above considerations in mind, we will now look at five specific, selective areas of law that intersect with economics: media of exchange, marriage and sexual relations, real and immovable property, slavery, and poverty. In each case there are distinctive differences between circumstances in the villages and those in the cities. Multiple other legal areas could also be discussed, but these five should serve as useful examples of the interface of law and economics.

Media of Exchange

We begin with the basic media of exchange in ancient Israel. A substantial variety of media, as well as subtypes, can be mentioned, but here we will look at three general types.

The first and probably the most widespread, consistently used medium was the system of bartering. It prevailed in village contexts from early times and continued long after money, precious metals, and other media came to dominate the market at the national and international levels. In barter one party exchanges some type of desirable goods—whether crops, animals, pottery, textiles, or other subsistence commodities—for other goods or services. The services can include labor, special skills, advice, childcare, education or training, mediation, transportation, and much more. Whatever the case, a reciprocal arrangement between parties establishes an ad hoc agreement about the equivalence of the bartered items or services, and such agreements can in turn become precedent setting if later parties find them fair. Customary law will not regulate the exchange rates as much as the processes by which the agreements are made, the exchange is executed, and failures to deliver are adjudicated. An alternative form of exchange is the gift, which is not necessarily given freely with no expectation of reciprocal response. Indeed, implicit to a gift is some form of anticipated reciprocity. In this sense, the difference between a barter and a gift lies mainly in the intention and transparency of the act.

Even before the sixth century BCE when a moneyed economy emerged, that is, one with quantifiable currency and coins, certain rare and precious items acquired special distinction and became the means for exchange at the level of commerce and politics, well beyond the reach of the ubiquitous villages and seldom if ever found there. The stories of Solomon, while not part of the legal corpus, provide a glimpse of the affluent—or idealized—worlds of monarchic and imperial affairs. According to the legends, Solomon receives from the queen of Sheba—and other monarchs—vast gifts of gold, silver, precious stones, ivory, exotic animals and birds, spices, weaponry, horses, textiles, and special woods. Whatever the historicity of such accounts may be, these commodities were indeed exchanged among kings, merchants, and the elite. Silver became a medium of exchange, especially as it could be weighed and thus standardized for purposes of payment. Silver, not coins, is the medium most frequently cited in laws and narratives, and it is measured in shekels. There are references to the one-quarter shekel, the one-third shekel, the one-half shekel, and many higher quantities. Unfortunately, we cannot be certain of the weight of silver in a shekel, and it quite likely fluctuated over the centuries. There is also a category called the "holy shekel" or the "shekel of the sanctuary" (šeqel haqqōdeš), mentioned in Lev 27:25. Whatever its value might be in today's terms, the ancient Israelites must have known its worth, even if it varied over time.

Coinage appears to have been invented in three places, China, India, and Lydia, at nearly the same time, ca. 600–500 BCE, spreading soon thereafter throughout ancient Southwest Asia, including to Israel.[13] Coins were minted of durable metals, standardized in size or weight, and usually stamped with the image of the reigning emperor or ruler. Used to pay wages to soldiers and to buy goods, they spread throughout the region and became the common currency for commerce, taxes, and tribute. Barter as well as possession of and trade in luxury goods continued to thrive in their respective contexts, but coins circulated widely as known quantities of value.

Beyond these three media of exchange, a system of banking and credit arose in ancient Israel as elsewhere. It became a further exercise of power and influence of the elites over the less advantaged, and probably a source of contention among the elites as well. The customary laws of the villages held little sway vis-à-vis this financial world, other than for villagers to caution each other how to avoid disaster at its hands. Some biblical laws, even if they were crafted in the urban contexts, urged lenders not to charge their fellow Israelites interest on loans (Exod 22:25 [22:24 MT]; Deut 23:19 [23:20 MT]) or to profit at another's expense (Lev 25:36–37), although charging interest on a loan to a foreigner is explicitly permitted in Deuteronomic law (Deut 23:20 [23:21 MT]). It is entirely believable that such exploitative practices were commonplace among the elites. Urging themselves to practice some restraint toward the poor, widow, orphan, and slave may have been a strategic way for the wealthy to keep the poorer class mollified, and expressing this impulse in moral or religious terms surely gave it added weight.

Marriage and Sexual Relations

Marriage and sexual relations must have been vital issues in both the village cultures and the urban environments, although differences between these two social worlds are likely to have affected the respective set of customs. The weightiness of these subjects is not to be underestimated. Marriage, reproduction, and sex would not have been associated mythically with divinity if they were insignificant matters in the human and animal world. Among Israel's neighbors the gods and goddesses cavort together among themselves and with humans, produce offspring, exhibit jealousy and revenge—in short, act almost like humans, although with enhanced powers. What is commonplace among deities, however, is not necessarily sanctioned among humans, even though

13. See the discussion and references in Boer, *Sacred Economy*, 188–92, 208–9, 212–14.

some interpreters have conjectured that these myths point to real practices among humans as well. Be that as it may, the economic dimensions of marital and sexual relations in general are distinctly evident and affect the laws significantly in both villages and cities.

Endogamy—the custom of marrying exclusively within one's own community—was the prevailing practice in villages, ensuring close ties, security, and support among community members. It also provided a safeguard for keeping property within the kinship group rather than having it pass to unrelated families. The two stories of the five daughters of Zelophehad (Num 27:1–11; 36:1–12), which may also be indicative of the process whereby the community developed new provisions when faced with unusual circumstances, deal with both property and family issues. With no brother to inherit their father's land, the daughters petition and are granted the right to inherit the property themselves; if there are no children at all, the property is to go to the father's nearest kin. The second story stipulates that any daughter inheriting property must marry within her clan, not to someone in another tribe lest her land become transferred to her husband's tribe. In the cities, endogamy may well have been attenuated since the urbanites, being wealthier and more powerful than the peasants in the countryside, could find it propitious to marry outside their clan in order to enhance their property or business interests, just as kings could marry foreigners for political or economic reasons.

The legal and economic status of women in ancient Israel needs to be highlighted more explicitly in these contexts, particularly because of the linkage of gender to class, as well as to ethnicity or race. With rare but notable exceptions, women appear in biblical laws and narratives typically in the roles of wives, mothers, daughters, or daughters-in-law. In villages, however, women played a much more active role in the domestic economy than they may have in urban contexts, and their standing in villages vis-à-vis men was probably correspondingly higher than the status of women in the cities. In contrast to the situation in Egyptian and Mesopotamian cultures at any rate, there is not much biblical evidence of women in Israelite villages or cities owning property or entering into legal contracts.

The intersection of law and economics is evident with respect to sexuality, particularly when the acceptable standards of sexual relations were transgressed. Adultery (nā'ap) in ancient Israel was understood to be sex between a married or engaged woman and a man who was not her spouse or fiancé. We have no evidence from ancient Israel that a man would be considered adulterous if he was married or engaged and had sex with another woman; the woman's own marital status seems to have been determinative for her alone. Such an act threatened the social fabric so severely that certain laws consider it a capital offense (Lev 20:10; Deut 22:23–27 regarding an engaged woman; 22:13–21 concerning a newly married woman; and 22:22 involving a married woman), even though the Hebrew Bible reports no such execution, the story involving Judah and Tamar (Gen 38) coming the closest to it. It is called "the great sin" (ḥăṭā 'â gĕdōlâ)[14] in Gen 20:9 as also in Egyptian and Ugaritic sources.[15] In village contexts people lived and worked in such close proximity that such misdeeds may have been seldom, whereas more possibilities for liaisons may have existed in cities.

But were wives and daughters considered property, as slaves were? There are texts that suggest it, such as Exod 20:17 (the commandment not to covet a neighbor's wife, slave, ox, donkey, or anything else belonging to the male neighbor), Exod 21:7–11 (a father can sell his daughter as a slave, although with certain conditions), and Deut 21:10–14 (a warrior can take a captive woman home and marry her, although he may not thereafter sell her as he could a slave).[16] According to biblical laws and narratives, a transaction occurs when a young Israelite woman passes from her father's domain to her fiancé's or to her husband's, whereas no comparable transaction attaches to the man's transition from bachelorhood to marriage. Furthermore, the woman's virginity and, after marriage, her sexual activity seem to have been commodified. In addition to the biblical laws just cited regarding the extramarital sexual activity of an engaged or married woman, there is another law dealing with the case of a man who has sex with a virgin to whom he is neither engaged nor married: he must pay her father—not her—a compensation or fine, either a set amount (the mōhar, Exod 22:16–17 [22:15–16 MT]) or fifty silver shekels (Deut 22:29); Middle Assyrian law (nr. A 56) sets the fine at triple the amount of silver of her value as a virgin. Beyond this evident inferior status of women, there can also be an attendant impact on the reputation and economic stability of other family members, whether in the rural or urban social settings. Certainly within the delicate workings of a subsistence economy, the loss of a productive contributor such as a wife or a daughter put the already tenuous conditions of survival at increased

14. While the implication in the text may be that the "great sin" by Abimelech is adultery, it may also be something else if we are to believe that he had not "approached" Sarah, as Gen 20:4 avers.

15. For the latter texts see Rabinowitz, "Great Sin," 73; and Moran, "Scandal."

16. See the discussion in Wright, "'She Shall not Go Free.'"

risk. The same can be said of a husband or son, but there are details attending the status and rights of a female that are absent from a male's standing.

More discussion of the bride-price, *mōhar*, is warranted, even if it is mentioned only slightly in the Hebrew Bible (Gen 34:12; 1 Sam 18:25; Ps 16:4) and just once in legal texts (Exod 22:16–17 [22:15–16 MT]). In an effort to dispel any notion that the fiancé is buying his wife, some interpreters have insisted that the *mōhar* is merely a compensation given to the bride's father[17] or have translated the word as "marriage present" (Gen 34:12 NRSV), but such readings belie the fact that a monetary transaction is required before the marriage can occur. This custom may have seemed acceptable in ancient societies, just as it can continue to be practiced in certain cultures today, but it does not indicate that women and men shared equal esteem or standing—quite the contrary. Both village and urban social contexts in ancient Israel must have had comparable traditions regarding marriage, sexuality, and the bride-price, although the poor villagers could not match the level of expenditures of their affluent compatriots in the cities. The same pertained to the dowry (*šilluḥîm*) that the bride brings with her to the marriage. While the dowry is not mentioned in biblical laws, the Code of Hammurabi and other Southwest Asian texts specify various conditions affecting it, such as divorce.

A marriage contract of some type probably existed in ancient Israel— whether it was an oral agreement in the nonliterate environment of villages or a written document in cities where more literacy was present. Financial issues could be addressed in either context—the amount of the bride-price and the dowry; provisions relating to adultery, divorce, property, inheritance, support after the death of the spouse, compensation if the contract is breached; and various other matters not directly bearing on economic concerns. Such details are present in the numerous marriage contracts found in neighboring countries, including the Jewish contracts from Elephantine in Egypt during the Persian period.[18] No contracts are retained in the Hebrew Bible; only Deut 24:1–4 refers to a "writ of divorce" (*sēper kĕrîtut*) that the husband is to hand the wife he is divorcing. It mentions nothing of a financial nature, although contracts from other ancient cultures generally do. Economic considerations were likely in Israel as well, though, especially if significant property or other assets were at stake.

17. See, e.g., de Vaux, *Ancient Israel*, 27.

18. For examples, see Westbrook, ed., *History*. For Egyptian marriage contracts, see Porten, *Elephantine Papyri*; and Porten and Yardeni, *Textbook*.

A woman who survived her husband was in a particularly vulnerable position. In a village context a widow probably stood a chance of getting support from her adult children and other relatives because of an ethic of caring for the disadvantaged in a kinship group. In this respect her lot was not much different from that of an orphan, who was doubly vulnerable after losing both parents. But there may not have been comparable protections for widows in the cities, where the kinship network was probably replaced by a more class- and property-oriented structure. Exod 22:22–24 (22:21–23 MT; see also Deut 27:19) explicitly forbids abusing widows and orphans in their need—which suggests that this must have been a problem in the urban settings where these laws were written. A widow's right to remarry was also carefully controlled in this patriarchal world.

Just because women were not chattel slaves does not suggest they were equal in rights and powers with the Israelite men; far from it. Yet it may well be the case that in their respective contexts women in the villages enjoyed a status higher than that of their urban counterparts. If so, it was surely because the village women were more central to their economy than were the city women to theirs. And to be sure, all the poor women and men in the villages were legally and economically disadvantaged in comparison to the upper-class women and men in the cities.

Property, Both Immovable and Movable

Land ownership and land use in ancient Israel are issues lying at the heart of the economic system, as can be expected for agrarian societies in general.[19] Several different kinds of real property were owned and operated: small plots held by the farmers and families who worked them; community property for shared use, such as common fields and pasturage, threshing floors, cisterns, storage areas, waste areas; larger estates owned by wealthy landowners; crown land under the control of the palace; and temple land used not just for religious buildings and personnel but also for agricultural purposes by tenants and hired laborers as well as slaves.[20] The question of private ownership is itself debatable; Boer, for example, argues that in rural and village contexts land was more likely shared within the community than owned by individuals.[21] In any case the village owners, whether individually or collectively, were responsible

19. See especially the landmark study by Lenski, *Power and Privilege.*
20. For more details, see Knight, *Law, Power, and Justice*, 144–48, 202–7, and 236–40.
21. Boer, *Sacred Economy*, 70–75 and 229–31.

for cultivation and care of livestock, and their livelihood depended on it. Even
if a family owned a portion of ancestral land, it was probably too small to support them, and they needed the help and produce of their neighbors, just as
they would have been motivated to help their kin and kind. The estates, on the
other hand, were controlled by large landowners, the palace, or the temple, and
they were worked not by their owners but by laborers, tenants, or slaves. Such
is the difference between the allocative and the extractive economic systems
described above, and the laws were designed to protect the special interests in
each case.

To assess land use among villagers we are once again without much in the
way of written records to offer a clear sense of the legal issues and ordinances at
play in ancient Israel. The problem of securing the boundaries between properties existed more among large landowners than among small-scale farmers,
although to the extent poor farmers owned their own plots they would have
been mindful of every square centimeter of their already meager holdings. For
land commonly shared among villagers, little need existed to secure property
lines. The law in Deut 19:14 proscribing the moving of boundaries makes most
sense as an issue for large landowners, many of whom probably lived in cities
away from their estates and hired overseers to manage their affairs. If the owners did not have daily supervision of their holdings, they may have harbored
well-founded concerns that they could lose some of their property, especially
through the illicit moving of boundary markers. Hence the law in Deut 19:14,
which served more to benefit estate owners than the village peasants. And it
should be noted that the mover of an estate's boundary marker is just as likely,
or more so, to have been the owner of an adjacent estate, not a poor farmer who
stood powerless, if resentful, when viewing the imposing property.

Several avenues were open to acquire livable or productive land, such as inheritance, purchase, foreclosure on a debt, illegal or unfair seizure, or conquest.
Inheritance was perhaps the most regularized form, although the amount of
property varied dramatically depending on one's socioeconomic class. A peasant's plot was certainly tiny, if for no other reason than that over the generations it could have been subdivided several times among the heirs. While the
law in Deut 21:17 provides for a double portion of the inheritance to go to the
firstborn son, such a custom would be impractical for such a small piece of land
since the portions going to younger sons would have been too small to sustain
a family. More likely among poor landowners was a system of partible inheritance, equal division among heirs, each of whom then had to supplement the
small shares by other means. The land shared among villagers was not subject

to inheritance by individuals; rather, it passed seamlessly from one generation to the next, often with their common, or putative, ancestor viewed as the original owner and their successors as the beneficiaries. A large estate, on the other hand, became a matter of considerable concern for the owner, who was eager to preserve all that had been amassed. The prophet Isaiah rails against such exploitative practices when he says, "Woe to you who join house with house and field with field, until no room remains and you dwell alone in the land" (Isa 5:8). Such estates, similar to the latifundia in ancient Rome, assumed the position of economic centers of agrarian production and labor. Quite possibly, these estates were so valuable that their owners were reluctant to divide them among heirs, which would diminish their power as well as the reputation of the ones who founded them. A biblical law forbids passing over the firstborn son and bequeathing the land to a younger, favorite son (Deut 21:15–17), an arbitrary act that certain landowners may well have preferred. Not only private owners but also the royal house and the temple depended on the income and power that accrued to them from their control over productive land. In an effort to guard against loss of value or income, biblical laws require restitution for causing a fire that destroys another's crops or for allowing livestock to graze over another's field or vineyard (Exod 22:5–6 [22:4–5 MT]).

Movable property ranged from livestock and tools to domestic items and luxury goods. Again, the poor population in rural and village contexts possessed only sparse belongings, items essential to their livelihood. Within the small villages and their kinship networks, everyone was probably quite aware of each other's belongings, and the chance of theft by neighbors or kinfolk was relatively low because of this familiarity among community members. Everyone would have noticed if an animal or tool belonging to one family turned up in another's household, and the community would adjudicate it according to their traditional processes. Given their economic constraints, the villagers had only a limited number of livestock and work animals such as oxen, and many of these animals belonged to the village as a whole. The situation differed vastly among the wealthy, though, both in their living environment within cities and on their estates where they had less direct oversight over the affairs of all those who worked on or passed through the property. To secure ownership, it was possible to draw up a contract to confirm a purchase or to have witnesses who could attest to it.[22]

Issues of liability and theft were at play, especially considering the more valuable commodities in the cities and on the estates, and are addressed in

22. For an example, see Knight, *Law, Power, and Justice,* 198–202, 207–8.

biblical laws. Theft could result in steep penalties for the thief: payment of five oxen for one ox stolen and slaughtered and four sheep for one sheep, but only two for one if the animal is recovered alive (Exod 22:1, 4 [21:37 and 22:3 MT]); with an eye specifically on the poor who may not be able to provide such compensation, the law even stipulates that the thief is to be sold into slavery if necessary to pay the fine. One can justifiably wonder whether such demands were enforceable if both parties were poor villagers. If royal goods or temple belongings are stolen, the crime is punished harshly in other laws in ancient Southwest Asia. Another situation involves items deposited by the owner with another person or borrowed by another person. The complex set of laws in Exod 22:7–15 (22:6–14 MT) details the liability that the recipient has, but it also provides for the possibility that the recipient in certain instances (for example, if the borrowed animal is killed by a wild beast) should not be held liable. Responsibility also extends to negligent acts, as in the case of someone who digs a pit, fails to cover it, and then must compensate the owner of an animal that falls into it and dies (Exod 21:33–34). The laws about the goring ox (Exod 21:28–32, 35–36) are also nuanced in assessing liability and penalties. The biblical law about burglary potentially affects both movable and immovable property: if a burglar breaks into a house at nighttime, the homeowner is justified in killing the burglar, but not if it happens during the daytime; the rationale seems to be that there is more danger of harm coming to the inhabitants during the night (Exod 22:2–3 [22:1–2 MT]).

Slavery

Israel's economy was not based as much on slavery as were the economies of ancient Greece, Rome, and the large empires in ancient Southwest Asia. Still it existed as a prevalent legal custom in Israel. Several routes led individuals and groups into slavery: birth to parents who were slaves, capture in warfare, indentured slavery, slave trade, and the king's mandate. Whichever course resulted in slavery for anyone, it was an extremely undesirable, demeaning position from which one could scarcely become free. Any society that allows—much less fosters—slavery can scarcely free itself from the stigma of brutality and exploitation.

The Hebrew Bible develops no denunciation of systemic slavery. Only one text comes close to considering the humanity of a slave. In Job 31:15 the poet states, referring to a slave: "Did not the one who made me in the womb make him? And did not he fashion us in the same womb?" Such a sentiment did not make its way into the laws. Even later translators occasionally sought to downplay the significance of slavery in the Bible by domesticizing the Hebrew term ʿebed from the harsh, subservient term "slave" to the household version of "servant" or "helper"; instead, it is better to preserve the radicalism of the metaphor in Isa 52:13—53:12 by referring not to the "suffering servant" but the "suffering slave." The tragic lot of slaves in the ancient world is not to be minimized. While some interpreters have speculated that slaves in Israel were really only laborers, their reality was closer to that of being property than to that of being hired workers. Far from refuting it, the biblical laws legitimated the owning and controlling of enslaved persons.

Slavery is one of the few sectors of the economy that exclusively benefited one class—the wealthy and powerful. Peasants living in rural villages had no resources to own slaves. If anything, they faced the prospect of themselves becoming slaves, whether through royal command or the elites' exploitation. Those who possessed slaves were the well-to-do: the merchants, the creditors, the royalty, the military officers, and the temple personnel. Some others in society may have acquired slaves as wartime booty, but we have no way of knowing how extensively plunder of this type became distributed among the general population. Slaves often found themselves working in agriculture, in the mines, in construction, in artisan workshops, and in any number of menial tasks. They could also be educated to serve in such capacities as household management, domestic service, scribal roles, even responsible positions in training, overseeing, and fulfilling various tasks needed by their owners. Their subservient status, however, ranged from chattel slaves (with virtually no control over their own lives) to debt slaves (working off the amount they owed) to slaves granted more responsibility in the household, commerce, government, and the cult. The biblical laws are primarily intended not to provide avenues for slaves to be freed (the exception may be the laws of release, although they may have had a more ulterior motive, as will be discussed shortly); rather, the laws ensure that the slaves will be of maximal benefit to their masters, as will become evident in the following examples. The legal provisions are not unconcerned with the slaves' well-being, but the property and the power of the owners are of paramount importance. Since only the wealthy and the powerful were able to own slaves, we can safely assume that any slave owner here mentioned is a person of the upper class, whether a private person or a representative of the palace or the temple.

Slaves are explicitly identified in Exod 21:21 as being their owner's property (kesep, usually translated "silver" but here in the sense of valuables that someone owns: "for the slave is the owner's kesep"). If the owner strikes a male

or female slave and the slave survives two days, the owner suffers no punishment for the injury; but if the slave dies, the owner will be punished, although it
is unclear how or how much (Exod 21:20–21). However, if the injury amounts
to the loss of an eye or a tooth, then the slave is to be set free (Exod 21:26–27).
If an ox gores a slave (presumably to death), the owner of the ox is to compensate the slave owner by paying thirty silver shekels—unlike the case in which
the ox gores a free person, which can result in a steeper fine and perhaps even
the death of the ox's owner (Exod 21:29–32). A slave owner can take his female
slave as his wife but must then treat and support her as a wife, or she is to be
freed (Exod 21:8–11; Deut 21:10–14). If a man has sexual relations with a
female slave, it is not counted as adultery; he is not to be executed since she
is not free, and he will be forgiven of the act if he brings a guilt offering to the
priest (Lev 19:20–22). Special provisions govern marriage between slaves, with
different treatments for men and women. If a male slave has a chance to go
free but is married and chooses to remain with his owner, then the owner can
pierce his ear as a sign that he is a permanent slave (Exod 21:3–6; Deut 15:16–
17). Biblical laws also seek to differentiate between Hebrew and foreign-born
slaves: a Hebrew slave is to be set free after six years of service (Exod 21:2), and
Lev 25:39–55 contains numerous stipulations providing preferential treatment
for Israelite slaves in comparison to foreign slaves.

Debt slavery was a common occurrence, and not only the male head of
the household but also his wife and children could be sold to discharge the
debt (e.g., Exod 21:7; Lev 25:39, 47). Slaves could be emancipated when they
had worked off their debt or when someone, usually a kin, redeemed them, but
several laws also provide for a general release of slaves (except the foreign slaves,
Lev 25:44–46) in the Sabbatical or the Jubilee Year (Lev 25; Deut 15:12–18).
Unlike laws common in neighboring countries, the Hebrew Bible contains a
rule that a runaway slave is not to be given back to the owner but should be
allowed to remain wherever he or she wishes, without fear of oppression (Deut
23:15–16 [15:16–17 MT].)

Employing the method of ideological criticism leads us to a quite different perspective on these biblical laws. Unless one wants to argue that these laws
were manufactured out of thin air and had no bearing on what was happening
in the real world, it is reasonable to assume that they in some way reflect certain
conditions and practices of that time. Slave owners *could* treat their slaves as
chattel; Hebrew slaves *were* being considered similarly to foreign slaves; female
slaves *were* at risk of being sexually mistreated and abandoned; slaves *could* be
kept in slavery indefinitely; escaped slaves *were* returned to their owners. In a

word, slave owners—including the king and the temple personnel—had considerable, virtually full power over their slaves, and even biblical laws and customary laws could not guarantee humane treatment of these powerless persons.

Poverty

"There will never cease to be poor in the land" (Deut 15:11a). Why is such a statement contained in the Hebrew Bible when many other texts readily acknowledge the presence of the poor, and when external evidence reinforces it? A conventional answer to this question emerges from the text itself in which it is embedded. Deut 15 belongs to the so-called humanitarian laws present in the book of Deuteronomy—laws or directives that seem to espouse a just, equitable, and charitable treatment of the poor and powerless within the society of ancient Israel. The several sections of this chapter set the tone for this interpretation. The first six verses enjoin the Israelites to practice the seventh-year remission of debts for fellow Israelites ("neighbors"), explicitly excluding foreigners from this benefit. Oddly, however, v. 4 almost seems to consider this law of remission to be unnecessary since, it idealistically states, there will be no one in need within the community as long as the people obey Yнwн's commandments. The second section (15:7–11), which concludes with our verse, presupposes that poor persons will populate the land; or at least it starts with the hypothetical "If someone from your community is in need" (literally, "if there is someone in need from among your brothers"). Completely left out of the picture are the many poor women—not the needy "brothers" but the destitute "sisters."[23] Furthermore, if this "humanitarian" law in fact focuses on Israelites (implied also by the term "brother"), then the many strangers and foreigners in the community are likewise disregarded. Instead, the text moves on quickly to direct those with means to lend liberally to those it recognizes in need, not holding back because the year of remission is at hand. The third section (15:12–18) applies this principle of liberality to slave ownership: slaves should not be kept in servitude against their will for longer than six years but should be set free in the seventh year and provided with food and livestock as provisions for their life in freedom. The fourth and final section in the chapter

---

23. Phyllis Bird has poignantly observed that biblical texts concerning poverty, particularly prophetic texts, seem far more focused on poor men than poor women, and it is vacuous, we might add, simply to say that āḥ "brother" is meant to include "sister" when so many women suffered a kind of poverty not experienced by their male counterparts. See Bird, "Poor Man."

(15:19–23) moves in a quite different direction, not concerned with poor or powerless persons but with the cultic status of firstborn cattle and sheep. Aside from this closing section, the chapter is thus devoted to the treatment of those in debt, in need, and in slavery. It seems to espouse what has generally been regarded as a high ethic of compassion and generosity.

But to whom is this text directed, and what is at stake for them? The addressees and the referents reveal enough to subvert the text itself. First we should note that all the second-person pronouns and verbal forms are in the singular, as if the addressee were a single person or, more likely, a collective. The variation between the singular and plural in Deuteronomy and the Deuteronomistic literature is a well-known conundrum and has been used, though not persuasively for all, to distinguish between the Deuteronomic source material (using the singular pronoun) and the Deuteronomistic redactional sections (using the plural pronoun).[24] Our verse—in fact the whole section of Deut 15:7–11— uses the second-person singular exclusively, but this feature alone does not preclude the possible presence of Deuteronomistic redaction. Rather, what is more telling about the intention of this text is its ideological underpinning.

To determine the addressee, we should look first at what the text expects of this ideal person or persons (and we will use the plural form here simply because this directive is hardly meant to apply to only one person). Most importantly, the addressees possess sufficient resources or assets to lend (15:8) or give (15:10) liberally to those in need. The preceding section also references creditors, in fact even those who have sufficient assets to lend to other nations, and the following section addresses slaveholders in the community. These wealthy persons are furthermore, according to the text, tempted or inclined to be hard-hearted and tight-fisted, exhibiting behavior against which the chapter rails. The addressees are, in other words, not the poor but the prosperous. At one level the text may be directed to the whole people of Israel, but here the authors seem to be explicitly singling out the well-to-do as the ones with a special responsibility toward the needy. At the same time the authors recognize—realistically, we can suspect—that these wealthy persons will not be inclined to part with their holdings but need to be pressed with promises or threats. Even their motivations can be suspect, according to the text: if the year of remission is near, they may strategize ways to withhold loans until later so as not to lose their capital. As noted above, addressing and imploring the wealthy elites should not be surprising since the biblical text, including Deut 15, was produced primarily in the urban contexts where many or most of them lived.

24. Minette, "Sections."

Such considerations cast a quite different light on this chapter than we are accustomed to entertain. Is it really advocating an upending of the systems that define the statewide economy—the amassing of wealth in the hands of the few, the exploitation of slaves, the control of power? It clearly does not reflect the subsistence economy of the poor villagers but the extractive system described by Boer.[25] In fact, we are hard put to imagine that anyone in need is likely to benefit from the high rhetoric of this chapter. Small wonder, then, that there is scarcely any evidence that the laws of remission, whether of debts or of slaves, were actually practiced or enforced in ancient Israel.[26] Such compassionate sentiment toward the vulnerable is much more thinkable among the poor population, who themselves knew their own vulnerability, than it is among the sheltered and privileged powerful.

This sentence itself, "There will never cease to be poor in the land," stands out in its context almost as a platitude, a common saying that circulated in the culture and was inserted into this context in Deut 15:11 because it seemed to fit the subject matter. It does not serve well as a motive clause: the wealthy are not more likely to show compassion to the poor simply because there are so many who live in destitution. The authors of Deuteronomy also do not turn it into an indictment of the whole society; an earlier verse in this chapter (v. 4) has already denied that there are any in need among the people. In the mouth of the poor, the sentence would seem to convey hopelessness and acquiescence or, alternatively, bitterness and resentment. But the poor are not being heard in this chapter; they are supposed to be the beneficiaries of the wealthy population's putative compassion. There is only a hint of a threat by the poor—that they may "cry out to YHWH against" the wealthy (15:9). This is suggestive of Weber's notion that "the curse of the poor" is the "weapon of democracy."[27] Absent any divine punishment, the status quo with the few prosperous and the multitudinous poor will certainly continue.

Conclusion

This chapter has focused especially on the dissymmetry existing in the socioeconomic contexts of ancient Israel and the effects it had on the legal worlds of the country, among both the haves and the have-nots. It is easy for us to let categories like money, marriage, property, powerlessness, and poverty remain as

25. Boer, *Sacred Economy*, 110–45.

26. See the discussion in Knight, *Law, Power, and Justice*, 217–22; and Knight, "Herrens Bud"; and the translated and expanded version: Knight, "Whose Agony?"

27. Weber, *Ancient Judaism*, 256–57.

abstract, depersonalized terms, and we do well to reconstruct as fully as possible what those terms actually might have meant in ancient times. The same can be said of the categories wealthy and powerful. If the actual economic and social conditions of the haves and the have-nots are ascertained and described, we are in a better position to assess the tensions between them, and the options available to each group. It follows that the biblical text needs to be interpreted critically in light of these economic, social, and political factors, for ulterior motives may be lurking behind the pronouncements included in the Hebrew Bible. Texts, and in particular here the laws, can conceal intents not at first evident on the surface. To ask who benefits from a given law or other text can disclose manipulative maneuvers by its authors and transmitters. A healthy dose of suspicion belongs to a critical, resistant reading of the text and clears the way to appropriate it in constructive and liberating ways.

Bibliography

Adams, Samuel L. *Social and Economic Life in Second Temple Judea.* Louisville: Westminster John Knox, 2014.

Bird, Phyllis. "Poor Man or Poor Woman: Gendering the Poor in Prophetic Texts." In *On Reading Prophetic Texts: Gender-Specific and Related Studies in Memory of Fokklien van Dijk-Hemmes,* edited by Bob Becking and Meindert Dijkstra, 37–51. BibInt 18. Leiden: Brill, 1996.

Boer, Roland. *The Sacred Economy of Ancient Israel.* LAI. Louisville: Westminster John Knox, 2015.

Broshi, Magen, and Israel Finkelstein. "'The Population of Palestine in Iron Age II." *BASOR* 287 (1992) 47–60.

Brueggemann, Walter. *Money and Possessions.* Interpretation: Resources for the Use of Scripture in the Church. Louisville: Westminster John Knox, 2016.

Giddens, Anthony. *The Constitution of Society: Outline of the Theory of Structuration.* Berkeley: University of California Press, 1984.

Knight, Douglas. "Herrens Bud—Elitens Interesser? Lov, Makt, og Rettferdighet i Det Gamle Testamente." *NTT* 97 (1996) 235–45.

———. *Law, Power, and Justice in Ancient Israel.* LAI. Louisville: Westminster John Knox, 2011.

———. "Whose Agony? Whose Ecstasy? The Politics of Deuteronomic Law." In *Shall Not the Judge of All the Earth Do What Is Right? Studies on the Nature of God in Tribute to James L. Crenshaw,* edited by David Penchansky and Paul L. Redditt, 97–112. Winona Lake, IN: Eisenbrauns, 2000.

Lenski, Gerhard. *Power and Privilege: A Theory of Social Stratification.* 1966. Reprint, Chapel Hill: University of North Carolina Press, 1984.

Minette de Tillesse, Georges. "Sections 'tu' et sections 'vous' dans le Deutéronome." *VT* 12 (1962) 29–87.

Moran, William L. "'The Scandal of the 'Great Sin' at Ugarit." *JNES* 18.4 (1959) 280–81.

Pirngruber, Reinhard. *The Economy of Late Achaemenid and Seleucid Babylonia.* Cambridge: Cambridge University Press, 2017.

Porten, Bezalel. *The Elephantine Papyri in English: Three Millennia of Cross-Cultural Continuity and Change.* DMOA 22. Leiden: Brill, 1996.

Porten, Bezalel, and Ada Yardeni. *Textbook of Aramaic Documents from Ancient Egypt, Newly Copied, Edited, and Translated into Hebrew and English.* 4 vols. Jerusalem: Academon, 1986–1999.

Rabinowitz, Jacob J. "The 'Great Sin' in Ancient Egyptian Marriage Contracts." *JNES* 18 (1959) 73.

Vaux, Roland de. *Ancient Israel.* Vol. 1, *Social Institutions.* Translated by John McHugh. 2 vols. New York: McGraw-Hill, 1965.

Weber, Max. *Ancient Judaism.* German original published 1917–1919. Translated and edited by Hans H. Gerth and Don Martindale. New York: Free Press, 1952.

Westbrook, Raymond, ed. *A History of Ancient Near Eastern Law.* 2 vols. HdO 72. Leiden: Brill, 2003.

Wright, David. P. "'She Shall Not Go Free as Male Slaves Do': Developing Views About Slavery and Gender in the Laws of the Hebrew Bible." In *Beyond Slavery: Overcoming Its Religious and Sexual Legacy,* edited by Bernadette Brooten, with the editorial assistance of Jacqueline L. Hazelton, 125–42. New York: Palgrave Macmillan, 2010.

8. Ideologies of Kingship and the Sacred in the Ancient Near East

RAINER KESSLER

Within a volume called *Economics and Empire in the Ancient Near East*, the following contribution deals with ideologies instead of economics. My task will be to demonstrate that there is an inner link between some ideologies (especially ideologies of kingship and the sacred) and the realities of the economic life of ancient societies, and in what this inner link between ideology and ancient economic life consists.

The term "ideologies of kingship" is well introduced in studies of the ancient world. It signifies a complex of ideas about the role of the king in front of the gods, his position in society, and his task as leader of his country, including his responsibility for welfare and economic growth. As we have very different societies in the ancient Near East, the term "ideologies of kingship" is only a generic term for a variety of concepts. According to the monumental study of Henri Frankfort (1897–1954) on *Kingship and the Gods* (1948), "Egypt and Mesopotamia held very different views as to the nature of their king and the temper of the universe in which he functioned."[1] However, especially in the field of economics, the function of the king is rather similar in the different cultures. It embraces more than what we would call economic policy in a modern sense. It always has to do with the sacred. Consequently, not only the king but also the temples with their priesthoods played an important role in the economic life of the ancient empires.

---

1. Frankfort, *Kingship and the Gods*, 3.

This chapter will begin with the worlds of Mesopotamia and Egypt and then pass to Israel and Judah.

Ideologies of Kingship in the Ancient World

The term "ideologies of kingship" is not a self-description of ancient cultures but a scientific term to describe a complex of ideas around the institution of monarchy in the societies of the ancient Near East. This complex of ideas is "ideological" because it does not reflect the reality of the monarchical institution but rather the idea how it should be. However, in its main aspects it has to do with reality, though in an exaggerated way.

The most prominent areas covered by the term "ideologies of kingship" are the king's relation to the divine world, his military task, his role in social relations between the wealthy and the poor, or between the strong and the weak, and his obligations to promote the land's fertility.

The King's Relation to the Divine World

A fundamental part of the concept of the "ideology of kingship" covers the relation of the monarch to the deities. However different the concrete ideologies may be in the individual societies, the king is always linked to the gods in a manner that is superior to that of normal human beings. The pyramid texts from the Egyptian Old Kingdom (c. 2868–2181 BCE) had a magical function—"to aid the resurrection of the dead king and ensure his supremacy as a god in the afterlife."[2] However, Amélie Kuhrt points out that in this early epoch "different ideas concerning the divine nature of kingship were current and debated within contemporary Egyptian society."[3]

In the Middle Kingdom (c. 2040–1730 BCE), Pharaoh Amen-em-het (or Ammenemes) III is identified with the highest god. A text framed as a father's instruction to his children has this among the attributes of the king: "He is Re by whose beams one sees, He is one who illumines the Two Lands more than the sun disc."[4] In the New Kingdom (c. 1550–1069 BCE), one of the titles of Pharaohs Thutmose III and Amenhotep II was "(Bodily) Son of Re."[5]

---

2. Kuhrt, *Ancient Near East*, 146.
3. Kuhrt, *Ancient Near East*, 146.
4. Pritchard, ed., *Ancient Near Eastern Texts*, 431.
5. Hallo, ed., *Monumental Inscriptions*, 14, 18, 20.

In Mesopotamia, we find similar tendencies of divinization of the king especially in the early times. Sargon, the ruler of the Mesopotamian empire of Agade (2340–2284 BCE), "attained a special status after his death—he was deified, and a cult existed for him."[6] Naram-Sim (2260–2223 BCE), Sargon's grandson and one of his successors, was portrayed with a horned helmet on his head, the exclusive attribute of the gods.[7] According to a contemporary inscription, the inhabitants of his city, Agade, requested that the gods become Naram-Sim, "the god of their city." As a sign of his divinization they built him a temple.[8] King Shulgi from the next dynasty, the third dynasty of Ur (2112–2004 BCE), was "deified in his lifetime."[9]

The Old Babylonian kings, who reigned from c. 2000 BCE onward, still were seen as descendants of the gods. Lipit-Ishtar (1934–1924 BCE) is frequently called "son of Enlil": "I, Lipit-Ishtar, the son of the god Enlil" is written on a clay cone recording the construction, by the king, of a storehouse for the gods Enlil and Ninlil.[10] Hammurabi (1793–1750 BCE) (in the prologue to his famous law code) and his successors had the title of "Sun(-God) of Babylon," which means that they were in the likeness of the god Shamash (= Sun). In the same prologue, however, Hammurabi says that he is the king who obeys the sun-god. As intermediary between the world of the humans and that of the gods, the king is like the god and, at the same time, a humble servant in the name of the gods.[11] He was believed to be called by the gods. "Hammurabi, the shepherd, called by Enlil," says the prologue, and the epilogue adds: "The great gods called me, so I became the beneficent shepherd whose scepter is righteous."[12]

For the Assyrian kings from the Old Assyrian period (c. 2000–1800 BCE) up until the Neo-Assyrian Empire (934–610 BCE) the true king was the god Ashur. The "fundamental ideology of the Assyrian king" describes him "as the human servant of the divine overlord."[13] While the god Ashur is the true king, the king Assurbanipal (668–630 BCE) is the warrior who establishes order on behalf of the god.[14] In his coronation hymn he proclaims: "Assur is

6. Van de Mierop, *Cuneiform Texts*, 63.

7. Cf. fig. 5 in Kuhrt, *Ancient Near East*, 52.

8. See Hallo, ed., *Monumental Inscriptions*, 244.

9. Kuhrt, *Ancient Near East*, 64.

10. Pritchard, ed., *Ancient Near Eastern Texts*, 159; Hallo, *Monumental Inscriptions*, 247.

11. Cf. Maul, "Assyrische König," 70–71.

12. Pritchard, ed., *Ancient Near Eastern Texts*, 164, 178.

13. Kuhrt, *Ancient Near East*, 365.

14. Maul, "Assyrische König," 75.

king—indeed Assur is king! Assurbanipal is the [representative] of Assur, the creation of his hands!"[15]

The Persian kings, though not of Semitic origin like the Babylonians and Assyrians, adopted a great part of the ideology from their predecessors. Darius I (522–486 BCE) presents himself as the great god Ahuramazda's creature: "A great god is Ahuramazda, . . . who made Darius king, one king over many, one lord of many."[16] In the same sense, Darius' son and successor Xerxes (486–465 BCE) proclaims: "Ahuramazda is the great god . . . who made Xerxes, the king, (rule) the multitudes (as) only king, give alone orders to the other (kings)."[17]

To sum up, whether deified, called a son of a god, called a god's likeness, or only called the one who acts in the name of a god and who is his loyal servant, always the king is highly elevated above normal humans. He is part of the divine sphere, or at least intermediary between the world of the gods and the humans.

The King as Military Leader

One of the first tasks of every king in the ancient Near East is to make war against their enemies. A papyrus from the Egyptian Middle Kingdom containing a royal hymn is typical for the "heroic, warrior-like image of the king":[18]

Land's protector who widens its borders,
Who smites foreign countries with his crown.
Who holds the Two Lands in his arms' embrace,
[Who subdues foreign] lands by a motion of his hands.

The idea of the king as the first soldier of his country never disappears from texts praising the pharaoh. The most important king of the Egyptian New Kingdom, Ramesses II (1290–1224 BCE), is praised in the so-called poem composed after the battle of Qadesh against the Hittite empire:

Now, his Majesty was a youthful lord, a hero without peer;
arms were powerful, his heart bold,
. . . Mighty in victories over all foreign countries,
one never knows when he may begin to fight.
Strong rampart around his army, their shield on the day of fighting.[19]

15. Hallo, ed., *Canonical Compositions*, 473.
16. Quoted in Kuhrt, *Ancient Near East*, 676.
17. Pritchard, ed., *Ancient Near Eastern Texts*, 316.
18. Quotation and text in Kuhrt, *Ancient Near East*, 165.
19. Hallo, ed., *Monumental Inscriptions*, 33.

Also in Mesopotamia the idea of the heroic king is an integral part of the ideology of kingship. The already-mentioned Naram-Sim is portrayed as victorious over the whole world: "when the four corners of the world opposed him with hostility, he remained victorious in nine battles."[20]

Passing from Naram-Sim in the third millennium to the Neo-Assyrian royal inscriptions of the first millennium, the picture is similar. Marc Van de Mieroop summarizes his study of the inscriptions in the following words: "the royal inscriptions appear as tools in an ideological project of the Assyrian elite. Conquest and domination of foreign lands are natural; they are necessitated by their disorder and chaos, negative characteristics that need to be rectified by the Assyrian king."[21]

It is not necessary to quote more witnesses because nearly any inscription or hymn containing elements of the ideology of kingship stresses the king's military role. However, one should underline what Stefan Maul states about the Assyrian kings, but which is also true about the Egyptians (at least of the New Kingdom), about the Neo-Babylonians, and about the Persians. Maul says that the Assyrian ideology of kingship is the prerequisite if not the motor of Assyrian imperialism.[22] As far as kingdoms of the ancient world were empires, their imperialism was based on their ideology of kingship.

Justice and Righteousness and the King as Protector of the Weak

An imperial king can only be successful when his country is strong and his rule is not disputed. According to the ideology of kingship, the foundation of successful rule is the promotion of justice and righteousness. In the ancient Near East, a king's justice and righteousness are marked by his role as protector of the weak. We find this "definition" of justice in Egypt and more elaborated in Mesopotamia. In the instruction for the new pharaoh, Merikare, his father gives him this advice:

> Do justice, then you endure on earth;
> Calm the weeper, don't oppress the widow,
> Don't expel a man from his father's property.[23]

According to Ur-Nammu, second king of the third dynasty of Ur (end of the

---

20. Text quoted in Kuhrt, *Ancient Near East*, 51.
21. Van de Mierop, *Cuneiform Texts*, 56.
22. Maul, "Assyrische König," 76.
23. Hallo, ed., *Canonical Compositions*, 62.

third millennium) the advice given to his Egyptian counterpart, Merikare, was fulfilled by himself: "The orphan I certainly did not consign to the rich man, the widow I certainly did not consign to the powerful man."[24]

These two examples demonstrate that the king must not offend the poor. Hammurabi goes a step further by not only abstaining from harming the weak, but also by intervening actively in the social conflicts of his time. In the prologue to the law code he claims to be named by the gods Anum and Enlil "to cause justice to prevail in the land, to destroy the wicked and the evil, that the strong might not oppress the weak." Again in the epilogue he reiterates that he acts "in order that the strong might not oppress the weak."[25]

The ideology behind this image of the king as protector of the weak is that the king is not part of the interested and often antagonistic groups within society. The king stands above them; he stands with at least one leg in the divine world. That enables him to be neutral, or better yet, to restore justice even at the cost of the mighty.

The King and the Fertility of the Land

According to our modern understanding, it is no surprise that the kings of the old world acted as military leaders. Consequently, in the ideology of kingship, they are always portrayed as the victorious heroes. Neither is it astonishing that kings are expected to observe justice and righteousness. Much more difficult to comprehend is the role the kings played concerning what we call nature. Nature, as distinct and separated from the divine and human spheres, is a modern concept unknown to the people of the ancient Near East. For them, nature always had to do with the gods. As the king was part of the world of the gods, or at least as he reigned in their name, he was also responsible for the fertility of the land. A good reign brings good harvests.

An Egyptian example is Pharaoh Amen-em-het I (1991–1962 BCE), who in his probably fictitious instructions for his successor says about his own reign:

24. Quoted in Kuhrt, *Ancient Near East*, 66. She ascribes the text to Ur-Nammu's successor, Shulgi. The full text in German translation in Kaiser, *Rechts- und Wirtschaftsurkunden*, 17–23, however, clearly indicates that it is Ur-Nammu who is speaking.

25. Pritchard, ed., *ANET*, 164, 178.

I was grain-maker, beloved by Nepri,
Hapy honored me on every field.
None hungered in my years,
None thirsted in them.[26]

One of his successors, Amen-em-het III (1843–1798 BCE), the one who is identified with the high god Re (see above), is said to be "one who makes the land greener than (does) a high Nile."[27]

For Mesopotamia it suffices to quote again the law code of Hammurabi. According to the prologue, he is "the one who makes affluence and plenty abound"; in the epilogue the ruler claims: "I promoted the welfare of the land."[28] In one of his inscriptions, the Neo-Assyrian King Esarhaddon (681–669 BCE) prays that the gods might produce rich harvests and abundance of grain and bring plenty and copiousness to the land.[29] During the coronation ritual for his successor, Assurbanipal, the following plea is recited: "During his years may rains from heaven and floods from the underground source be steady."[30]

It is crucial to understand that these expectations and wishes have nothing to do with concrete political actions. They are part of the sacred sphere that surrounds the king. The king was responsible for the fertility of the land because he was responsible for contact with the divine world. Fertility depended on the will of the gods. It was the king's obligation to push their will in a positive direction. This explains the phenomenon, so strange for modern thinking, that the king was even responsible for earthquakes. When such a catastrophe occurred, the king must have provoked the wrath of the gods, or at least he did not hinder it.[31]

However, this idea of a sacred sphere that brings fertility to the land is only half of the truth. I repeat the words from Hammurabi's prologue quoted above that he is "the one who makes affluence and plenty abound." Some lines later, we can read that Hammurabi is "the lord, who revived Uruk; who supplied water in abundance to its people."[32] Supplying water in this region means constructing and maintaining the system of canals. And this is the king's obligation, not by prayers or sacrifices but by practical politics. A Sumerian hymn

26. Hallo, ed., *Canonical Compositions*, 67.
27. Pritchard, ed., *ANET*, 431–32.
28. Pritchard, ed., *ANET*, 164, 178.
29. Arneth, "*Sonne der Gerechtikeit*," 55–56.
30. Hallo, ed., *Canonical Compositions*, 473.
31. Cf. Maul, "*Assyrische König*."
32. Pritchard, ed., *ANET*, 164.

of King Lipit-Ishtar, "son of Enlil" (see above), demonstrates how fluent the transition was from the sacred to the practical. The hymn ends by stating that the king brings abundance of water to the canals, which he does by practical measures.[33]

To sum up the main aspects of the ideology of kingship in this rough sketch, it is possible to quote what Kuhrt writes about the royal hymns from the third dynasty of Ur:

> Although each hymn is different, they all contain the same essential elements ... which emphasize the legitimacy of the king, through his royal descent, divinely born and appointed by the highest gods. His strength and physical beauty are also stressed: he is the perfect soldier and military commander, exceptionally strong and brave and an expert in handling all kinds of weapons. He always leads his troops into battle; the fame of his military triumphs is known throughout the world and inspires terror in his enemies ... Other themes are the king's care for the temples, the prosperity of the land, his justice and protection of the weak.[34]

This quote mentions "the king's care for the temples." The fundament of the whole ideology of kingship was the king's close relationship with the world of the gods. But, of course, temples are also institutions for the mediation between heaven and earth. This leads to the question of the role of the temples compared with that of the kings.

The Role of Temples in Ancient Economy

Just as there was no uniform "ideology of kingship" in the different cultures of the old world during the various epochs of their history, so no unchanging role of the temples can be identified. What is clear is the fact that kings did not only have the privilege of contact with the sacred, but they were part of the system. Generally, they had the function of the highest priest but did not act as priests except in some clearly defined special situations. Kings were responsible for the construction and functioning of temples. But within the system, temples and their priesthoods were strong, had their own hierarchies and rules, and benefited from a certain degree of autonomy. All this was not only a question of ideology but had its material fundament in the fact that the temples owned landed property.

33. Text in Falkenstein and von Soden, eds., *Sumerische*, 126–30, lines 43–48.
34. Kuhrt, *Ancient Near East*, 68.

Both in Egypt and in Mesopotamia an important part of the economic activities of the country was performed by the temples. Sometimes in older descriptions of the economy of the ancient world the idea prevailed that the *whole* economy was directed by the institutions of temples and palaces, and that everyone had to work for these institutions. However, one must consider two facts pointing in other directions and differentiating the picture.

The first point is made by Marc Van de Mieroop. He states that in Mesopotamia "three types of landownership are attested . . .: institutional, private, and communal, corresponding to three sectors of society: the public institutions of temples and palaces; the private citizenry; and village communities."[35] It is acknowledged in studies of ancient economy that institutions owned a lot of land. However, Van de Mieroop writes,

> it remains hard to determine how dominant they were. A great danger lies in a positivistic approach to these matters. Indeed, the majority of records will refer to institutional land, but that is due to the fact that most large archives are institutional. The communal sector is hardly documented because its economic activities were not so complex as to require written records to keep track of them.[36]

This is even more evident for the private sector. The great number of documents about transactions with people working for the temple or the palace gives the impression that these persons worked exclusively for the institutions. This is probably wrong. Van de Mierop claims that "The actual workers provided their services, and received rations, only for part of the year. In the last decade it has become clear that many of the workers in this seemingly highly centralized state-economy, worked part-time for the state, and consequently are only visible in the record part of the year."[37] We have to admit that we do not know how much time they spent on their own land producing for themselves.

A second warning is brought forward by Michael Jursa and the research group Economic History of Babylonia in the First Millennium BC, which he directed between 2002 and 2009.[38] For a long period in research history, the idea prevailed that Egypt and Mesopotamia were characterized by the assumed dominance of institutional land ownership by palaces or temples. This picture, however, which may be true for the third and second millennia BCE, changes when we move forward to the first millennium. Jursa and his team, who

35. Van de Mierop, *Cuneiform Texts*, 106–7.
36. Van de Mierop, *Cuneiform Texts*, 107.
37. Van de Mierop, *Cuneiform Texts*, 91.
38. Jursa, *Aspects*.

scrutinized the economic developments in Babylonia in the first millennium, especially in the so-called *long* sixth century, summarize that "in the structural differences separating this Iron Age economy [i.e. of the sixth century] from its Bronze-Age predecessors, lies the principal importance of the economic developments treated in this book."[39] Main characteristics of this development are the loss of importance for the institutional sectors of palace and temple. Jursa states that the importance of temple economies depends not only on the quantity of land that they own. He writes,

> Of all the economic agents documented by our sources, the temples owned the largest estates. But this is of less importance than has often been assumed. The economic power of the two temples that are well known through huge archives [those of Eanna in Uruk and of Ebabbar in Sippar] was demonstrably limited by their chronic lack of the other means of production (labour, ploughs and plough oxen, water); the overall productivity of their agricultural sector was correspondingly modest.[40]

In contrast, "the productivity of private, intensively farmed land owned by city dwellers was such that it matched, and cumulatively may well have exceeded, the output of the large, but under-staffed and often poorly managed temple estates with their extensive farming regime."[41] Whereas in the third and second millennia the temple and palace economies formed a more closed system of redistribution within a self-sufficient institutional household, this is no longer true in the first millennium. It is necessary to accept this diachronic factor when evaluating the importance of temple economy.

The role of temple economies was important, but it must not be overestimated. It was more important in the beginning, but it lost part of its influence in the first millennium. And it did not absorb all other economic activities: a deception produced by the unequal spread of written documents.

The Ideology of Kingship in Israel and Judah

Focus will now be given to Israel and Judah, two petty states existing at the margins of the great empires. These states were products of the first millennium, but they inherited a lot of ideas and perhaps even institutions from the great powers that preceded or surrounded them. Among the heritage we find law traditions. For example, the law of the biblical Covenant Code on the

39. Jursa, *Aspects*, 816.
40. Jursa, *Aspects*, 759.
41. Jursa, *Aspects*, 759.

goring ox (Exod 21:28–32) is nearly identical with paragraphs 250–252 of Hammurabi's Code, which is about a thousand years older than the biblical collection. Another example is the wisdom tradition. Proverbs 22:17—24:22 is very similar to a part of the Egyptian teachings of Amenemope; in a certain sense, it is a kind of translation or adaptation.

When Israel and Judah introduced royal rule from the turn of the first millennium onward, they inherited from their neighbors not only the institution of kingship (the elders saying to Samuel, "appoint for us a king to govern us, like the nations" [1 Sam 8:5]). Together with the institution they also inherited the ideology of kingship.

In the texts of the Hebrew Bible, the role of the king is highly disputed. We find a strong layer of texts opposed to the institution of monarchy. Their arguments are situated on different levels. One argumentation is purely political or sociological. Jotham's fable in Judges 9:8–15 portrays a king whom the lords of Shechem had just established as a useless person. All the noble plants in the fable (i.e., the olive tree, the fig tree, and the vine) refuse to become king over the trees. Only the bramble agrees, which means that the king is nothing but a useless bramble among all the noble plants of the country.

More direct than the fable is Samuel's speech to the elders of the Israelites who ask him to appoint a king for them. In the "ways of the king," which Samuel proclaims to the Israelites, the future king is portrayed as a brutal despot (1 Sam 8:10–17). Two verbs dominate the framework of the text: "to take" and "to give." The king is expected to take the young men as commanders for the army and the young women as specialists for the royal household. He is supposed to take fields and vineyards and olive orchards, a tenth of all products and male and female slaves. And he will, says Samuel, give all this to his officers and courtiers. The last sentence in Samuel's speech sums up the place of the people as it relates to the place of the king: "you will be his slaves."

Beside this politically motivated resistance to monarchy, some texts reject the rule of a human king on merely religious grounds. According to these texts, there can only be one king—either God or a human: the two are in opposition to each other. According to the book of Judges, the Israelites offer the kingdom to Gideon, but he answers: "I will not rule over you, and my son will not rule over you; YHWH will rule over you" (Judg 8:23). The same opposition between divine and human kingship occurs in the story about the introduction of royal rule in 1 Sam 8, where we have already found the above-mentioned "ways of the king." God tells Samuel that it is not him whom the people have rejected, but YHWH "from being king over them" (1 Sam 8:7). Later, Samuel summarizes the events, saying to the Israelites: "you said to me, 'No, but a king shall reign over us,' though Yhwh your God was your king" (12:12).

In these texts, whether they use political or religious arguments, the idea of God as king over Israel and the idea of a human king exclude each other. All these texts are strictly opposed to another layer of texts that represent the "ideology of kingship" in ancient Israel and Judah.

The Textual Evidence

Witnesses for the ideology of kingship can be found in nearly all parts of the Hebrew Bible. They take different shapes in the distinct texts, but the general traits of the kingship ideology are identical.[42] And they cover the same fields as do the texts from the other ancient Near Eastern sources we have discussed.

The Psalms

The book of Psalms includes a number of individual psalms that can be named as "royal psalms," and that present nearly all elements of the traditional ideology of kingship. In Ps 2 the king himself proclaims that he is the *son of God*: "He said to me, 'You are my son; today I have begotten you'" (v. 7). "You are my son" clearly represents adoption terminology. The formula is augmented by "today I have begotten you."[43] It is left open as to whether these words point to physical *sonship* or legitimation by adoption.[44] The counterpart to the formula "You are my son" is pronounced by the king himself in Ps 89:27 (ET Ps 89:26): "You are my father." The intimacy of father and son providing the main metaphor for the very close relationship between Yhwh and the king also appears when the king is addressed as God's "firstborn" (Ps 89:28 [ET v. 27]).[45]

In the royal wedding song in Ps 45—sung by a singer in the royal court during official wedding festivities either in Jerusalem or Samaria[46]—the king is even called *'elōhîm*. This could be translated as "God" (NRSV), but here it does

42. A short overview is given in Oswald, "Königtum und Staat," 202–4.

43. Erhard Blum has shown that the use of the perfect ("I have begotten you") commonly accepted from the Septuagint and the Vulgate up until the majority of modern translations is not precise. The speech act marked by the Hebrew perfect, the first person of the speaker plus the marker "today" has to be qualified as performative. An adequate translation would be, "Herewith I make you my son." Cf. Blum, "Psalm 2,7c," 129–32.

44. Cf. Gerstenberger, *Psalms: Part 1*, 47.

45. Cf. Gerstenberger, *Psalms: Part 2*, 152.

46. Cf. Gerstenberger, *Psalms: Part 2*, 189.

not identify the king with Yhwh the high God. It just means that the king in some way belongs to the divine sphere. He is "godlike." Ps 89:4 (ET v. 3) points in another direction. The king is not part of the world of the gods, but he is distinguished from all other humans by God's personal covenant with David and all his descendants. A similar motif appears in Ps 132:11, which does not speak of a covenant but of "a sure oath" sworn by Yhwh to David and his dynasty.

The king, adopted by God, claims *world dominion*. He overcomes hostile nations who at the same time are his own and God's enemies (Ps 2). God himself invites the king to sit at his right hand until he makes the king's enemies his footstool (Ps 110:1). This is reminiscent of Egyptian paintings showing the pharaoh sitting in the lap of a deity with the traditional nine enemies as the pharaoh's footstool.[47] The singer during the wedding ceremony urges the king: "Gird your sword on your thigh, / O mighty one, / in your glory and majesty. / In your majesty ride on victoriously" (Ps 45:3–4). Psalm 72 is a prayer for the king during the ceremony of enthronement. The speaker or the community wish, "May he have dominion from sea to sea, / and from the River to the ends of the earth. / May his foes bow down before him, / and his enemies lick the dust" (vv. 8–9). Finally, in Ps 18 the king is portrayed as the "royal hero," fighting like God himself fights.[48]

Also, the third element of the traditional ideology of kingship is found in royal psalms in the Hebrew Bible: that is, the king's *commitment on behalf of the weak and poor*. When we compare Hammurabi's words in the prologue of his law code with the wishes of Ps 72 for the newly enthroned king, we detect a very close similarity. Hammurabi wrote that he was made king "to cause justice to prevail in the land, to destroy the wicked and the evil, that the strong might not oppress the weak."[49] The prayer on behalf of the Judean king says, "May he judge your people with righteousness, / and your poor with justice. / . . . May he defend the cause of the poor of the people, / give deliverance to the needy, / and crush the oppressor" (vv. 2, 4). What here is formulated as a wish, later in the psalm reappears as an utterance about the attributes of the king: "For he delivers the needy when they call, / the poor and those who have no helper. / He has pity on the weak and the needy, / and saves the lives of the needy. / From oppression and violence he redeems their life; / and precious is their blood in his sight" (vv. 12–14).

47. See the reproduction in Nordheim, *Geboren von der Morgenröte*, 59.
48. See Adam, "Der königliche Held."
49. Pritchard, ed., *ANET*, 164.

Psalm 72, the intercession for the king at his enthronement, not only speaks of his military power and his commitment to justice but also of his role in favor of the *fertility of the land*: "May there be abundance of grain in the land; / may it wave on the tops of the mountains; / may its fruit be like Lebanon" (v. 16). I will come back to this point further below in the section, *The Sacred Role of the King*.

The parallels between the royal psalms and other ancient Near Eastern texts featuring the elements of the kingship ideology are evident. Israel and Judah are part of the world of the ancient Near East and share a lot of ideas with it. Martin Arneth in his study of Ps 72 goes so far as to contend that this psalm in its original layer is formed according to a Neo-Assyrian *Vorlage*, only slightly adopted by the Judean authors. He believes that the psalm was composed at the occasion of King Josiah's accession to the throne.[50]

The Narrative Tradition

It is not astonishing that the first texts that embrace elements of the ideology of kingship appear in the context of the introduction of monarchical rule in Israel. The first kings, Saul and David, are no longer elected like the charismatic leaders of the preceding epoch—the so-called judges—for only one special task. From the beginning they are chosen to form a dynasty. The one who makes them king is YHWH, who acts through his prophet Samuel (cf. 1 Sam 9–10 for Saul and 1 Sam 16:1–13 for David). The *special relationship between the deity and the king*, which is typical for the ideology of kingship, is symbolized by the anointment of the king. When Samuel anoints Saul king, he says to him: "YHWH has anointed you ruler over his people Israel. You shall reign over the people of YHWH and you will save them from the hand of their enemies all around" (1 Sam 10:1). After Saul's rejection, David, his future successor, is also anointed by Samuel (1 Sam 16:1–13). David Tsumura writes that "The anointing rite was believed to impart something of the divine sanctity to the king."[51] "To anoint" in Hebrew is *māšaḥ*, from which the noun *māšiaḥ*, "the anointed," the "messiah," is derived. No one must "raise his hand against YHWH's anointed" (1 Sam 26:9, cf. 24:7 [ET v. 6]). The king was sacrosanct. His inviolability was a clear sign that he was placed between the divine and the human spheres.[52]

While Saul and his son only reign for a short time, David is the founder of a dynasty that rules for about four hundred years. The foundational document

50. Arneth, "*Sonne der Gerechtigkeit*," 96–100.

51. Tsumura, *First Book of Samuel*, 274.

52. Cf. Hartenstein and Krispenz, "König, Gott als König," 275.

for the "house of David" is the prophecy of Nathan (2 Sam 7:1–17; cf. 1 Chr 17:1–15). As it is in Ps 2:7 and Ps 89:27 (ET v. 26), the relationship between the deity and the king is denominated metaphorically as a relationship between a father and son. God says about David's successor: "I will be a father to him, and he shall be a son to me" (2 Sam 7:14; 1 Chr 17:13).

Like the royal psalms, the narrative tradition stresses the king's *military function*. The people's wish to have a king over them is to have a ruler who "may govern us und go out before us and fight our battles" (1 Sam 8:20). Nearly all kings of Israel and Judah are portrayed as more or less successful military leaders.

The third element of the common Near Eastern ideology of kingship—the *protection of the poor and needy*—is nearly absent in the narrative tradition of the books about the epoch of the kingdoms (i.e., the books of Samuel and Kings). This may be due to the special interest of the (Deuteronomistic) authors or redactors of these books, who judge the kings not according to their social behavior but according to their religious behavior.

The last element of the ideology of kingship, the *economic role* of the king, is of special interest for this chapter. In the narrative texts, it appears in two different perspectives. The first is what we would call economic activities of the state. The books of Samuel and Kings give only some hints about a royal economic sector. There are few more allusions in Chronicles, which might reflect the situation of the Persian or even Hellenistic epochs.

The second perspective is on royal activities that have an impact on the economy of the land but are ritual or cultic in their form. They represent what we in modern terminology call the ideology of kingship. Of special interest are two stories which demonstrate that a situation of economic distress is seen as a consequence of royal misbehavior (2 Sam 21:1–14; 24). The section on *King and Economy*, below, will deal with the correspondence between the ideology of the king as guarantor of the land's fertility and what we today would call his economic activities.

Prophetic Texts

In the prophetic literature, we find some texts which judge kings in conformity with the traditional ideology of kingship. A good example is Jeremiah's attack on King Jehoiakim of Judah. The prophet contrasts Jehoiakim with his father, King Josiah, whom he portrays as an ideal king (Jer 22:15–16):

Did not your father eat and drink
and do justice and righteousness?
Then it was well with him.
He judged the cause of the poor and needy;
then it was well.
Is not this to know me?
says YHWH.

In the introduction to the collection of oracles on the kings with the superscription "To the house of the king of Judah" (Jer 21:11—23:8), the prophet (or rather the redactors of the prophetic book) underlines the king's responsibility for "justice and righteousness": "Execute justice in the morning, and deliver from the hand of the oppressor anyone who has been robbed" (Jer 21:12), and: "O King of Judah ... Thus says YHWH: Act with justice and righteousness, and deliver from the hand of the oppressor anyone who has been robbed. And do no wrong or violence to the alien, the orphan, and the widow, nor shed innocent blood in this place" (Jer 22:2–3).

Jeremiah's collection ends with an oracle about a future king. This king again will be an ideal ruler in the sense of the traditional ideology: "I will raise up for David a righteous Branch, and he shall reign as king and deal wisely, and shall execute justice and righteousness in the land. In his days Judah will be saved and Israel will live in safety" (Jer 23:5–6). In these few words, three characteristics of the ideology of kingship are bound together: the dependence of the king on the deity, his obligation to execute justice, and the military safety he guarantees.

With Jer 23:1–6 we have already reached the sort of texts which traditionally are called "messianic oracles." The name is misleading because it suggests a messianic concept which is only developed in later times. Within the framework of the Hebrew Bible one should speak of announcements of a just ruler, nothing more.[53] In these oracles the ideology of kingship survives in a transformed way. It achieves new traces and is projected into the future. The most important texts are Isa 8:23—9:6 (ET 9:1–7); Isa 11:1–9; Mic 4:13—5:5 (ET 5:1–6); and Zech 9:9–10.

Isaiah 8:23—9:6 (ET 9:1–7) stresses the military success of the future king, which will lead to everlasting peace. His power is founded on justice and righteousness: "there shall be endless peace for the throne of David and his kingdom. He will establish and uphold it with justice and with righteousness

---

53. Cf. the word "Herrscherverheißungen" (*Promises of a Ruler*) in the title of Seebass, *Herrscherverheißungen.*

from this time onwards and for evermore" (Isa 9:6 [ET v. 7]). The future king described in Isa 11:1–5 "shall come out from the stock of Jesse" (v. 1). On him, the spirit of Yhwh shall rest (v. 2). The text interprets the righteousness of the king in the sense of help for the poor and suppression of the mighty: "with righteousness he shall judge the poor, and decide with equity for the meek of the earth; he shall strike the earth with the rod of his mouth, and with the wreath of his lips he shall kill the wicked" (v. 4). In an addition to the original oracle, the messianic time is described as a paradise characterized by peace between wild beasts on the one hand and between domesticated animals and humans on the other (vv. 6–9). Micah 4:13—5:5 (ET 5:1–5) like Isa 8:23—9:6 (ET 9:1–7) highlights the military victories of the king from Bethlehem. Peace is guaranteed by military strength. Zechariah 9:9–10 also describes the future king as "triumphant and victorious." But his strength is based on humility, and peace is not ensured by military power but by the destruction of weapons: "He will cut off the chariot from Ephraim and the warhorse from Jerusalem; and the battle-bow shall be cut off" (v. 10). This is no longer the ideology of a present king but of a future messianic ruler.

In sum, three of the traditional characteristics of the royal ideology are at hand for the ruler of the times to come: he rules in the name of God, his kingdom is founded on justice and righteousness, and he will guarantee peace either by military success or by general disarmament. No mention is made of the fertility of nature or of any economic measures taken on the part of the king.[54]

Wisdom Literature

The king plays an important role in wisdom literature. This is due to the fact that this genre of literature, especially in the book of Proverbs, not only encompasses collections of popular sayings but is also part of the educational program in royal society. A short description of the office of the king in Proverbs by David Pleins demonstrates that two elements of the ideology of kingship are crucial for the wisdom picture: the king's commitment to justice and righteousness, and his close relationship with the deity. Pleins writes: "The king is important to the maintenance of order and justice in society (Prov 8:15–16; 16:12; 20:8, 26; 22:11; 29:4, 14; 30:22). In particular, he is the protector of the weak (29:14). The king has special access to the divine, and therefore has

---

54. For the so-called messianic texts cf. Jeremias, *Theologie des Alten Testaments*, 417–26. He includes some of the royal psalms which in their present form (from post-exilic times) are to be read as "messianic" or "eschatological" (Jeremias, *Theologie des Alten Testaments*, 36).

extraordinary knowledge and powers of judgment (16:10; 21:1; 25:2–3; cf. 1 Kgs 3:4–14)."[55] Not mentioned are the military abilities of the king, probably because they played no role in the wisdom education of the king's future servants. Like in the majority of texts which can be linked with the phenomenon of ideology of kingship, economic activities of the king are absent.

In summary: The textual evidence looked upon in this section shows that the four main elements of the ideology of kingship in the ancient Near East can also be found in the Hebrew Bible. First, the kings live in a close relationship to the deity. They are called by God's prophet, they are anointed (i.e., sacrosanct). They are, in an exclusive way, sons of God, and he is their father, by adoption. The future king will be filled with God's spirit. Second, they are successful military leaders. Their victories will lead to everlasting peace. Third, this is possible because the foundations of their thrones are justice and righteousness. They act in favor of the poor and needy, and they oppress the mighty.

The fourth element of the ideology of kingship, the role of the king for the fertility of the land, is the least developed in the Hebrew Bible, for in Hebrew society this had more to do with the cult than with political acting. Good rule—under the guidance of God, founded on justice—will lead to fertility (Ps 72). Famine can be interpreted as a consequence of royal misbehavior (2 Sam 21:1–14; 24). However, there are only few allusions to what could be called economic politics of the kings.

These observations lead to the sociohistorical question about the place of the kings in the economies of Israel and Judah.

The King and Economy

Sociohistorical and Archeological Evidence

The fundament of Israelite and Judean economy was neither the king (palace) nor the temple; it was the subsistence economy of small farmers. This did not change during all the epochs of ancient history until Roman times and later. The royal economy was the economy of the king's household. It was led by the (ašer) al-habbajit, "the one over the house," a royal official. The household was formed by the king's family heritage. Saul is said to be the son of a wealthy family (1 Sam 9:1–2). He claims to be able to give fields and vineyards to his followers (22:7). His successor, David, decides over the landed property of Saul (2 Sam 9; 16:1–4; 19:25–31). David is also portrayed as stemming from a wealthy

55. Pleins, *Social Visions*, 455.

family (1 Sam 16:1–13). David's son Absalom owns flocks at Baal-hazor in Ephraim (2 Sam 13:23). We cannot be sure whether we have historically reliable knowledge in these texts. However, the sociohistorical structure is evident: family property is the basis of the king's household.

A special part of the personal property of the kings of Judah are towns obtained in early times. The first book of Samuel tells that David became a vassal of the Philistine king Achish, and that this king gave him the city of Ziklag as a residence for him and his six hundred men with their families. Then the text reads: "therefore Ziklag has belonged *to the kings of Judah* to this day" (1 Sam 27:6). Later, when King Azariah of Judah conquered Elath, it is said that he "restored it *to Judah*" (2 Kgs 14:22). This city is not part of the personal property of the Judean kings. Ziklag, indeed, seems to be an exception belonging directly to the king's household. The same may be true with the stronghold of Zion, which was named "city of David" after the conquest of Jerusalem (2 Sam 5:9).

The kings are able to expand their property by several means. They can acquire land by buying it from private owners. David as well as Omri bought land for construction projects (2 Sam 24:18–24; 1 Kgs 16:24). King Ahab at least tried to buy a piece of land from Naboth, offering him a fair compensation or a good price for his vineyard—though the transaction ended in a different way (1 Kgs 21).

Probably, land belonging to people judged as disloyal (like Meribaal, 2 Sam 9; 16:1–4; 19:25–31) or belonging to those condemned to death (like Naboth, 1 Kgs 21) fell into the hands of the king.[56] The same seems to be true for property of people who had left the country (2 Kgs 8:1–6).

Aside from holding royal property with its agricultural production, the state (that is to say the king) is active in two more economic areas. The first is international trade. It is probably a projection into the past when King Solomon is described as a great international trader, but it reflects the reality of later epochs of the monarchy when international trade was the monopoly of the state. Solomon is said to have sent ships to East Africa to bring gold and precious goods from there (1 Kgs 9:26–28; 10:11, 22). There is also some trade in horses (1 Kgs 10:28–29). The details are difficult to understand, but what is important is that it was "the king's traders" who managed the transactions. Another form of international trade is cited in 1 Kgs 20:34 where Israelite bazaars in Damascus are mentioned, as well as Aramean bazaars in Samaria. The

---

56. In the case of Naboth this is evident. For Meribaal cf. the argumentation in Ben-Barak, "Meribaal."

main object of this sort of trade was to obtain luxury goods, which are not available in the Hebrews' own territory. This means that it had no great impact on the national economy as a whole.

A second field of royal commitment in economic affairs was craftsmanship. Large building projects in Jerusalem, Samaria, and other smaller cities needed specialists. Again we are confronted with projections into the past which nevertheless give an idea as to where the state was active. The texts mention carpenters and masons (2 Sam 5:11), stonecutters (1 Kgs 5:29 [ET v. 15]), an "artisan in bronze" (1 Kgs 7:14), and a production place for items in bronze (7:46), all in the context of the construction of the temple. For its maintenance, again masons and stonecutters, carpenters and builders (2 Kgs 12:12; 22:6) were necessary. The army also needed specialists besides the soldiers. The texts mention artisans and smiths (2 Kgs 24:14, 16). Together with the soldiers they were "strong and fit for war" (v. 16).

As in the case of international trade, the impact of these activities on the national economy was not great. It was limited to the immediate needs of the state itself. The majority of economic activities remained in the frame of subsistence economy. Families produced what they needed. Greater projects were executed on a local level. Trade was small-scale trade.

A step further in the direction of a centralized royal economy was made after Judah became an Assyrian vassal kingdom. Judah had to pay tribute in kind, so the kings took measures to increase agricultural production. In the late eighth century one can observe an increase in the number of farms. Pottery is standardized, a system of marked weights is introduced. This hints at a form of production that goes beyond that of a royal household in a narrower sense. This is best demonstrated by the jar handles with the stamp impression *lmlk*, "belonging to the king," which appear from the end of the eighth century onwards.[57] The four names incised together with *lmlk*, Hebron, Socoh, Ziph, and the unidentified *mmšt*, are places of royal property. All the above-mentioned changes "point to a centralized royal economy, which improved agricultural production and its transportation under the guidance of a central authority."[58]

However, the basis of production was still subsistence economy, and it was the aim of the central power to collect as much of the surplus as possible. The more developed the monarchical state became, the more elaborated was the system of collection of goods and manpower. The texts give few hints to a taxation system. Menahem, one of the last kings of the Northern Kingdom, is

57. *Lmlk* is a Hebrew seal imprint commonly found on jars, meaning "to/for the king."
58. Lipschits, et al., "Royal Judahite Jar Handles," 7.

said to have exacted fifty shekels of silver from the wealthy people to pay the tribute that he owed to the Assyrian king (2 Kgs 15:20). Whether this action is an indication of a regular taxation system is not clear, whereas the taxation of the land by the Judean king Jehoiakim (2 Kgs 23:35) would not have been possible without an elaborate taxation system. The existence of such a system is proved by the so-called fiscal bullae from the second half of the seventh century BCE (HAE II/2 No. 30.11—30.17). They all display the number of a year (i.e., the regnal year of a king) plus the name of a village. This means that the taxes were collected within the villages and then sent to a central place. The use of a seal with the regnal year of the ruling king demonstrates that such a transaction took place several times a year.

The excavations of the last decades at Ramat Rahel have shown that this place near the Old City of Jerusalem (nowadays within the borders of the modern city of Jerusalem) was the most important location for the collection of taxes during the late Judean monarchy (and later).[59]

The collection of agricultural products by the kings was mainly dedicated to maintaining tribute payments to the imperial powers. However, it could also have had a positive impact on the economic situation of their own population. Palestine is a land "watered by rain from the sky," and not by irrigation (Deut 11:11). Consequently, the construction and upkeep of canals was not among the royal tasks, as it was Egypt and Mesopotamia. But a land dependent on rainfall is always threatened by the failure of precipitation and in consequence by famine. In the story of Joseph in Egypt, an impending famine is managed by erecting storehouses to have a reserve for the land (Gen 41:25–57). This, precisely, is also an economic obligation for the kings in Israel and Judah. In this sense, Solomon, an ideal king to a certain extent, is said to have constructed storage cities (1 Kgs 9:19). By doing this, he acted as a king responsible for the economic welfare of his country.[60]

To conclude this section, during the times of the monarchy in Israel and Judah there was relevant economic activity by the kings. Towards the end of the epoch these activities increased as they became part of the state's income (mainly to pay tribute). However, the royal economy remained a household economy. Certainly, the household of the king was the most important one in the country, but it was one among thousands of other family households. The king's influence on economic production was primarily indirect insofar as the king collected goods in a taxation system that forced producers to produce

59. Lipschits et al., "Palace and Village."
60. Cf. Kessler, "Gott und König."

the products that they would have produced anyway (e.g., grain, oil, wine, and fruit). Insofar as they stored part of this income as supply for the population in times of distress, the kings took care for the people's economic welfare.

Compared with the cultures of Egypt and Mesopotamia, a Hebrew king's function pertaining to the economy of the land was of lesser importance. There were no water systems that he was responsible to maintain. He was not the owner of large estates managed as a palace economy—though we cannot be sure how large the palace economy in Mesopotamia really was or how much it dominated the economic system as a whole (see above). This lower degree of influence that the Hebrew kings had on the economic development of their country is probably the main reason why the king's importance to the land's fertility plays such a small role within the royal ideology in its Israelite form.

The other elements of this ideology are far more developed: the close relationship between king and the divine, his military role, and his responsibility for justice and righteousness. In all of these areas, the kings in Israel and Judah played an active role. They were the masters of the state sanctuaries: see Solomon's role for the temple of Jerusalem (1 Kgs 6–8) and the designation of the sanctuary of Bethel as "the king's sanctuary" and "a temple of the kingdom" in Amos 7:13. The kings were the commanders in chief of their army, which was directed by the "commander of the army" (1 Sam 14:50; 2 Sam 8:16; 20:23, etc.). But they had no "minister for economic affairs." This explains the marginal role of the Hebrew kings' responsibility for the fertility of the land within the biblical form of the common Near Eastern ideology of kingship.

However, there is one form of influence on the economic development of the country that has not yet been addressed. It has nothing to do with economic politics in a modern sense, but with the cult.

The Sacral Role of the King

In ancient Near-Eastern texts the king is held to be responsible for the fertility of the land. It is shown that this idea has two aspects: the first is the king's role as mediator between heaven and earth. This is the fundament of the concept. The second aspect is the practical responsibility of the kings for maintaining the water systems along the great rivers: the Nile, the Euphrates, and the Tigris. Though this function of the king is absent in Palestine, which does not have great rivers and irrigation systems, Israelite and Judean royal ideology adopts the idea of the king's responsibility for the fertility of nature. This has to do with the cultic role of the king.

Two stories in the Second Book of Samuel highlight this special function of the king. The story of Rizpah and David (2 Sam 21:1–14) demonstrates that the king is indeed responsible in a situation of economic distress. After a famine of three years, the king feels obliged to inquire of YHWH. He does not act in a manner that we today would describe as "economic," but rather he engages in a ritual or religious act. Because bloodguilt is the cause of the famine, the king has to remove this guilt to improve the economic situation. It is the king's position between God and the people which makes him responsible for the economic welfare of his land. In accordance with this thinking, in a second story in 2 Sam 24 a famine of seven years is described as a potential consequence of the king's misbehavior (v. 13; NRSV has three years in 1 Chr 21:12 and the Greek text). Speaking of sin and guilt (2 Sam 24:10), the text uses cultic categories for an economic disaster.

In terms of practical politics, a king had only few possibilities to bring forward the economy of his country. The foundation of the national economy in monarchic Israel and Judah was not of land owned by the king but land owned by small farmers. Karl Marx already has seen this point. He makes a distinction between the "Asiatic mode of production" with collective property sometimes owned by the king and a mode of production based on private property. For him, "the Jews" were part of this mode of production. Marx writes: "Alle alten Gesetzgeber, und vor allen Moses, gründeten den Erfolg ihrer Anordnungen für Tugend, Rechtlichkeit und gute Sitte, auf *Landeigenthum*, oder wenigstens *gesicherten erblichen Landbesitz*, für die möglich größte Zahl der Bürger."[61] The king was not the (fictitious) owner of all land.[62] The king's main task in the field of practical economy was restricted to collecting the surplus produced by the farmers and redistributing it to the respective overlords, to the king's palace, to his servants, and perhaps also as provisions in times of need. However, on a religious level the king was responsible for the fertility of the land.

The importance of the king's cultic role as reflected in the two stories on David consists in legitimizing the power of the king. The logic is simple: fertility in Palestine depends on rain; God is the one who can send or withhold

61. "All the old legislators, and above all Moses, founded the success of their orders for virtue, legality and good morals, on land ownership, or at least on secured hereditary land ownership, for the greatest possible number of citizens." Marx, "Ökonomische Manuskripte 1857/58," 383.

62. Compare Lowery, who takes his starting point from the following thesis: "In monarchical Judah, state ownership of all land was the practical reality . . . Royal theology completed the picture: the king was the vicar of Yahweh, true owner of all Israel's land." Lowery, *Reforming Kings*, 59.

rainfall; God will only send rain when the king is a just and pious ruler; as a just and pious king, he by his cultic behavior guarantees the fertility of the land and has the right to collect the surplus product from his population to fulfill his tasks. Psalm 72 is the best example for this network of ideas that forms what we call ideology of kingship:

> ¹ Give the king your justice, O God,
>   and your righteousness to a king's son.
> ² May he judge your people with righteousness,
>   and your poor with justice.
> ³ May the mountains yield prosperity for the people,
>   and the hills, in righteousness.
> ⁴ May he defend the cause of the poor of the people,
>   give deliverance to the needy,
>   and crush the oppressor . . .
> ⁶ May he be like rain that falls on the mown grass,
>   like showers that water the earth.
> ⁷ In his days may righteousness flourish
>   and peace abound, until the moon is no more.
> ⁸ May he have dominion from sea to sea,
>   and from the river to the ends of the earth.
> ⁹ May his foes bow down before him,
>   and his enemies lick the dust . . .
> ¹² For he delivers the needy when they call,
>   the poor and those who have no helper . . .
> ¹⁶ May there be abundance of grain in the land;
>   may it wave on the tops of the mountains;
>   may its fruit be like Lebanon . . .

The outstanding place of the king's cultic role within the area of royal ideology leads to the question of the place of temples in the economy of ancient Israel and Judah.

Temple and Economy in Ancient Israel and Judah

In the second section of this chapter it has been revealed that the role of the temple economy was important in Egypt and Mesopotamia, but also that its role should not be overestimated. Temples did not absorb all other economic activities. They even lost part of their influence in the first millennium. In turning to Israel and Judah it should be recognized that the direct economic role of the temples was even less developed than in the neighboring countries. And again, the difference between *real* economic activities and the place of temple cult in the ideological system needs to be appreciated.

The Epoch of the Monarchies

Already before the rise of monarchy, and for a long time during the monarchic period, there existed local sanctuaries in all parts of the country. Biblical texts mention the temples of Shiloh (1 Sam 1–4; 14:3; Jer 7:12, etc.), Mizpah (1 Sam 7:5—7, etc.), Gilgal (1 Sam 11:14–15; Amos 4:4; 5:5, etc.), Beer-sheba (Amos 5:5), and others. A wonderful excavation is the temple of Arad from the late monarchic epoch in Judah. All these temples had their income, according to the general rule in all cults: "No one shall appear before the deity empty-handed" (cf. Exod 23:15). However, whether the temples owned land and how they organized the cultivation is unknown.

Beside the local sanctuaries stood the royal temples, "the king's sanctuary" and "temple of the kingdom" (Amos 7:13). For Israel, this temple was in Bethel (and probably there was a second one in Dan); for Judah it was in Jerusalem. The king was the master of the temple. The priests of the royal temples were ministers among other servants of the king, and never the most important ones (cf. the lists of officials in 2 Sam 8:15–18; 20:23–26; 1 Kgs 4:1–6). Amaziah, the priest of Bethel, reported to the king when a rebellious prophet appeared at the sanctuary (Amos 7:10–17). The priest of the Jerusalem temple under the last kings of Judah is called "chief priest" (2 Kgs 25:18), but not yet "high priest," as he is called after the exile.

Temples of course had their income, donations from the king, and gifts from the people who visited the temple. Second Kings 20:4 enumerates different forms of donations, and v. 9 mentions a chest where the money is placed (cf. 2 Kgs 22:4–7). On different occasions, the texts mention "the treasures of the house of YHWH" and "the treasures of the king's house" (1 Kgs 14:26; cf. 1 Kgs 15:18; 2 Kgs 12:19; 16:8; 18:15). Obviously the temple had its own treasure, and it is never confused with the king's treasure. However, it is always the king who "took away the treasures of the house of YHWH" (see 1 Kgs 14:26; 2 Chr 12:9). Whether he consulted the priests before taking the temple's treasures is not mentioned, and it is not very probable.

Nothing is stated about economic activities directed by the temple. We do not even know whether temples had landed property. Of course, they included people who worked for the maintenance of the buildings, "the workers who had the oversight of the house of YHWH" (2 Kgs 12:11). But these were internal affairs.

The situation changed after the destruction of the first temple and the construction of the second temple.

The Second Temple Period

After the exile, the temple acquired growing importance. The master of the sanctuary was no longer the king who resided next to the temple, but the Persian king who was represented by a governor. This increased the importance of the high priest, as he then came to be called. He represented, in a certain way, the people of Jerusalem and Judah. In Hellenistic times he would become the official speaker of the Judean *ethnos*.

It is not known whether the growing political role of the priesthood was accompanied by growing economic activities of the temple. For sure, the cultic activities within the temple area of Jerusalem—and certainly also on Mount Gerizim where less evidence exists—were widened compared with the preexilic situation. When we read a book like Ezra, we get the impression that everything was organized around the temple. However, the excavations at Ramat Raḥel already mentioned in the section on the sociohistorical and archeological evidence, above, make it probable that there were two centers for the collection of goods: one in Jerusalem centered in the temple and one at the site of Ramat Raḥel some miles away. And this had only to do with the sphere of redistribution, not that of production, itself. We still have no hints that the second temple owned such an amount of landed property as to be of economic relevance.

While there is little evidence for growing economic activities of the temple before Hellenistic times, it is obvious that the ideological importance of the temple reached a new dimension. The land's fertility and the population's wealth no longer depended on the correct behavior of the Davidic king—who indeed was replaced by the Persian king and his governor—but on the existence and functioning of the temple.

The extant witnesses for this development are the two postexilic prophets Haggai and Malachi. Haggai prophesied in the time after the return of a first group of exiled Judeans to Jerusalem. His oracles are dated to the second year of King Darius I (i.e., 520 BCE). Haggai's main concern is the reconstruction of the temple. According to Haggai's first oracle (1:2–11), the land suffers an economic crisis. Harvests are poor ("You have sown much, and harvested little," v. 6a), the wages of the workers are of no value ("and you that earn wages

earn wages to put them into a bag with holes," v. 6b), and a drought threatens
the entire agricultural production (vv. 10–11). From this situation the people
draw the conclusion that it is not yet time to rebuild the destroyed Solomonic
temple ("These people say the time has not yet come to rebuild Yнwн's house,"
v. 2). The prophet turns this logic upside down. For him, the difficult economic
situation must not be taken as a *reason* not to build the temple, but is a *consequence* of the refusal to do it. He promises that as soon as the building activities
begin, God will send his blessing (v. 8).

The prophet seems to have convinced his fellow countrymen and the authorities of Jerusalem. The reconstruction of the second temple began. Nearly
four months later, Haggai confirms his position (2:10–19). Before the beginning of the work, he says, harvests were poor (vv. 16–17). But now, as the foundation of the temple is laid, the situation will change: "From this day on I will
bless you," says Yнwн (v. 19). We have no data to confirm or refute Haggai's
prediction. However, we can conceive of the ideological importance that the
temple had achieved in the Persian period.

The book of Malachi was written later in the epoch of Persian dominance, whether in the middle of the fifth century BCE[63] or in the first half of
the fourth century BCE.[64] It is marked by a theology of gift and blessing. In
the fifth of his six discussions (3:6–12), Malachi accuses the people of having
"robbed" Yнwн by not bringing the tithes and offerings to the temple. The consequence is a curse on the land (v. 9). The prophet calls on the people to bring
the full tithe into the storehouse and promises as a consequence that Yнwн
will "open the windows of heaven for you and pour down for you an overflow-
ing blessing" (v. 10). The gift of the people will lead to the blessing of God, and
God's blessing obliges the people to bring their gifts to the temple. Gift and
blessing form a perfect circuit.

Conclusion

The link between the sphere of the sacred (whether represented by the kings
or by temples or by other institutions) and economic life remained intact until
the times of modern capitalism (which, according to Walter Benjamin, is a religion in itself).[65] However, a new development began soon after the completion
of the writings of Haggai and Malachi: money entered the economic world
in a way until then unknown. Monetization changed not only the economy

63. Cf. Snyman, *Malachi*, 1–3.
64. Kessler, *Maleachi*, 75–77.
65. Cf. the title of Benjamin, "Kapitalismus als Religion" (Capitalism as Religion).

but also the thinking of humankind. Greek philosophers reflect this development. In search of the first principle of the world, Heraclitus, Haggai's younger contemporary, holds that it is fire; and he compares the function of fire for philosophical explanation with the function of money for the economy, writing that "all things are an exchange for fire and fire for all things, like goods for gold and gold for goods."[66] Aristotle, perhaps a contemporary of Malachi, introduces the distinction between utility value and exchange value and is the first philosopher to discuss monetary economics as an ethical problem. The category of money also enters biblical writings of the Hellenistic period.[67] Qohelet writes: "The lover of money will not be satisfied with money," recognizing the nature of money, which has no natural limits and opposing the love of money to the love of God (Eccl 5:9 [ET v. 10]). And he knows the omnipotence of money: "Money answers every thing" (Eccl 10:19 KJV).

This development, however, opens a new chapter.

Bibliography

Adam, Klaus-Peter. *Der königliche Held: Die Entsprechung von kämpfendem Gott und kämpfendem König in Psalm 18.* WMANT 91. Neukirchen-Vluyn: Neukirchener, 2001.

Altmann, Peter. *Economics in Persian-Period Biblical Texts: Their Interactions with Economic Developments in the Persian Period and Earlier Biblical Traditions.* FAT 109. Tübingen: Mohr Siebeck, 2016.

Arneth, Martin. *"Sonne der Gerechtigkeit": Studien zur Solarisierung der Jahwe-Religion im Lichte von Psalm 72.* BZABR 1. Wiesbaden: Harrassowitz 2000.

Ben-Barak, Zafrira. "Meribaal and the System of Land Grants in Ancient Israel." *Bib* 62 (1981) 73–91.

Benjamin, Walter. "Kapitalismus als Religion [Fragment]." In *Gesammelte Schriften*, vol. 6, edited by Rolf Tiedemann and Hermann Schweppenhäuser, 100–103. 7 vols. Frankfurt: Suhrkamp, 1991.

Blum, Erhard. "Psalm 2,7c—Eine Performative Aussage." In *Grundfragen der Historischen Exegese: Methodologische, Philologische und Hermeneutische Beiträge zum Alten Testament*, edited by Wolfgang Oswald and Kristin Weingart, 295–314. FAT 95. Tübingen: Mohr Siebeck, 2015.

Falkenstein, Adam, and Wolfram von Soden, eds. *Sumerische und akkadische Hymnen und Gebete.* Die Bibliothek der alten Welt. Der alte Orient. Zürich: Artemis, 1953.

---

66. Fragment B90, quoted and commented in Seaford, *Money and the Early Greek Mind*, 232.

67. Peter Altmann, who studied economics in Persian-period biblical texts claims that "the Persian biblical rejected the rise of economically defined value" and "instead repeatedly placed community cohesion around their sanctuary as the highest value." Altmann, *Economics in Persian-Period Biblical Texts*, 304.

Frankfort, Henri. *Kingship and the Gods: A Study of Ancient Near Eastern Religion as the Integration of Society & Nature*. Oriental Institute Essay. Chicago: University of Chicago Press, 1948.

Gerstenberger, Erhard S. *Psalms: Part 1 with an Introduction to Cultic Poetry*. FOTL 14. 1988. Reprint, Grand Rapids: Eerdmans, 1991.

———. *Psalms: Part 2 and Lamentations*. FOTL 15. Grand Rapids: Eerdmans, 2001.

Hallo, William W., ed. *The Context of Scripture*. Vol. 1, *Canonical Compositions from the Biblical World*. 4 vols. Leiden: Brill, 1997.

———, ed. *The Context of Scripture*. Vol. 2, *Monumental Inscriptions from the Biblical World*. 4 vols. Leiden: Brill, 2000.

Hartenstein, Friedhelm, and Jutta Krispenz. "König, Gott als König." In *Wörterbuch alttestamentlicher Motive*, edited by Michael Flieger et al., 272–79. Darmstadt: Wissenschaftliche Buchgesellschaft, 2013.

Jeremias, Jörg. *Theologie Des Alten Testaments*. GAT 6. Göttingen: Vandenhoeck & Ruprecht, 2015.

Jursa, Michael, ed. *Aspects of the Economic History of Babylonia in the First Millennium BC: Economic Geography, Economic Mentalities, Agriculture, the Use of Money and the Problem of Economic Growth*. AOAT 377. Münster: Ugarit, 2010.

Kaiser, Otto, ed. *Texte aus der Umwelt des Alten Testaments*. Vol. 1, *Rechts- und Wirtschaftsurkunden: Historisch-chronologische Texte*. Gütersloh: Mohn, 1982.

Kessler, Rainer. "Gott und König, Grundeigentum und Fruchtbarkeit." In *Studien zur Sozialgeschichte Israels*, 167–84. SBAB 46. Stuttgart: Katholisches Bibelwerk, 2009.

———. *Maleachi*. HThKAT. Freiburg: Herder, 2011.

Kuhrt, Amélie. *The Ancient Near East c. 3000–300 BC*. 2 vols. Routledge History of the Ancient World 2. 1995. Reprint, London: Routledge, 2010.

Lipschits, Oded, et al. "Royal Judahite Jar Handles: Reconsidering the Chronology of the LMLK Stamp Impressions." *Tel Aviv* 37.1 (2010) 3–32.

Lipschits, Oded, et al. "Palace and Village, Paradise and Oblivion: Unraveling the Riddles of Ramat Raḥel." *NEA* 74 (2011) 1–49.

Lowery, R. H. *The Reforming Kings: Cult and Society in First Temple Judah*. JSOTSup 120. Sheffield: Sheffield Academic, 1991.

Marx, Karl. "Ökonomische Manuskripte 1857/58." In *Gesamtausgabe*, by Friedrich Engels. MEGA 11/1,2. Berlin: Akademie, 1981.

Maul, Stefan M. "Der Assyrische König—Hüter der Weltordnung." In *Gerechtigkeit: Richten und Retten in der abendländischen Tradition und ihren altorientalischen Ursprüngen*, edited by Jan Assmann et al., 65–77. Reihe Kulte / Kulturen. Munich: Fink, 1998.

Nordheim, Miriam von. *Geboren von der Morgenröte? Psalm 110 in Tradition, Redaktion und Rezeption*. WMANT 118. Neukirchen-Vluyn: Neukirchener, 2008.

Oswald, Wolfgang. "Königtum und Staat." In *Die Welt der Hebräischen Bibel: Umfeld— Inhalte—Grundthemen*, edited by Walter Dietrich, 197–210. Stuttgart: Kohlhammer, 2017.

Pleins, J. David. *The Social Visions of the Hebrew Bible: A Theological Introduction*. Louisville: Westminster John Knox, 2001.

Pritchard, James B., ed. *Ancient Near Eastern Texts: Relating to the Old Testament*. 2nd ed., corr. and enlarged. Princeton: Princeton University Press, 1956.

Seaford, Richard. *Money and the Early Greek Mind: Homer, Philosophy, Tragedy*. Cambridge: Cambridge University Press, 2004.

Seebass, Horst, *Herrscherverheißungen im Alten Testament*. BThSt 19. Neukirchen-Vluyn: Neukirchener, 1992.

Snyman, S. D. *Malachi*. HCOT 23. Leuven: Peeters, 2015.

Tsumura, David Toshio. *The First Book of Samuel*. NICOT. Grand Rapids: Eerdmans, 2007.

Van de Mieroop, Marc. *Cuneiform Texts and the Writing of History*. Approaching the Ancient World. London: Routledge, 1999.

9. The Economy and Israelite Prophecy from the Eighth to the Sixth Centuries BCE

Davis Hankins

Introduction

At first glance, an ancient Israelite prophet may appear to have little in common with an economist. On the one hand, prophets speak for God, engage in supernatural speculation, and are generally concerned with a future that differs from the present in both space and time. Prophetic imaginations are often preoccupied with potential transformations of the status quo and the emergence of new situations—for good or ill. An economist, on the other hand, is concerned with analyzing the world as it is, here and now—with demographics, patterns of land tenure, and the most elemental social relations of production, exchange, distribution, and consumption, as well as the technological forces currently deployed in such relations. But these oversimplified definitions do not tell the whole story. Since the future inevitably impinges upon every economic situation, economists are not focused solely on the present, and they often study and theorize about societal transformations. Likewise, no actual example of prophecy, ancient or modern, can be fully grasped apart from economic circumstances—and thus prophets have never been merely consumed by spiritual abstractions.

Consider, for example, the confrontation between the high priest Amaziah and the prophet Amos at Israel's national sanctuary in Bethel as depicted in

Amos 7:10–17. The story may initially seem to prove that there is a fundamental opposition between prophecy and economics: the prophet speaks about a future that is at odds with the present (see 7:9, 11), and the priest reveals his commitment to the status quo by censuring and attempting to deport the prophet (7:12–13). Sounding like an economic advisor, Amaziah implores the deplorable prophet to find a more receptive market for his message: "Go, flee away to the land of Judah, earn your bread there, and prophesy there" (7:12). And this high priest describes Bethel—which literally means "God's house"—as "the king's sanctuary, and it is a temple of the kingdom" (7:13). Although he is a priest, Amaziah's imagination appears constrained to the terrestrial perspective of a national economist committed to the reigning order and its royal sovereign.

Amos' response, however, casts Amaziah in a quite different light. Amaziah appears out of touch with his circumstances and engaged in a desperate, even idealistic effort to suppress any hint that an element within his world may open it to an alternative future. First, Amos rejects Amaziah's suggestion that his prophetic activity has anything to do with an economic logic of exchange, i.e., for bread (7:14–15). The prophet is uninterested in profit. In fact, he describes gaining the prophetic position from which he speaks through Yahweh's removal of him from economic activities (7:15). Amaziah thus appears to misunderstand Amos' prophecy because he considers it only from the limited, economic perspective of a job. Moreover, the content of Amos' prophetic critique is primarily concerned with present and past circumstances, including economic conditions. And the futures that he predicts for Amaziah, for the king, and for Israel involve deeply economic matters. Amaziah even betrays some degree of awareness of the vulnerability of the status quo when he reports to the king, "the land is not able to bear all [Amos'] words" (7:10). In short, the conflict initially appears to be between a royal bureaucrat concerned with present realities and a prophet speaking about an alternative future. But ultimately, this is a story about a priest's idealistic effort to constrain all possible futures within the framework of the status quo, and the prophet's insistence on viewing the present as shaped by and toward alternative possible futures. Far from being opposed to economics, prophecy in biblical literature turns out to be inextricably entwined with economic matters. Perhaps they did not have the tools of modern economists, but ancient Israelite prophets addressed the entire range of matters under the purview of the academic discipline.

This chapter focuses on what we can say with some confidence about economic conditions in Southwestern Asia from the late eighth through the early sixth century BCE, as well as on how these economic realities shaped the lives, discourse, and concerns of the Israelite prophets whose words ultimately and through complex processes of mediation made their way into what would become biblical literature. Of course, the economy cannot be isolated from larger social, political, legal, cultural, religious, and other factors. So those factors will necessarily be considered in their relation with the economy even though the primary concern will remain the economy and how it matters for our understanding of Judahite and Israelite prophecy in roughly the final two centuries of the Iron Age.

Theorizing the Ancient Economy

This chapter approaches the ancient economy informed by the long, rich tradition of Marxist economic analysis, especially as developed in Roland Boer's 2015 book, *The Sacred Economy of Ancient Israel*.[1] In that work, Boer identifies five institutional forms within the ancient economies of Southwest Asia: subsistence survival, kinship-household, patronage, (e)states, and tribute-exchange. The changing and different relations among these institutional forms enable Boer to track changes over time and differences between places. Boer demonstrates that one or another of the institutional forms functions as dominant within a particular regime. The three regimes that Boer distinguishes include the subsistence regime, in which the institution of subsistence-survival is dominant; the palatine regime, in which the institution of patronage or (e) states is dominant; and the plunder regime, in which tribute-exchange is the dominant institutional form. These three regimes variously coexisted in different times and places in ancient Southwest Asia, and together, Boer writes, they constitute "the internal workings of the mode of production I call *the sacred economy*."[2]

More historical details are provided below, but in the eighth and seventh centuries BCE the Neo-Assyrian Empire's regime of plunder became as insatiable as it was unsustainable. It relied on directly plundering subjugated populations, and it supplemented that wealth and value acquired through booty with regular income that was extracted through another form of plunder, albeit less direct, namely, the requirement of tribute from subjugated peoples.

---

1. Boer, *Sacred Economy*. See also the review essays by Hankins ("Introduction"), Chaney ("Some Choreographic Notes"), Sharp ("Fields and Forced Labor"), Keefe ("Religion"), Erickson ("Rethinking"), Adams ("Benevolence"), and Brueggemann ("Reading Mistakenly"), plus Boer's response ("Reply"), published in *Horizons in Biblical Theology* 38.

2. Boer, *Sacred Economy*, 2 (italics original).

In both cases, the empire demanded direct payment as well as various forms of compulsory labor. The empire required such plunder to fund numerous construction and rebuilding projects, large armies that annually moved many miles and engaged in violent conflict, and finally, a large administrative bureaucracy of scribes, priests, prophets, artists, artisans, and their ilk. In addition to the direct compulsory labor for imperial projects, the plunder of booty no less than the plunder of tribute depended upon surpluses extracted from local laborers, largely through palatine (e)states. The palatine regime and the plunder regime are both regimes of extraction. Only the subsistence regime organizes social life and labor for nonextractive ends, namely, for allocation. The subsistence regime is driven by the need to allocate and reallocate labor, technology, and produce for the purpose of survival rather than surplus.

As is already clear from this brief economic sketch of ancient Southwest Asia, such a Marxist analysis always approaches the economy as already shaped by the dynamics of politics, society, culture, law and other spheres. At times Marxist analyses have been criticized for adopting a reductive approach to political, religious, and cultural forms as mere expressions of a foundational economic base that is determined by control over the means of production. But among the various Marxist approaches developed over the last half century in particular, many have advanced nonreductive frameworks that are capable of attending to the relative autonomy of various aspects within a social formation such as the juridical, political, or cultural. The corresponding risk of this approach, of course, is that the semiautonomous nature of religion, for example, becomes a permission slip for the critic to treat religious phenomena as uninflected by economic and other conditions. The point, however, is to grasp both how a particular cultural form is constituted within particular economic conditions as well as how it may function with relative autonomy with respect to those conditions. And relatedly, power dynamics and political relations are always present prior to or at least coconstitutive with economic relations. Power differentials and hierarchical relations, which paradigmatically function through relations of credit and debt, condition who produces what, with what kind of labor and technology, and the relations of humans to their economic activities.[3]

As a final comment about the Marxist economic approach adopted here, just as the economy ultimately cannot be approached in isolation, so too is it insufficient to approach the economy simply in conjunction with the other facets of political and social life mentioned above. The ultimate object of analysis

3. For more on this in the current climate, see Lazzarato, *Making of the Indebted Man.*

needs to be what Kojin Karatani, for example, refers to as social formations that consist of combinations of distinct *modes of exchange*.[4] Social formations are not constituted by combining a particular political regime with a particular economic structure or with particular norms or legal regulations, for instance. There is instead an intersectional dynamic among these various spheres such that a social formation always possesses characteristics and powers that are more than the sum of its constituent parts. This point is especially clear when considering particular examples. To take some that are directly pertinent to this chapter, the function of credit, debt, land tenure, or even genealogical and ethnic relations, will not be identical in different social formations. Nomadic or seminomadic peoples in places and times where land is abundant tend to have much looser ethnic sensibilities and highly malleable genealogies, as people regularly join and depart the group. Where land is more scarce and/or the social group is more sedentary, genealogies can become more rigid and ethnic sensibilities more determinative of one's labor and status. This brings me to the second theoretical foundation for this chapter's approach to the economy, namely, comparative analyses across cultures by scholars informed by the social sciences.

Comparative sociological and cultural anthropological studies have shrewdly discerned deep economic patterns that characterize different types of social formations. Here again, I am influenced by the work of other economic historians. Roland Boer, for example, relies on Soviet-era Russian scholars who advanced our understanding of what Marx called the Asiatic mode of production.[5] In particular, they illuminate the relations between ruling-class estates that extract from producers and allocative villages geared toward subsistence survival. Across various cultural contexts, the emergence of palatine and temple estates occurs in tension with rural agriculture as the former struggle to secure laborers and the latter resists such attempts in various ways. Boer also benefits from the insights into ideology, social stability, and change that were initially developed by so-called *régulation* theorists in France.[6]

Régulation theory focuses on the particular cultural forms, beliefs, assumptions, and institutions that offer ideological support for any specific organization of the economy. In light of *régulation* theory, changes and continuities in the ancient economy can be understood as a result of shifts in the institutional forms that play a determinative role in different regimes. So, for example,

4. Karatani, *Structure of World History*.
5. See, for example, Boer, *Sacred Economy*, 28–31.
6. See, for example, Boer, *Sacred Economy*, 31–41.

the period on which this chapter focuses can be grasped as a period in which the politically dominant institutional form in Israel and then in Judah shifts from ruling class (e)states to tribute-exchange that aims primarily at provisioning foreign empires.

In this chapter I also draw from the work of biblical scholars such as Marvin Chaney, D. N. Premnath, and Norman Gottwald, whose analyses of Israelite and Judahite societies have benefited from the evolutionary sociohistorical work of Gerhard Lenski and Marvin Harris. Despite their differences, the latter theorists propose that human societies can be separated into distinct types primarily on the basis of the "society's *overall technological efficiency*," which is determined on the basis "of their basic techniques of subsistence."[7] These comparativists also consider the influence of other factors such as environmental differences, the rate of participation in the military, political differences, and more. On the basis of Lenski's typology, ancient Israel and Judah fit the generic category of agrarian societies primarily because (i) unlike *horticultural* societies, their use of the plow and traction animals to cultivate fields enables a significant increase in economic production; (ii) unlike *maritime* societies, agricultural rather than commercial activities provide the chief source of economic surplus; and finally, (iii) unlike modern *industrial* societies, humans and animals supply the chief sources of energy for production. Of course, significant differences exist among societies that fit the generic type of agrarian, but a disciplined comparison between Israel, Judah, and similar societies can contribute to more informed questions that one may pose about the structures, processes, and related phenomena within any one of those societies.

The Economies of Late Iron Age Israel and Judah

Evidence from multiple sources attained through various disciplines strongly attests to major changes in the political economies of Israel and Judah in the Iron III period, which covers roughly 800–587 BCE. Several scholars in the last half century have produced syntheses of these societal shifts. Although there are some differences and disagreements about particular details, historians largely agree about the broader contours of the changes that occurred. Archaeological and other material evidence suggests that the separate kingdoms of Israel and Judah experienced relatively stable conditions early in this period, up to the middle of the eighth century. At the local level, Neo-Assyrian military campaigns neutralized the threats posed to the kingdom of Israel by

7. Lenski, *Power and Privilege*, 93 (italics original).

neighboring Syria at the turn of the eighth century.[8] At the imperial level, the Neo-Assyrian Empire did not begin reasserting its presence in ways that deeply impacted the area until Tiglath-Pilesar III began a series of military campaigns in 738. This early period of stability permitted some demographic and territorial growth, as well as the production and accumulation of an increased amount of wealth.

Evidence from the material record suggests that an increased level of centralized control over agricultural production emerged in the late eighth century BCE. Storage jars become standardized in shape and size and stamped with a label (*lmlk*) that associated them with the king.[9] They appear to have functioned as part of distribution networks that were broader than before. The type of jar that later gets stamped already appears in the record in the late ninth and early eighth centuries.[10] The system of stamp impression appears in the late eighth century, as attested by the data from Lachish III and related destruction layers confidently dated to 701.[11] Multiple seal types are attested at Lachish, and recent analysis suggests that there are early and late types already by 701, and that this administrative system continues for six more centuries.[12] These stamped jars likely functioned as part of an administrative transformation of agricultural production as a result of Judah's increased integration into the Neo-Assyrian Empire, but the political significance of this administered economy surely changed over time given the protracted history of the system. This economic system begins in earnest with the reestablishment of Assyrian sovereignty over Syria-Palestine in the mid-eighth century, so it was likely inaugurated as an effort to accommodate imperial demands. "We have an Assyrian administrative document that clearly details the arrival of Judean tribute bearers during the reign of Sargon [r. 721–705] (SAA vol. 1 letter 110, Nimrud Letter 16), and it is highly likely that Judah continued to pay tribute during much of this period."[13] For the subsequent century of Assyrian rule in the area, biological remains "point to the heavy intrusion of Assyrian imperial policy into local economies."[14] In short, the shock and weight of Assyrian demands for tribute likely instigated efforts to administer the economy to increase production.

8. See, for example, Miller and Hayes, *History*, 327–47.

9. *Lmlk* is a Hebrew seal imprint commonly found on jars, meaning "to/for the king."

10. See Shai and Maeir, "Pre-*lmlk* Jars"; and Sergi et al., "Royal."

11. See, for example, Na'aman, "Sennacherib's Campaign," 72–73.

12. See Lipschits, "Judah."

13. Aster, "Shock," 481.

14. Chaney, "Political Economy," 39.

The storage jars strongly suggest an increased level of centralized control over the economy, and while their appearance is correlated with increased pressure on Southwest Asia from Assyrian rulers, the political significance of the jars and the changes to which they attest remain uncertain, especially for the late eighth century when Judah, under King Hezekiah, rebelled against Assyria. Many jars were discovered at sites concentrated in the Shephelah, which were destroyed by Sennacherib's devastatingly punitive campaign in 701 BCE. The significance for the Assyrians of subduing this rebellion is evident in the most elaborate and memorable reliefs from Sennacherib's palace in Nineveh. These in fact provide the only battle portrait of Sennacherib ever discovered.

As others have suggested, the agricultural production that filled Judah's jars may have been driven by the Judahite kingdom's anti-imperial resistance against Assyrian hegemony—and thus not primarily by the desire to extract surpluses for the acquisition of luxury items for a few elites. That is, the need to provision the people in anticipation of an imperial response to colonial resistance may have led to the accumulation of these storage jars. Or if their contents were collected for the purposes of trade organized to import military and/or building materials into Judah, this trade could plausibly have been motivated by the realistic awareness that an assertion of sovereignty in opposition to the empire needed to be backed by a well-heeled military and strong defensive fortifications.

Of course, none of these scenarios precludes the possibility that native elites were perpetuating imperial and domestic exploitation of the peasant majority before, during, or after Hezekiah's revolt. And of course, there are imported items in the material record that would not have helped resist imperial troops. Even still, given the anti-imperial rebellion that instigated the counterrevolutionary violence, it is surely conceivable that this administrative system served purposes beyond exploitation sanguine to imperial and/or elite interests. And Assyria's response certainly suggests that they viewed the revolt as a serious offensive. In other words, the *lmlk* jars could signify several things at once: increased production, increased centralization, but also a potential, namely, the potential for regional power that, coupled with Judahite resistance, led to the Assyrian aggression.

Regardless of the various potential political valences at the end of the eighth century, the royal storage jars and other evidence from the material record strongly suggests that economic practices and social relations underwent significant transformations in the Iron III period. And despite ongoing subjection to foreign imperial rule, these changes clearly strengthened the power of the crown and the ruling elites centered in Jerusalem. Power is complex, however, and rarely serves a singular interest. These shifting power dynamics also constituted the conditions for the contemporaneous changes that occurred in the nature of prophecy in Israel.

Before turning directly to prophecy, however, there is more evidence from the material record that helps paint a fuller picture of these changes in late Iron Age Israel and Judah. First, ostraca discovered in Samaria "document the flow of oil and wine to Israelite court officials from upland estates."[15] The ostraca refer to "vintage wine" as well as "washed oil," which likely refers to a special labor-intensive refining process for producing olive oil in the form of a luxury good.[16] As Boer writes, "for subsistence agriculture, the only time luxury foods are eaten is during feasts; for societies marked by sharp class distinctions, luxury becomes an everyday item for the ruling class."[17] Hundreds of imported ivory fragments, some inlayed with stone and glass, have been recovered in archaeological excavations, and the increase in social stratification that they index is suggested by the fact that most were concentrated in the royal palace in Samaria, the capital city of Israel.[18] Early in this period, however, the Northern kingdom of Israel quickly declined in the face of Assyrian might. First they submitted to Assyrian rule and ceded the territories of Gilead, Dor, and Megiddo. After their subsequent rebellion against Assyria, Samaria was taken and destroyed in 721 BCE, and the ruling elite were forcibly deported to other areas of the empire. Israel's territories then became provinces in the Assyrian Empire, with parts of them inhabited by newly arrived settlers.

With the destruction of the Israelite kingdom, including many major regional centers in addition to Samaria, Judah and its capital city of Jerusalem soon became considerably more impressive and influential even as this increased urbanization and integration into the imperial economy placed a considerable burden on the majority of the populace Various extensive construction projects, including numerous new domestic structures that appear in the seventh-century strata of the capital city, transformed Jerusalem and other parts of Judah. As Daniel Pioske notes, a number of these new domiciles "were built for more affluent citizens . . . as indicated by the incorporation of fine ashlar masonry, porto-Ionic capitals, and sheer size." In short, "Jerusalem came to

15. Chaney, "Political Economy," 38.
16. See Veen, "When Is Food a Luxury?" Cf. King and Stager, *Life in Biblical Israel*, 96.
17. Boer, *Sacred Economy*, 62 n.22.
18. See Dever, "Social Structure," 424.

dominate Judah as it never had before in the city's history."[19] Outside Jerusalem, new settlements also appear in patterns that suggest a centralized authority organized their development.[20] In addition, "Marine archaeology has discovered two Phoenician ships dating to this period, still laden with the standardized wine amphorae they were carrying to Egypt when they were sunk by a storm off the Philistine coast."[21] These ships provide some evidence of trade exports in bulk goods, just as increases in evidence of luxury items, building supplies, and military equipment attest to some importing of goods.

The exact political significance of these findings remains unclear. We do not know whether the Phoenician ships carrying Judahite wine amphorae to Egypt were intended to return with luxury items to display the wealth and secure the power of a few elites, with military *matériel* to help deliver the nation from imperial power, or something else entirely. The fact that Sennacherib's officials taunt King Hezekiah for relying on Egypt in 2 Kgs 18:21 may suggest that trade with Egypt at the time was more likely to have been motivated by military interest in independence rather than economic efforts at extraction. And even if the exportation of Judahite wine was intended to secure independence, what was driving such efforts? A local elite attempting to increase their wealth and power? Or, perhaps it was a desire to return to a subsistence economy such that, as Isaiah says to Hezekiah, the people shall again eat what they sow, and eat what they reap, and "the surviving remnant of the house of Judah shall again take root downward and bear fruit upward" (19:29–30)? Regardless, Judahite efforts to resist imperial domination were unsuccessful, so history offers no further evidence for such motivations. I raise such alternative possibilities (i) to account for the historical evidence for anti-imperial rebellion, and (ii) because I am theoretically committed to approach the political sphere as, in Althusser's words, semiautonomous in relation to the economy.[22] In any case, such trade could only have occurred by means of the production and extraction of a surplus, and there was clearly a lot of extraction following Hezekiah's reign.

Such extraction and the growing class stratification that it served are evident in the material remains of luxury and imported items dating to the late Iron Age. For example, Pioske lists the following evidence of Jerusalem's prosperity and participation in international trade: "ornate boxwood (*buxus*

19. Pioske, *David's Jerusalem*, 86.
20. See Premnath, *Eighth Century Prophets*, 45–56.
21. Chaney, "Political Economy," 36.
22. See Jameson, *Political Unconscious*, 260–78.

sp.) furniture imported from southern Turkey and northern Syria, wine jars brought into the capital from Greece and Cyprus, intricately decorated shells from the Red Sea, fine pottery from Assyria, and ostraca detailing the export of grain and olive oil."[23] Moreover, Jerusalem appears to have tripled in size in the mid-eighth century BCE. A recent archaeological study of its population estimates that it reached a population of around eight thousand inhabitants in the late eighth century BCE, after the fall of Samaria in 722 and before the destruction wrought by Sennacherib in 701 that reduced the population to around six thousand.[24] As noted above, it apparently grew again over the course of the seventh century BCE, as did the kingdom of Judah, until it reached another zenith during the reign of Josiah as the center of economic, political, and religious life in the region while the Assyrian Empire crumbled.[25]

Archaeological evidence attests to several different types of habitations in the Iron III period, which likely correspond to different roles played in the administration of the kingdom.[26] In addition to the haphazardly constructed residences in small villages, one also finds small towns with buildings that likely functioned as storage facilities for grain and/or for the fermentation of wine made from grapes collected from peasants in the town's vicinity. These towns also contained presses for the grapes and olives used in the production of wine and oil. The density of such towns increases in proximity to the capital cities of Jerusalem and Samaria, which suggests that the monarchic administrations likely used many such towns as sources of labor and revenue, but it is unlikely that they all participated in the royal economy. They arose primarily in order to meet local "needs in production and trade. Agriculturalists lived here and worked the surrounding lands, just as the villagers in their own settings, but these towns also lent themselves well to the small-scale manufacture of goods such as pottery, textiles, and metal objects."[27]

Administrative structures also appear in the record. These arose to serve the extractive economic needs of the kingdom. Unlike the towns previously

23. Pioske, *David's Jerusalem*, 88.

24. Geva, "Jerusalem's Population."

25. See Keel, *Geschichte Jerusalems*, 512–17; Lipschits, *Fall and Rise*, 20–29; and Na'aman, "Josiah," 216–17. Scholars debate whether Jerusalem's population peaked in the late eighth or later in the seventh century. For the former, consensus position, see, e.g., Broshi and Finkelstein, "Population of Palestine." For the latter, see, e.g., Faust, "Settlement Dynamics," 28.

26. For more information on the following classifications, see Knight, *Law, Power, and Justice*, 161–73. See also Herzog, "Settlement"; Herzog, "Cities"; Herzog, *Archaeology of the City*; and Frick, *City in Ancient Israel*.

27. Knight, *Law, Power, and Justice*, 163.

mentioned, these were often fortified and contained large production centers for wine and olive oil, and storage facilities for collecting taxes in goods in kind. These also likely housed some military presence in addition to administrative officials. Even larger and fewer in number, royal cities also appear that seem to have been most important for the kingdoms' control of regions in the eighth and seventh centuries BCE. In the Northern Kingdom of Israel, these include Megiddo, Hazor, Gezer, and Dan. In the smaller Southern Kingdom of Judah, these include Lachish and Azekah. Royal cities differ from the administrative centers in that they have monumental architecture associated with the kingdom such as a palace, temple, open ceremonial and gathering spaces, large four- or six-chambered gates, "quarters for the military, stables, water systems, storehouses, courtyards, and the like. Some could have had special functions; for example, Megiddo may well have been a large breeding and training center for horses . . . All of these cities were built according to comprehensive plans developed by official architects working in the service of the king."[28] Finally, there were the capital cities of Samaria and Jerusalem that were much like the royal cities, only larger and more impressive in size and in constructed space. Whereas Samaria was destroyed in 722 BCE and then rebuilt by the Assyrians, Jerusalem ballooned in size and area over the late eighth and throughout the seventh century BCE, likely a result of a combination of factors, including reproduction and immigration from the former kingdom of Israel and from the western regions that Sennacherib took from Judah and gave to the Philistine cities on the coast. At the end of the Iron Age, Jerusalem's size, power, and prominence within the kingdom of Judah had grown so dramatically that when Nebuchandrezzar destroyed it in the early sixth century BCE, the kingdom of Judah was utterly decimated and quickly disintegrated "into a decentralized and de-urbanized region of humble villages and small towns."[29]

Among the complex factors responsible for making Jerusalem's consolidation and extension of royal power possible, population levels—although notoriously difficult to estimate—appear to have been enormously important. Population levels in general were major determinants in the distribution and concentration of power in the ancient world. In the macrosociological work of Gerhard Lenski, for example, population and technology largely determine the shape of different types of human societies.[30] As Boer emphasizes, land was rarely scarce in the ancient world. Consequently, there was often some degree

28. Knight, *Law, Power, and Justice*, 166.
29. Pioske, *David's Jerusalem*, 137. Cf. Carter, *Emergence of Yehud*, 216–25.
30. See Lenski, *Power and Privilege*.

236 ECONOMICS AND EMPIRE IN THE ANCIENT NEAR EAST

of freedom for peasants to live outside the large estates directly supporting the elite who were concentrated in urban areas. This relative freedom may have meant a life working less efficiently on difficult land, but such a tradeoff was likely more favorable than the alternative. However, evidence shows that the population density in Judah increased significantly in the late Iron Age.[31]

The extent to which there was "population saturation," as Chaney puts it, is a matter of some dispute.[32] For example, Zertal's twenty-three-year survey of Manasseh concluded that the density of inhabited sites reduced by two-thirds in the region around the former capital of the Northern Kingdom.[33] Nevertheless, the demographic rise in Judah predictably accompanied an increase in urban centers and the appearance of settlements in previously uninviting areas such as western Samaria and south into the Negev.[34] The majority of the population remained as peasants in villages and towns. Yet the demographic rise and the increase in urban centers limited peasant mobility and facilitated the ability of the elite to control peasant labor and extract higher surpluses. Douglas Knight writes, "Even though ancient Israelite cities were very small by today's standards, in comparison to the villages around them they loomed as centers of power and resources, visibly evident in their fortifications, gates, palaces, temples, public spaces, and wealthier dwellings."[35] The extension of the kingdom of Judah into previously unsettled areas in the southern desert both compensated for the fertile land lost in the Shephelah after Sennacherib's campaign and linked Judah with the Arabian trade routes prized by the Assyrian

31. See Chaney, "Political Economy," 38, 48; Chaney, "Some Choreographic Notes," 139–40; and Premnath, *Eighth Century Prophets*, 70–72.

32. According to Faust, *Archaeology*, 3: "The intensity of settlement in Iron Age II, particularly in the eighth century (and in parts of Judah also the seventh century), also contributes to our knowledge, since this was a period of demographic peak: a large proportion of the *tells* were settled, usually over extensive areas." Yet, as Faust elsewhere reports, "following Sennacherib's campaign, much of Judah was underpopulated during the seventh century BCE." (Faust and Weiss, "Judah, Philistia," 74.).

33. See the figures and table depicting the distributions of inhabited sites in the kingdom of Israel versus the Assyrian province of Samaria in Zertal, "Province of Samaria," 402–3. Zertal concludes from his survey that only one in three sites remained in the region of Samaria (401). See also Itach, "Kingdom of Israel," 67: "Most of the devastated sites were not rebuilt. In some of the cities, a poor settlement presence was identified and no evidence exists of fortified sites, following the Assyrian destruction. The state administration was gone, and the industrial centers shifted to other countries in the vicinity, such as Judah and Philistia."

34. See Premnath, *Eighth Century Prophets*, 51–56; Chaney, "Political Economy," 38; and Chaney, "Some Choreographic Notes," 140.

35. Knight, *Law, Power, and Justice*, 75.

elite.[36] This extension involved an enormous outlay of labor in the seventh century not only in construction projects including multiple fortresses, but also in the development of dry-farming practices.[37]

The means by which a surplus was produced in Iron III also appears to have left traces in the material record. A variety of evidence suggests that agricultural practices changed in this period such that regional specialization increased as did the uniformity of productive technologies, which in turn increased the productive capacities of land and labor. The pottery record transitions from varied, locally produced, and small-type wares to "mass-produced, limited variety forms ideal for more efficient transport and distribution of goods."[38] Some technological developments also appear in the material record. For example, the beam press became more widely used in olive oil production.[39] And archaeological surveys indicate that rock-cut processing installations for olives and grapes increased markedly in the eighth century BCE.[40] Though significant, such technological innovation was likely less significant for the increased levels of production and efficiency than the shift to regional specialization of agricultural activities.[41] Grains were increasingly grown in the lowlands and foothills, herding increased in the Negev and less arable areas, more cisterns were hewed for seasonal watering holes, and terraces were built in the uplands to increase the output of viticultural and olive planting activities.

While village life persisted for those who remained engaged in subsistence-based production, in the Iron III period the centralized power of the cities to command economic practices increased in ways that were geared toward increased efficiency. The cost of such measures included decreased sustainability, which taxed the lives and labor of village inhabitants caught in the web of such power. These changes had a transformative effect on the Judahite economy and society. Chaney explains, "Upland fields previously intercropped to provide a mixed subsistence for peasant families were combined into large

36. See Byrne, "Early Assyrian Contacts."

37. The fortresses include Tel Ira, Horvat 'Uza, and Horvat Radum, on which see Beit-Arieh, Tel 'Ira; and Beit-Arieh, Horvat 'Uza and Horvat Radum. On the agricultural practices in the Negev, see Herzog, "Beer-Sheba Valley."

38. Pioske, David's Jerusalem, 90. Pioske cites Zimhoni, Iron Age Pottery, 171–72; and Zimhoni, "Pottery Levels," 1705–7.

39. See Chaney, "Political Economy," 38–39.

40. See Dar, Landscape and Pattern, 147–90.

41. See Chaney, "Political Economy," 37–38; and Premnath, Eighth Century Prophets, 56–70.

vineyards and olive orchards producing a single crop for market."[42] Regional specialization clearly increased in this period, even if the record is in reality more mixed than the previous quotation suggests.[43] Pioske nicely summarizes some of the consequences: "The destruction of traditional agrarian networks, the loss of territory to Judah's neighbors after Sennacherib's campaign, and state acquisition of agricultural land by Jerusalem for the increased production needed to satisfy tributary requirements would have transitioned Judah from a patrimonial society centered on kin-based agrarian structures and land holdings to one in which geographical dislocation and loss of family property made the Judahite population increasingly vulnerable to the policy decisions of the Jerusalem ruling elite."[44]

As highlighted in the work of Chaney, Coomber, Pioske, Premnath, Yee, and others, stark social antagonisms shaped the end of Israel's and Judah's histories in Iron III. The political economies in monarchic Israel and Judah were split between two distinct and competing logics that funded "two conflicting systems of land tenure."[45] Much like Boer's distinction mentioned above between regimes of allocation for subsistence and reproduction versus regimes of extraction for surplus, Chaney characterizes this conflict in multiple places as an opposition between a commitment to sufficiency versus the pursuit of efficiencies.[46] And studies of peasant economies over the last sixty years have confirmed the appropriateness of drawing such distinctions.[47] The logic of the peasant economy defies what neoclassical economic theory would anticipate by adjusting labor and consumption practices for the purposes of optimal reproduction rather than, for example, maximal surpluses. In villages that typically only had seventy-five to one hundred members, each family and clan "had to be largely self-sufficient in food production, maintenance of shelter, and manufacture of everyday tools and utensils . . . producing all that it consumed and needed. In doing so, each community diversified in order to reduce risk, for example, by combining agriculture with herding, and transhumance was

---

42. Chaney, "Coveting," 312.

43. See, for example, Faust and Weiss ("Judah, Philistia," 75–76), who discuss the evidence that grain was grown in Judah in the seventh century in areas that are actually more ecologically suited for vines and trees, and grapes were grown and wine produced on the coastal plain near Ashkelon and not only in upland fields.

44. Pioske, David's Jerusalem, 89.

45. See Chaney, "Systematic Study," 68.

46. E.g., Chaney, "Bitter Bounty," 17; Chaney, "Coveting," 312; and Chaney, "Systematic Study," 73.

47. As attested, for example, by publications in the Journal of Peasant Studies.

practiced by others. Production was labor intensive, requiring as much involvement as possible from both genders and all ages in a family."[48] The competing logic that aims for maximal efficiency tends to compromise mechanisms that ensure the sustainable reproduction of an agrarian peasant society, such as crop rotation and diversification, fallowed fields, the extension of credit, and more.[49]

Prophets and Prophecy in Late Iron Age Israel and Judah

The prophetic figures from this period cluster around three distinct periods of political unrest. Four eighth-century BCE prophets lived in and around the period from 744 to 701 BCE, in which the Neo-Assyrian Empire reasserted its hegemony over Mesopotamia and the rest of Southwest Asia. The Neo-Assyrian Empire established this hegemony through violent domination, including massive military campaigns: first, in 734 when the kingdoms of Syria and Israel suffered heavily; second, in 722 when the capital city of Samaria and the kingdom of Israel were destroyed and transformed into a province of Assyria ruled by provincial governors; finally, in 701 when Assyria destroyed many towns in the kingdom of Judah, especially in the Shephelah, including the large royal city of Lachish.

Next, several other prophetic books in the Bible preserve texts related to the waning and downfall of the Neo-Assyrian Empire in the late seventh century BCE that was instigated in part by—and also paved the way for—the resurgence of the Babylonian Empire. Finally, the third set of texts considered in this chapter include those that deal with the devastation wrought by the Babylonians in the early sixth century BCE that led to significant population depletion, the destruction of the kingdom of Judah, and the territorial constriction of those living in the vicinity of Jerusalem. Primarily for reasons of spatial constraint, but also because of these major social, political, and economic

48. Knight, *Law, Power, and Justice*, 124–25.

49. See Chaney, "Political Economy," 40–42. For others, "urbanization in Jerusalem in the eighth and seventh centuries BCE was not accompanied ... by a transformation in the means of economic production" (Kaplan, "Credibility of Liberty," 198). While Kaplan is correct that this urbanization did not involve a shift from farm to factory akin to Western urbanization in the nineteenth and twentieth centuries CE, his emphasis on continuity obscures important changes in the content and character of agricultural practices influenced by (e)state organization during this period. Similarly, he rightly notes that village agriculture for subsistence-survival continued throughout the monarchic and postmonarchic periods: "tribal organization persisted ... Land-ownership practices and modes of agricultural production likewise continued" (199). However, he downplays and obscures the evidence that such regimes persisted in varying degrees of conflict and competition with (e)state-organized regimes of extraction. To Kaplan's larger point, however, such conflict makes ancient Israel and Judah only more suitable for the jubilee practices legislated in Lev 25.

devastations of the early sixth century, I do not consider prophetic texts that concern the events surrounding the downfall of the Babylonian Empire, the rise of the Persian Empire, and the constitution of a new social order in what becomes known as the province of Yehud. Thus I am largely eschewing later redactional materials in the books considered here as well as the books of Haggai, Zechariah, Joel, and Malachi.[50]

The ancient Israelite and Judahite books now preserved in Bibles and elsewhere do not provide direct access to the lives of the historical figures with which they are associated. The texts now rendered as books underwent long periods of redaction and recomposition and did not exist as books until periods much later than the centuries that concern us. Israel's traditions coalesced very late and exhibit complex pluriformity in periods when earlier scholarship tended to presume too much stability. Among others, recent works by scholars such as Ingrid Lilly, Eva Mroczek, and Nathan Mastnjak strongly suggest that the so-called biblical books did not initially exist in the material form of books on long scrolls. Lilly's analysis of the witness to Ezekiel in Papyrus 967,[51] Mroczek's discussion of the Dead Sea Scrolls manuscripts containing psalms as well as other texts,[52] and Mastnjak's article on the differing Greek and Hebrew versions of Jeremiah,[53] suggest that these books did not exist as extended, linear books on long scrolls, but rather as a multiplicity of shorter scrolls that were arranged independently and distinctly as extended books at times later than the original composition of their parts.

Because portions of the materials in these witnesses overlap whereas other portions differ to varying degrees, it appears that portions of these books may have stabilized earlier than others. That is, the differences between the versions suggest that stabilization occurred only in stages or partially with respect to the larger body of traditions associated with the Psalms, Jeremiah, and Ezekiel. This is in part a result of the textual material culture. Already in 1982 Menahem Haram argued that papyrus was likely used until the Second Temple period, before the writing material shifted to parchment and vellum by the time of the Dead Sea Scrolls in the Hellenistic and Roman periods.[54] Many traditions that were composed or compiled in the late monarchic, exilic,

50. Of course, determining what counts as early or late is a matter of wide scholarly debate.

51. Lilly, *Two Books of Ezekiel.*

52. See Mroczek, "Thinking Digitally"; and Mroczek, *Literary Imagination.*

53. Mastnjak, "Jeremiah as Collection."

54. Haran, "Book-Scrolls in Israel."

and early Persian periods likely existed as collections of shorter papyrus scrolls rather than as single, extended scrolls. Thus, for example, the different locations of the OAN and their different order in the LXX versus the MT of Jeremiah may not be a matter of the redaction of one version by the other, but rather a consequence of the technological shift to long-form leather scrolls that led to different, independent efforts at organizing a collection of literary traditions that existed on separate scrolls without a definitive rule for or a governing sense of their internal ordering.[55]

In what follows, I have sought to avoid such debates, even though it may occasionally be necessary to comment on the date of one text or another. While attempts have been made to avoid conclusions that depend on texts that scholars judge for good reason to be redactional additions from later periods, and to focus instead on those that offer some significant connections with economic matters in the late Iron Age, it is acknowledged that scholars take a great deal for granted in dating these texts. If Amos, for example, really existed as a historical figure in the late eighth century BCE, it is equally true that he said and did much more than we now have in the book of Amos, and that some of the materials now in the book originated with later scribes and prophets. So I have sought to begin with archaeological research and a reliable sociological framework in order to make sense of the texts within the Iron III period, but admits that some of these texts may be better understood as products of later periods.

A further methodological comment is necessary, however, for later texts can actually preserve traces and memories that better align with earlier periods than the material world in which they were composed. As Pioske writes, this is especially true "in texts that purport to portray a past. As Homeric scholars have illustrated . . . subtle references to a Mycenaean Bronze Age world are embedded within texts that were composed in a late Iron Age milieu; and, though written in the third century BCE, the fragments of Berossus' *Babyloniaca* included detailed information on a Neo-Assyrian past supported by (and likely based on) sources composed in the eighth–seventh centuries."[56] Furthermore, the decision to treat the material record first and the literary texts second is pragmatic and, as Pioske also notes, "not intended to suggest that the information gleaned from an archaeological analysis will always prove to be more meaningful, historically speaking, than that of the textual record."[57] Pioske's

55. See Mastnjak, "Jeremiah as Collection," 37.

56. Pioske, *David's Jerusalem*, 29.

57. Pioske, *David's Jerusalem*, 43. While this point is correct in principle, it can also be true that "archaeological material's one significant advantage over the literary evidence is that

methodological chapter offers an extended and insightful discussion of the sources, practices, and epistemological frameworks of modern historians, and he advocates for a dialectical approach that critically engages both the material and the literary record, as well as the relationship between the two.[58] In this chapter I have attempted to adopt a similar approach.

Most scholars agree that a scribal class emerged in the mid- to late eighth century BCE to such an extent that it could support the existence of prophetic figures such as Amos, Hosea, Isaiah, and Micah, as well as the recording and transmission of traditions surrounding them. Those traditions may not have become popular during the prophets' lifetimes, and they were certainly shaped and supplemented by later scribal tradents, but early materials are likely present in the books of Amos, Hosea (especially in the core of the book in chapters 4–11), Isaiah (especially in chapters 2–11 and 28–32), and Micah (especially in chapters 1–3).[59] Late in the seventh century BCE and early in the sixth, similar early materials are likely present in Nahum, Jeremiah, and Zephaniah. Even where scholars hypothesize the presence of early materials on the basis of linguistic and contextual evidence and arguments, we still cannot be sure about the full meaning of a particular text. Most contemporary scholars think that the earliest materials from the prophets, like similar materials from Israel's neighbors in Mesopotamia, consisted of oracular pronouncements such as the judgment against Israel in Hos 5:8–11. And many think that this specific oracle reflects the prophet's stance against the Syro-Ephraimite coalition resisting Assyrian hegemony around 735 BCE. However, this still does not inform us about the prophet's attitude toward the prophesied destruction of the Northern Kingdom. That is, is Hosea welcoming this destruction, trying to deflect it, or doing something else entirely? We simply cannot answer such questions.

I have decided to organize the following discussion of the biblical texts thematically for two main reasons. One is the previously mentioned distance separating the prophetic collections that we now have in Bibles from the historical figures and events to which they attest. Second, as discussed in the previous section, the underlying socioeconomic dynamic and issues remain fairly stable throughout the Iron III period despite particular changes and developments over time. A major transformation occurs in the sixth century BCE with the devastation brought by the Neo-Babylonian imperial armies, which essentially

---

it does not run the risk of being reflective of only one individual or a limited elite, but represents a wide spectrum of society" (Levine, *Visual Judaism*, 467).

58. See Pioske, *David's Jerusalem*, 8–62.

59. See Schmid, "Biblical Writings," esp. 495–97; and Kratz, "Prophetic Discourse."

decimated urban life in Judah, drastically depleting the population and severely constricting the size of the Judahite territory.[60]

The ensuing discussions do not aim to be exhaustive but should rather be taken as indicative of the importance of economic matters for prophetic texts and figures. And my isolating the economic issues from each other is artificial and potentially misleading because they are interrelated. Plus, the prophetic texts tend to address the economic issues as embedded within and intersected by moral, political, and religious dimensions. And of course, the prophetic texts also characteristically treat all these intersectional dimensions of human communities as fundamentally related to a divine dimension that modern Western thought tends to exclude from historical analysis.

One could scarcely find a passage in the prophetic corpus of materials from the late eighth to the early sixth centuries BCE that could be definitively described as unconcerned with economic issues. This is in part because economies are *embedded* in larger social realities, to use a term inextricably tied to the work of Karl Polanyi, by which I mean that all economies are inalienably intersected by other social dimensions. More specifically, however, numerous passages are concerned with what have been understood traditionally as directly economic matters. For example, interest and debt are the primary issue in the most detailed economic transaction recorded in biblical literature. In Jer 32, Jeremiah's cousin Hanamel is in danger of forfeiting his rights to some arable land because he apparently cannot meet his debt obligations and so will lose the land as collateral. The story resembles that of the widow who nearly loses her children to a creditor in 2 Kgs 4:1–7. Whereas Elisha saves the widow's sons by miraculously mobilizing her community around an abundance of oil, Jeremiah simply pays for the land in order to keep the rights to its usufruct in the family (Jer 32:1–44).[61]

As detailed above, a major trend in the Neo-Assyrian and Neo-Babylonian periods was the use of debt to transfer wealth from laborers to a class of creditors. The debtor who could not pay the interest owed on a loan was obligated to forfeit the land to the creditor, who could then lease the land back to the debtor. The land's occupancy and use may not have changed, but now the creditor received rent from the debtor and had access to the usufruct of the land.[62] As Mario Liverani argues, over the course of the first millennium BCE land becomes increasingly controlled by the elite and taken out of

60. See Lipschits, "Demographic Changes"; Lipschits, *Fall and Rise*.
61. On the Elisha story, see Brueggemann, *Tenacious Solidarity*, 14–16, 23–25.
62. See Wunsch, "Egibi Family's Real Estate," 408.

the hands of the families and kin groups.[63] Jeremiah's purchase of the land apparently saves his cousin from this general trend. In a context where scarcity can lead to such predation, Hanamel likely experienced Jeremiah's redemption as no less miraculous than the widow's encounter with Elisha's abundant oil.

In Ezekiel, debt and interest are also a primary concern. In Ezek 18, debt and interest actually define the identities of righteous versus wicked people, as well as what constitutes the difference between the two. The righteous person "returns the debtor's pledge . . . gives his food to a hungry person and covers the naked with a garment," apparently without putting the latter into debt, and "neither lends with interest (nešek) nor receives interest (tarbît)" (18:7–8; cf. 18:16–17). In contrast, the wicked person "oppresses the poor and needy . . . fails to return a pledge . . . lends with interest (nešek) and receives interest (tarbît)" (18:12–13; cf. 18:18). Of course, there are laws already in the Torah against taking interest (see Exod 22:25; Lev 25:36–37; Deut 23:19), but Ezekiel's claims are asserted independently and not based upon any legal authority (cf. Ezek 22:12).

Moreover, the prophets go even further by recognizing that law itself can become a tool wielded by those who are more economically secure to prey upon impoverished persons made vulnerable by their poverty. So, for example, Isaiah inveighs against lawmakers:

Ah, you who make iniquitous decrees,
    who write oppressive statutes,
to turn aside the needy from justice
    and to rob the poor of my people of their right,
that widows may be your spoil,
    and that you may make the orphans your prey!
(Isa 10:1–2; cf. 5:22–23; 33:15)

As Walter Brueggemann has written about this passage, "The writing of law turns out to be 'the writing of oppression' whereby exploitation of the vulnerable—widows and orphans [and, we should add, the poor]—is completely legal."[64] Jeremiah similarly attacks the failures of a legal system that is socially destructive, "their houses are full of deceit; consequently they have grown rich . . . they do not judge justly such that the orphan could prosper, nor do they defend justice for the needy" (5:27–28; cf. 8:10). In the following passage Jeremiah says nothing about legality but determines what is just or unjust and morally

63. See Liverani, "Land Tenure."
64. Brueggemann, Isaiah 1–39, 90.

acceptable or reprehensible on the basis of economic activities such as wage theft and the use of ostentatious building supplies:

> Woe to him who builds his house by unrighteousness,
>   and his upper rooms by injustice;
> who makes his neighbors work for nothing,
>   and does not give them their wages;
> who says, 'I will build myself a spacious house with large upper rooms',
> and who cuts out windows for it,
>   paneling it with cedar, and painting it with vermilion.
> Are you a king because you compete in cedar?
> Did not your father eat and drink and do justice and righteousness?
>   Then it was well with him.
> He judged the cause of the poor and needy;
>   then it was well.
> Is not this to know me? says the LORD.
> But your eyes and heart are only on your dishonest gain,
> for shedding innocent blood,
>   and for practicing oppression and violence. (Jer 22:13–17)

The praise of Josiah for judging "the cause of the poor and needy," immediately following the direct indictment against the crown for wage theft ("does not give them their wages") has led some to suggest that the praise "may actually be a reference to wage laborers on royal construction projects who replaced corvée."[65] In other words, Gottwald suggests that the prophet here praises the king's compensation to laborers for work previously completed as an unpaid obligation to the crown. In any case, the generational contrast is grounded in economic relations between the ruling elite and the laboring classes.

In a passage that happens also to be quoted in the book of Jeremiah (26:18), Micah similarly indicts the ruling elites, specifically naming military leaders and the support staff of religious functionaries:[66]

> Hear this, you rulers of the house of Jacob
>   and chiefs of the house of Israel,
> who abhor justice

---

65. Gottwald, "Social Class," 14. Corvée is a common form of forced labor feature in most agrarian societies.

66. Although there is some debate among commentators about whether the second term, here "chiefs," carries military connotations, Smith-Christopher's recent commentary makes a compelling case concerning the prominence of the military in the target of Micah's critiques, including here. See Smith-Christopher, *Micah*, 121–22.

and pervert all equity,
who build Zion with blood
    and Jerusalem with wrong!
Its rulers give judgment for a bribe,
    its priests teach for a price,
    its prophets give oracles for money;
yet they lean upon the LORD and say,
    'Surely the LORD is with us!
    No harm shall come upon us.'
Therefore because of you
    Zion shall be plowed as a field;
Jerusalem shall become a heap of ruins,
    and the mountain of the house a wooded height. (Mic 3:9–12)

Just prior to this passage, "Micah uses the imagery of cannibalism to speak of robbery and economic exploitation of the populace" (3:1–4).[67] Here in vv. 9–12 Micah attacks the urban elite for unjust and inequitable urban planning that brings bloodshed. Micah targets three classes of leaders for specifically economic iniquities: those with authority over legal matters take bribes, priests sell their religious instruction for a price, and prophets offer oracles for sale. Without making the connection explicit, Micah suggests that these corrupt leaders have developed a false sense of safety and security through the economic funding that they receive for their labor.

A similar indictment in Isaiah suggests that greed functions like a set of blinders preventing corrupt rulers from seeing or being concerned with those who are in need and likely also harmed by their own nefarious actions:

Your princes are rebels
    and companions of thieves.
Everyone loves a bribe
    and runs after gifts.
They do not defend the orphan,
    and the widow's cause does not come before them. (1:23)

A few verses earlier Isaiah attacks ritual sacrifices offered to the elites amid social injustice and without accompanying moral actions (see Isa 1:10–17). Highlighting the political context of Judah's vassalage to Assyria, Aster emphasizes the extent to which God's rejection of sacrifice here should be understood

---

67. Smith-Christopher, *Micah*, 110.

in contrast to Assyria's interest in tribute.[68] In Isa 2, the prophet speaks more vaguely against those who are "forsaking your people" (2:6 AT), yet the contributing factors are clearly described as economic matters of trade ("they high-five foreigners"; 2:6 AT) and treasury ("their land is full of silver and gold"; 2:7 AT), which of course also involve military *matériel* ("their land is full of horses and there is no end to their chariots"; 2:7 AT) and religious idolatry ("their land is full of idols"; 2:8). In short, the prophets could, and often did, speak about particular economic activities, such as kings collecting tribute and taking plunder (e.g., Isa 10:13–14; Hos 10:6); offerings to priests (e.g., Hos 6:6; Amos 5:21–24); using and abusing weights, scales, and measures (e.g., Ezek 45:10; Amos 8:5; Mic 6:10–12); trade, wages, profits, and commodities (e.g., Isa 23:17–18; Ezek 27); as well as debt instruments and interests (e.g., Ezek 22:12; Amos 2:6–8). In the following section, however, I turn to the more fundamental economic antagonism described above that defined the struggles of much of the population in the late Iron Age.

The Defining Economic Antagonism of Late Iron Age Israel and Judah

Although the concrete socioeconomic conditions serving as the background for prophetic critiques are often unclear, the sorts of economic changes described above in relation to the material record from Iron III repeatedly appear to provide what the "prophets presumed but did not state," to borrow a formulation from Marvin Chaney.[69] Beginning in the late eighth century BCE, key passages in prophetic literature reflect the struggle to name, understand, and respond to the kind of rapid agricultural intensification, political pressuring, legal finagling, and outright corruption associated with the material conditions described above and known from cultural-evolutionary studies of agrarian societies that transition from an economy aimed at allocation to one that is driven by extraction.[70] In several articles in particular, Chaney has closely analyzed examples of such passages in Isa 5:1–7; Amos 2:6–8, 13–16; Mic 6:9–15; and in Hosea's rhetoric of promiscuity.[71] These passages and others appear to allude to elite efforts to alter agricultural practices and replace the peasants' customary

68. See Aster, *Reflections of Empire*, chap. 7.

69. This is the subtitle of Chaney, "Political Economy."

70. In addition to the resources discussed and cited below, see also Coomber, "Prophets to Profits," esp. 217–19.

71. See Chaney, "Whose Sour Grapes?"; Chaney, "Producing Peasant Poverty"; Chaney, "Micah—Models Matter"; and Chaney, "Accusing Whom of What?"

rights to the land with the rights of their creditors to amass large estates for specialized crop production on which the peasantry would work, although now without the freedom to determine their labor practices or the fate of their land's surplus crops, and thus also in greater dependence upon, quite literally, the fruits of other people's labors.

For example, early in the book of Isaiah the prophet proclaims:

> My people—every one of their exactors is a gleaner,
>   and creditors rule over them.
> My people, your leaders mislead you,
>   and the course of your paths they confuse.
> Yahweh has taken his stand to litigate;
>   he stands to vindicate his people.
> Yahweh comes in judgement
>   against the elders of his people and their officials.
> "It is you who devour the vineyard;
>   the spoil of the poor is in your houses!
> What do you mean by crushing my people,
>   by grinding the face of the poor?" (3:12–15)[72]

Shortly thereafter the prophet sings the "Song of the Vineyard," which is followed by the first of a series of "Woe Oracles," strategically placed in response to the issues raised in the Song:

> Alas for those who, annexing homestead after homestead,
>   join field to field, until there is no place left,
>   and you are made to dwell alone in the midst of the land!
> Yahweh of hosts in my hearing:
> "I swear that the great houses shall be desolate,
>   large and fine ones without lordly inhabitant!
> For ten acres of vineyard shall produce but one bath,
>   and a homer of seed shall produce only an ephah!" (5:8–10)[73]

Both of these passages in 3:12–15 and 5:8–10 surround the "Song of the Vineyard" and castigate the elite for crimes concerning vineyards. The elite are indicted for devouring vineyards, exploiting the poor, and appropriating peasant-held landholdings for the purposes of accumulating excessive wealth that results in a tragically low yield from that land. In context, the elite are

72. This translation is taken from Chaney, "Whose Sour Grapes?," 110.

73. This translation is adapted from Chaney, "Whose Sour Grapes?," 110; and Davis, *Biblical Prophecy*, 71.

constructing many new vineyards, about which the prophet sings in 5:1–2, and as in that Song they are *expecting* high yields from maximized efficiencies (vv. 2, 4). So it is a bitter irony that the prophet's attack in the Song and in the Woe Oracle anticipates a devastatingly low yield. Grounded in the subsistence economy of agrarian peasants laboring to survive via sufficient production, the prophet is able to see past the mechanisms for maximizing efficiencies in the production of cash crops so as to criticize the social disintegration already underway and to foretell the economic devastation that will surely follow.

Hosea accuses the "rulers of Judah" of becoming "like those who remove boundaries" (5:10). While we cannot recover the full significance of this accusation, it suggests that an elite class both existed in the Southern Kingdom and engaged in the practice of (re)moving boundaries. The mere presence of marked boundaries likely implies the existence of a ruling class in control of lands at some distance from their daily lives. Agrarian peasant communities intimately familiar with their lands, every square cubit, do not require or use boundary markers. "Wealthier landowners," as Douglas Knight states, "especially those living in towns or cities and thus removed from their holdings, were not nearly so familiar with their lands and thus depended on boundary markers."[74] Clear boundaries are not typical in agrarian village life. Arable land was allocated and regularly redistributed among social units on various bases, including the social unit's abilities and resources, proximity to the plot, previous seasonal assignments, and more. Thus, references to a boundary, portion, or delimited plot of land in the context of village life are best understood as either a misleading projection of urban relations to the land onto rural villagers, or as references to "a moveable and reallocated land share" rather than "a field or plot of land."[75] In the context of Hosea's critique, both possibilities may be at play insofar as the urban elite were extending their relations with the land into additional regions with the result that the peasants' abilities to allocate their lands and determine agricultural practices were being directly undermined.[76]

In Jer 22:13–17, quoted above, Jeremiah offers a poignant critique of the ruling class for offenses similar to those discussed here. Yet he contrasts the current rulers with the previous reign of Josiah. For Jeremiah, Josiah raised the possibility that a ruler could be guided by the Torah's concern for justice. Josiah's descendants, however, have perpetuated a reality of exploitation. The excessive accumulation of luxury items by the ruling class, here represented by

74. Knight, *Law, Power, and Justice*, 147, see also 205–7.
75. Boer, *Sacred Economy*, 72–73.
76. See also, Premnath, *Eighth Century Prophets*, 107–8.

the spacious house of Josiah's son Jehoiakim, is made possible by wage theft and other practices that violate justice and lead to violence against neighbors and the ultimate annihilation of the ruling class (vv. 18–19). The prophet momentarily considers an alternative possibility in vv. 15–16, which Brueggemann has characterized as "one of the most stunning lines in the Bible." Brueggemann continues: "Yʜwʜ says, 'This is to know me!' Knowledge of God is intervention for the poor and the needy. Josiah knew that. He knew that solidarity of haves and have-nots is the way to well-being."[77] But, as Jeremiah recalls, Josiah's descendants did not link their future with the poor and needy, and so God promises them a bitter end.

Often, as is evident in numerous passages already discussed, the prophets' criticisms of the ruling classes attack their luxury items and other material displays of affluence that either brazenly disregarded or callously mocked their neighbors who were made socially and economically vulnerable by their own extractive practices. For example, Isaiah proclaims that the day of Yahweh will sink the fancy ships of Tarshish (2:16) just as it will bring down "every high tower" and "every fortified wall" (2:15). Taken together, the fortifications and the ships symbolize urban life, constructed by the labor of peasants pressed into corvée, supported by military might, and enriched by the exchange of goods like "cedars of Lebanon" and "oaks of Bashan" (2:13). Hosea similarly attacks the "palaces," "fortified cities," and "strongholds" of Israel and Judah (8:14). For Micah too, on the day of Yahweh the military *matériel* of horses, chariots, and fortifications will be destroyed (5:10–11 [Heb. 9–10]). And Amos inveighs against "houses of ivory" (3:15) and "beds of ivory" (6:4) upon which the nonproducing urban elites engage in conspicuous consumption and idle leisure.

In addition to offering severe criticisms of the ruling elite's exploitation of peasants and threats to their agrarian economy, the prophets also encouraged their communities to adopt more sustainable social and economic practices in the future. Moreover, the prophets were capable of offering such encouragement from more than one perspective. At times the prophets stood squarely in the midst of the peasant majority to imagine a future in which their subsistence-based agrarian economy would achieve hegemony and function outside the extractive mechanisms of large aristocratic (e)states. For example, Isaiah imagines the day when "the palace will be forsaken" (32:14), "the city will be laid low" (32:19), and justice and righteousness will be established in the wilderness and in the cultivated fields (32:16), which will bring peace, quiet, and

---

77. Brueggemann, *Tenacious Solidarity*, 330.

confidence (32:17) such that all Israelites will be happy agrarians with free-range oxen and donkeys (32:20).

Micah 3:9–12, quoted above, paints a similar picture of Jerusalem's monumental architecture crumbling so that "Zion should become a cultivated field" (v. 12). The best example, however, is probably Micah's well-known peace oracle that imagines the following future:

> He shall judge between many peoples,
>> and shall arbitrate between strong nations far away;
> they shall beat their swords into plowshares,
>> and their spears into pruning-hooks;
> nation shall not lift up sword against nation,
>> neither shall they learn war anymore;
> but they shall all sit under their own vines and under their own fig trees,
>> and no one shall make them afraid;
> for the mouth of the LORD of hosts has spoken.
> For all the peoples walk, each in the name of its god,
>> but we will walk in the name of the LORD our God forever and ever.
> (Mic 4:3–5)

A very similar although slightly shorter poem also appears in Isa 2:4. It may be that a shared tradition became associated with both prophets, or perhaps Micah creatively adapts an earlier oracle now found in Isaiah. If Micah supplemented an earlier version of an oracle that was more like the one currently found in Isaiah, then the additions may provide a window onto Micah's (or its editors') interests. Micah grounds Isaiah's vision of peaceful international relations in the classic Israelite ideal of a peasant economy characterized by egalitarian social relations. With demilitarization comes freedom from the burdens of the tax and labor systems that supported the military, as well as an end to the dominance of the elite whose interests the military primarily served.[78] And, in Mic 4:5, the prophet even imagines that the resulting circumstances will include a peaceful ecumenism among devotees of diverse religious traditions!

Another example of prophetic hope offered from the perspective of the peasantry is found in Jeremiah. Above I mentioned Jeremiah's vision of the ultimate destruction of exploitative institutions and players in Judah at the hands of the Neo-Babylonians. Beyond the destruction, however, Jeremiah envisions a future renewal of the people that is grounded, in Ellen Davis' words, in "a sustainable local economy composed of small landholders. That is the

---

78. See Brueggemann, "Vine and Fig Tree."

significance of the story (32:1–44) of Jeremiah's acquisition of a field in his village of Anathoth on behalf of his cousin Hanamel, who has evidently fallen into straits and been forced to sell off the family land, or some portion of it, as collateral for debt."[79] Jeremiah's purchase of the land redeems it from the control of the creditor class. This act symbolizes the future redemption of the people (v. 11) while also grounding, quite literally, that redemption in a specified plot of arable land, thereby, to quote Davis again, "giving hope a place."[80]

A second mode adopted by some prophets for imagining a more sustainable future in the late Iron Age may come as a surprise. Not without reason, many scholars for whom class is an essential analytic category tend to conflate the interests and actions of the king with other elites. Of course, it is true that elites are often able to link their interests and concerns. However, it is also true that the ruling classes are incapable of establishing a fully cohesive platform for their interests because those interests necessarily compete with one another, structured as they are by a logic of monopolization. Their interests inevitably come into conflict with one another and/or become impinged upon by other interests striving for monopolization. It is in this sense that Marx refers to the ruling class as a "struggle of enemy brothers."[81] They do at times band together in concerted efforts to maintain privilege and expand their power, but they are ultimately at war with one another in the interest of reducing another's share of surplus product so as to increase one's own share.[82]

In ancient Southwest Asia there were no businesses investing in various market strategies in order to put others out of business. However, the structural logic remains the same in that the ruling class functions as a band of warring brothers in contrast with the peasantry and the dispossessed, who share class interests with one another. This is perhaps most evident if we consider the practice of forgiving debts carried out by kings in this ancient world. Evidence that debts were canceled on a fairly regular basis exists from about 2500 BCE through the period under analysis in this chapter.[83] The result of

79. Davis, *Biblical Prophecy*, 162.

80. Davis, *Biblical Prophecy*, 162–66.

81. Marx, *Capital*, 3:362.

82. See also Lenski, *Power and Privilege*, 231: "Throughout the history of every agrarian society there has always been an almost continuous struggle for power between the ruler and the governing class. Though the outward form of these struggles has been highly variable, their basic character has always been the same: each party has constantly fought to maximize its own rights and privileges."

83. For more on this and the ensuing discussion, see Hudson, *And Forgive Them Their Debts*.

debt forgiveness was economic solvency, that is, the preservation of a functioning economy with "a land-tenured citizenry free from bondage. The effect was to restore balance and sustain economic growth" for the economy as a whole.[84] For those in the lending class to whom some of those debts were owed, however, such an act constituted a check on their efforts to accumulate wealth and to maintain an indebted underclass obliged to labor for them and not, needless to say, for themselves or for the king, the royal treasury, tax collector, and the like. The consequences of debt forgiveness did not disrupt the fundamental structure of society or eliminate inequalities, but rather offered reform measures that preserved a functioning social and political system. The class of those indebted and/or dispossessed, however, tends not to perceive the difference between reform and revolution as such a rigid dichotomy. Thus, in addition to the prophets' ability to articulate hopeful visions of the destruction of extractive regimes and of the constitution of subsistence-based, sustainable agrarian economies, they also sometimes sought to leverage the royal legion within the "warring brothers" to fight against their brethren in the creditor/predator class and on behalf of the peasantry and the dispossessed.

In 2 Kgs 18 we have evidence of such an alliance across class divisions being instigated from the top down, so to speak. There the Assyrian royal officer offers the inhabitants of Jerusalem terms of their vassalage. He promises the Judahites that surrendering to Assyria will bring peace and enable them to prosper and "eat from your own vine and your own fig tree" (2 Kgs 18:31). Accepting the terms offered by the Assyrian Empire would end the Judahite resistance. In other words, the officer sought a diplomatic alliance with the peasantry on terms that appealed to their desire for a citizenry free to work their own lands and in opposition to the military policies of the Judahite leadership. In his commentary on Micah, Daniel Smith-Christopher offers the following intriguing suggestion at the end of his discussion of this diplomatic effort: "*The book of Micah may well represent precisely the kind of insurrectionist thinking that the Neo-Assyrian armies hoped to instigate.*"[85]

If we grant Smith-Christopher's suggestive reading of Micah, we can add that Micah is not alone among the prophets. Jeremiah also provides a compelling example of a prophet participating in such an alliance with a faction from the ruling class. Jer 34 provides a fascinating narrative account of such an interclass alliance, even if it is ultimately a negative example without evidence attesting to its historicity. According to the narrative, after Babylonian forces

84. Hudson, *And Forgive Them Their Debts*, xi.
85. Smith-Christopher, *Micah*, 13 (italics original).

temporarily withdrew from the siege of Jerusalem in 588 BCE (Jer 34:21), the king was able to secure a commitment from the creditor class to forgive the debts of fellow Judahites and to free those who had become debt slaves (vv. 8–10, 15).[86] However, the text immediately reports that the creditor class of oligarchs was quickly able to reinstitute the debt economy and regain subjugated debt slaves (vv. 11, 16). From our perspective, several aspects of this story are particularly noteworthy. First, it suggests that the various Jubilee laws prescribing the manumission of debt slaves were at least on the horizon of Judah's social and political imagination.[87] Jer 34:14 refers explicitly to principles recorded in Deut 15:1–11 and Exod 21:1–6, without exactly corresponding to the circumstances underlying those laws. Whereas the latter concern individuals who are freed after seven years, the story in Jeremiah tells of a collective liberty for all debt slaves. Consequently, Carroll suggests that this situation is actually more similar to the Jubilee Year in Lev 25 than it is to the instructions for debt release in Exodus and Deuteronomy.[88] Carroll also notes that the regulations in Deuteronomy and Exodus curtail the practice of debt slavery, whereas the motivation for the act in Jeremiah suggests an end to it altogether: "so that no one should enslave their fellow Judean" (34:9).

Second, this story portrays the creditor class in the early sixth century BCE as so powerful that they were able to recuperate the losses incurred by the king's command for them to forgive the accumulated obligations of their indebted neighbors. Nevertheless, and however temporary, this story portrays the king as a primary agent behind a policy that would directly benefit the indebted class and cost the creditor class a significant amount of social power and economic wealth. Even if the liberty proclamation serves the crown's interests in some sense, this does not diminish the positive consequences of this liberty (again, however temporary) for those who were enslaved and indebted.

Commentators tend to speculate thoroughly about royal self-interests, and to downplay the potential consequences of such freedom for the indebted and enslaved. Moreover, many assume that the king is among those whom the prophet attacks for reneging on the covenant. However, the king is not mentioned in the lists of offenders in Jer 34:10 and 19. Those lists refer to officials and specifically mention the involvement of priests, which we expect in light of the fact that the covenant ceremony took place in the temple (v. 15). And while

86. According to Jer 37:5, 11, Babylon's temporary withdrawal occurred in response to Egypt's mobilization of forces to support the besieged Judahite towns.

87. Cf. Kaplan, "Credibility of Liberty."

88. Carroll, *Jeremiah*, 648.

it might otherwise be plausible to assume that the king participated with the offenders of this covenant, when Jeremiah next mentions the king in v. 21, it is as if the king were not part of the group criticized and cursed in vv. 19–20. Thus the text suggests that the king instigated the covenant to undermine competing upper-class interests and to garner the support and allegiance of the indebted class but was not part of those who reneged on the covenant. Nevertheless, when he reappears in v. 21, it is because Jeremiah includes him among those who would suffer negative consequences as a result of this violation of the covenant and the ensuing economic exploitation. Thus this text appears to illustrate a scene in which a faction of the upper class temporarily or strategically allies with the lower classes, yet that faction cannot ultimately alter their fate so long as they maintain their class affiliation.

Third, whereas this story pays minimal attention to the motivations and political wrangling that would have accompanied any such act, a brief detail in Jer 34:16 may suggest that it involved a direct concession of the creditors to the interests of those who were enslaved and indebted. According to the NRSV, the creditors set the male and female slaves "free according to their desire" (*ḥopšîm lĕnapšām*). Some understand this to mean that the slaves were simply freed so as to pursue their desires.[89] Yet it is certainly possible and, in my opinion, more plausible that the proclamation of liberty met the slaves' desire *for their freedom*. That is, the slaves' desire that the proclamation of liberty meets is not some vague set of differing interests but the concrete desire to be free from debt. When the text says that the slaves were freed according to their desire, it means that they were freed to live their lives rather than to satisfy their debts.[90]

Finally, the prophet appears to be involved in all of this in some way but the precise role that he plays remains unspecified. The introductory formula in Jer 34:8 initially seems awkward since no "word of Yahweh" appears until v. 12. This may be a narrative strategy of deferral that appears elsewhere in Jeremiah (see 32:1–6).[91] However, it also creates some ambivalence that implicates the prophet in the covenant and proclamation that the king makes "with all the people in Jerusalem" (v. 8). And we may be further inclined to imagine that Jeremiah played a part in such a covenant in light of the discussion above about the role that prophets could play as mediators in interclass alliances, and especially insofar as the story portrays Jeremiah in the midst of the conflict and

89. See, for example, Carroll, *Jeremiah*, 645.

90. The root of the word here translated "desire" is *npš*, which means "life."

91. See Brueggemann, *Commentary on Jeremiah*, 325n1.

clearly speaking on behalf of the debtors against the creditors once the latter break the covenant with the former.

This second mode through which prophets could encourage their communities toward more sustainable economic futures is often neglected in analyses that take class seriously. To my mind this is a serious blunder, since it neglects the extent to which class struggle is always intersected by various interests. Even Marx recognized that the proletariat had to form alliances lest, as he put it, their solo song become a swan song.[92] Finally, just as prophets could find common cause with factions in the conflicts among ruling elites, and just as a faction of the ruling elite could strategically concede to certain interests of the peasantry to gain stability if not an upper hand against a competitor, so this chapter would be incomplete without mentioning the many passages that remember Israelite prophets who raised their voices in support of reigning injustices and the ruling elite's interests in ways that were complicit with resource exploitation, patriarchal misogyny, expansive nationalistic militarism, mistreatment of the poor and vulnerable, and the like (e.g., Isa 9:14–16; 11:14; Jer 2:8; 8:8–11; Ezek 13:1–23; Mic 3:5–8, 11; 4:8, 13; Nah 3:1–7, 13; Zeph 2:9). That is, prophets were not universally linked with the interests of the peasantry, but were capable of siding both with as well as against them.

Conclusion

While Hebrew prophetic literature offers important insights into the first-millennium economics in Southwest Asia, a consideration of the economy is necessary for a sufficient understanding of prophetic literature and the peoples of the region. However, much work on biblical texts continues to be produced with little attention to economic issues.[93] No investigation of the biblical texts or consideration of the significance of the prophets is complete without attending in some way to such economic dynamics. Yet those considerations do not paint a singular or straightforward picture of the relationship between prophets and the political economy. On the one hand, as mentioned above, this is obvious from the many conflicts the texts report among prophets regarding the social, political, and economic content of their messages (e.g., 1 Kgs 22:1–28; Jer 28; cf. Deut 18:15–22). On the other hand, however, a more profound degree of

92. Karl Marx wrote this in the 1852 edition of "Eighteenth Brumaire," but then deleted it from the 1869 reprint. I owe this observation to my colleague Joe Weiss.

93. This was the central message of Gottwald's 1992 presidential address to the Society of Biblical Literature. So Gottwald, "Social Class," 21: "Our analysis of a text is never complete until we pose questions about social class, the answers to which will be more or less substantial or persuasive from case to case, as is true of any method."

uncertainty if not ambivalence characterizes even those prophets who were the most vehement social critics when we consider their role and their discourse against the broader horizon of Israel's and Judah's historical development. However critical prophets were within their particular contexts, and however supported they were by some among their peers with significant social capital (e.g., the family of Shaphan for Jeremiah in Jer 26:24; 29:3; 39:14; 40:5; 43:6), their critical voices repeatedly (even if to varying degrees) appear to be isolated and distanced from those in positions of public power. Moreover, we possess little evidence of the effectiveness of prophetic voices at effecting change.

Perhaps we simply lack evidence. But if in fact prophets were not especially effective agents of social change, then they were not only critics but also symptoms of social situations that merited their critiques but resisted the changes they recommended. The point here, in part, is that the extent to which we should understand prophetic voices as reactionary or progressive is a complex and delicate question that permits no clear or singular answer. Of course any answer depends in part on the particular prophets and their different social and historical situations, but I think that every answer will likely be some form of "both." Prophetic voices could be reactionary, at least

+ insofar as their socioeconomic critique aims at times at merely reforming what are structural circumstances of exploitation;

+ insofar as their messages reproduce some aspect of the exploitative situation such as through the use of patriarchal and misogynistic metaphors[94];

+ or insofar as their critique enables the displacement of political agency from an exploited collective onto the prophets' own relatively marginalized and isolated selves.

Yet prophetic voices were also progressive, at least

+ insofar as their prophetic critique captures the deep, structural social problems of their time;

+ insofar as their discourse about alternative futures summons their communities toward more tenacious social solidarity;

+ and insofar as their relatively marginalized positions both represent the

---

94. For differently insightful studies of gender, misogyny, and prophetic literature, see Weems, *Battered Love*; Yee, *Poor Banished Children*, esp. 81–134; and Graybill, *Are We Not Men?*

possibility of life outside the exploitative state, and indeed foreshadow the demise of the exploitative state at the end of the Iron Age.

In an age when the economy is no less (and in fact is much more) geared toward extraction as well as beset by fundamental limits foreshadowing its demise—whether through ecological catastrophe, nuclear warfare, global pandemic, financial collapse, political transformation, or some combination of these and more—the prophets occupy a particularly meaningful position for those who dream of an alternative and more sustainable future. They offer lessons about the temptation to and dangers of reactionary positions that preserve some sense of subjective distance and freedom (for the prophets among us) but fail to threaten the dominant ideology in any way. Yet the prophets also testify to the potential of and exemplify the life-altering consequences of faith in a God who desires and pursues alternative social, political, and economic realities that are geared toward more sustainable reproduction, committed to newfound disarmament, and devoted to developing deep attachments that enable vast social renewal. The prophets could be reactionary and progressive, wedded to the status quo and fierce social critics, strikingly vivid poets and beautiful theologians. They have bequeathed to us a rich legacy that yields no easy answers but rather issues an invitation to participate in their practices of witnessing, storytelling, testifying, complaining, caring, sharing, singing, performing, wondering, and praising.

Bibliography

Adams, Samuel L. "Benevolence and Justice in Extraction Economies." *HBT* 38.2 (2016) 167–72.

Aster, Shawn Zelig. *Reflections of Empire in Isaiah 1–39: Responses to Assyrian Ideology.* ANEM 19. Atlanta: SBL Press, 2017.

———. "The Shock of Assyrian Imperial Ideology and the Responses of Biblical Authors in the Late Eighth Century." In *Archaeology and History of Eighth-Century Judah*, edited by Zev I. Farver and Jacob L. Wright, 475–87. ANEM 23. Atlanta: SBL Press, 2018.

Beit-Arieh, Itzhaq. *Horvat ʿUza and Horvat Radum: Two Fortresses in the Biblical Negev.* Sonia and Marco Nadler Institute of Archaeology Monograph Series 25. Tel Aviv: Emery and Claire Yass Publications in Archaeology, 2007.

———, ed. *Tel ʿIra: A Stronghold in the Biblical Negev.* Tel Aviv: Emery and Claire Yass Publications in Archaeology, 1999.

Boer, Roland. "The Sacred Economy: A Reply to Interlocutors." *HBT* 38.2 (2016) 185–99.

———. *The Sacred Economy of Ancient Israel.* LAI. Louisville: Westminster John Knox, 2015.

Broshi, Magen, and Israel Finkelstein. "The Population of Palestine in Iron Age II." *BASOR* 287 (1992) 47–60.

Brueggemann, Walter. *A Commentary on Jeremiah: Exile and Homecoming*. Grand Rapids: Eerdmans, 1998.

———. *Isaiah 1–39*. Westminster Bible Companion. Louisville: Westminster John Knox, 1998.

———. "On Reading Mistakenly . . . and Otherwise." *HBT* 38.2 (2016) 173–84.

———. *Tenacious Solidarity: Biblical Provocations on Race, Religion, Climate, and the Economy*. Edited by Davis Hankins. Minneapolis: Fortress, 2018.

———. "Vine and Fig Tree: A Case Study in Imagination and Criticism." *CBQ* 43 (1981) 188–204.

Byrne, Ryan. "Early Assyrian Contacts with Arabs and the Impact on Levantine Vassal Tribute." *BASOR* 331 (2003) 11–25.

Carroll, Robert P. *Jeremiah: A Commentary*. OTL. Philadelphia: Westminster, 1986.

Carter, Charles E. *The Emergence of Yehud in the Persian Period: A Social and Demographic Study*. JSOTSup 294. Sheffield: Sheffield Academic, 1999.

Chaney, Marvin L. "Accusing Whom of What? Hosea's Rhetoric of Promiscuity." In *Distant Voices Drawing Near: Essays in Honor of Antoinette Clark Wire*, edited by Holly E. Hearon, 97–115. Collegeville, MN: Liturgical, 2004. Reprinted in Chaney, *Peasants, Prophets and Political Economy*, 175–90.

———. "Bitter Bounty: The Dynamics of Political Economy Critiqued by the Eighth-Century Prophets." In *Reformed Faith and Economics*, edited by Robert L. Stivers, 15–30. Lanham, MD: University Press of America, 1989. Reprinted in Chaney, *Peasants, Prophets and Political Economy*, 147–59.

———. "Coveting Your Neighbor's House in Social Context." In *The Ten Commandments: The Reciprocity of Faithfulness*, edited by William P. Brown, 302–17. Library of Theological Ethics. Louisville: Westminster John Knox, 2004. Reprinted in Chaney, *Peasants, Prophets and Political Economy*, 67–82.

———. "Micah—Models Matter: Political Economy and Micah 6:9–15." In *Ancient Israel: The Old Testament in Its Social Context*, edited by Philip F. Esler, 145–60, 329–30. Minneapolis: Fortress, 2006. Reprinted in Chaney, *Peasants, Prophets and Political Economy*, 205–19.

———. *Peasants, Prophets, and Political Economy: The Hebrew Bible and Social Analysis*. Eugene, OR: Cascade Books, 2017.

———. "The Political Economy of Peasant Poverty: What the Eighth-Century Prophets Presumed but Did Not State." In *The Bible, the Economy, and the Poor*, edited by Ronald Simkins and Thomas Kelly, 34–60. Journal of Religion and Society Supplement Series 10. Omaha: Creighton University Press, 2014. Reprinted in Chaney, *Peasants, Prophets and Political Economy*, 121–46.

———. "Producing Peasant Poverty: Debt Instruments in Amos 2:6b–8, 13–16." In *Reading a Tendentious Bible: Essays in Honor of Robert B. Coote*, edited by Marvin L. Chaney et al., 19–34. Hebrew Bible Monographs 66. Sheffield: Sheffield Phoenix, 2014. Reprinted in Chaney, *Peasants, Prophets and Political Economy*, 191–204.

———. "Some Choreographic Notes on the Dance of Theory with Data: A Response to Roland Boer, *The Sacred Economy of Ancient Israel*." *HBT* 38 (2016) 137–44.

———. "Systematic Study of the Israelite Monarchy." *Semeia* 37 (1986) 53–76. Reprinted in Chaney, *Peasants, Prophets and Political Economy*, 83–105.

———. "Whose Sour Grapes? The Addressees of Isaiah 5:1–7." *Semeia* 87 (1999) 105–22. Reprinted in Chaney, *Peasants, Prophets and Political Economy*, 160–74.

Coomber, Matthew J. M. "Prophets to Profits: Ancient Judah and Corporate Globalization." In *Bible and Justice: Ancient Texts, Modern Challenges,* edited by Matthew J. M. Coomber, 211–37. BibleWorld. London: Equinox, 2011.

Dar, Shimon. *Landscape and Pattern: An Archaeological Survey of Samaria 800 B.C.E.–636 C.E.* British Archeological Report 308. Oxford: British Archaeological Report, 1986.

Davis, Ellen F. *Biblical Prophecy: Perspectives for Christian Theology, Discipleship, and Ministry.* IBC. Louisville: Westminster John Knox, 2014.

Dever, William G. "Social Structure in Palestine in the Iron II Period on the Eve of Destruction." In *The Archaeology of Society in the Holy Land,* edited by Thomas E. Levy, 416–30. New York: Facts on File, 1995.

Erickson, Amy. "Rethinking Religion and Economics in Ancient Israel." *HBT* 38.2 (2016) 161–66.

Faust, Avraham. *The Archaeology of Israelite Society in Iron Age II.* Translated by Ruth Ludlum. Winona Lake, IN: Eisenbrauns, 2012.

———. "Settlement Dynamics and Demographic Fluctuations in Judah from the Late Iron Age to the Hellenistic Period and the Archaeology of Persian-Period *Yehud.*" In *A Time of Change: Judah and Its Neighbors in the Persian and Early Hellenistic Periods,* edited by Yigal Levin, 23–51. LSTS 65. London: T. & T. Clark, 2008.

Faust, Avraham, and Ehud Weiss. "Judah, Philistia, and the Mediterranean World: Reconstructing the Economic System of the Seventh Century BCE." *BASOR* 338 (2005) 71–92.

Frick, Frank. *The City in Ancient Israel.* SBLDS 36. Missoula, MT: Scholars, 1977.

Geva, Hillel. "Jerusalem's Population in Antiquity: A Minimalist View." *Tel Aviv* 41 (2014) 131–60.

Gottwald, Norman K. "Social Class as an Analytic and Hermeneutical Category in Biblical Studies." *JBL* 112 (1993) 3–22.

Graybill, Rhiannon. *Are We Not Men? Unstable Masculinity in the Hebrew Prophets.* New York: Oxford University Press, 2016.

Hankins, Davis. "Introduction to Reviews of Roland Boer, *The Sacred Economy of Ancient Israel.*" *HBT* 38.2 (2016) 133–36.

Haran, Menahem. "Book-Scrolls in Israel in Pre-Exilic Times." *JJS* 33 (1982) 161–73.

Herzog, Ze'ev. *Archaeology of the City: Urban Planning in Ancient Israel and Its Social Implications.* Tel Aviv University, Sonia and Marco Nadler Institute of Archaeology Monograph Series 13. Tel Aviv: Emery and Claire Yass Archaeology Press, 1997.

———. "The Beer-Sheba Valley: From Nomadism to Monarchy." In *From Nomadism to Monarchy: Archaeological and Historical Aspects of Early Israel,* edited by Israel Finkelstein and Nadav Na'aman, 122–49. Jerusalem: Israel Exploration Society, 1994.

———. "Cities." In *ABD* 1:1031–43.

———. "Settlement and Fortification Planning in the Iron Age." In *The Architecture of Ancient Israel from the Prehistoric to the Persian Period: In Memory of Immanuel (Munya) Dunayevsky,* edited by Aharon Kempinski and Ronny Reich, 231–274. Jerusalem: Israel Exploration Society, 1992.

Hudson, Michael. . . . *And Forgive Them Their Debts: Lending, Foreclosure, and Redemption from Bronze Age Finance to the Jubilee Year.* Dresden: ISLET, 2018.

Itach, Gilad. "The Kingdom of Israel in the Eighth Century: From a Regional Power to Assyrian Provinces." In *Archaeology and History of Eighth-Century Judah,* edited by Zev I. Farver and Jacob L. Wright, 57–77. ANEM 23. Atlanta: SBL Press, 2018.

Jameson, Fredric. *The Political Unconscious: Narrative as a Socially Symbolic Act*. Ithaca, NY: Cornell University Press, 1981.

Kaplan, Jonathan. "The Credibility of Liberty: The Plausibility of the Jubilee Legislation of Leviticus 25 in Ancient Israel and Judah." *CBQ* 81 (2019) 183–203.

Karatani, Kojin. *The Structure of World History: From Modes of Production to Modes of Exchange*. Translated by Michael K. Bourdaghs. Durham: Duke University Press, 2014.

Keefe, Alice A. "Religion, Gender, and the Liberation of Bodies." *HBT* 38 (2016) 153–60.

Keel, Othmar. *Die Geschichte Jerusalems und die Entstehung des Monotheismus*. 2 vols. Orte und Landschaften der Bibel: Ein Handbuch und Studien-Reisefuhrer zum Heiligen Land 4/1. Göttingen: Vandenhoek & Ruprecht, 2007.

King, Philip J., and Lawrence E. Stager, *Life in Biblical Israel*. LAI. Louisville, London: Westminster John Knox, 2001.

Knight, Douglas A. *Law, Power, and Justice in Ancient Israel*. LAI. Louisville: Westminster John Knox, 2011.

Kratz, Reinhard G. "Prophetic Discourse on 'Israel.'" In *Archaeology and History of Eighth-Century Judah*, edited by Zev I. Farver and Jacob L. Wright, 503–15. ANEM 23. Atlanta: SBL Press, 2018.

Lazzarato, Maurizio. *The Making of the Indebted Man: An Essay on the Neoliberal Condition*. Semiotext(e) Intervention Series 13. Los Angeles: Semiotext(e), 2012.

Lenski, Gerhard E. *Power and Privilege: A Theory of Social Stratification*. 2nd ed. Chapel Hill: University of North Carolina Press, 1984.

Levine, Lee I. *Visual Judaism in Late Antiquity: Historical Contexts of Jewish Art*. New Haven: Yale University Press, 2012.

Lilly, Ingrid. *Two Books of Ezekiel: Papyrus 967 and the Masoretic Text as Variant Literary Editions*. VTSup 150. Leiden: Brill, 2012.

Lipschits, Oded. "Demographic Changes in Judah between the Seventh and Fifth Centuries B.C.E." In *Judah and the Judeans in the Neo-Babylonian Period*, edited by Oded Lipschits and Joseph Blenkinsopp, 323–76. Winona Lake, IN: Eisenbrauns, 2003.

———. *The Fall and Rise of Jerusalem: Judah under Babylonian Rule*. Winona Lake, IN: Eisenbrauns, 2005.

———. "Judah under Assyrian Rule and the Early Phase of Stamping Jar Handles." In *Archaeology and History of Eighth-Century Judah*, edited by Zev I. Farver and Jacob L. Wright, 337–55. ANEM 23. Atlanta: SBL Press, 2018.

Liverani, Mario. "Land Tenure and Family Inheritance in the Ancient Near East: The Interaction between 'Place' and 'Family' Sectors." In *Land Tenure and Social Transformation in the Middle East*, edited by Tarif Khalidi, 33–44. Beirut: American University of Beirut, 1984.

Marx, Karl. *Capital: A Critique of Political Economy*. Vol. 3. Translated by David Fernbach. London: Penguin, 1981.

———. "The Eighteenth Brumaire of Louis Bonaparte." In *Marx: Later Political Writings*, edited and translated by Terrell Carver, 31–127. Cambridge: Cambridge University Press, 1996.

Mastnjak, Nathan. "Jeremiah as Collection: Scrolls, Sheets, and the Problem of Textual Arrangement." *CBQ* 80 (2018) 25–44.

Miller, J. Maxwell, and John H. Hayes. *A History of Ancient Israel and Judah*. 2nd ed. Louisville: Westminster John Knox, 2006.

Mroczek, Eva. *The Literary Imagination in Jewish Antiquity.* Oxford: Oxford University Press, 2016.

———. "Thinking Digitally about the Dead Sea Scrolls: Book History before and beyond the Book." *Book History* 14 (2011) 235–63.

Na'aman, Nadav. "Josiah and the Kingdom of Judah." In *Good Kings and Bad Kings*, edited by Lester L. Grabbe, 189–247. LHBOTS 393. London: T. & T. Clark, 2005.

———. "Sennacherib's Campaign to Judah and the Date of the LMLK Stamps." *VT* 29 (1979) 61–86.

Pioske, Daniel D. *David's Jerusalem: Between Memory and History.* Routledge Studies in Religion. London: Routledge, 2015.

Premnath, D. N. *Eighth Century Prophets: A Social Analysis.* St. Louis: Chalice, 2003.

Schmid, Konrad. "The Biblical Writings in the Late Eighth Century BCE." In *Archaeology and History of Eighth-Century Judah*, edited by Zev I. Farver and Jacob L. Wright, 489–501. ANEM 23. Atlanta: SBL Press, 2018.

Sergi, Omer, et al. "The Royal Judahite Storage Jar: A Computer-Generated Typology and Its Archaeological and Historical Implications." *Tel Aviv* 39 (2012) 64–92.

Shai, Itzhack, and Aren M. Maeir. "Pre-*lmlk* Jars: A New Class of Iron Age IIA Storage Jars." *Tel Aviv* 30 (2003) 108–23.

Sharp, Carolyn J. "Of Fields and Forced Labor." *HBT* 38 (2016) 145–52.

Smith-Christopher, Daniel L. *The Book of Micah.* OTL. Louisville: Westminster John Knox, 2015.

Veen, Marijke van der. "When Is Food a Luxury?" *World Archaeology* 34.3 (2003) 405–27.

Weems, Renita J. *Battered Love: Marriage, Sex, and Violence in the Hebrew Prophets.* OBT. Minneapolis: Fortress, 1995.

Wunsch, Cornelia. "The Egibi Family's Real Estate in Babylon (6th Century BC)." In *Urbanization and Land Ownership in the Ancient Near East*, edited by Michael Hudson and Baruch A. Levine, 391–419. Peabody Museum Bulletin 7. Cambridge: Harvard University, Peabody Museum of Archaeology and Ethnology, 1999.

Yee, Gale A. *Poor Banished Children of Eve: Woman as Evil in the Hebrew Bible.* Minneapolis: Fortress, 2003.

Zertal, Adam. "The Province of Samaria (Assyrian Samerina) in the Late Iron Age (Iron Age III)." In *Judah and the Judeans in the Neo-Babylonian Period*, edited by Oded Lipschits and Joseph Blenkinsopp, 377–412. Winona Lake, IN: Eisenbrauns, 2003.

Zimhoni, Orna. "The Pottery Levels V and IV and Its Archaeological and Chronological Implications." In *The Renewed Archaeological Excavations at Lachish (1973–1994)*, vol. 4, edited by David Ussishkin, 1643–788. Tel Aviv: Emery and Claire Yass Archaeology, 2004.

———. *Studies in the Iron Age Pottery of Israel: Typological, Archaeological, and Chronological Aspects.* Tel Aviv: Occasional Publications 2. Tel Aviv: Tel Aviv University Press, 1997.

10. Economic Aspects of Wisdom and Apocalypticism

Samuel L. Adams

Introduction

The history of ancient Israel and Judah was marked by cultural shifts, colonial occupation, economic transformation, and ongoing hardship for the majority of the population. After the fall of Israel (722 BCE) and Judah (586 BCE), and the events of the Babylonian exile, a series of foreign powers held sway over Judea and its environs, extracting significant resources and tax revenues. Some merchants and elite property owners benefitted from the stratified system, as they had the collateral and connections to turn a profit. Certain well-placed Judeans joined in the extraction, in effect becoming conduits between foreign rulers and the local populace (e.g., tax collectors). The flourishing of Persian and then Hellenistic culture meant new influences and economic opportunities for such individuals. Yet the vast majority of people living in Judea remained poor agriculturalists, subject to the fluctuations of the region's weather cycles and the imposing demands of local and foreign leaders. Most households lived at the subsistence level or only slightly above it, and crisis—rather than relative stability—was the norm. Life remained cyclical, precarious, and arduous for the majority of persons in Judea who placed their faith in the God of Israel.[1]

---

1. Boer applies *régulation* theory to the ancient Near East and concludes that crisis rather than stability was the norm for the vast majority of the population. The prevailing question then becomes "how periods of stability are achieved through compromises or complex patterns of *régulation*." Boer, *Sacred Economy*, 33–34.

Difficult circumstances are apparent in extant sources from this larger period. Papyri from the Jewish colony at Elephantine, commercial documents from the Dead Sea, and the pointed descriptions in certain biblical texts underscore the gap between rich and poor and the vulnerability of most persons within a hierarchical and corrupt economic structure.[2] A demanding system of local and imperial taxation, difficult farming conditions, and the widespread practice of usury created an economic climate where profit could be made by a select few, but a household in distress might lose their long-standing family plot. For example, Neh 5 depicts a famine where certain lenders are taking advantage of their vulnerable neighbors: "There were also those who said, 'We are having to pledge our fields, our vineyards, and our houses in order to get grain during the famine'" (Neh 5:3). The perpetrators in this endeavor are fellow Judeans (v. 5) who lent grain at predatory rates in order to appropriate land, resources, and even people. There are also references in this chapter to debt slavery and the onerous nature of imperial and local taxation (Neh 5:4, 14–15).

In the midst of these trying circumstances, many Judeans wrestled with a lack of fairness in the marketplace, the possibility of divine retributive justice for both the dishonest (e.g., Prov 1:19) and the virtuous (e.g., Prov 22:4), and how best to handle household finances. Legal codes were created and refined, prophets railed against injustice, and local scribes tried to document transactions through greater reliance on contracts (e.g., the contracts from Elephantine and the Babatha archive). Coinage became more commonplace during the Second Temple period, and trade increased rapidly, especially along the coastal cities most susceptible to Hellenistic influence.[3] All of these developments provide necessary context for understanding the response of Judeans to the economic landscape.

Wisdom literature was an important vehicle for diverse reflection on financial challenges and opportunities, and this occurred both during the monarchical period and after the Babylonian exile. For millennia, ancient Near Eastern sages had offered maxims on numerous topics, including wealth and poverty, and the content was varied.[4] Some sayings offered descriptive, pragmatic advice on the correct way to navigate a corrupt marketplace, such as warnings about the threat of swindlers (e.g., Sir 26:29—27:2). Alternatively,

2. For examples of primary texts, see Porten, *Textbook*; Durand, *Grecs*.

3. For further background, see Horsley, *Scribes*; Pastor, *Land and Economy*; Tcherikover, *Hellenistic Civilization*; Hengel, *Judaism and Hellenism*.

4. See the instructional literature in Simpson, *Literature of Ancient Egypt*. For Mesopotamian wisdom texts, COS 1.151–54; 1.174–86.

certain maxims promised that cheaters would receive their justified comeup-
pance (e.g., Prov 11:28). Still other admonitions urged those with resources to
share what they had with the poor (e.g., Sir 29:8).

Value of Sapiential and Apocalyptic Literature
in Unearthing Economic Realities

Sapiential Literature

During the Second Temple period in particular, advice on economic matters seems to take on a special urgency, as evidenced by the vivid nature of
the descriptions in sapiential literature and the fact that corruption, inequality, and foreign incursions became a permanent part of many people's experience. The specificity of the economic advice in Second Temple wisdom texts
points to actual social realities more than the traditional platitudes of anteced-
ent instructions. In this respect, postexilic wisdom writings from Proverbs to
4QInstruction (from the corpus of the Dead Sea Scrolls) represented one of
the more important mechanisms for incisive commentary and the shaping of
human behavior. This essay will argue that instructional literature provides a
significant resource for understanding social and economic life during this critical period, and that a striking number of voices speak out against stratification
and the corruption that is often endemic to commerce. These instructions are
underutilized when considering the social history of Judea after the exile.

In studying this sapiential material, one of the salient features of certain
Second Temple instructions is the introduction of an otherworldly framework as a means of adjudicating proper and improper conduct and guarantee-
ing fair recompense for the righteous. In texts like 4QInstruction, and in the
Wisdom of Solomon, the authors promise eternal life for those persons who
adhere to practical advice and honor God. Other sapiential voices, most notably Qoheleth and Ben Sira, are aware of instructional frameworks involving an
afterlife and speak in protest against such a possibility. The appeal to an afterlife
indicates both Hellenistic influence regarding the immortality of the soul, as in
the Wisdom of Solomon, and apocalyptic ideas about a final judgment, as in
4QInstruction. Such a shift marks a major development in the wisdom tradition and deserves special attention in the context of economics.[5]

---

5. On this development, see Goff, *Worldly*; Adams, *Wisdom in Transition*. See below for
further discussion.

Apocalyptic Literature

Along with incisive discourse in wisdom texts on economics, apocalyptic ideas and terminology emerged as a form of social commentary and means of dealing with colonial occupation and persecution.[6] When presenting this type of discourse, the authors of such works frequently address financial issues. The texts often labeled as "apocalyptic" recognize some of the structural inequalities in their culture, especially as these relate to empire.[7] Such a shift had a transformative impact on early Judaism and Christianity, since an otherworldly framework offers innovative horizons for interpreting current events and circumstances, including a reversal of fortune for the rich and poor.

When analyzing such apocalyptic texts as the Epistle of Enoch, Dan 7–12, and documents from the Dead Sea Scrolls corpus, particularly in the context of economics, it is pertinent to ask the question of social location. Many texts labeled as apocalyptic rail against the wealthy and economic injustice by promising eschatological reward for those experiencing difficulty. Does such rhetoric originate on the margins of society as a means of protesting inequality and offering eternal recompense to struggling persons (whether economically, socially, or both), or does it represent the efforts of the more elite classes to maintain an unjust status quo by promising future rewards? Max Weber famously argued that apocalyptic frameworks usually originate on the periphery of a society, among "pariah groups" rather than the ruling classes. According to this understanding, millennial expectation often comes from those who lack power, whether because of political oppression and/or penury.[8] Weber's idea of "pariah intelligentsia" has been highly influential, as many subsequent analyses have assumed that "marginal sects" are the primary locus for apocalyptic ideas and texts. Yet some question this assumption, instead claiming that apocalyptic language can be an effective tool for reform among elite classes and in many instances a means of oppression.[9] According to this latter interpretation, the afterlife functions as a disingenuous balm that seeks to assuage the anxious concerns of the larger population in the wake of injustice; by promising future

6. One has to distinguish between the genre "apocalypse" and those works with apocalyptic elements when exploring this literature, but it is undeniable that a new form of discourse emerged in the Second Temple period that included cosmological speculation, the promise of earthly deliverance from foreign oppressors, messianic expectation, and in many instances a beatific afterlife as compensation for present economic and social hardship.

7. Portier-Young, *Apocalypse against Empire*.

8. Weber, *Sociology of Religion*.

9. See Boer, *Sacred Economy*.

rewards and a reversal of present struggles, it becomes possible to perpetuate economic injustice.

Subsequent discussion will consider the nature of apocalyptic discourse on economic injustice, with careful attention to the historical context for this literature. When a text like the Epistle of Enoch critiques "the rich" and cites "the poor" as an elect category worthy of salvific rewards—a framework also present in the Gospel of Luke—we must explore the intricacies of the textual description and also ask questions of social location for author and audience. It will be argued that one should not posit a neat dichotomy between establishment circles and dissident scribes when it comes to this type of framework/literature. The language of redemption for the poor in some cases originates more on the periphery of Judean society, among groups Weber correctly labeled as pariah intelligentsia. In other cases, this type of discourse could derive from those who promised future reversal as a means of social control. It is not an either/or decision, and therefore each text has to be examined on its own merits and in its own context in order to consider the nature of the economic message and the author's agenda.

Proverbs

Our inquiry begins with the book of Proverbs, which is the largest anthology of sapiential literature in the Hebrew Bible. In terms of background, the book is composed of two major sections: chapters 1–9 and 10–31. The first section (chapters 1–9) is a series of sermons or lectures on proper behavior and the figure of Wisdom; the subunits in chapters 10–31 consist largely of two-line sayings and admonitions. In a great many cases, the sayings are built around antithetic and synonymous parallelism. One concept or element is likened or contrasted with another. For example, "Wisdom is a fountain of life to one who has it, but folly is the punishment of fools" (Prov 16:22). With regard to authorship, the book of Proverbs as we have it comes from scribal officials ("learned clerks") who collected, catalogued, and in some cases authored sayings.[10] There is a reference in Prov 25:1 to the maxims "that the officials of King Hezekiah of Judah copied." The social location for the content is pivotal for our inquiry: some of the proverbs are relevant to the more elite setting of scribal officials, such as appropriate behavior around the ruler and how best to handle servants (e.g., Prov 29). Other sayings address farming matters, household relationships, and other issues tied to family and village life. At least some of these sayings would seem

---

10. Fox, "Social Location," 237.

to reflect a more popular or folk origin.[11]

Because of the lack of historical markers, it is more or less impossible to assign a date to this collection, especially since many of the sayings address timeless issues. The editing and cataloguing of sayings was an ongoing process in ancient Israel and Judah, and we have no way of knowing when a saying was first uttered. Most of the sayings had an oral history, and there is clear evidence of intercultural borrowing, especially from the Egyptians, whose wisdom tradition stretched back millennia. A number of observations describe kingship as a reality, which most likely points to the preexilic period. Except for those interpreters who cling to Solomonic authorship for the book, there is overwhelming consensus that the anthology continued to take shape after the exile. The lectures in Prov 1–9 are thought by most interpreters to be later, perhaps dating to the Persian period. This especially appears to be the case when one takes into account terminological (including a number of late Aramaic forms) and thematic issues.[12]

Material Rewards for Righteousness

Even if the date remains uncertain for both the collection as a whole and also for individual sayings, one thing is clear: a great deal of the content in Proverbs addresses economic concerns, and the type of advice is diverse and often conflicting. One can find at least four different lines of argumentation related to economics, with some sayings frequently at odds with others.[13] First is the optimistic (or perhaps simplistic) association of material rewards with righteousness and sinfulness with loss. According to this perspective, the one who demonstrates virtue and the reverential awe (i.e. "fear of the LORD") that is required of faithful pupils, will enjoy financial gain. For the righteous individual, "your barns will be filled with plenty, and your vats will be bursting with wine" (3:10). A good distillation of this perspective is Prov 22:4: "The reward for humility and fear of the LORD is riches and honor and life." Conversely, the sinner who seeks to accumulate riches will stumble as a result of his treachery. Even if

---

11. Yet it is important to note that the subject matter of a saying does not necessarily indicate provenance. A proverb about laziness in the fields does not necessarily originate in an agrarian community but could be a scribal commentary on the need for industriousness.

12. Yoder's *Wisdom as a Woman of Substance* uses linguistic evidence as a means of dating the opening section and final chapter of the books, with special attention to economic terminology. Cf. Fox, *Proverbs 1–9*, 6, 48–49.

13. For a more complete treatment of these categories, see Adams, *Social and Economic Life*, 184–89.

he enjoys temporary success, prosperity will elude him. The most famous negative example is the description of the adolescent thugs in Prov 1:10–19 who seek to entice a vulnerable lad into petty larceny. What they do not realize, according to the speaker, is that their temporary gain will eventually lead to their self-destruction: "Such is the end of all who are greedy for gain; it takes away the life of its possessors" (Prov 1:19).

When examining such sayings in isolation, the conclusion often follows that Proverbs offers a rudimentary understanding of economics and human behavior: an act-consequence nexus where cheaters automatically suffer and the honest prosper. Aphorisms such as Prov 22:23 contribute to this interpretation: "Whoever digs a pit will fall into it, and a stone will come back on the one who starts it rolling" (Prov 26:27). This idea of a facile *Tun-Ergehen Zusammenhang* ("act-consequence connection") might seem self-evident from such sayings.[14] Yet it is always risky to take a single proverb as indicative of an entire instruction, since other sayings directly contradict this assertion of a fair society. For example, Prov 24:16 admits that the righteous might "fall." Moreover, we must remember the pedagogical intent of sapiential literature: the baseline goal is to shape behavior such that the claim about falling into a pit is not meant to indicate a one-to-one correspondence but rather to serve as a warning about the long-term benefits of good character. For this reason, commentators have sometimes referred to a "character-consequence relationship" in the collection.[15] Consequently, this first category intends to show that wealth comes to righteous persons over a lengthy period, along with other benefits such as long life and progeny.

Wisdom over Wealth

This first category does not exhaust the nuanced presentation of wealth and poverty in the book of Proverbs, however. A second set of sayings repeatedly highlights the superiority of wisdom over wealth. Many warnings and observations in the collection emphasize the importance of measured behavior and loyalty to God, as opposed to unbridled avarice. For example, "How much better to get wisdom than gold! To get understanding is to be chosen rather than silver" (Prov 16:16). The preferability of household contentment over material possessions is a related concern: "Better is a dinner of vegetables where love is than a fatted ox and hatred with it" (15:17). This line of thought emphasizes

14. Koch, "Is There a Doctrine?"
15. Boström, *God of the Sages.*

the benefits of sapiential learning as far superior to an acquisitive mindset. In this respect, the second category has a mitigating effect on the association of wisdom with wealth in the proverbs mentioned above.

Plight of the Poor

A third category of sayings brings realism to pecuniary matters, including a special concern for the plight of the poor. These sayings consist of insightful observations on the duplicity that can characterize financial transactions and the necessary caution that should mark participation in the marketplace. A searing example is Prov 13:23: "The field of the poor may yield much food, but it is swept away through injustice." Such an admission severely undercuts the character-consequence sayings in the first category that offer material blessings for the righteous. These and other sayings acknowledge the vulnerability of the poor in the social structure, especially of those who lack the security of an established household. Just as the legal language of the Torah does, so in the book of Proverbs several statements and warnings speak on behalf of those struggling in the society: "Do not rob the poor because they are poor, or crush the afflicted at the gate; for the LORD pleads their cause and despoils of life those who despoil them" (Prov 22:22–23). Here and elsewhere with similar admonitions there is clear acknowledgment of stratification, the vulnerability of the poor in the public square, and the assertion of divine protection for those in difficult straits.

Along with this type of honesty about swindlers is a pragmatism in Proverbs about financial transactions. Lending money at exorbitant interest rates is frowned upon (e.g., Prov 28:8), and the sages responsible for this collection warn against standing as guarantor for someone else's loan, even a close friend or associate. The reason for this type of caution is twofold: loans among friends can ruin relationships, and the possibility always exists that the neighbor or associate might not be able to repay the amount, thereby making the guarantor a responsible party. The book of Proverbs contains vivid descriptions of what can happen in such a situation: "Do not be one of those who give pledges, who become surety for debts. If you have nothing with which to pay, why should your bed be taken from under you?" (Prov 22:26–27; cf. 11:15; 17:18; 20:16). An extended section in Prov 6:1–5 presents a scenario where a person underwrites the loan of an associate and thereby owes money to a neighbor. In such descriptions, the preference for self-preservation over benevolence is striking, especially in a sapiential collection that prizes kindness to the poor. With the wariness about surety, we find a pragmatic tone based on experience and some of the most practical advice in all of the Hebrew Bible.

The historical setting of the Persian and early Hellenistic periods merits this type of caution. We mentioned the vivid description in Neh 5, where interest charges are threatening vulnerable households. In order to survive, the "people" pledge land, belongings, and in some cases their relatives as collateral. The creditors in this scenario are making extraordinary demands of fellow Judeans, and thus raising the ire of Nehemiah because they have breached the solidarity requirement in the Torah when it comes to usury (Deut 23:19–20). Even if the narrative in Neh 5 has legendary elements, the mentions of famine, usury, and stratification all conform with the historical record from this period. Extracanonical evidence points to usury as an intrinsic part of many transactions during this period.[16] By the Persian period, Judean society could have been accurately characterized as an "advanced agrarian economy" (using the terminology of Gerhard Lenski), with an entrenched upper class and a ruling power with sophisticated mechanisms for taxation and the usurpation of resources.[17] When considering the different levels of taxation, imperial demands on the populace, and the tendency of nonagricultural elites to extract as much as possible from poor farmers—including and especially during periods of crisis—the cautious tone on surety makes sense during the Persian and early Ptolemaic periods. This type of setting makes borrowing money or getting involved in lending arrangements a precarious enterprise.

Instruction on Right Behavior

The fourth and final category has a didactic intent, focusing on industrious behavior. The proverbs here are more honest than the first, character-consequence type discussed above. The sayings in this category exhibit a preoccupation with diligence and wariness against idleness. A good example is the contrast between a lazy person and an ant in Prov 6:6–11: "Go to the ant, you lazybones; consider its ways, and be wise" (v. 6). For the individual who persists in idleness, destitution lies near: "poverty will come upon you like a robber, and want, like an armed warrior" (v. 11). Here and with similar maxims, the pedagogical intent is

16. See Adams, *Social and Economic Life*, 110–14.

17. Many economic theorists and historians have studied the tendency for unscrupulous practices to occur in sophisticated agrarian economies marked by stratification, including the unfair extraction of interest and other goods. This type of economy often emerges when there is a strong colonial power. For further background on the characteristics of an "advanced agrarian economies," see Lenski, *Power and Privilege*.

to foster dutiful, measured behavior, not reckless indulgence.

Alcohol abuse is a preoccupation within this category, and not just due to the deleterious effects on one's health, but because excessive intake can compromise a person's financial well-being. For example, "Whoever loves pleasure will suffer want; whoever loves wine and oil will not be rich" (Prov 21:17). Any temporary bliss from strong drink is illusory, according to the sayings in this category: "At the last it [wine] bites like a serpent, and stings like an adder" (23:32).

These four categories on economic matters are noteworthy for their diverse and perhaps contradictory messaging.[18] How does one reconcile the conflicting advice, when one proverb lauds wealth as a gift for the virtuous, and then another declares that the acquisitive person will suffer anxiety and never attain happiness? These diverse sayings might seem contradictory when placed side by side, but the various assessments of economic life do not seem to represent editorial stages, nor do they necessarily come from different backgrounds. Rather, the seeming discrepancies in Proverbs reflect the ambiguous and complex nature of money, particularly in instructional literature. The ancient sages responsible for Proverbs could argue simultaneously that wealth leads to disingenuous flatterers *and* that diligence brings material possessions. These are lucid and timeless insights, even if they seem inherently contradictory. Such divergent assertions reflect the complex nature of money in any society. In many of the sayings on economics, the book of Proverbs offers an honest and nuanced assessment of the complexities involved in financial matters.

When examining the interplay between the four categories, Roland Boer's assertion that the book of Proverbs represents the attempts of a controlling elite to justify an oppressive status quo misses the mark somewhat.[19] Boer seems quite correct in his arguments about *régulation* theory and crisis as the norm in ancient Israel, and it is undoubtedly the case that many of these sayings come from an upper-class provenance. Yet the frequent candor about wealth and poverty and attentiveness to the poor in Proverbs, even if not

18. Sandoval, *Discourse*, 56–66, has similar categories in his assessment of Proverbs: (1) the *wisdom's virtues discourse*, which is equivalent to the second category discussed above; (2) a "*discourse of social justice*," which also falls into our second category; (3) a "*discourse of social observation*," which describes daily occurrences as the sages observe them and correlates with our third category (p. 69). Sandoval also highlights the "two ways" discourse in Proverbs (something we also find in Deuteronomy and Psalms), the use of wealth as a "motivational symbol," and the act-consequence (or "wisdom prosperity") nexus in the book (our first category).

19. Boer, *Sacred Economy*, 125, argues that in Proverbs "the origin of ethics is very much a justification of ruling-class mores."

offered with the same prophetic urgency and frequency as Amos, is neverthe-less a distinguishing feature of the book.[20] It is inaccurate to characterize the social ethic in Proverbs as completely elitist or naïve: as our review has shown, plenty of sayings prize virtue over acquisitiveness, and the plight of the poor is recognized in just about every section of this instructional document. There is a great deal of honest realism in Proverbs.

One final aspect before moving to the next instruction: the book of Proverbs does not offer a beatific afterlife for the individual as consolation for poverty or a virtuous life. Moreover, the sages responsible for this collection seem unaware of emergent proposals in this regard concerning an afterlife. Despite a few arguments that indicate more confessional hope on the part of the modern interpreter making the claim, there is no possibility of eternal exis-tence in Proverbs, even for the righteous.[21] "Life" in Proverbs entails a fulfilling reality in the earthly sphere: "For whoever finds me finds life and obtains favor from the LORD; but those who miss me injure themselves; all who hate me love death" (Prov 8:35–36). In this and similar sayings, there is no promise of a heavenly journey or reward to compensate for life's afflictions, even for those who have suffered economically. Even as the sages responsible for Proverbs wrestled with the complexities of financial holdings, this entire instruction is devoid of eschatological expectation.

Ecclesiastes/Qoheleth

The book of Qoheleth (Ecclesiastes) struggles more pointedly than Proverbs with the unfair aspects of human existence, including with issues of wealth and poverty. This sapiential document clearly dates from the Second Temple period, due to the presence of Persian loanwords (Qoh 2:5; 8:11), Aramaisms, and the probable influence of Hellenistic philosophical ideas.[22] In searching for a more precise date, one finds a number of features that match up with the Ptolemaic era in Judea (third century BCE). According to Thomas Krüger, the "royal autobiography" section in Qoh 1:12—2:26 correlates with the sys-tem of local rulers in Judea during this period, including the succession of high

20. Boer, *Sacred Economy*, 125n41, claims that the sayings privileging righteousness over wealth (e.g., 11:4: the second category discussed above) are veiled instructions on how to manage one's money, "keeping in mind a higher calling of righteousness, which is the path to true wealth."

21. Waltke, *Book of Proverbs*, argues for eschatological expectation in Proverbs.

22. On the probable influence of Hellenistic ideas, see Braun, *Kohelet*. Even if he overes-timates the extent of borrowing, some of his examples are convincing.

priests and the Tobiad family, one of the elite clans that controlled Judea.[23] Krüger claims that Qoh 10:5–7, where the author sees "slaves on horseback, and princes walking on foot like slaves" (v. 7), is highlighting the fluid economic climate of the Ptolemaic period.[24] Moreover, it is possible to associate Qoh 5:7 [8] with the royal network of property, corrupt officials, and taxation under the Ptolemies: "If you see in a province the oppression of the poor and the viola-tion of justice and right, do not be amazed at the matter; for the high official is watched by a higher, and there are yet higher ones over them." The bureaucracy under the Ptolemaic administration had layers of intricate detail, demanding taxation on farmers and other subject peoples, and the pharaonic administra-tion exercised a great deal of proprietary control over its territories.[25]

Qoheleth in Its Historical Economic Context

While some commentators on Qoheleth have utilized these and other passages to argue for a Persian-period date, the economic material in the book tilts more strongly in favor of a Ptolemaic setting, particularly when we also consider the probable influence of Hellenistic philosophy.[26] For example, a stratified, colo-nial context is described in the Zeno correspondence, which dates from the middle of the third century (261–229 BCE). Appollonius, who was *dioketes* ("chief financial officer") under Ptolemy II Philadelphus (282–246), had an underling named Zeno, who traveled in the countryside on imperial business. While in the Galilee region, Zeno visited an estate under the direct control of the *dioketes*, and the extant documents from this collection demonstrate an elaborate property system that was tightly controlled. There is evidence of co-operation among Ptolemaic officials, local elites, and property owners.[27] Savvy officials might receive and maintain land, but property could also revert to the crown. In certain cases, tensions arose between Ptolemaic officials and local property owners in the region.[28] Such an atmosphere is not incidental to the

23. Krüger, *Qoheleth*.

24. Krüger, *Qoheleth*, 20.

25. See Adams, *Social and Economic Life*, 145–55.

26. Seow, *Ecclesiastes*, examines the commercial terminology in the book to argue for a Persian period date.

27. See Hölbl, *History*, 58–61. He highlights military settlements, which opened the door for greater Hellenistic influence in terms of civic organization, exposure to philosophy, and agricultural advancements.

28. A good example is a papyrus (P.Cair.Zen. 59018) from the Zeno archives that men-tions a landowner named Jeddous. According to the description, Jeddous refuses to return

economic passages in Qoheleth. For example, a fluid economic climate correlates well with the hypothetical situation in Qoh 6:1–2, where a property owner has to leave his inheritance to a complete stranger.

Material evidence also helps us to contextualize the socioeconomic background for Qoheleth's probable era. Along the Mediterranean coastal cities of this region one finds evidence of commerce and greater engagement with foreign powers.[29] Monument remains and extant coins at various sites demonstrate significant activity in this regard.[30] The impact of Hellenistic culture on the interior regions is more difficult to determine but was almost certainly more modest. Many agrarian villages would have experienced little exposure to Ptolemaic culture, even if they had to meet significant taxation demands. In some cases, Greek settlements arose in close proximity to older towns, creating opportunities for cultural and financial exchange.[31] The Ptolemies increased slave trading, and this enhanced agricultural efficiency and wealth for the elite. Such a system might lie in the background of Qoh 2:7: "I bought male and female slaves, and had slaves who were born in my house." The vast majority or all of the royal autobiography in Qoh 1:12—2:26 could be fictional, and yet it does point to actual circumstances during this period. The persona created in the book, "Qoheleth" would have bargained with foreign officials, negotiated for more property and a favorable tax situation, and enjoyed the benefits of his wealth.[32] Certain passages about economics appear to have a Hellenistic flavor (e.g., 2:4–9 and the reference to elaborate gardens, which is a staple of Greek culture), and they reflect an elitist perspective about enjoying one's wealth and maximizing resources.[33]

Poverty also receives considerable attention in this book. Misfortune and unfairness strike the needy in much greater proportion, and the author behind this incisive set of timeless reflections acknowledges the plight of the poor, even as he also addresses the problematic nature of material possessions.

---

debts to the local Ptolemaic officials, suggesting a power struggle of some sort. This document and other examples from the Zeno papyri point to a system of wealthy locals who partnered with officials, sometimes disagreeing and in many instances working with them to extract revenue from the populace. It is important to note here that unclaimed property was usually the possession of the king/pharaoh and his administration.

29. Berlin, "Archaeological Sources."

30. Berlin, "Archaeological Sources," 6. Several coastal areas were enhanced under the Ptolemies, including Gaza and Mareshah. Archaeologists have demonstrated that oil, wine, and wheat were traded widely during this period.

31. Harrison, "Hellenization."

32. Berlin, "Archaeological Sources," 9.

33. See Harrison, "Hellenization," 108.

Social exclusion is one of the more overlooked aspects of poverty, but Qoheleth depicts it vividly: "There was a little city with few people in it. A great king came against it and besieged it, building great siegeworks against it. Now there was found in it a poor wise man, and he by his wisdom delivered the city. Yet no one remembered that poor man" (Qoh 9:14–15). Here the author acknowledges the marginal social location of a poor individual and the intrinsic obstacles to respectability. We have already cited the author's reference to "the oppression of the poor and the violation of justice and right" (5:7[8]) as a common occurrence, especially in a stratified economy with layers of bureaucracy and heavy taxation on the farmers who make up the bulk of the population. Yet even as he characterizes poverty with honesty, Qoheleth does not glorify wealth as unambiguously blissful. In this same section, he declares that "The lover of money will not be satisfied with money; nor the lover of wealth, with gain" (Qoh 5:9[10]). The next few sayings in chapter 5 (vv. 9–11[10–12]) all deal with the anxieties that accompany the accumulation of riches. The timelessness of these observations is a primary reason for the enduring appeal of the book of Ecclesiastes. The author understands the persistent dynamics that characterize the relationship between humans and money.

As Qoheleth explores wealth and poverty, he notes the frequent unfairness that occurs "under the sun." Whatever the precise financial status of the author behind this book, Qoheleth is galled by the injustices he and others witness or experience and the inability of human beings to maintain their earthly status or possessions. He bristles much more strongly than the sages of Proverbs at what he perceives to be a fundamental problem: everything and everyone is ultimately forgotten in an impermanent and cyclical world. In several passages on this topic, Qoheleth asks practical, concrete questions, is concerned with "profit" or "gain" (Heb. *yitrōn*), and is exasperated that the ledger sheets of human experience are uneven and unfair. He asks the fundamental question in this regard: "What do people gain (*yitrōn*) from all the toil at which they toil under the sun?" (Qoh 1:3). In a related passage, he sounds like a hopeless accountant seeking a consistency that is elusive: "See, this is what I found, says the Teacher, adding one thing to another to find the sum (*ḥešbôn*), which my mind has sought repeatedly, but I have not found" (Qoh 7:27–28).

The finality of death looms over Qoheleth's discourses on economics and indeed the entire book. According to the author, there is no possibility for immortality, no chance for individuals or their possessions to transcend earthly existence. This state of affairs is exasperating, particularly the lack of correlation between ability and results: "Again I saw that under the sun the race is not to the swift, nor the battle to the strong, nor bread to the wise, nor riches to the intelligent, nor favor to the skillful; but time and chance happen to them all" (Qoh 9:11). Because of the brevity of life, the best recourse is for a person to enjoy close relationships, blessings from God, and any possessions in life (his or her "portion" [*ḥēleq*], as in Qoh 2:10; 3:22; 5:17[18]; 9:7): "for there is no work or thought or knowledge or wisdom in Sheol, to which you are going" (Qoh 9:10). In framing human existence in this manner, the author seems to be aware of alternative proposals concerning the possibility of an afterlife, such as one finds in the Epistle of the Enoch and other apocalyptic texts, and he categorically rejects them as fanciful (cf. Qoh 3:19–22).[34] For present purposes, the most critical implication of this worldview is that unfair outcomes, whether in relationships or finances, are often permanent and final.

Ben Sira

The Jewish sage responsible for the book of Ben Sira/Sirach presents similar beliefs to the author of Qoheleth concerning marketplace ethics and the finality of death, but he is more orthodox and hopeful in his reflections. This instruction derives from a scribal figure who utilizes and largely adheres to the discourses of Proverbs, while also incorporating the Torah as an explicit source of authority. The ethical template found in the Mosaic legislation becomes central to this author's message, and he takes great efforts to rail against unjust financial practices. In trying to encourage virtuous behavior, Ben Sira offers his steadfast belief that what truly matters is the "good name" of a person, which will bring favor from the Lord and last forever. Such a reputation is cultivated through faithfulness to the Deity (i.e., "fear of the Lord") and honesty in the public square, especially in one's financial dealings. Ben Sira's nuanced presentation and palpable concern with economic issues merit careful attention in our discussion.

As with the books of Proverbs and Qoheleth, the historical circumstances of Ben Sira's instruction have tremendous bearing on the presentation of financial topics. Because of the grandson's prologue to the book of Ben Sira/Sirach (lines 27–30), written in Greek and praising his grandfather as an erudite man who was well-versed in Jewish tradition, we can date the instruction with relative precision to the beginning of the second-century BCE.[35]

---

34. We are not arguing for a direct response by Qoheleth to any of the apocalyptic texts discussed below, but the author is clearly aware of emergent ideas related to individual eschatology.

35. Moreover, Ben Sira is familiar with the high priest Simon II, a figure who lived

Ben Sira reveals no awareness of the tumultuous reign of the Seleucid king Antiochus IV Epiphanes from 175 to 164 BCE and the persecutions he instigated. Consequently, the instruction dates from a period of foreign control in Judea under a succession of foreign rulers, Seleucid and Ptolemaic, whose administrations worked with local elites to maximize revenue and establish a network of control. One can point to numerous passages in Sirach that reflect this complex sociopolitical environment. The book came about during an era in which the Seleucids were seeking to usurp Jerusalem from the Ptolemies during the Fifth Syrian War (202–195 BCE). This was a time of cultural shift and rapid social change, as Judeans had to negotiate Hellenistic influences and a changing economy.

When looking at archival evidence from this period for insights about Ben Sira's presentation on wealth and poverty, the Zeno papyri are clearly an important source for understanding both this instruction and Qoheleth; we should also note the account of the Tobiads in Josephus and the section often designated the Tobiad Romance (*Ant.* 12.154–236). This description points to wealth accumulation among Judean officials and the ability of well-connected persons to enjoy a meteoric rise to wealth and power. Tobiah came from an important Judean family (the Tobiads). According to the account in Josephus, the high priest Onias II would not pay the required tribute to the Ptolemaic king, and the ruler then threatened to parcel up the land into military colonies, or cleruchies. Tobiah's son Joseph intervened by entertaining the royal diplomat from Egypt and even offered the necessary tribute from borrowed funds. Through his subsequent negotiations, he became a tax collector for the empire and confidante of the royal administration. According to Josephus, this individual, Joseph, collected taxes from many different localities and squashed revolts through force. Whatever the historical accuracy of this account may be, it speaks to the topsy-turvy nature of this period and the potential for resourceful hucksters to succeed quickly. Ben Sira's concerns about trickery and the corruption that can occur in a stratified economy make sense in the context of the Tobiad Romance.

Ben Sira offered his maxims as a "scribal-sage" in the midst of this climate. As many commentators have noted, the author of this instruction belonged to the "retainer class," as he taught aspiring scribes and other members of the elite classes about ethics, Torah-piety, and the wisdom tradition (among other things).[36] His teaching role in this regard is apparent in his famous in-

during this same time period.

36. Wright, "Fear the Lord," 195–96, classifies this author as a "scribal-sage" who served

vitation for potential pupils to "lodge in my house of instruction" (Sir 51:23). Scribal-sages of this type shared the wisdom tradition, wrote and preserved texts that were cultural identity markers, and performed other administrative functions, primarily for the elite.[37] Ben Sira self-identifies as a "scribe" in 38:24, and he wants his charges to follow a similar path. Some of the language elsewhere in the instruction highlights his petitions to his students and the future he envisions for them. Along with the study of the Torah, he demands attentiveness to earlier wisdom: "Do not slight the discourse of the sages, but busy yourself with their maxims; because from them you will learn discipline and how to serve princes" (8:8). According to this author, other occupations, especially those that involve manual labor, do not afford one the opportunity to "attain eminence in the public assembly" or "expound discipline or judgment" (38:33). In this section of the work (Sir 38:24—39:11), Ben Sira highlights the perks of wealth and the drudgery of physical tasks.[38] Even those with highly refined manual skills do not have the time for thoughtful reflection that a scribe does (Sir 38:24).

Within this cultural setting, scribes like Ben Sira had a tightrope to walk as they traveled among the elite classes. Ben Sira had a delicate balancing act in the sense that he relied on wealthy individuals as benefactors and did not want to alienate the famous and powerful (priestly and nonpriestly). Yet he also felt compelled to speak against injustices. For example, his allegiance to the Torah required him to adhere to the charity requirements characteristic of early Judaism (e.g., almsgiving), and yet he had to be careful to avoid reactionary language that could threaten his social standing. Scribes like Ben Sira certainly had opportunities for social advancement and influence (20:27–28; 38:31—39:4), along with access to various luxuries (14:3–19; 31:12—32:13), and opportunities for travel abroad (39:4; 51:13). Such retainers were somewhat at the whims of the powerful classes, who frequently engaged in reckless and corrupt behavior, especially in the realm of economics. This state of affairs leads to a cautious tone in Ben Sira's teaching (e.g., 8:1–19; 13:1–13), as he is both social critic and servant to the wealthy.[39]

---

the elite classes. Cf. Horsley and Tiller, "Ben Sira," discuss Ben Sira's close relationship with the priesthood. While one must be circumspect about how much we can understand the author's personal biography, the instruction does have thematic consistency and can be dated to a specific period.

37. For further discussion on the role of scribes, see Adams, "Social Location."

38. This section of the book is dependent on the Middle Kingdom Egyptian instruction of Dua-khety.

39. See Gregory, "Sirach/Ben Sira"; Sanders, "Ben Sira's Ethic."

Despite his caution, Ben Sira does offer an array of reflections on financial topics, and a brief summary of central themes demonstrates both this author's allegiance to the Torah and wisdom tradition and his admirable determination to become a critic of severe injustice.[40] First, Ben Sira's acknowledges the intrinsic advantages of the wealthy and the frequent animosity between rich and poor: "The rich person speaks and all are silent; they extol to the clouds what he says. The poor person speaks and they say, 'Who is this fellow?'" (Sir 13:23).[41] Along with the idea that poverty is an unenviable state, Ben Sira allows that a person might accumulate wealth quickly or lose it just as fast. His reflections in this regard mark the spirit of his age: "In the time of plenty think of the time of hunger; in days of wealth think of poverty and need. From morning to evening conditions change; all things move swiftly before the Lord" (Sir 18:25–26; cf. 11:10–21). This admission speaks to the author's belief in divine control, but it also correlates with the fluid economy described in the Zeno papyri, Josephus' description of the Tobiads, and other sources.

Corruption in the Marketplace

This author offers pointed reflections on the corruption that he observes with financial exchanges. Earlier figures had also commented on the tendency for manipulative tactics to occur in the public square, but Ben Sira brings a sharp rebuke that should be attributed to his particular historical context:

> A merchant can hardly keep from wrongdoing,
>   nor is a tradesman innocent of sin.
> Many have committed sin for gain,
>   and those who seek to get rich will avert their eyes.
> As a stake is driven firmly into a fissure between stones,
>   so sin is wedged in between selling and buying. (Sir 26:29—27:1)

This statement recognizes with brutal honesty the inherent temptations of the marketplace and the probability of widespread fraud, particularly in a stratified economy. In his descriptions of the various tradesmen, Ben Sira does not even mention the merchant, perhaps because he did not consider the person engaged in commerce to be pursuing a noble occupation. As Collins observes, "Insofar as Hellenism is associated with the brash entrepreneurial ethos of the

---

40. For a useful summary of key themes, see Wright and Camp, "Ben Sira's Discourse."

41. The author qualifies this elsewhere with the statement that the "The poor are honored for their knowledge, while the rich are honored for their wealth" (Sir 10:30).

Tobiads, Ben Sira was indeed opposed to it. But this does not mean he was opposed to Hellenistic culture, or even Hellenistic commerce, if it could be combined with the traditional, reverential fear of the Lord."[42]

The question Ben Sira asks in this regard is whether a person can be simultaneously wealthy and faithful to the Deity. This author declares that "Riches are good if they are free from sin" (Sir 13:24). Elsewhere he wonders about whether this is even possible:

> Blessed is the rich person who is found blameless,
>   and who does not go after gold.
> Who is he, that we may praise him?
>   For he has done wonders among his people. (Sir 31:8–9)

The possibility of combining reverential awe ("fear of the Lord") with savvy financial maneuvering is not likely for the sage; he considers a wealthy *and* blameless person to be highly implausible. Ben Sira is anxious about an unfettered marketplace that gives no heed to the principles in the Torah, and he offers warnings about riches in the interest of restraint.

Ben Sira is well aware of the fact that his charges and the elite individuals he serves are going to indulge in luxuries. In response he urges moderation, not abstemious behavior. For example, he gives advice on appropriate behavior at banquets, a staple tradition of the Hellenistic age. The author's extensive discourse on this topic (Sir 31:12—32:13) is noteworthy for its nuance and specificity: "Do not reach out your hand for everything you see, and do not crowd your neighbor at the dish" (31:14). Throughout this section and in similar passages, Ben Sira encourages restraint, with an eye towards fostering civility and appropriate decorum. Contrary to some influential readings of the instruction, Ben Sira does not advocate withdrawal from Hellenistic culture or the marketplace.[43] His stance is more subtle, for he allows and even encourages his pupils to enjoy the finer things in life provided that they are cautious, generous, and seek to preserve a positive reputation for themselves and their families. Like Qoheleth, Ben Sira does not posit a belief in a blessed afterlife. Consequently, current delights are the only option for the righteous individual: "Give, and take, and indulge yourself, because in Hades one cannot look for luxury" (Sir 14:16). While not as fretful as Qoheleth about the finality of death, the urgency of present enjoyment is apparent in the discourses of Sirach.

---

42. Collins, *Jewish Wisdom*, 31.

43. See Hengel, *Judaism and Hellenism*.

Duty toward the Impoverished

Benevolence is also part of the presentation on wealth and poverty matters. The generosity requirement stems from allegiance to the Torah (and Proverbs), but also strategic self-interest. Like Proverbs (e.g., Prov 22:22–23), Ben Sira claims that God sympathizes with the destitute and even becomes their champion. As a result, generous acts are obligatory (Sir 29:9; cf. Deut 15:7–11). This sage also becomes an enthusiastic advocate of almsgiving (e.g., Sir 7:10 12:3; 29:8; 35:4), a practice that apparently become more widespread in the Second Temple period. Those with resources have an obligation to share what they have because of the stratified economy and because the Torah requires it. Moreover, Ben Sira advises that one should stand surety for a neighbor who is in trouble (29:14–20), a marked contrast from Proverbs. Although he warns the person vouching for a loan to exercise caution, he encourages kindness whenever possible. This can be beneficial when an individual encounters adversity in the future, because aid can be expected as a reciprocal act (Sir 3:31).[44]

Ben Sira claims that the most important thing a person can do is preserve a positive reputation, or "good name." The individual who cultivates a favorable status through attentiveness to the Mosaic commandments and the wisdom tradition can expect blessings from the Lord, but also an eternal reputation (Sir 15:6; 37:26; 39:9; 41:11–13; 44:8). This author declares that "The human body is a fleeting thing, but a virtuous name will never be blotted out" (41:11). In contrast, the descendants of a sinner will have to face the repercussions of his grievous acts for generations (41:5). Ben Sira gives more pronounced attention to this motif of a good name than any of his sapiential predecessors. There are several probable reasons for this, including a desire to affirm a character-consequence relationship without the possibility of an afterlife. Based on the many discourses and sayings related to economics, a desire to lead his audience to fairness and honesty in their financial activity was also part of the rationale. More than any other sapiential author of the Second Temple period, Ben Sira sought to impress upon his listeners that Jewish tradition requires virtuous behavior in the marketplace if one wishes to secure favor from God and a lasting reputation.

The 4QInstruction Document and the Blending of "Wisdom" and "Apocalyptic"

A major shift occurs with 4QInstruction, the largest wisdom text in the Dead

---

44. In this respect, Ben Sira's ethics on wealth and poverty is eudaemonistic.

Sea Scrolls corpus. This sapiential document most likely dates to the second century BCE, the same general period as Ben Sira. As our earlier discussion indicated, this was an era of stratification and widespread corruption, and the advice in 4QInstruction reflects such a context.[45] Although fragmentary, this text clearly combines mundane advice on such matters as loans and crop harvests with lengthier discourses that include mystery language and eschatological speculation. Certain phrases in 4QInstruction offer a beatific afterlife for the virtuous person, a guarantee that Proverbs, Qoheleth, and Ben Sira do not extend. In terms of vocabulary and content, we witness a blending of generic categories that modern scholarship tends to separate too neatly into "wisdom" and "apocalyptic."[46] The author(s) responsible for 4QInstruction do(es) not know such a distinction: virtuous behavior in the earthly sphere and attentiveness to the central revelatory concept in this text (the *raz nihyeh* or "mystery that is to be") lead to salvific rewards.

On one level, 4QInstruction offers financial advice in the same spirit as earlier sages. For example, there are warnings about vouching for the loan of another in 4Q415 VIII, 2 and 4Q418, 88 3. In a related passage, the text of 4Q416 2 II, 5–6 is fragmentary, but the subject matter is about becoming a guarantor: "For the purse of your treasure/s/ [you] have ha[nded over to your creditor on account of your neighbors]; (in so doing) you [have given] your life. Quickly give what is his and take your purse back."[47] Such caution about surety reflects the same type of attitude one finds in Proverbs, but not Ben Sira. The addressees of 4QInstruction probably had practical reasons for avoiding messy financial entanglements due to their more precarious position in the social structure.

Wisdom for the Marginalized

Much advice in this text warns the addressee of 4QInstruction (referred to as a *mevin* or "discerning one") about how to avoid financial ruin, including a striking refrain: "You are poor."[48] This declaration does not appear in the other Second Temple instructions we have examined, and some commentators have argued that it is a reference to metaphorical poverty, similar to being "poor in spirit" (cf.

45. For the primary text, Strugnell and Harrington, *Qumran Cave*. For a discussion of the date see Goff, *Worldly*, 228–32.

46. On the simplistic dichotomy that scholarship has often drawn between "wisdom" and "apocalyptic," see the collection of essays in Wright and Wills, eds., *Conflicted Boundaries*.

47. My translation follows Strugnell and Harrington, *Qumran Cave*.

48. See 4Q415 6 2; 4Q416 2 II, 20; 4Q416 2 III, 2, 8, 12, 19.

Matt 5:3).[49] Yet this refrain is probably not symbolic, but an acknowledgment of real financial difficulties. The advice about economic matters in 4QInstruction assumes challenging financial scenarios for the recipients of this advice.[50] For example, a "needy" individual will likely find a "tight-fisted" lender when seeking basic necessities (4Q417 2 II 21–24). This is a concrete situation and not a depiction of spiritual poverty. While perhaps not destitute, the audience for 4QInstruction does not belong in the same upper-class category as the pupils under Ben Sira's tutelage. In another example, the instruction takes up the situation of working for a difficult superior (4Q416 2 II, 9–15). The audience also receives advice about meager resources, including lack of food, and then getting entangled with an opportunistic creditor (4Q417 2 II, 17–18). Such examples are far removed from advice about how to behave in a wealthy banquet hall.

Consequently, we can categorize the audience for 4QInstruction as a segment of the populace with a more precarious social status than Ben Sira and his charges. These are struggling farmers, merchants, and craftsmen who are trying to survive in the stratified colonial economy of Judea under the Ptolemies and Seleucids. While not as tightly organized as the sectarian groups outlined in the rule books of the Dead Sea Scrolls, 4QInstruction clearly has in mind a confederation of persons whose present struggles might be mitigated by an esoteric mystery concept and specific advice on how to navigate a corrupt marketplace.

An Emphasis on Immortality and Its Significance

The "discerning one" of 4QInstruction can take consolation in his eternal inheritance, whatever his struggles might be. Even if present financial adversity means ongoing challenges—including and perhaps especially in the financial arena—immortality offers the ultimate consolation. As a course of discipline, meditation on the "mystery that is to be," and adherence to key aspects of the wisdom tradition and the Torah are in order.[51] For example and in a clear

49. Wold, "Metaphorical Poverty," 149, maintains that the poverty refrain in 4QInstruction is symbolic, and that the point is to emphasize the secondary status of human beings in relation to angels. In contrast, Wright, "Categories," understands most of the references to be to actual poverty. The latter position is more persuasive: even though some of the economic vocabulary in 4QInstruction may be symbolic/eschatological (e.g., "an inheritance of glory" in 4Q416 2 III, 11–12), there are many references to concrete difficulties throughout the text.

50. Jefferies, *Wisdom at Qumran*, 160–209, catalogues all the economic references in the extant fragments.

51. Thomas, *Mysteries of Qumran*.

allusion to the Decalogue, the addressee is commanded to "Honor your father in your poverty and your mother in your steps" (4Q416 2 III, 15–16). For persons who adhere to such commandments, Ben Sira could only offer a lasting reputation and a peaceful death. In contrast, 4QInstruction promises "eternal joy" (4Q417 2 i 12) to the ones who heed the advice in this document. For those who demonstrate the proper conduct and allegiance to the esoteric mystery concept, God will act "to lift up the head of the poor one [...] with eternal glory and everlasting peace" (4Q418 126 II, 7–8). The reference here to "poor ones" is significant: divine favor, including heavenly reward, shines on "weak" or "poor" individuals who heed the advice. Consequently, we find an explicit association between poverty and election in this document.[52]

Other passages, many of them fragmentary, mention heavenly rewards for the faithful and terrible punishment for the wicked. One key example is the warning against fraudulent activity when dealing with money from a stranger. For those who follow the proper path, "Then you may lie down with the truth, and when you die your memory will blos[som for ev]er, *w'hrytch* will inherit joy" (4Q416 2 III, 7–8). The precise meaning of this Hebrew designation is difficult to determine: one legitimate possibility is that it refers to "the hereafter" for the righteous person, such that the best translation would be "In the hereafter you will inherit joy."[53] This would provide yet another example of the association between righteous conduct and eschatological promise in 4QInstruction. Conversely, those who stray from the program of discipline face serious consequences. The "foolish-minded" and "children of iniquity" category will have to suffer punishment in the "everlasting pit" (4Q418 69 II, 6–9).[54]

Moral Nature of Wealth

Even with this language about poverty and wariness about creditors, those responsible for 4QInstruction do not categorize financial assets as intrinsically

52. Unlike Proverbs and Ben Sira, 4QInstuction is directed to a particular community or segment of the population and not to a more general audience. A great deal of debate and disagreement has centered on how closely we can tie this text to the undisputed sectarian literature of the Dead Sea Scrolls corpus.

53. Collins, "Mysteries of God," 294.

54. In one key passage (4Q417 1 I, 13–18), 4QInstruction contrasts the fate of the spiritual people from the "fleshly spirit," using a variety of phrases from the book of Genesis. The fragments of 4QInstruction do not include any detailed portrait of the heavenly realm, but there is a clear promise of individual immortality. One finds similar language in the book of Mysteries from the Dead Sea Scrolls corpus, particularly the rhetoric of harsh judgment for the non-elect (e.g., 1Q27 1 I, 5–6).

evil. Although this text appears to derive from a non-elite provenance, material holdings are not necessarily an obstacle to right relations with the Deity. The traditional belief in Proverbs about the righteous receiving wealth, progeny, and other blessings from God (our first category of financial saying) does appear in modified form in 4QInstruction. For example, 4Q417 2 I, 19–20: "for the storehouse [of God] has no lack, [and on] his command everything will be." Moreover, 4QInstruction does not rail against the rich in the manner of the Epistle of Enoch or the Synoptics. Wealth acquisition, like other occurrences in life, is a gift from God.[55] Even as it depicts an otherworldly framework for retribution, 4QInstruction allows that it is possible for a person to receive material benefits in the present, and this is a cause for celebration rather than concern (4Q416 2 III, 8–9). Although immense financial gains might be implausible for the recipients of this advice, those who do enjoy earthly success should welcome it. The instruction even advises its audience to "Be an advocate for your own business interests" (4Q417 2 I, 12, author's translation).[56] Such language demonstrates that some of the long-standing assumptions about material wealth persisted, even in instructional texts that had apocalyptic elements.

Wisdom of Solomon

Other instructional texts from the late Second Temple period, including the Wisdom of Solomon (henceforth called Wisdom), offer individual immortality to the righteous sinner and warn against the eternal consequences of wayward behavior.[57] Wisdom differs from 4QInstruction through intricate engagement with Hellenistic philosophical traditions, most notably Neoplatonic ideas. Even so, the association of honesty in the marketplace with eschatological reward is a critical feature of both works. In the "book of Eschatology" that composes the first section of Wisdom (Wis 1:1—6:21), the author depicts a group of miscreants who believe that the brevity of human existence and opportunities for instant wealth should lead to aggressive, unsavory tactics. These rebellious characters reason that the lack of an afterlife provides license to act with impunity. In chapter 2, the author quotes their perspective, which consists of a primary belief in the fleeting nature of individual existence: "For our allotted time is the passing of a shadow, and there is no return from our death . . . Let us take our fill of costly wine and perfumes, and let no flower of spring pass

55. Adams, "Poverty and "Otherness."

56. On the difficulties with translating this phrase, see Goff, *Worldly*, 157.

57. The date for the Wisdom of Solomon is uncertain. Winston, *Wisdom of Solomon*, 22–23, situates the text around the turn of the era.

us by . . . Let us oppress the righteous poor man; let us not spare the widow or regard the gray hairs of the aged" (Wis 2:5–10). The use of economic terminology here is noteworthy, as the sinners in this passage plan to disobey the Torah through oppressive action against vulnerable persons. The recall of logic from Qoheleth is also evident, especially acute despondency over the finality of death. The earlier sage did not recommend destructive action like the sinners in this passage from Wisdom (e.g., Qoh 9:7–10), but he shared their belief in Sheol as the universal destination of humanity.

In contrast, the righteous in this scenario understand the eternal repercussions of sinful behavior and the retributive system that the Deity has put in place. These faithful persons will receive a blessed afterlife: "For though in the sight of others they were punished, their hope is full of immortality" (Wis 3:4). The influence of Platonic concepts is evident in this section and elsewhere, including the use of such terms as "incorruption" (Greek *aphtharsia*) in Wis 2:23 and 6:18. Righteous individuals, at the time of their judgment "will shine forth, and will run like sparks through the stubble" (Wis 3:7). These persons understand the "mysteries" of God (2:22) and enjoy their "lot among the saints (5:5).[58] In addition to some of the parallel terminology and concepts between Wisdom and 4QInstruction, we should note here the shared interest of both works in honest financial dealings. Persons who do not take care of their own household and choose the corrupt path will not only be judged harshly by God but will face eternal punishment (4QInstruction) or a cessation of their existence (Wisdom).[59]

In both of these instructional documents, there is clear indebtedness to ideas and terminology that are often classified as "apocalyptic." This move is significant in an instructional document, because the earthly frameworks have been transformed, and we have what scholars have referred to as the "eschatologizing of wisdom."[60] The combination of practical advice, including warnings about economics, with heavenly speculation also occurs in works that we classify as apocalyptic, and it is to these texts we now turn.

58. Collins, "Mysteries of God," 293, argues that the language of immortality correlates with astral imagery in other texts (both Jewish and Hellenistic).

59. There is no concept of Sheol in the Wisdom of Solomon; the wicked simply cease to exist.

60. Collins, "Eschatologizing of Wisdom."

The Social Setting for Apocalyptic Literature and the Election of the Poor

When exploring economics and the apocalyptic literature of the Second Temple period, it is essential to consider social location. Do otherworldly constructs and the language of election for the poor, such as we find in the Epistle of Enoch, necessarily derive from marginal sects, *or* do they come from the more influential scribal classes? Should we add greater nuance to this question? A great deal of scholarly discussion has arisen in recent decades concerning the larger intent and background for apocalyptic literature. Debates have continued over whether the promise of heavenly reward in a text functions as hopeful consolation or as a mechanism for justifying present injustices, including economic oppression.

Social-scientific analysis can help us with this type of inquiry. The introduction to this essay mentions the influential theory of Max Weber concerning *"pariah intellgentsia."* When examining various sects and orders across cultures, Weber claimed that apocalyptic ideas usually derive from a position of social marginality. According to what is often referred to as "deprivation theory," a primary assertion is that eschatological frameworks originate on the periphery of a society rather than among the ruling classes. According to Weber and subsequent disciples of this approach, millennial expectation finds a natural home among those who lack power in society, whether because of oppression, penury, or both. Such a perspective also appears in Norman Cohn's influential work, *Pursuit of the Millennium*, where he argued that economic oppression led to apocalyptic movements among the struggling classes of medieval Europe.[61]

Certain scholars have applied this theory to the Second Temple period, none more influential than Paul Hanson. In using Weber's argument and that of Karl Mannheim, along with the work of Ernst Troeltsch on churches and sects, Hanson has maintained that "Temple priests are not likely candidates for apocalyptic seers."[62] The assertion that early postexilic, proto-apocalyptic Second Temple texts came from "antihierocratic visionaries" opposing the establishment of the Zadokite elites has influenced basic assumptions, as Hanson delineated various factions in the society and the texts he associated with outsiders. Even if doubts persist about the thrust of Hanson's argument, the categorization of the book of Joel and of Zech 9–14 as the work of opposition

61. Cohn, *Pursuit of the Millennium.*

62. Hanson, *Dawn of Apocalyptic,* 232; Mannheim, *Ideology and Utopia*; Troeltsch, *Social Teaching.*

figures led many to conclude in turn that Dan 7–12 and certain sections of the Enochic corpus also originated within circles of protest and deprivation.

In posing the question of social location, we must allow that traumatic experience, including and especially political/religious persecution, is a driving force behind the imagery and formulations we find in many, but not all, apocalyptic texts. For example, whatever else we want to say about the *maskilim* ("learned ones") responsible for Dan 7–12, their response to the atrocities of Antiochus IV Epiphanes stems from a specific situation of religious oppression and in turn economic struggle.[63] Within this context of imperial aggression, there is intentional marginality in the last section of Daniel, as the text interprets earlier prophetic traditions. The *maskilim* depict the actions of this Seleucid ruler as a desperate situation for themselves and fellow believers. As Carol Newsom argues, the articulation of marginality "represents an odd combination of conscious deference to and unconscious power over received tradition."[64] Newsom is circumspect about what we can say regarding the social location of "apocalyptic scribes," other than they probably did not control social institutions but nevertheless had a certain degree of power stemming from their scribal training and material resources.[65] This question of social location becomes very difficult to assess if trauma lies in the foreground of a document, as with Daniel. Whenever literary constructs stem from a specific crisis, it is a complex matter to ascertain other cultural propellants that might have influenced the construction and reception of a text, including economic factors.

When commentary on economics is present in apocalyptic texts, the preferred approach is often to interpret such works through the lens of class warfare. The argument frequently proceeds that pariah intelligentsia are responsible for giving voice to class consciousness. For example, Richard Horsley refers to the *maskilim* of Daniel as "dissident retainers" who worked against the prevailing power structures: "Indeed, in a crisis of authority, dissident scribes were capable of mounting stubborn resistance to the oppressive and repressive practices of the empire and/or its client regime in Jerusalem. The *maskilim* stood firm in the covenant against the dominant aristocratic faction that, in collusion with the imperial regime, abandoned it (Dan 11:28–35)."[66] While this

---

63. For historical background on the actions of Antiochus, see Collins, *Daniel*, 62–65. The religious nature of the persecution that began in 168 is confirmed by the content of 2 Macc 4–6.

64. Newsom, *Self as Symbolic Space*, 50.

65. See further, Newsom with Breed, *Daniel*.

66. Horsley, *Scribes*, 174.

type of understanding might be possible in certain instances with apocalyptic texts, caution is in order when using terms like "dissident retainer." As Collins, Newsom, and other have shown, the *maskilim* and any audience associated with Daniel are difficult to pinpoint in relation to a *distinctive* scribal or social class.

When turning to the Enochic books, we can certainly categorize some of the individuals mentioned in this corpus as "learned scribes," with expertise in sacred traditions.[67] The figure at the heart of the Book of the Watchers is a "scribe of righteousness" (1 Enoch 12:4; 15:1). Even if we do not know the precise nature of what this entails, such an appellation speaks to a lofty understanding of the authors for this work. The Epistle of Enoch contains similar logic: "[The Epistle of Enoch] which he wrote and gave to his son Methusaleh . . ."(1 Enoch 92:1). Ethiopic translations of this passage refer to Enoch as a "most skilled scribe" in what appears to be a clear allusion to the title given in Ezra 7:6. As with Ben Sira, such references present a specific portrait of the scribe: these figures dutifully preserve the sacred traditions of Israel's Deity, produce books, and are conversant in a variety of literary genres.[68] The nature of the audience for such apocalyptic reflections, including their economic status, is a more complex matter to determine. In some cases, as with 4QInstruction, the poverty is explicit for the elect group. The same is true for the Epistle of Enoch (see below).

When exploring these questions, the work's preoccupation with mantic wisdom, calendrical concerns, and the marked antipathy towards imperial power structures perhaps warrant the "dissident scribe" label. Even so, Portier-Young's caution is helpful, especially since we know so little of the "Enochic scribes" other than about their erudition and intricate knowledge of an array of literary antecedents: "Far from an alienated group, they were engaged in regional affairs and deeply concerned with the global and local exercise of power. We can place them among the class of scribes and sages. This suggests a connection to the Jerusalem Temple establishment and to the regional government and its imperial superstructure, as these are the major employers of scribes known to us in this period. Yet the exact nature of the connection is unclear."[69] Similarly, Annette Reed questions our capacity to locate a "movement" of scribes in the first place, with such a diverse corpus that was written and compiled over a lengthy period: "To what degree does the unity within 1 *Enoch* reflect the production of its parts within a single socio-religious sphere, and to what degree is

67. Adams, "Social Location," 32.

68. Schams, *Jewish Scribes*, 105.

69. Portier-Young, *Apocalypse*, 309–10.

the appearance of unity created retrospectively by the act of collection?"[70] This type of caveat complicates our exploration of social location.

When considering this issue, it is important to remember the fundamental goal of apocalyptic texts: to reveal heavenly mysteries and assure the audience of God's ultimate deliverance of persons in the elect category. As DiTommaso explains, the larger aim is "to pull aside the veil and allow its audience to glimpse the deep mechanisms of time and space that underpin the divine plan for human destiny."[71] When offering apocalyptic discourse, Collins notes, the texts regularly involve angelic mediators, eschatological expectation of a final judgment, and the belief that the world is in a less than perfect state.[72] There is the promise of a new beginning within such a schema: the predetermined plan of the Deity will reward the virtuous, punish the wicked, and inaugurate a new age. While the imagery and contours of apocalyptic literature can differ widely, these common features are usually present in Second Temple texts of this type.

Such speculative, esoteric content does not mean that apocalyptic literature is removed from concern about the present, including economic matters. Otherworldly constructs and provocative images often make for the most acute social commentary. The invocation of the heavenly realm does not render present difficulties irrelevant, as has sometimes been argued. Rather, heavenly images and mystery often indicate present struggles and difficulties, whether systemic injustice or everyday economic hardship. For example, we need only remember the combination of practical advice and heavenly speculation in 4QInstruction, where ethical concerns appear in conjunction with personal and group eschatology.

Effects of Class and Oppression on Apocalyptic Composition

It is very difficult to answer with certainty how class consciousness and economic oppression contribute to the tenor of apocalyptic discourse. Perhaps this line of inquiry could include an acknowledgment that there are complex reasons for presenting an apocalyptic understanding of the created order, with economic factors being one element of a larger set of cultural propellants. To take a more recent example, James Cone's important work *The Cross and the Lynching Tree* examines a host of factors that have contributed to apocalyptic

70. Reed, "Interrogating," 341. For more detailed discussion, see Adams, "Social Location," 29–36.

71. DiTommaso, "Class Rhetoric," 5.

72. Collins, "Wisdom, Apocalypticism."

language among African American communities throughout their history. Primary factors include the language of White supremacy, economic oppression, and of course the forced subjugation of an entire race.[73] When examining discourses in such a complex cultural context, it becomes difficult to separate one factor apart from another.

Perhaps the best way of pursuing this question is to return to the actual apocalyptic texts of the Second Temple period. One of the more pivotal examples of class consciousness occurs in the Epistle of Enoch, where we find a vivid contrast between the rich and the poor.[74] The wicked group is actually categorized as "rich," and the "poor" compose the elect category. For example, "Woe to you, rich, for in your riches you have trusted; and from your riches you will depart, because you have not remembered the Most High in the day of your riches" (1 Enoch 94:8).[75] Such an assertion is very much in the tradition of anti-establishment prophets such as Amos. The "poor" in this section receive a favorable designation: they are the "pious ones." Persons in this category can take comfort in a promised reversal: "Take courage, then; for formerly you were worn out by evils and tribulations, but now you will shine like the luminaries of heaven; you will shine and appear, and the portals of heaven will be opened for you" (1 Enoch 104:2). Even if present circumstances are a struggle, these poor individuals can take comfort that their lot is among the angels/stars, the "luminaries of heaven." As many commentators have noted, we find a similar contrast in the Gospel of Luke, as the "poor" constitute the elect category (see the Sermon on the Plain [6:17–49] and the parable of the rich man and Lazarus [16:19–31]).

Economic commentary is clearly at work in this vivid contrast between the "pious"/"poor" ones and the "wicked"/"rich" ones, and our larger question about the level of class consciousness is pertinent here. DiTommaso captures the essence of the timeless contrast in the Epistle of Enoch: "It is a fierce diatribe against self-indulgent wealth and ostentation, which, with only a few changes, could function as a blistering denunciation of Wall Street today."[76] Yet the polemic against the rich in this document occurs alongside a laundry list of additional sins, including drunkenness, idolatry, lying, and a host of other iniquities. DiTommaso compares the "woe" statements in the Epistle of Enoch

73. Cone, *Cross and the Lynching Tree.*

74. The Epistle of Enoch is usually dated to the second century BCE. See Nickelsburg and VanderKam, *1 Enoch,* 1:8.

75. Translation is from Nickelsburg and VanderKam, *1 Enoch.*

76. DiTommaso, "Class Rhetoric," 6.

to the "roster of sins" in the second Sibylline Oracle and other early Christian apocalypses, "where miasmic greed is one among many things for which male-factors are tormented at the end-time."[77] Economic marginalization is certainly part of the worldview in the Epistle of Enoch, and the depiction of a heavenly realm for the righteous poor offers the same type of consolation we find in 4QInstruction and in the Wisdom of Solomon. The Revelation to John and the Synoptics also offer contrasts based on poverty, and the relevant passages are receiving attention elsewhere in these volumes.

Claudia Setzer highlights the power of an eschatological horizon for struggling persons and the manner in which "resurrection constructs commu-nity." Reflecting on Paul's attitude in the Corinthian correspondence, Setzer argues that the apostle's peripheral status as a member of a small sect and his belief in the afterlife are closely related. His reflections on resurrection breed confidence: "Resisting the economic patronage system in place, he works for himself and takes up collections for other churches. He promotes different cus-toms in prayer, banquets, legal disputes, and personal conduct, all at odds with the surrounding society."[78] One can say the same about many of the texts we have examined: the community behind 4QInstruction, however loosely con-figured, and the elect audience for the Epistle of Enoch can take solace that present economic struggles are not permanent. The corrupt marketplace and stratified economy that lies in the background of these texts provide context for the appeals to a beatific afterlife. Such eschatological promise can function to create solidarity and hope. It allows for acceptance of present circumstances, and it functions to identify a specific set of people (e.g., Pharisees, Essenes, and the first Christians) who have access to an eschatological banquet, while others (e.g., Sadducees) do not. This promise of heavenly fulfillment had the benefit of appealing to a cross-section of believers and providing hope to the marginal-ized, even if some of the authors for these texts perhaps enjoyed a more lofty status.

Yet it can also be argued that the promise of an afterlife functions as a mechanism of social control. Elites can excuse present circumstances, including onerous taxation and widespread corruption, as inconsequential when one also considers personal eschatology. In other words, the promise of heavenly reward becomes a mechanism for ongoing economic oppression. The images, texts, and public utterances providing eschatological consolation can be an effective tool.

77. DiTommaso, "Class Rhetoric," 7. This section of the Sibylline Oracle is from Ps-Phocylides, sapiential reflections that are located within the larger instruction.

78. Setzer, *Resurrection*, 68.

Focus on the afterlife and the irrelevance of present conditions becomes a diversion from unjust economic practices and ongoing exploitation of the poor. Whether such an agenda is at work in any of the Second Temple texts we have examined is an open question. The present writer is more inclined to see the protest of economic injustice in a text like the Epistle of Enoch or the admonitions in 4QInstruction about how to avoid destitution as legitimate expressions of financial difficulty with the resultant hope in a "settling of accounts" at the end of days.

Conclusion

This essay has pointed to intense engagement with economic issues in the sapiential and apocalyptic texts of the Second Temple period, with varying responses to financial dynamics. Some instructional texts such as Proverbs and Sirach acknowledge the plight of the poor and the existence of inequality, but there is also reticence about challenging the status quo too much or advocating for systemic change. Part of this hesitation stems from social location: many wisdom texts, such as Sirach, are the products of learned figures who clearly saw rampant corruption but did not want to risk their status as scribal retainers to the wealthy. Other sources, such as 4QInstruction, also refrain from socially disruptive language, while promising individual immortality. Still other texts, such as the Epistle of Enoch, categorize the poor as an elect category and offer anti-establishment rhetoric through the lens of economics. While it is very difficult to determine social location for texts that lack an explicit author and audience, the class-based tone of certain apocalyptic texts reflects, at least in part, dissident voices ("pariah intelligentsia") and courageous advocacy on behalf of the poor.

Discourses on wealth and poverty are one of the enduring features of wisdom and apocalyptic texts from this period. The engagement is specific in that these texts offer nuanced criticism of actual cultural realities (e.g., the depiction of bribery in Qohelet), but there is also a timeless aspect to this material. These sages and scribes depict a world in which cheaters often prosper, rich people have situational "friends," and poverty can be a desperate, unenviable state that stems from corruption and a system that offers many intrinsic advantages to the wealthy. In our current age of financial inequality, huge disparities in wealth, and political polarization, these voices from ancient Judea offer a helpful reminder that greed and obsessiveness over money are enduring, intractable aspects of what it means to be human.

Bibliography

Adams, Samuel L. "Poverty and 'Otherness' in Second Temple Instructions." In *The 'Other' in Second Temple Judaism: Essays in Honor of John J. Collins*, edited by Daniel C. Harlow et al., 189–203. Grand Rapids: Eerdmans, 2011.

———. *Social and Economic Life in Second Temple Judea.* Louisville: Westminster John Knox, 2014.

———. "The Social Location of the Scribe in the Second Temple Period." In *Sibyls, Scriptures, and Scrolls: John Collins at Seventy*, edited by Joel Baden et al. 22–37. JSJSup 175. Leiden: Brill, 2017.

———. *Wisdom in Transition: Act and Consequence in Second Temple Instruction.* JSJSup 125. Leiden: Brill, 2008.

Berlin, Andrea M. "Archaeological Sources for the History of Palestine: Between Large Forces: Palestine in the Hellenistic Period." *BA* 60.1 (1997) 2–51.

Boer, Roland. *The Sacred Economy of Ancient Israel.* LAI. Louisville: Westminster John Knox, 2015.

Boström, Lennart. *The God of the Sages: The Portrayal of God in the Book of Proverbs.* CBOTS 29. Stockholm: Almqvist & Wiksell, 1990.

Braun, Rainer, *Kohelet und die Frühhellenistiche Popularphilosophie.* BZAW 130. Berlin: de Gruyter, 1973.

Cohn, Norman. *The Pursuit of the Millennium.* London: Secker & Warburg, 1957.

Collins, John J. *Daniel.* Hermeneia. Minneapolis: Fortress, 1993.

———. "The Eschatologizing of Wisdom in the Dead Sea Scrolls." In *Sapiential Perspectives: Wisdom Literature in Light of the Dead Sea Scrolls; Proceedings of the Sixth International Symposium of the Orion Center for the Study of the Dead Sea Scrolls and Associated Literature, 20–22 May, 2001*, edited by John J. Collins et al., 49–65. STDJ 51. Leiden: Brill, 2004.

———. *Jewish Wisdom in the Hellenistic Age.* OTL. Louisville: Westminster John Knox, 1997.

———. "The Mysteries of God: Creation and Eschatology in 4QInstruction and the Wisdom of Solomon." In *Wisdom and Apocalypticism in the Dead Sea Scrolls and in the Biblical Tradition*, edited by Florentino García Martínez. BETL 168. Leuven: Leuven University Press/Peeters, 2003.

———. "Wisdom, Apocalypticism, and Generic Compatibility." In *In Search of Wisdom: Essays in Memory of John G. Gammie*, edited by Leo G. Perdue et al., 165–85. Louisville: Westminster John Knox, 1993.

Cone, James H. *The Cross and the Lynching Tree.* Maryknoll, NY: Orbis, 2011.

DiTommaso, Lorenzo. "Class Consciousness, Group Affiliation, and Apocalyptic Speculation." In *The Struggle over Class: Socioeconomic Analysis of Ancient Christian Texts*, edited by G. Anthony Keddie et al., 277–312. WGRW 19. Atlanta: SBL Press, 2021.

Durand, Xavier. *Des Grecs en Palestine au IIIe siècle avant Jésus-Christ: Le dossier syrien des archives de Zénon de Caunos (261–252).* CahRB 38. Paris: Gabalda, 1997.

Fox, Michael V. *Proverbs 1–9.* AB 18A. New York: Doubleday, 2000.

———. "The Social Location of the Book of Proverbs." In *Texts, Temples, and Traditions: A Tribute to Menahem Haran*, edited by Michael V. Fox et al. Winona Lake, IN: Eisenbrauns, 1996.

Goff, Matthew J. *The Worldly and Heavenly Wisdom of 4QInstruction.* STDJ 50. Leiden: Brill, 2003.

Gregory, Bradley C. "Sirach/Ben Sira." In *The Wiley Blackwell Companion to Wisdom Literature*, edited by Samuel L. Adams and Matthew J. Goff, 87–103. Wiley Blackwell Companions to Religion. Hoboken, NJ: Wiley, 2020.

Gropp, Douglas M., and James C. VanderKam. *Wadi Daliyeh II and Qumran Miscellanea, Part 2: The Samaria Papyri from Wadi Daliyeh*. DJD 28, Pt. 2. Oxford: Oxford University Press, 2001.

Hanson, Paul D. *The Dawn of Apocalyptic: The Historical and Sociological Roots of Jewish Apocalyptic Eschatology*. Rev. ed. Philadelphia: Fortress, 1979.

Harrison, Robert C. "Hellenization in Syria-Palestine: The Case of Judea in the Third Century BCE." *BA* 57.2 (1994) 98–108.

———. "Qoheleth in Social-Historical Perspective." PhD diss., Duke University, 2008.

Hengel, Martin. *Judaism and Hellenism: Studies in Their Encounter in Palestine during the Early Hellenistic Period*. Translated by John Bowden. 2 vols. 1974. Reprint, Eugene, OR: Wipf & Stock, 2003.

Hölbl, Günther. *A History of the Ptolemaic Empire*. Translated by Tina Saavedra. New York: Rout-ledge, 2001.

Horsley, Richard A. *Scribes, Visionaries, and the Politics of Second Temple Judea*. Louisville: Westminster John Knox, 2007.

Horsely, Richard A., and Patrick A. Tiller. "Ben Sira and the Sociology of the Second Temple." In *Second Temple Studies III: Studies in Politics, Class, and Material Culture*, edited by Philip R. Davies and John M. Halligan, 74–107. JSOTSup 340. London: Sheffield Academic, 2002. Reprinted in Horsley and Tiller, *After Apocalyptic and Wisdom: Rethinking Texts in Context*, 19–55. Eugene, OR: Cascade Books, 2012.

Jefferies, Daryl F. *Wisdom at Qumran: A Form-Critical Analysis of the Admonitions in 4QInstruction*. Gorgias Dissertations, Near Eastern Studies 3. Piscataway, NJ: Gorgias, 2004.

Koch, Klaus. "Is There a Doctrine of Retribution in the Old Testament?" In *Theodicy in the Old Testament*, edited by James L. Crenshaw, 57–87. Translated by Thomas H. Trapp. Issues in Religion and Theology 4. Philadelphia: Fortress, 1983.

Krüger, Thomas. *Qoheleth*. Translated by O. C. Dean Jr. Hermeneia. Minneapolis: Fortress, 2004.

Lenski, Gerhard E. *Power and Privilege: A Theory of Social Stratification*. 1966. 2nd ed., Chapel Hill: University of North Carolina Press, 1984.

Mannheim, Karl. *Ideology and Utopia*. Translated by Louis Wirth and Edward Shils. New York: Harcourt, Brace, 1936.

Newsom, Carol. *The Self as Symbolic Space: Constructing Identity and Community at Qumran*. STDJ 52. Leiden: Brill, 2004.

Newsom, Carol, and Brennan W. Breed. *Daniel*. OTL. Louisville: Westminster John Knox, 2014.

Nickelsburg, George W. E., and James C. VanderKam. *1 Enoch: A New Translation; Based on the Hermeneia Commentary*. Minneapolis: Fortress, 2004.

Pastor, Jack. *Land and Economy in Ancient Palestine*. London: Routledge, 1997.

Porten, Bezalel, and Ada Yardeni. *Textbook of Aramaic Documents from Ancient Egypt*. Vol. 2, *Contracts*. Winona Lake, IN: Eisenbrauns, 1989.

Portier-Young, Anathea E. *Apocalypse against Empire: Theologies of Resistance in Early Judaism*. Grand Rapids: Eerdmans, 2011.

Reed, Annette. "Interrogating 'Enochic Judaism': 1 Enoch as Evidence for Intellectual History, Social Realities, and Literary Tradition." In *Enoch and Qumran Origins: New*

Light on Forgotten Connections, edited by Gabriele Boccaccini, 336–44. Grand Rapid: Eerdmans, 2005.

Sanders, Jack. "Ben Sira's Ethic of Caution." *HUCA* 50 (1979) 73–106.

Sandoval, Timothy J. *The Discourse of Wealth and Poverty in the Book of Proverbs*. BibIntSer 77. Leiden: Brill, 2006.

Schams, Christine. *Jewish Scribes*. JSOTSup 291. Sheffield: Sheffield Academic, 1998.

Seow, C. L. *Ecclesiastes*. AB 18C. New York: Doubleday, 1997.

Setzer, Claudia. *Resurrection of the Body in Early Judaism and Early Christianity: Doctrine, Community, and Self-Definition*. Boston: Brill Academic, 2004.

Simpson, William Kelly, ed. *The Literature of Ancient Egypt: An Anthology of Stories, Instructions, Stelae, Autobiographies, and Poetry*. With an introduction by William Kelly Simpson and translations by Robert K. Ritner et al. 3rd ed. New Haven: Yale University Press, 2003.

Strugnell, John, and Daniel J. Harrington. *Qumran Cave 4.XXIV: Sapiential Texts, Part 2. 4QInstruction (Mûsār Lĕ Mēvîn): 4Q415ff. With a re-edition of 1Q26*. DJD 34. Oxford: Clarendon, 1999.

Tcherikover, Victor. *Hellenistic Civilization and the Jews*. Reprint, Peabody, MA: Hendrickson, 1999.

Thomas, Samuel I. *The Mysteries of Qumran: Mystery, Secrecy, and Esotericism in the Dead Sea Scrolls*. EJL 25. Atlanta: Society of Biblical Literature, 2009.

Troeltsch, Ernst. *The Social Teaching of the Christian Churches*. Translated by Olive Wyon. 2 vols. Harper Torchbooks. Cloister Library. New York: Harper & Row, 1960.

Waltke, Bruce K. *The Book of Proverbs: Chapters 1–15*. NICOT. Grand Rapids: Eerdmans, 2004.

Weber, Max. *The Sociology of Religion*. Translated by Ephraim Fischoff. 1920. Reprint, Boston: Beacon, 1963.

Winston, David. *The Wisdom of Solomon: A New Translation with introduction and Commentary* AB 43. Garden City, NY: Doubleday, 1979.

Wold, Benjamin G. "Metaphorical Poverty in 'Musar le Mevin.'" *JJS* 58 (2007) 140–53.

Wright, Benjamin G. "The Categories of Rich and Poor in the Qumran Sapiential Literature." In *Sapiential Perspectives: Wisdom Literature in Light of the Dead Sea Scrolls, Proceedings of the Sixth International Symposium of the Orion Center for the Study of the Dead Sea Scrolls and Associated Literature, 20–22 May, 2001*, edited by John J. Collins et al., 101–25. STDJ 51. Leiden: Brill, 2004.

———. "'Fear the Lord and Honor the Priest': Ben Sira as Defender of the Jerusalem Priesthood." In *The Book of Ben Sira in Modern Research: Proceedings of the First International Ben Sira Conference, 28–31 July 1996, Soesterberg, Netherlands*, edited by Pancratius C. Beentjes, 189–222. BZAW 255. Berlin: de Gruyter, 1997.

Wright, Benjamin G., and Claudia V. Camp. "Ben Sira's Discourse of Riches and Poverty." *Henoch* 23 (2001) 153–74.

Wright, Benjamin G., and Lawrence W. Wills, eds. *Conflicted Boundaries in Wisdom and Apocalypticism*. SymS 35. Atlanta: SBL, 2005.

Yoder, Christine R. *Wisdom as a Woman of Substance: A Socioeconomic Reading of Proverbs 1–9 and 31:10–31*. BZAW 304. Berlin: de Gruyter, 2001.

Ancient Documents Index

2 Samuel

2	87
2:13	54
2:17	54
5:2	49
5:9	212
5:11	213
7:1–17	208
7:8	49
7:14	208
8:2	89
8:15–18	218
8:16	215
9	211, 212
11–12	135
13:5	123
13:23	212, 212
14:7	78, 208
14:30–31	87
16:1–4	211, 212
17	54
19:25–31	211, 212
20:23–26	218
20:23	215
21:1–14	208, 211, 216
24	208, 211, 216
24:10	216
24:18–25	88
24:18–24	85, 212
30–31	54

1 Kings

1:2	123
1:9	77
1:19	77
1:25	77
3	134
3:4–14	211
3:15	134
4:1–6	218

4:6	64
4:7–19	64
4:20–26	82
4:20	57
4:22–23	64
4:26	64
4:29–34	57
5:11	84
5:13–16	64
5:15	213
6–8	64, 215
7:14	213
7:46	213
8:31–32	141
8:58	134
9:11–13	84
9:15–21	64
9:19	214
9:26–28	212
10	80
10:11–12	82
10:11	212
10:15	82
10:20	81
10:22	59, 80, 81, 212
10:28–29	82, 212
11	134
11:9–11	134
11:33	134
14:26	218
15:17	77
15:18	218
16:24	212
18	7
20:34	212
21	85, 170, 212
21:3	90
21:4	90
21:19	90
22:1–28	256
22:17	49, 61

Jeremiah

Author Index

Ekholm-Friedman, Kajsa, 4, 11
Elliger, Karl, 87, 103
Elliott, Neil, ix
Engels, Friedrich, 51–52, 69, 222
Erasmus, Charles, 24, 39
Erickson, Amy, 226, 260

Fall, Patricia, 29, 39
Faust, Avraham, 64, 69, 112, 126, 234, 236, 238, 260
Fine, Ben, 46, 69
Finkelstein, Israel, 31, 33, 39, 81, 103, 171, 192, 234, 258, 260
Finkelstein, Jacob, 140, 166
Firestone, Ya'akov, 50, 69
Firth, Raymond, 17, 39, 51
Fischbach, Michael R., 48, 69
Fitzpatrick-McKinley, Anne, xviii, 29, 31, 36, 128–68
Flannery, Kent, 18, 25, 39
Fox, Michael V., 267, 268, 295
Frankfort, Henri, 194, 222
Fried, Lisbeth, 133, 166
Fried, Morton, 18, 39
Friedman, Jonathan, 18, 39, 58, 69
Friesen, Stephen J., 105
Frilingos, Chris, 95, 104

Gaines, Janet Howe, 153, 166
Gallant, Thomas, 21, 39
Garraty, Christopher P., 36, 39, 40
Geertz, Clifford, 20, 39
Gerstenberger, Erhard S., 205, 222
Geus, Cornelis de. H. J., 86, 103
Geva, Hillel, 234, 260
Giddens, Anthony, 172, 192
Giorgadze, G. G., 60, 69
Glancy, Jennifer A., 95, 96, 98, 99, 100, 104
Glascock, Michael, 40, 41
Godelier, Maurice, 86, 104
Goff, Matthew J., 265, 283, 286, 295, 296
Goody, Jack, 24, 39, 129, 141, 151, 166

Gottwald, Norman K., ii, v, x, 70, 74, 229, 245, 256, 260
Grabbe, Lester L., 64, 69, 132, 133, 163, 166, 162
Graeber, David, 58, 69
Granott, Abraham, 48, 70
Grant, Robert L., xi
Gray, Robert, 17, 39
Graybill, Rhiannon, 257, 260
Greenfield, Jonas, 149, 167
Gregory, Bradley C., 279, 296
Grmek, Mirko, 51, 70
Gropp, Douglas M., 296
Guijarro, Santiago, 91, 104
Guillaume, Philippe, 48, 70, 86, 88, 90, 104

Hagstrum, Melissa, 16, 22, 39
Håkansson, Thomas, 24, 29, 40
Halbe, Jurgen, 138, 167
Hald, Mette Marie, 48, 70
Hall, Crystal L., xi
Hall, Thomas D., 81, 103
Hallo, William W., xiv, 195, 196, 197, 198, 200, 222
Halstead, Paul, 16, 21, 40, 42
Hands, Arthur, 27, 40
Hankins, Davis, x, xviii, 224–62
Hanson, K. C., ix
Hanson, Paul D., 288, 296
Haran, Menahem, 240, 260
Hardin, James W., 112, 113, 122, 126
Harding, Thomas, 17, 40
Hardt, Michael, 65, 70
Harrill, J. Albert, 95, 104
Harrington, Daniel J., 283, 297
Harris, Marvin, 18, 40, 229
Harrison, Robert C., 275, 296
Harriss, John, 42
Hastorf, Christine, 118, 119, 126
Hartenstein, Friedhelm, 207, 222
Havea, Jione, x
Hayden, Brian, 24, 39, 40, 50, 70